Studies in Diversity Linguistics

Editor: Martin Haspelmath

In this series:

1. Handschuh, Corinna. A typology of marked-S languages.
2. Rießler, Michael. Adjective attribution.
3. Klamer, Marian (ed.). The Alor-Pantar languages: History and typology.
4. Berghäll, Liisa. A grammar of Mauwake (Papua New Guinea).
5. Wilbur, Joshua. A grammar of Pite Saami.
6. Dahl, Östen. Grammaticalization in the North: Noun phrase morphosyntax in Scandinavian vernaculars.
7. Schackow, Diana. A grammar of Yakkha.
8. Liljegren, Henrik. A grammar of Palula.
9. Shimelman, Aviva. A grammar of Yauyos Quechua.
10. Rudin, Catherine & Bryan James Gordon (eds.). Advances in the study of Siouan languages and linguistics.
11. Kluge, Angela. A grammar of Papuan Malay.
12. Kieviet, Paulus. A grammar of Rapa Nui.
13. Michaud, Alexis. Tone in Yongning Na: Lexical tones and morphotonology.
14. Enfield, N. J (ed.). Dependencies in language: On the causal ontology of linguistic systems .
15. Gutman, Ariel. Attributive constructions in North-Eastern Neo-Aramaic.
16. Bisang, Walter & Andrej Malchukov (eds.). Unity and diversity in grammaticalization scenarios.
17. Stenzel, Kristine & Patrizia Paggio (eds.). On this and other worlds: Voices from Amazonia.
18. Paggio, Patrizia and Albert Gatt (eds.). The languages of Malta.

ISSN: 2363-5568

Attributive constructions in North-Eastern Neo-Aramaic

Ariel Gutman

Ariel Gutman. 2018. *Attributive constructions in North-Eastern Neo-Aramaic* (Studies in Diversity Linguistics 15). Berlin: Language Science Press.

This title can be downloaded at:
http://langsci-press.org/catalog/book/123

ISBN: 978-3-96110-081-1 (Digital)
978-3-96110-082-8 (Hardcover)

ISSN: 2363-5568
DOI:10.5281/zenodo.1182527
Source code available from www.github.com/langsci/123
Collaborative reading: paperhive.org/documents/remote?type=langsci&id=123

Cover and concept of design: Ulrike Harbort
Typesetting: Ariel Gutman, Sebastian Nordhoff
Illustration: Sebastian Nordhoff
Proofreading: Andreas Hölzl, Andrew Spencer, Aviva Shimelman, Christian Döhler, Eitan Grossman, Jean Nitzke, Jezia Talavera, Michael Rießler
Fonts: Linux Libertine, Arimo, DejaVu Sans Mono, Arabtype, Estrangelo Edessa, SBL Hebrew
Typesetting software: XƎLaTeX

Language Science Press
Unter den Linden 6
10099 Berlin, Germany
langsci-press.org

Storage and cataloguing done by FU Berlin

À mes enfants, Or et Tal

לילדיי, אוֹר וטַל

Contents

Preface

This book is a revised version of my doctoral thesis, defended at the university of Konstanz on the 22nd of April 2016 (see Gutman 2016). As a supporter of the open access philosophy, it is a great honour for me to publish it with Language Science Press. I thank Martin Haspelmath, the editor-in-chief, for his encouragement and acceptance of the book.

The next section reproduces verbatim the acknowledgements of my doctoral dissertation. I would like to add to these my sincere thanks to Sebastian Nordhoff for his editorial support and his invaluable contribution in drawing the two maps which adorn the book.

I would also like to thank the three anonymous reviewers of the manuscript. Although I could not follow amply all their suggestions due to unfortunate time constraints, their comments permitted me to clarify and correct some points, elaborate on others, altogether making this a better book. Reading the reviews, moreover, was a great pleasure. I would like to thank especially one reviewer who described my thesis as "a truly bewildering study but also very fascinating". Reading these sweet words made the entire enterprise worth its while.

Ariel Gutman
Zürich, April 2017

Acknowledgements

יא כסי, סי אכזי אימי סלעא דילא כסאד ונפלתא ונאשא לא גמאינך אבה – אאיא זון! דלאבד בד
נפלא בקימה וגרנא, ובד מרמא רישא לאזם אי סלעא! (פשט ויהי בשלח)

O my kinsman, go and see which merchandise is little in demand and whose value is gone down and no one looks at it – that you buy! For its value will certainly go up and increase; that merchandise will surely rise in value! (Pəšaṭ Wayəhî Bəšallaḥ 5:16, edition and translation by Sabar 1976)

Many people inspired, aided, and supported me in the long road leading to the writing of this dissertation, and the few paragraphs ahead are dedicated to them.

First and foremost, I would like to express my immense gratitude to my doctoral supervisor, *Doktormutter* in the true sense of the word, Eleanor Coghill. I believe that few doctoral students have the luck I had of enjoying such a wonderful supervisor. Eleanor turned out to be much more than an academic supervisor, but also a true friend: On numerous occasions she fed me, provided me with drink and shelter, and lent her ear upon necessity. All this, it goes without saying, while keeping the highest academic standards, and giving me thorough and frequent guidance and critique. It is fair to say that most of the good ideas in this dissertation are hers, while most of the not-so-good ones were included despite her better advice.

Eran Cohen served as an external supervisor throughout my work on the thesis. Much of the methodology of this research, as well as many of the ideas, are based on his work, and at the same time, he served as an excellent opponent for refining my own ideas. Yet his influence on my research goes much further back, as in fact he is responsible for attracting me to the field of Neo-Aramaic: While I was just a freshman of the linguistics department at the Hebrew University of Jerusalem, he advised me to take the course on Neo-Aramaic, which incidentally he was teaching. Little did we know the dire consequences of this...[1]

[1] In my third year of studies, moreover, I took his course about the Jewish Nerwa texts, where I got acquainted with the above citation. If I understood it as a recommendation to further my studies in Aramaic, I bear sole responsibility for this...

Upon my arrival at the University of Konstanz, Frans Plank kindly agreed to serve as my second doctoral supervisor.[2] As such, I had the pleasure of attending some of his seminars and benefited from his sharp questions and critique. Indeed, the typological underpinnings of this research are, in a large part, based on his work. Moreover, the decision to concentrate on the topic of adnominal modification and construct state in NENA crystallised during the DEM GENITIV workshop, held in Konstanz in October 2012, which was organised by Frans.[3]

A fourth person deserving special thanks is Pollet Samvelian. Before moving to Konstanz, I started the project as a doctoral student at the Sorbonne Nouvelle University (Paris III) under the supervision of Pollet Samvelian. Indeed, Pollet encouraged me to take on this research project and, as is evident from the results, many of the research questions were inspired by her guidance.

On the inspirational level, moreover, my interest in contact linguistics and realization of the vast research possibilities related to Neo-Aramaic in this domain were spurred after attending Don Stilo's course "Typological Features and the Areal Dimension in the Languages of the Southern Caucasus, Northern Iran-Iraq and Eastern Turkey" given at the Leipzig Spring School on Linguistic Diversity (March-April 2008).[4] This was a true eye-opener and Don's meticulous level of research served as a constant (unreachable) horizon for me.

The choice, however, of continuing my graduate research in the domain of Neo-Aramaic was not always clear. In this respect, a person whom I don't know personally played a crucial role. Ariel Sabar's book "My Father's Paradise: A Son's Search for His Jewish Past in Kurdish Iraq" (Algonquin Books, 2008), in which he tells the fascinating story of his father, Prof. Yona Sabar, a native speaker and renowned researcher of Neo-Aramaic, convinced me to pursue research in the domain of Neo-Aramaic, not only because of my fascination for the language, but also for its speakers. In this respect I am grateful as well to my friend Ashley Kagan (née Burdick) who sent me a copy of the book from LA.

As the dissertation is in fact a culmination of my entire linguistics curriculum, I would like to thank all my linguistic teachers (in the broadest sense) during

[2] A small anecdote is here apposite: When I was about to finish my studies at the Hebrew University, I asked the late professor Gideon Goldenberg, who introduced me to typology with the course "Semitic Languages: Historical and Typological Perspectives", to give me some advice as to where I could continue to study typology abroad. He recommended me to approach Frans Plank, the Editor-in-Chief of the Association of Linguistic Typology. Yet my route went elsewhere and I forgot all about it. Thus, it was a curious coincidence that I recalled this recommendation only after Frans agreed to act as my doctoral supervisor.

[3] See http://typo.uni-konstanz.de/ocs/index.php/dem-genitiv/.

[4] See http://www.eva.mpg.de/lingua/conference/08_springschool/.

the last 12 years (and some even before). Besides my aforementioned supervisors, these include Alain Desreumaux, Alain Lemaréchal, Anbessa Teferra, Anne Christophe, Ari Rappoport, Benoît Crabbé, Bruno Poizat, Dana Taube, David Gil, Dominique Sportiche, Eitan Grossman, Florence Villoing, Gideon Goldenberg, Gilles Authier, Jeroen van de Weijer, Kim Gerdes, Maarten Mous, Marian Klamer, Martine Mazaudon, Mori Rimon, Sérgio Meira, Sharon Peperkamp, Simon Hopkins, Uzzi Ornan, Vincent Homer, Wido van Peursen, Willem Adelaar, and Yishai Peled, among others.

I am thankful to Geoffrey Khan, Lidia Napiórkowska and Jasmin Sinha for answering my questions regarding their material. I am grateful as well to Miriam Butt, who during my doctoral colloquium provided me with some comments and criticism which permitted me to sharpen my discussion of clitics.

Thanks are due to my friend Ivri Bunis for reading an earlier draft of the manuscript and giving some useful comments and references. Thanks go also to Adam Pospíšil, who told me about the term "pertensive", which I would otherwise have overlooked. Special thanks go to my colleague Doris Penka who kindly translated the English abstract into German.[5]

During the research project (and before it) I conducted many fieldwork sessions with speakers of Neo-Aramaic. In this respect I am grateful to Hezy Mutzafi, who initiated me into NENA fieldwork, mentored me in this domain, put me in contact with speakers and was always happy to answer my questions.

While only a small part of the fieldwork data found its way into the dissertation (mainly due to time constraints related to the transcription) I would like to thank my many NENA consultants for their time, help and hospitality. These include the Audisho family in Sarcelles, Elie Avrahami, Hadassa Yeshurun and her father Rabbi Ḥaim Yeshurun, Isa Hamdo and his family, Ḥabib & Sara Nourani, Kara Hermez and her father Pinkhas, Lea & Nissim Sharoni, Nissan Bishana and his family, Oz Aloni and his mother Batia, Ya'aqov Mordechai, the Yaramis family in Sarcelles, Yoel Sabari, Ziad Mooshi, and Zvi Avraham.

Special thanks are due to Joseph Alichoran: first for teaching me (together with Bruno Poizat) conversational Neo-Aramaic at the INALCO, and secondly for helping me on numerous occasions with transcription of NENA data and answering various language questions. Thanks are also due to his lovely family for their hospitality.

At the institutional level, I would like to thank the *Zukunftskolleg* at the University of Konstanz for hosting me professionally during the research. As a Ph.D.

[5] [The English and German abstracts can be found in the original thesis manuscript (Gutman 2016).]

student I was spoiled with a spacious office and excellent working conditions, as well as enjoying the various interdisciplinary workshops and lectures. In this respect, I would like to thank especially the head of the Zukunftskolleg, Giovanni Galizia, as well as Martina Böttcher and Anda Lohan from the administration for their kindness and helpfulness. Thanks go also to my postdoctoral office-mates, Yaron McNabb and Sven Lauer, for enduring my presence and providing me with advice and coffee pads on occasion.

Adjacent to the Zukunftskolleg sits the Research Centre for Aramaean Studies. I enjoyed passing many afternoons there drinking coffee and chatting about Aramaeans and Aramaic. Special thanks are due to Zeki Bilgic and Ralph Barczok for their help with Modern Aramaic and Syriac.

At the University of Konstanz, I am especially thankful for two people for facilitating my move to Konstanz and dealing with the local bureaucracy: These are Johannes Dingler from the Welcome Center, as well as the wonderful Elisabeth Grübel from the HR department, who became a true friend.

The first year of my doctoral project, 2011–12, I spent at the Sorbonne Nouvelle University (Paris 3) and it was financed by a doctoral position granted by the French government through the *École Normale Supèrieure.* At that time I also benefited from the *entourage* of the research project "Langues, dialects et isoglosses dans l'aire Ouest-Asie", led by Pollet Samvelian and Anaïd Donabedian, which is part of the LabEx Empirical Foundations of Language. I am grateful for this initial funding and the company.

For the subsequent years, 2012–16, my position at the University of Konstanz and research needs were financed by the German Research Foundation project "Neo-Aramaic morphosyntax in its areal-linguistic context" led by Eleanor Coghill. Here again, I am thankful for this invaluable support.

I am grateful to Riki Manetsch for her warm hospitality in Zurich during the very final (and intensive!) phase of corrections of the manuscript.

To my parents, who inspired me to pursue the academic path, Hélène and Per-Olof, I offer many thanks and love.

Last but certainly not least, I would like to thank my beloved wife Solange for the passionate discussions about linguistics we held together and for the enduring moral support she gave me during the work on this thesis.

Ariel Gutman
Konstanz, September 2016

Abbreviations and symbols

AC	Attributive Construction	f., ff.	and following page(s)
Adj.	Adjective	fn.	footnote (in references)
ALC	Analytic Linker Construction	Intrg.	Interrogative pronoun
Ap.	Apocope (Construct State)	J	Jewish
alt.	alternative form	lit.	literally
BCE	Before the Common Era	N	Noun / Nominal
C	Christian	NE	North-Eastern
CE	Common Era	NENA	North-Eastern Neo-Aramaic
ch.	chapter (in references)	NP	Noun Phrase
Cl.	Clause	NW	North-Western
Conj.	Conjunction	NWNA	North-Western Neo-Aramaic
CSC	Construct State Construction	p.c.	personal communication
DAC	Double Annexation Construction	PP	Prepositional Phrase
		Prep.	Preposition
Diyana-Z.	Diyana-Zariwaw (NENA dialect)	Q.	Quantification
		SE	South-Eastern
DLC	Dative Linker Construction	W.	Western
ed.	edited (by), editor		

Gloss labels

The glossing of the examples follows the Leipzig Glossing Rules (Comrie et al. 2008), with some additions. Proper nouns are abbreviated in the glosses. The following gloss labels are used:

1, 2, 3	1st, 2nd, 3rd person	AUX	auxiliary
A	agent-like argument	CAUS	causative
ABS	absolute state	COMP	complementizer
ACC	accusative	COMPR	comparative
ADJ	adjectival derivation	COP	copula
AGR	agreement features	CST	construct state

DAT	dative	NEG	negation
DEF	definite	OBL	oblique
DEM	demonstrative	ORD	ordinal
DET	determiner	P	patient-like argument
DIR	directional	PASS	passive
EMPH	emphatic state	PL	plural
DIST	distal	POSS	possessive pronominal suffix
EZ	Ezafe	PRO	pronominal primary
EX	existential particle (∃)	PROG	progressive
F, FS	feminine (singular)	PST	past
FREE	free state	PTCP	active participle
FUT	future	PRF	perfect
GEN	genitive	PROX	proximal
IMP	imperative	REFL	reflexive
IMPF	imperfect	REL	relativizer
IND	indicative	RES	resultative participle
INDF	indefinite	SBJV	subjunctive
INF	infinitive	SG	singular
INV	invariable form	SUPER	superlative
LNK	linker	V_{CST}	vocalic nucleus of a CST suffix
M, MS	masculine (singular)		
NOM	nominative		

Notes regarding the glossing of verbs

1. The present and preterite bases of NENA and Kurdish verbs are not glossed explicitly. Instead, the verbal base is glossed by an English verb in base form (*do*) or past form (*did*) respectively. The past participle (*done*) is used as gloss for the NENA resultative (passive/perfect) participles, followed by the RES gloss.

2. The explicit glossing of agent (A) and patient (P) pronominal arguments of the verb is only done when both arguments appear.

3. A verb is glossed as subjunctive (SBJV) or indicative (IND) only when the two forms are different.

The general format of examples is detailed on page 18.

Brackets and symbols

C, V	Consonant, Vowel
X, Y	Primary, Secondary
( )	In gloss: gender of nouns In text or translation: context of an example In translation only: material added to clarify the translation In tables: form with restricted use
(?)	Uncertain gloss
[ ]	Important constituent
{ }	Optional element
/	Alternative formulations
*	In examples: unattested or ungrammatical form In historical discussions: reconstructed form
.	Gloss separator
-	Morpheme boundary
=	Clitic boundary
'	Intonation boundary
⁺, ⁽⁺⁾	Phonological velarization
V́, V̀	Word-stress, utterance-stress
...	Hesitation in speech; elided material
∅	Paradigmatic/Morphological Zero (lack of overt element)
↨, ↔	Apposition
↦	Dependency (Attributive) relation
⟺	Co-reference

SMALL CAPS are used to introduce key concepts.

1 Introduction

1.1 Aim and scope of the research

The current research can be situated at the crossroads of several sub-fields of linguistics: historical linguistics, areal linguistics and language contact, as well as dialectology, all informed by linguistic typology and framed within structuralist linguistics (see the second chapter for a more precise statement of the theoretical framework). More precisely, I wish to study the variation in a specific language group, namely the North-Eastern Neo-Aramaic dialects (=NENA, belonging to the Semitic language family – see below for further information), examine the diachronic origin of the attested variation, and relate it to language contact with neighbouring languages as well as to general typological tendencies.

The NENA group is well suited for such a study for several reasons: First and foremost, it offers a rich variety of dialects, of which many have in recent years been described, thus providing a firm empirical underpinning to the research.[1] Secondly, as these dialects span a large geographic area, covering north Iraq, south-east Turkey and west Iran, they have been in contact with different languages and language families (mostly Turkish, Azeri, Kurdish, Persian and Arabic), thus providing the possibility to study the effects of differing language contact situations. Thirdly, previous strata of Aramaic are known and documented, giving the possibility to add diachronic depth to the study. In short, the NENA languages are in a unique position, in which the linguistic community have access to both historical strata and to language contact data. Thus, they provide a "laboratory" setting in which it may be possible to disentangle the role of "pure" language-internal change from changes originating in particular language contact situations. My conclusions, I hope, could inform linguists looking at linguistic change in languages which do not have this wealth of information.

As I am working in a language contact framework, I am mainly interested in overt patterns, or – more technically, constructions – prone to replication from

[1] I use the traditional term "dialects", but it should be borne in mind not all these dialects are mutually intelligible, and they may represent varieties of different "languages" of the NENA group.

one language to another. Thus, a specific construction (with a given function) is defined in terms of the linear (syntagmatic) ordering of its elements, together with the morphological cues present on each element. In contrast to some formal approaches, I am less interested in covert elements, or the hierarchical (syntactic) relations between the elements. As such, the research is focused on the "surface" manifestation of linguistic content.

To establish the effects of language contact, I adopt the framework of Matras & Sakel (2007b), distinguishing between PATTERN REPLICATION and MATTER REPLICATION. The latter consists of a case of a foreign morpheme integrated in a recipient language's native system. Pattern replication, on the other hand, is a more complex process, where a construction, as defined above, is copied from a model language to a recipient language, without necessarily copying any specific morphemic material. This is typically done by the identification of a key element of a given construction in the model language (the PIVOT), finding a morphemic counter-part in the recipient language with a partial similarity in function, and then copying the construction using the morphemic material of the recipient language, effectively extending its functional load. When a construction is copied with (possible partial) transfer of morphemic material I speak of PATTERN-CUM-MATTER REPLICATION. On the other hand, when a certain construction is not attributed to effects of language contact, but reflects rather a (presumed) "natural" development of the language, I shall use the term INTERNAL DEVELOPMENT.

In order to achieve both breadth of dialectal coverage and depth of linguistic analysis, I was bound in this study to restrict my attention to one linguistic domain. Much attention has been given in the literature to the verbal system of NENA dialects, which presents a drastic change as compared to the pre-modern strata of Aramaic (see *inter alia* Goldenberg 2000; Coghill 2016; Gutman 2008). Less attention has been given to the nominal domain, although there too one finds important re-arrangement of linguistic material. For this reason, the current research concentrates on the nominal system of NENA, and in particular the domain of adnominal modification. As we shall see, this research domain may be of special interest for typologists, as the nominal system of NENA (as in Semitic languages in general) is marked by a preference for head-marked constructions. It is my impression that the research of head-marked constructions has been under-represented in typological literature, a lack which this work attempts to remedy.

In classical Semitic languages, Aramaic included, adnominal modification of one noun by another is typically expressed by the ANNEXATION construction (Hebrew: *smixut* סְמִיכוּת, Syriac: *smixūtā* ܣܡܝܟܘܬܐ, Arabic: *iḍāfa* إِضَافَة) in which the head-noun is marked by a special morphological form, the CONSTRUCT STATE. The NENA group exhibits both a functional retention of this category alongside morphological innovations regarding its formal manifestation, and functional innovations reflected in novel constructions. In this work, I subsume all such constructions involving adnominal modification under the term ATTRIBUTIVE CONSTRUCTIONS (=ACs) expressing the ATTRIBUTIVE RELATION (these terms are elaborated upon in the second chapter).

The NENA attributive constructions are especially interesting, as on the one hand they show traits typical of Semitic languages, but on the other hand they manifest effects of language contact. Thus, the research questions which I wish to answer are two-fold:

1. What is the extent of the variation among attributive constructions in the documented NENA dialects? Which different constructions exist in the various dialects to express the attributive relationship?
2. How do these constructions relate to the contact languages of NENA *vis à vis* the historical background of NENA? In other words, what was the role of language contact in shaping the synchronic manifestations of the attributive constructions in NENA dialects?

By answering the first question I expect to give a detailed typological view of the attributive constructions within the NENA group. Given the rich variation of structure within these dialects, I believe these results should be informative to any typologist or linguist interested in similar constructions. The answer to the second question will permit us to formulate plausible hypotheses as to how these constructions may develop over time, with or without influence from contact languages. These conclusions may in turn inform linguists working on language change and language contact in the nominal domain of other languages.

Structure of the book The rest of this introductory chapter gives some general information regarding the NENA dialects. The second section gives a rough outline of the Noun Phrase structure in NENA dialects, while the third section outlines the methodology used in the research, listing in particular the dialects surveyed.

The second chapter is devoted to the theoretical and methodological foundation of the research. It introduces the theoretical framework of this research, namely structuralist linguistics, and within it the notions of attributive relation and attributive constructions. These notions are anchored moreover within the traditions of linguistic typology and Semitic linguistics. A synthesis of these approaches yields the methodology used in the current research.

The third chapter presents the attributive system of Syriac, a well-documented Aramaic language of the Classical Aramaic period, which can serve as a good approximation of the language stratum preceding the NENA dialects. When appropriate, references to other Classical Aramaic languages (notably Jewish Babylonian Aramaic) are given as well.

The fourth chapter gives a "bird's-eye view" analysis of some of the most important AC markers present in NENA dialects, all related to the Classical Aramaic linker *d-*, and therefore dubbed D-MARKERS. This chapter, moreover, introduces the important theoretical notions of CLITIC and PHRASAL AFFIX, and relates them to the current research.

Chapters five to eight give an in-depth analysis of the attributive system of four select NENA dialects, representing different corners of the NENA-speaking area: these are the Jewish dialect of Zakho (Iraq), the Christian dialect of Qaraqosh (Iraq), the Jewish dialect of Urmi (Iran), and the Jewish dialect of Sanandaj (Iran). As all examples are glossed, I hope these chapters could be useful for typologists wishing to gain access to the data of these dialects.

The ninth chapter gives a cross-dialectal survey of attributive constructions in Kurdish dialects, being the main contact languages of NENA. Due to the lack of detailed description of Kurdish dialects, much information is drawn from pedagogical grammars of standard Kurmanji and Sorani. Some comments on other Iranic languages (often called Iranian languages), such as Persian and Gorani dialects, are given as well.

The tenth and eleventh chapters present the key results of the research, as they deal with the development of the AC systems of NENA dialects. Both chapters present a comparative synchronic view of each construction discussed, as well as hypotheses and claims regarding the development path of each construction and the relation to contact languages.

The tenth chapter deals especially with the development of D-marked constructions, i.e. those constructions which contain a reflex of the Classical Aramaic linker *d-*. These include the Neo-CST construction marked by the suffix *-əd*, the genitive marking by prefix *d-*, as well as the development of various alternative linker forms. This chapter is tightly related to the fourth chapter.

The eleventh chapter deals with the development of other constructions, being the apocopate construct state construction, various double-marked constructions, the juxtaposition construction and the borrowing of AC morphemes from Iranic languages (the Ezafe and the clausal subordinator). This chapter contains also a case study of the ordinal sub-system of NENA as compared to contact languages (both Kurdish and Iraqi Arabic) and to the anterior stratum approximated by Syriac.

Finally, the General Conclusions give an outlook on the main results, and suggest further research prospects.

1.2 Overview of the NENA dialects

1.2.1 Genetic affiliation and general information

The term Neo-Aramaic refers to a group of languages and dialects spoken today, which are descended from ancient Aramaic, a branch of Northwest Semitic. Aramaic, in its various forms, has been spoken continuously from the beginning of the 1st millennium BCE. I shall divide this long stretch of time into the following 3 periods (cf. Beyer 1986):[2]

1. Early Aramaic: c. 850 BCE (first attested inscriptions) – 200 CE

2. Classical Aramaic: c. 200–700 CE (decline of spoken use)

3. Neo-Aramaic: The present-day dialects, attested since the 16th century

With the emergence of Classical Aramaic, around the 2nd century CE, a major split between its western and eastern branches became visible. The western branch has only one surviving descendent, namely the *Western Neo-Aramaic* language (=Western Neo-Aramaic), spoken in 3 villages in Syria.[3]

In this book, I shall concentrate on the eastern branch, and thus use the unqualified term Classical Aramaic to refer specifically to Eastern Classical Aramaic. This branch has many surviving contemporary dialects, which are divided into 3 major groups:[4]

Neo-Mandaic This is the smallest group, which is spoken by the Mandaean community in Iran and diaspora countries (in the past also in southern Iraq). The number of speakers is estimated to be some hundreds (Poizat 2008: 16).

[2]The Early Aramaic period is sometimes divided into 3 distinct phases: Ancient Aramaic (c. 850–700 BCE), Imperial Aramaic (c. 700–200 BCE) and Middle Aramaic (c. 200 BCE – 200 CE) (Fitzmyer 1979; Kaufman 1997), but this level of detail is not needed in the current research.

[3]The current geographic situation of these speakers is unclear, as at least some of the speakers have been dislocated due to Syrian civil war (see Gutman 2015a).

[4]See also the discussion of Hoberman (1988: 557, fn. 2), who coined the term North-Eastern Neo-Aramaic.

North-Western Neo-Aramaic This group consists today of the *Ṭuroyo* language (known natively as *Surayt*), which is mainly spoken by Syriac Orthodox Christians originating from the Ṭur ʿAbdin region in south-eastern Turkey. Poizat (2008: 16) estimates the number of speakers to be around 50,000. Another documented language of this group, Mlaḥsô, is considered today to be extinct.

North-Eastern Neo-Aramaic This is the most diverse language group, geographically, ethnically and linguistically. It has been spoken mainly in northern Iraq and to a lesser extent in western Iran, south-eastern Turkey, and north-eastern Syria by Jews and Christians, though by now many speakers have moved to western countries.[5] The number of speakers does not exceed half a million.[6]

As mentioned above, the present research concentrates on the North-Eastern Neo-Aramaic group (=NENA), as it shows the greatest linguistic variation. The high diversity of this group can be attributed first and foremost to its wide geographic spread, leading to diverse contact situations (see below). There exists, moreover, a major socio-linguistic divide between the dialects spoken by Jews (now mostly in Israel) and those spoken by Christians (now both in their homelands and in diaspora), even when they are in close geographical proximity (this point is neatly exemplified by Mutzafi 2015 regarding the dialects of Salamas).

Texts in NENA can be dated as far back as the 16th–17th centuries, these being Christian and Jewish religious texts (Jewish: Sabar 1976; 1984b; Christian: Mengozzi 2002; 2011). Earlier strata are undocumented, but it is reasonable to take Syriac, a form of Classical Aramaic spoken from the 1st century up to (at least) the eight century, as an approximation of the pre-NENA dialects.[7] Indeed, as Syriac is continuously used as a liturgical language of the Christian NENA speakers, they often see it as the classical form of their own language. This view has led to the usage of the somewhat misleading term "Neo-Syriac" for NENA.

---

[5]A short history of the speakers and their language, including their move to diaspora communities with a special emphasis on France, is given by Alichoran & Sibille (2013).

[6]This estimate is based on the summation of the number of speakers of North-Eastern Aramaic languages according to the *Ethnologue* (Lewis et al. 2013), which yields 466,000 speakers. A slightly more conservative estimate (375,000 speakers) can be found by summing the number of speakers per country given by Poizat (2008: 16–18).

[7]At this stage of the research, it is unclear whether a unique proto-NENA language dating to the Classical Aramaic period existed, or whether the NENA dialects are descendants of various unattested dialects, which were contemporary with Syriac. The latter option may be more plausible, as some NENA dialects show stronger affinities with Jewish Babylonian Aramaic. See also the discussion of Kim (2008).

1.2.2 Dialectal division of the NENA group

As mentioned, NENA dialects are often divided into Christian and Jewish dialects. From the genealogical point of view, however, one cannot simply postulate a Proto-Jewish-NENA versus a Proto-Christian-NENA. The picture is rather more complex and still unknown to a large extent, especially since the anterior strata of NENA dialects were undocumented spoken varieties.

While the internal classification of the Christian dialects is yet unclear, the Jewish dialects can be divided on a phonological and morphological basis into 3 main groups (Mutzafi 2008b) which are related geographically to the Zab river:

- The Cis-Zab group (also called *Lišana Deni* 'our language'), spoken in western Iraq, for instance in the cities of JZakho * and Dohok.
- Central-Zab, such as the dialects of Sandu and Barzani.
- The Trans-Zab group, which itself is divided into 3 major clusters:
  - The Inter-Zab group, around the town of Arbel (in Iraq).
  - The North-Eastern Trans-Zab group, around the city of JUrmi * (in the Iranian West Azerbaijan province). This group came under the influence of the Azeri language.
  - The South-Eastern Trans-Zab group (also called *Hulaula* 'Judaism, Jewish Language'), spoken around the towns of JSanandaj * (in the Iranian Kurdistan province) and Khanaqin (in Iraq).

Many of the Christian dialects, regardless of their geographic location, show affinities with the Jewish Cis-Zab group.

1.2.3 Geographical spread of NENA and contact situation

The NENA group spans a large geographic area: It spreads from South-Eastern Turkey (as far north as the city of Van and as far west as the city of Cizre in the Şırnak Province), through northern and eastern Iraq (as far south as Khanaqin) up to western Iran (as far north as Salamas in Iranian Azerbaijan, as far south as Kerend and as far east as Bijar in Iranian Kurdistan).

The area covered by the NENA dialects is largely contained within the Kurdish language zone, and indeed the NENA dialects have been in close contact with Kurdish dialects, both of the Kurmanji group and the Sorani group. The divide between NENA speakers and Kurdish speakers within this language area is related to religious and ethnic factors: While Kurds, both Muslims and Yezidis, speak Kurdish, Jews and Christians of various denominations speak different dialects of NENA (the latter also speak NWNA). It is clear that the religious differences have prevented to some extent the mixing of these groups, and thus acted as a guardian of the linguistic diversity. Yet the close proximity of the speakers, spanning possibly several millennia, has led to mutual influence both regarding the language and other aspects of society (for a historical and socio-linguistic survey of the contact situation see Chyet 1995; a detailed linguistic treatment of the contact situation of the NE-Trans-Zab dialects is given by Garbell 1965a; Pennacchietti & Orengo 1995 offer a bird's-eye linguistic view while a comprehensive linguistic treatment is presented by Coghill 2018). Today Aramaic is a minority language, and thus NENA scholars have generally focused on the influence Kurdish exerted on it (but see Chyet 1997 for a study of Aramaic loanwords in Kurdish). In the past, however, Aramaic enjoyed a large prestige (at least up to the Arabic conquest starting at the seventh century), and thus the possibility of it acting as a donor language should not be neglected.

Another Iranic language which has been in contact with NENA is Persian. In modern times, it came into contact with NENA speakers of Iran (living in the provinces of Iranian Azerbaijan and Iranian Kurdistan) as an official state language. The contact, however, is much longer in time.

On some dialects (mostly those of Iranian Azerbaijan) there has been, moreover, an extensive influence from Azeri (see Garbell 1965a, which treats Azeri as a Turkish dialect).

Amongst Semitic languages Arabic (both standard and vernacular) had an influence, being the state language of Iraq, and spoken in the area since the Arab conquest. Indeed, some Jewish communities of the region, as well as the inhabitants of Mosul, spoke Arabic (see map of Jastrow 1990: 4). Hebrew and Syriac have been used as liturgical languages by the Jewish and Christian communities respectively, and thus also had an influence on the spoken language, though this influence may be mostly lexical.

In this work, I shall concentrate especially on the contact effects of Kurdish dialects, due to their prominent situation with regard to NENA.

1.3 Noun phrase structure in NENA

Aramaic nominals (nouns, adjectives as well as pronominal forms) are marked morphologically by two grammatical features, number (SG vs. PL) and gender (M vs. F). In NENA, The gender feature is normally only marked for the singular nominals; some animate nouns (typically gentilic nouns) may inflect for gender also in the plural forms (e.g. in Qaraqosh: Khan 2002a: 212). These features are typically morphologically overt on nominals of Aramaic origin, while loan-nouns and loan-adjectives may be non-inflecting or show only partial inflection for the number feature.

Attributes typically follow the head noun. One type of attribute, namely adjectives, inflects to show agreement in its grammatical features with its head noun. For this reason, Semitic adjectives are traditionally said to be in APPOSITION with the head noun, in the sense that they share the same grammatical features as the head noun and are co-referential with it.[8] Other types of attributes, particularly nouns, are not necessarily in apposition with their head noun, but rather stand in an ATTRIBUTIVE RELATION with it. In this case the head-noun is normally marked morphologically by a special form, the CONSTRUCT STATE. These concepts will be explained in greater detail in the next chapter. In either case, the attribute is best analysed as a phrasal element, as it may itself be expanded by an attributive complement, or be determined independently of the head noun.

As described by Jastrow (2005), Early Aramaic varieties, such as Biblical Aramaic, mark also the category of determination by means of morphological inflection. In this system, the so-called EMPHATIC STATE marks definite nominals, while the ABSOLUTE STATE marks indefinite nominals. Attributive adjectives, moreover, agree in this feature as well with their head-noun. With time, however, the definite value of the emphatic state had became eroded, such that in Classical Aramaic, represented for instance by Syriac, the emphatic state became the unmarked form of the noun. Jastrow (2005: 146) notes that this situation has led NENA to mark definiteness by various periphrastic strategies, such as indexing on the verb (for nouns in object position), or the usage of demonstrative pronouns. According to Jastrow, only NWNA Ṭur ʿAbdin dialects have developed a fully consistent definite article paradigm pre-posed to the NP (see also Jastrow 2002: 20f.).[9]

(1) Mīdin : **Determiner–Noun Phrase**
u= *bayto=* *rabo*
DEF.MS= house(MS)= big.MS
'the big house' (Jastrow 2002: 21)

[8]Cf. Cohen (2008: 28): "Apposition is here defined as the property of two or more entities sharing the same syntactic status in a given syntactic setting: a characteristic example is the Semitic Adjective, which reflects the same syntactic information as the entity to which it refers." See also §2.1.1.

[9]The general format of examples is given on on page 18.

In NENA the marking of definiteness is less consistent, as various discourse and syntactic strategies can be used. Nonetheless, according to the analysis put forward by Cohen (2012: 20–27), the dialect of JZakho has a set of elements which act as determiners, both definite and indefinite.[10] These include short forms of the inflecting demonstrative pronouns for marking definiteness, as well as the numeral *xa* 'one', which marks indefinite specific nouns. Complicating the picture is the fact that also a ∅ acts as a *±def., generic* determiner. According to Cohen (2012: 22) this is a true determiner standing in paradigmatic opposition with the overt determiners, and not merely a lack of such an element. In the example (3) below I render it explicit, but subsequently I shall not mark its presence.

(2) JZakho: **Determiner–Noun**
əs-wa xa gōra ... aw gōra
EX-PST INDF man DEF.MS man
'There was a man... the man...' (Cohen 2012: 22 (3))

(3) JZakho: ∅ **Determiner–Noun**
∅ ʾarya lá =g- dāməx lá =hoya rəš ∅ xəzēna
DET lion NEG =IND lie NEG =be.SBJV on DET treasure
'A lion (any lion) does not lie down, unless it is on top of a treasure' (Cohen 2012: 23 (13))

Table 1.1 presents the main components of the determiner system of JZakho, extracted from Cohen (2012: 21).[11]

Table 1.1: The Determiner system of JZakho

	MS	FS	PL
Definite	*aw*	*ay*	*an*
Indefinite		*xa*	
Interrogative		*ēma* 'which'	
Unmarked/Generic		∅	

[10] Eran Cohen kindly shared with me an as yet unpublished paper elaborating this analysis. See Cohen (2018) in the bibliography.

[11] Cohen's table includes more elements, some of which can act also as independent pronouns, but we do not need to go into these details here. Note that the use of *xa* as a plural indefinite determiner is only available before quantified plural nouns yielding a meaning of approximation (see example (7) on page 12).

The usage of these elements as indefinite and definite determiners has been recognized for other NENA dialects by other scholars. Thus, Khan (2008a: 287f.) writes:

> [T]he cardinal numeral "one" is often used as an indefinite article [...] Of special importance in this respect in all dialects is the system of demonstrative pronouns, which in some contexts are most idiomatically translated by the English definite article. Neither the cardinal numeral nor the demonstratives, however, correspond in distribution exactly to that of the indefinite and definite articles of English.

As English is by no means the standard by which articles (or determiners) should be defined, it seems safe to analyse these elements as definite and indefinite determiners, albeit less grammaticalised than the Germanic type. The determiner system presented in Table 1.1 on the facing page is in all likelihood present in most, if not all, NENA dialects, with some minor modifications.[12] Yet in the glossing, I follow in general the terminology used by the descriptions of the respective dialects, glossing these elements either as DEF (definite determiners) or DEM (attributive demonstrative pronoun).[13]

An important difference between this system and the Old Aramaic system is the fact that the determiners have phrasal scope: They typically open the NP and they appear only once. In this respect they are similar to the Western European articles.[14] Moreover, Cohen (2012: 21) analyses the determiners as being the *head* of the Noun Phrase ("noun group" in his terminology). Using an alternative terminology, the determined Noun Phrase may be called a Determiner Phrase, or DP. I shall however stick with the general term NOUN PHRASE, and distinguish only when necessary between a DETERMINED NP and a BARE NP.

Notwithstanding the above, it is worth noting that in some cases the determiner appears NP internally, intervening between a noun and its attribute.[15] In such cases one may prefer to analyse the determiner as being syntactically associated with the attribute (which is phrasal):

[12]One such difference is that in some dialects, the indefinite determiner (and numeral 'one') inflects as well, being *xða* or *da* for feminine (e.g. Bēṣpən: Sinha 2000: 165).

[13]In Barwar, there are three series of attributive demonstratives: Speaker deixis, Far deixis and Default (Khan 2008c: 148). I took the liberty to gloss the latter, representing short forms of the demonstratives, as definite determiners.

[14]Some dialects, such as Sulemaniyya, have borrowed a suffixed definite marker from Sorani, namely the suffix *-eke* (Khan 2004: 232).

[15]Interestingly, such a phrase-internal position correlates with the alleged original position of the Northwest Semitic article, which, according to the theory advanced by Pat-El (2009), was at first an adnominal marker.

(4) JZakho: **Noun–Determined Adjective**
axōna [aw rūwa]
brother DEF.MS big.SG
'the older brother' (Cohen 2012: 214)

Another paradigmatic slot of the Noun Phrase identified by Cohen (2012: 25) is that of a Quantifier, appearing between the Determiner and the nominal. As this is an optional slot, there is no need to posit a ∅ quantifier. Cohen gives examples as the following:

(5) JZakho: **Determiner-Quantifier–Noun**
ʾan ʾəṣra nāše
DEF.PL ten people
'the ten people' (Cohen 2012: 25 (30))

(6) JZakho: **Determiner-Quantifier–Noun**
xa xa yarxa
INDF one month
'about one month' (Cohen 2012: 25)

(7) JZakho: **Determiner-Quantifier–Noun**
xa ʾəṣra askar
INDF ten soldier(INV)
'some ten soldiers' (Cohen 2012: 25 (29))

Establishing a similar Quantifier slot (separate from the Determiner slot) in other NENA dialects would require further examination, but one finds similar examples in other dialects, as the following:

(8) Alqosh: **Determiner-Quantifier–Noun**
xā̃ʾ ʾárba=xamša gàrre.ˈ
INDF(?) four=five loops
'about four or five loops.' (Coghill 2003: 295 [A:90])

Judging by such examples, I tentatively generalize Cohen's analysis to the NENA group as a whole. The full pattern of the NENA Noun Phrase is given in Table 1.2, though the order of elements may vary.

The quantifier as well as the attribute are optional. The determiner, conversely, is always present, but it may be a ∅. The attribute is typically an NP on its own

Table 1.2: The NENA Noun Phrase structure

Det+{Quant}+Noun+{Attr$_{NP}$}
Noun+{Attr$_{NP}$}: Bare NP
Det+{Quant}+Noun+{Attr$_{NP}$}: Determined NP (=DP)

(either bare or determined), considering also adjectival phrases as a sub-type of NPs. Note, moreover, that the noun may be replaced by an adjective, and, as we shall see in the subsequent chapters, a special type of pronoun, namely a pronominal linker.

1.4 Data sources and methodology

The Cambridge NENA database (see in the bibliography under Khan, ed.) lists currently 137 different dialects, but only about 20 dialects have extensive grammatical descriptions. For this research, I have collected data from 26 different dialects using the available grammatical descriptions as well as published texts. When possible, the recordings of texts deposited in the *Semitisches Tonarchiv* (see in the bibliography under Arnold, ed.) were consulted as well to validate the examples. In some cases, moreover, I was able to conduct fieldwork with speakers of the dialects.

The dialects surveyed in this book are listed in Table 1.3 on the next page, alongside their geographical region (using the classification of the Cambridge database) and the religious community of the speakers (Jewish or Christian). The sources used for each dialect are listed as well. Sources whose audio recordings are publicly available are marked with a ♫ symbol (the URL is given in the bibliographic reference). A map showing the approximate locations of the dialects referred to in this study (reflecting the situation in the beginning of the 20th century) is given in Figure 1.1 on page 15.[16]

The amount of information gathered from the different sources varies considerably. Seven dialects (marked in **bold** in Table 1.3) contributed each between 100 and 200 examples to the research database, together amounting to two-thirds of the NENA data-points in it. Not surprisingly, amongst these are the 4 dialects to which survey chapters are devoted. The remaining dialects contributed each between 8 to 60 examples each. Data from the dialects of Khabur (Talay 2008) were

[16] I'm grateful to Eleanor Coghill, who assembled the locations of the dialects, as well as to Sebastian Nordhoff, who prepared the map figuring in the book. An online version of this map can be found at http://tinyurl.com/ac-nena-map.

Table 1.3: Dialects surveyed in the research, with most prominent dialects marked in **bold**.

Dialect		Location	Sources
Alqosh	C.	NW Iraq	Coghill 2003
Amədya	J.	NW Iraq	Greenblatt 2011
Aradhin	C.	NW Iraq	Krotkoff 1982
Aradhin	J.	NW Iraq	Mutzafi 2002b
Arbel	J.	NE Iraq	Khan 1999♫
Barwar	C.	NW Iraq	Khan 2008c; 2009a
Barzani	J.	NW Iraq	Mutzafi 2002a; 2004b♫
Baz	C.	SE Turkey	Mutzafi 2000
Bēṣpən	C.	SE Turkey	Sinha 2000♫
Betanure	J.	NW Iraq	Mutzafi 2008a♫
Bohtan	C.	SE Turkey	Fox 2009
Challa	J.	SE Turkey	Fassberg 2010
Diyana-Zariwaw	C.	NE Iraq	Napiorkowska 2015
Gaznax	C.	SE Turkey	Gutman 2015c; own fieldwork
Hertevin	C.	SE Turkey	Jastrow 1988♫
Jilu	C.	SE Turkey	Fox 1997
Koy Sanjaq	J.	NE Iraq	Mutzafi 2004a♫
Old Nerwa	J.	NW Iraq	Sabar 1976; 1984b
Qaraqosh	C.	NW Iraq	Khan 2002a♫
Rustaqa	J.	NE Iraq	Khan 2002b; own fieldwork
Sanandaj	C.	W Iran	McPherson & Caldani 2013♫; Panoussi 1990
Sanandaj	J.	W Iran	Khan 2009b; own fieldwork
Sardarid	C.	NW Iran	Younansardaroud 2001♫
Sulemaniyya and Ḥalabja	J.	NE Iraq	Khan 2007; 2004♫
Urmi	C.	NW Iran	Marogulov 1976
Urmi	J.	NW Iran	Garbell 1965b,a; Khan 2008b
Zakho	J.	NW Iraq	Avinery 1988; Cohen 2010; 2012; Sabar 2002; Goldenberg & Zaken 1990; Sabar 2007

Figure 1.1: Approximate locations of NENA dialects (and one NWNA dialect: Mīdin) at the beginning of the 20th century.

collected as well, but for methodological reasons are not treated in the book.

The data collected was registered in a Microsoft Access database. Accordingly, in this database all the various ACs found in the different NENA dialects surveyed, as well as other languages under investigation (mainly Kurdish and Syriac), were listed and linked to appropriate examples. The classification of the ACs in the database was done according to the principles outlined in §2.4 on page 41. An example of the data-entry form is given in Figure 1.2 on the following page. The database can be found online as part of Gutman (2016).[17]

While many of the consulted NENA grammars have sections labelled "Annexation", "Attributes" or the like, the concept of the attributive construction as defined in the current work is normally not described in any single section of the grammar, requiring collection of examples from numerous sections in a given grammar.[18] The data assembly started with the collection of ACs headed by nouns modified by various attributes (nouns, adjectives, clauses etc.). Only subsequently were examples with other types of primaries (pronouns, adjectives,

[17]In the electronic database the primary and secondary fields are referred to as Nucleus and Attribute respectively.

[18]An exception is the grammar of JZakho, Cohen (2012).

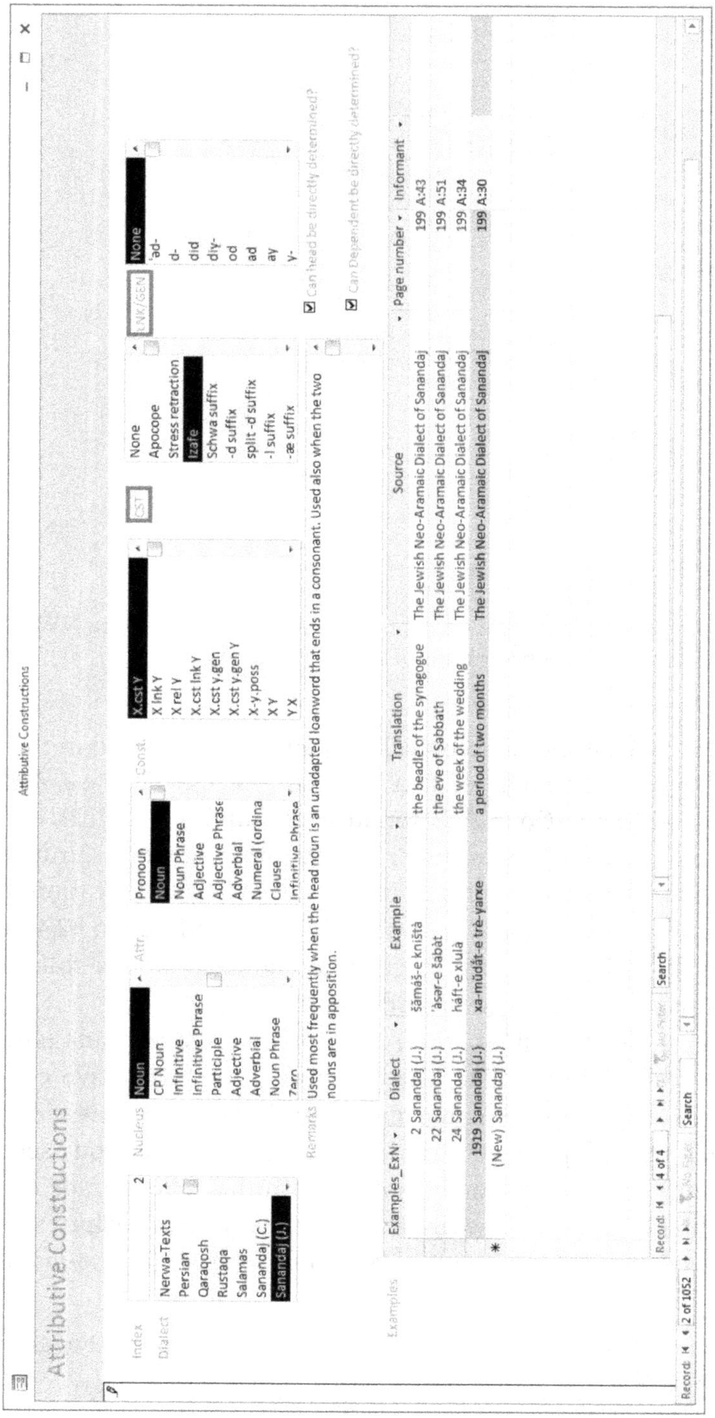

Figure 1.2: Example of data entry in the accompanying database

adverbials etc.) collected, yielding possibly a less systematic picture of these combinations.

It should be noted that the listing of the different constructions is purely qualitative, as no quantitative data were gathered from the corpora. Thus, any remark regarding the usage frequency of a given construction is based on comments given in the consulted grammars.

The database design permits to query cross-dialectally the presence of a specific construction, with or without limitations to the parts-of-speech involved. This possibility was invaluable for conducting the comparative research, constituting the core of the current study (see chapters 10–11).

Format of examples The NENA examples given in this work are all taken from the database. While the database conserves the original transcription system of each source, in the book I have attempted to normalize the different transcriptions to a standard system, namely that of Khan (2008c; 2009b; 2008b).[19]

All examples have a title stating the language (or dialect) of the example as well as the categories of the members of the AC under discussion. Thus, a title of **Noun Phrase-Adjective** means that the example illustrates an AC with a noun phrase modified by an adjective, irrespective of the question of the ordering of the adjective and the noun phrase in the example itself, and the possibility of other (typically embedded) ACs appearing in the example. The examples are glossed according to the Leipzig Glossing Rules (Comrie et al. 2008) with some additions (see list of glosses on page xv).

Typically, the examples are cited using the source's page number where they are discussed (unless they are cited directly from a corpus). The original example number (if available) is given in parenthesis. If the author gives a reference to his own corpus (typically a letter+number combination), this is given in square brackets.

The format of examples is illustrated on the following page.

[19] Note that older publications of Khan, such as Khan (1999; 2004) use a slightly different system. The main difference has to do with the transcription of a short [ɪ]~[ə] vowel, which in later works is transcribed as *ə*, while in earlier works it is transcribed as *ĭ*. Notwithstanding the question of transcription, it should be noted that not in all dialects is the difference between a tense [i] and a lax [ə] phonemic (see for instance the discussion of Gaznax phonemic inventory in Gutman 2015c). Another change concerns the rendering in NENA dialects of a fricative [θ] consistently as θ rather than *ṯ*. Especially affected is the transcription system of Younansardaroud (2001), which I have simplified by removing the vocalic-timbre marks as well as most timbre superscripts (cf. Younansardaroud 2001: 20). The hard timbre which is marked by her as superscript ʰ is marked here with a ⁺ sign, in accordance with Khan (2008b).

(9) Language: **Primary–Secondary**
Example text
Glosses
'Translation' (Source: page (example number) [Textual reference])

2 Attributive constructions: Typological and Semitic perspectives

2.1 Theoretical framework

The current research, while informed by advances in linguistic typology, is situated methodologically within the structuralist current of linguistics, which analyses language as a system of oppositions, be they between the consecutive constituents of an utterance (the so-called SYNTAGMATIC AXIS) or between possible constituents at a given point in discourse (the PARADIGMATIC AXIS). The usage of these analytical concepts will be further clarified below. While the structuralist tradition is interested mainly in the description of a single language, one can profitably extend these tools to compare and contrast several languages, as I do in the current study.

In structuralist linguistics, MORPHEMES are defined by way of opposition along the paradigmatic axis: Whenever an element of language (a SIGNIFIANT in Saussurian terms) stands in opposition in a given ENVIRONMENT (or SYNTAGM) with other elements and its exchange by these other elements co-varies systematically with a difference in *meaning* broadly conceived (a SIGNIFIÉ), this element can be identified as a LINGUISTIC SIGN. Minimal signs, i.e. those that are not analysable in terms of smaller signs, are considered to be MORPHEMES. As simple as this procedure is, it is possible to apply it in quite different ways, in accordance with the understanding of the term ENVIRONMENT used above. If by ENVIRONMENT one means a well-formed utterance, one gets the classical notion of a STRUCTURAL PARADIGM. If, on the contrary, one allows for opposition within smaller environments, such as word-forms, the above procedure yields the notion of a MORPHOLOGICAL PARADIGM. The elements identified as morphemes would be different in each case: For instance, a grammatical case marker attached to a noun-stem, whose usage is obligatory in certain environments may not be considered a morpheme within the classical approach (as it does not stand in opposition within a well-formed utterance), but it can be seen as a morpheme in the morphological approach, as the word in isolation shows variation in case. In this study I opt for the latter approach: namely, morphemes are defined relative to word-forms in isolation, and not relative to full utterances.

Linguistic structuralism is normally equated with no *a priori* categories of language, as these should be defined on a per-language basis using the analytical method sketched above. Yet, as this research follows the footsteps of previous scholars, I will operate within a framework assuming the existence of three general grammatical relations in language, described in the next section. Of these, the ATTRIBUTIVE RELATIONSHIP shall be seen as the abstract functional correlate of the concrete grammatical patterns examined, the ATTRIBUTIVE CONSTRUCTIONS (ACs). This is further explained in §2.1.2. In structural terms, the attributive relationship is the SIGNIFIÉ of several different SIGNIFIANTS.

The rest of the chapter is devoted to anchoring these terms in the traditions of linguistic typology (§2.2) and of Semitic linguistics (§2.3). §2.4 synthesizes from these different approaches one methodology used in this study.

2.1.1 The three relations

In this book, I rely on a simple dependency model of morpho-syntax admitting three basic dependency relations holding between elements of a clause:

1. The PREDICATIVE RELATION, holding between a subject and a predicate.
2. The ATTRIBUTIVE RELATION, holding between a head and its attribute.
3. The COMPLETIVE RELATION, holding between a predicative construction and a complement.

This theory, as presented here, was advocated by the Israeli linguist Gideon Goldenberg (1930–2013), who himself credited the German philologist Karl Ferdinand Becker (1775–1849) as being one of its early forefathers (see Becker 1830: 10; Goldenberg 1987; 2013a: Ch. 11; Cohen 2008: 37–38; Gutman 2015b).

Goldenberg saw the theory as both general in scope and at the same time especially adequate to the Semitic family:[1]

> The recognition of three essential types of grammatical relations, or bonds, has been a major approach to syntactic analysis commonly pursued in linguistics during the last two centuries. With regard to Semitic languages and

[1] Goldenberg clearly saw these relations as valid cross-linguistic notions, but he did not address the question whether they represent linguistic universals, nor did he tie them to any nativist conception of language. It seems, rather, that the cross-linguistic validity of these notions stems from the fact that they represent syntactic correlates of necessary communicative functions of language such as assertion (the predicative relation), qualification of referents (the attributive relation) and of events (the completive relation).

in connexion with case declension such a conception appositely reflects the very structure of the languages involved. (Goldenberg 2013a: 142)

This is so, since the case-marking classical Semitic languages (Classical Arabic, Akkadian and Ugaritic) have exactly three cases, which correspond well with the three mentioned relations. Regarding linguistic change in Semitic languages, he asserted that by using this theory "we may be able to better understand the meaning of changes in some innovative languages and thus perhaps even to measure typological innovation." (Goldenberg 2013a: 142). Since the aim of this book is exactly to investigate change in modern Semitic languages, namely the NENA branch, the usage of this theory seems especially adequate.

To the three above-mentioned dependency relations, one must add APPOSITION, not being a dependency relation, but rather an equivalence relation. In this framework, two elements are considered to be in APPOSITION, whenever both are governed by the same dependency relation, share potentially the same grammatical features (number, gender, case and definiteness – if explicitly marked), and are co-referential. In such conditions, they can replace each other syntactically, although the two may not be equivalent on semantic and discursive grounds, as one element may take a higher information load. In the latter case, my notion of apposition is similar to the notion of "appositional modification" defined by Rießler (2016: 13) as following: "Semantically, the appositional modifier is headed by the modified noun. Syntactically, however, the appositional modifier has an empty head which is co-referential with the head noun of the apposed noun phrase." His "empty head" is analysed in the current framework as a covert pronominal element.[2]

2.1.2 The attributive relationship and its manifestation

In this book, I am interested only in one of the relations mentioned above, namely the ATTRIBUTIVE RELATION. This is the dependency relationship within the NP domain which holds between a head noun (or pronoun) and a second nominal

[2]See also Cohen's definition of apposition given in footnote 8 on page 9. Acuña-Fariña (1999: 65) rejects a similar notion of apposition claiming that "[i]f a syntactic relationship of this type is to be posited, then that relationship must be applicable to a number of other constructions, and not just to one construction", and contrasts it with the widely applicable notion of dependency. Yet, in the current framework, apposition is not a syntactic relation *sensu stricto*, i.e. a dependency relation, but rather an equivalence relation. Compare again with Cohen (2008: 38): "It must be stressed that apposition [...] is not in itself a relationship, but rather a repetition of a syntagm, and occasionally, of the relationship itself." As such, the notion of apposition is applicable to a wide range of constructions.

element (the ATTRIBUTE or DEPENDENT) qualifying the head noun (cf. Goldenberg 1995: 1–2; Cohen 2013). This notion is closely related to Jespersen's notion of JUNCTION (Jespersen 1992 [1924]: Ch. 8). Note that semantically, there is no restriction on the type of the qualification involved, which may range from possession to qualification of some property of the head.

In structuralist terms, the attributive relation is a SIGNIFIÉ (function) whose SIGNIFIANT (form, i.e. morpho-syntactic exponent), is an ATTRIBUTIVE CONSTRUCTION (=AC). I use the term CONSTRUCTION here as denoting a linear ordering of segmental (and possibly super-segmental) material together with paradigmatic slots, "place-holders" so to speak, which can accommodate either an open group of elements (i.e., a lexical paradigm, often corresponding to some part of speech), or a closed group of elements (i.e., a functional paradigm, often corresponding to an inflectional paradigm of some morpheme), to which a specific function is tied.[3] In a given language, one may find many different attributive constructions. While all of these encode an attributive relationship, they may be used in different syntactic contexts, or convey different semantic or stylistic nuances. I will only linger upon these differences as far as they are insightful for my comparative purposes.

Every AC is defined as having two paradigmatic slots corresponding to the head and the attribute. In some cases, however, the two elements in question are split across two separate NPs which stand in apposition to each other, rather than in an attributive relationship. In such a configuration, it is often the case that the attributive relationship holds within one of the NPs, in which the other NP is being represented pronominally. In virtue of this, it is possible to identify one NP as being the qualified, and the second NP as being the qualification,[4] and posit an INDIRECT ATTRIBUTIVE RELATIONSHIP between them (cf. the term INDIRECT ANNEXATION used by Goldenberg 2000: 79). Yet in such a case one cannot accurately use the terms *head* and *attribute* for these NPs, as they imply a direct attributive relationship between the two elements. To overcome this terminological problem I shall use the notions of PRIMARY and SECONDARY to denote the two members, in line with Plank (1995: 38):[5]

[3]The notion of CONSTRUCTION was popularized by the proponents of Construction Grammar (e.g. Goldberg 1995; Croft 2011). It corresponds in fact to an abstract understanding of the long-standing Saussurian notion of LINGUISTIC SIGN, i.e. a coupling of FORM and FUNCTION.

[4]It is often the case that the qualifying NP follows in discourse the qualified NP, in accordance with the general tendency of pronouns to be anaphoric rather than cataphoric.

[5]These terms clearly bear affinity to the same terms introduced by Jespersen, but note that his usage is broader, as it applies equally well to cases of junction as well as nexus (Jespersen 1992 [1924]: 97).

> The nominals in relation will be neutrally referred to as PRIMARY and SECONDARY. Attributes are prototypical secondaries vis-a-vis their heads [...] but on referential and distributional grounds, secondary rank is also justified for the appositum in apposition or for a nominal indirectly related to another as a secondary predicate or the like.

Prototypically, the primary and the secondary are expected to be nouns, but this does not exclude other nominal elements, chiefly pronouns and adjectives. Moreover, as we shall see, the secondary can also be a prepositional phrase (a PP), or even a clause (Cl). Moreover, in Semitic languages the same constructions are often used with adverbial elements (prepositions or conjunctions) as primaries. While these uses can be seen as peripheral, and not strictly realizing an attributive relationship, they are sometimes illuminating for the study's comparative purposes, and thus will be taken into account.

2.2 Attributive constructions from a typological perspective

The notion of the attributive relationship, and the corresponding ACs, is clearly a very broad, unifying concept. Many typological studies, on the other hand, look at a restricted set of ACs as their object of study. Thus, Ultan (1978) establishes a typology of POSSESSIVE CONSTRUCTIONS, i.e. ACs whose secondary is a nominal possessor.[6] More recently, Koptjevskaja-Tamm (2003) discusses the *Possessive noun phrases in the languages of Europe*. A similar restriction is taken by Nichols & Bickel (2013), discussed further below. The restriction applied is basically a semantic one. Another quite common division of the domain of ACs is according to the syntactic category of the secondary: Dryer, looking at word-order phenomena, separates ACs whose secondary is a noun (a "genitive"), an adjective or a relative clause (Dryer 2013b,a,c). Gil (2013), on the other hand, examines to what extent these three categories are differentiated across the languages of the world.[7]

[6] Ultan elaborates a quite complex typology, taking into account both the LOCUS of marking (see §2.2.1), and the type of marking: whether it is syntactic or morphological on the one hand, and whether it indexes features of the possessed noun or the possessor. Yet at the end he reduces this typology to a simple LOCUS typology. Unfortunately, the lack of clear definitions of the various marking categories and the sparse use of examples renders his work less than insightful.

[7] Goldenberg (2013a: 235) comments on Gil's approach: "[t]he constitutional identity of constructions with genitive nominals, adjectives, and relative complexes will in any case belong to the profoundest level of language structure, not to be regarded as different semantic types

In the framework of Canonical Typology, Nikolaeva & Spencer (2013) pose inalienable possession and attributive modification (by adjectives) as two separate canonical constructions,[8] while alienable possession and modification by noun are their non-canonical counterparts. While they too split the AC domain, using both semantic and syntactic criteria, they do acknowledge that "there is some deeper link between the two constructions" (Nikolaeva & Spencer 2013: 209), by examining languages in which these functions are expressed identically, specifically the Ezafe marking of Iranic languages (which shall be examined carefully in this book; see §4.3).

It is not surprising that large scale typological studies attempt to focus on a restricted domain of constructions, using various semantic and syntactic criteria to delimit it. Such criteria, in line with Haspelmath's notion of COMPARATIVE CONCEPTS (Haspelmath 2010), assure the typologists they are comparing like with like. As this study is focused on a restricted and similarly shaped set of languages (namely, the NENA languages and their contact languages), I have had the leisure of defining a broader object of study. Of course, more comprehensive accounts can be found in the typological literature as well. Thus, Fairbanks (1979) starts by treating equally cases of adnominal modification by nouns, PPs and clauses, although his main interest is nominal modification. Another broad account, discussed in more detail below, is that of Plank (1995).

In the following, I shall examine in more detail the typologies of Nichols & Bickel (2013) and Plank (1995). To round of the picture, I shall present also the recent typology elaborated by Rießler (2016).

2.2.1 Head-marking vs. dependent-marking typology

Following the pioneering work of Nichols (1986), Nichols & Bickel (2013) classify possessive constructions (and subsequently languages[9]) according to the LOCUS of marking, i.e. whether the construction is marked morpho-syntactically on the head (primary in the current terminology) or the dependent (secondary), irrespective of the order of these two constituents.[10] Since the marking of each locus is independent, this simple typology yields 4 types of marking: head marking, dependent marking, double marking and no marking.[11]

of attributions that collapsed due to imperfect differentiation".

[8]Note that their use of the term CONSTRUCTION is different than ours, as it is not tied to a specific manifestation in language.

[9]For each language, they consider only one construction, which "is [the] default or has the fewest restrictions" (Nichols & Bickel 2013: §2).

[10]Such a classification has in fact been proposed earlier by Ultan (1978), but in less clear terms.

[11]A fifth category, is dedicated to "low-frequency but systematic further patterns" (Nichols & Bickel 2013: §1.5). These are cases where the markers could not be easily associated with either the head or the dependent, but they represent only 2.5% of their sample (i.e. 6 languages).

While this typology succeeds at capturing large geographical distributions, it suffers from two shortcomings rendering it somewhat simplistic at the descriptive level.

First, there is no differentiation between syntactic marking and morphological marking. Rather, the authors agglomerate the two under the heading "overt morphosyntactic marking".[12] Thus, the preposition *of* in the English phrase *the price of oil* is considered to be a case of dependent-marking, probably due to its syntactic co-constituency with the dependent, on par with an inflectional genitive case marker.[13] Since the syntactic constituency of an element may be disputed in some cases (especially if it cliticizes to another element), this can lead to analytical difficulties.[14]

Secondly, the typology does not differentiate between two quite distinct types of markers: pure relational markers versus pronominal markers, which represent the antipodal locus (i.e. the opposite member of the construction). Thus, in Turkish, in which one finds both head marking and dependent marking, the two markers are of quite distinct type:

(1) Turkish: **Noun–Noun**
çocuğ-{un} araba-sı
child-{GEN} car-POSS.3
'{the} child's car' (Bozdémir 1991: 49)

The dependent-marker is purely relational (a genitive case),[15] while the head-marker is pronominal. This is crucial, since the expression *araba-sı* is by itself a well-formed NP meaning 'his car'. A similar criticism is made by Goldenberg (2013a: 229):

> Attributive, or possessive, syntactic relations are commonly regarded as being marked either on the head or on the dependent attribute, not only by

[12] By syntactic marking I mean marking achieved by a separate syntactic element, typically bearing phrasal scope, while morphological marking is achieved by inflection of a word, possibly (but not necessarily) having narrow scope on that word only. Recently, Haspelmath (2011) has suggested that this distinction is void and cannot be applied consistently across various languages, yet I find it important in studies of language change, like the current one.

[13] Cf. Fairbanks (1979: 36): "The main distinction between the genitive inflection and the pre/postposition is that the genitive inflection is inseparable from its noun and it must be repeated in certain situations."

[14] Indeed, as we shall see in §4.3, such a controversy exists around the Persian Ezafe particle. Nichols & Bickel (2013) classify it without further comment as a head-marking instance.

[15] The usage of the genitive case in Turkish is in fact not obligatory. When it is used it usually marks the secondary as definite and specific. In this it is similar to Turkish accusative case, which marks only definite objects. See Bozdémir (1991: 49f.).

> stem form or case, but also by personal morphemes, as if the possessive relation in "the man his-house" (for "the man's house") is marked by "his" on the head term "house" [...] Pronominal morphemes, however, like other nominals or nominalizations, are not markers of the head-dependent relation, but belong with the *termini* [=loci, primary or secondary] between which the relation is apprehended.

These two shortcomings were addressed to some extent by a more elaborate typology, presented in the next section.

2.2.2 Plank's adnominal typology

A more elaborate typology of adnominal modification is presented by Plank (1995). It is not restricted to a specific semantic domain of ACs, and indeed no specific restrictions are put on the secondary, except it being of nominal nature. As Plank (1995: 38) puts it:

> The following taxonomy of marking patterns is therefore intended to be neutral (a) as to whether the nominal to be related to another is a noun or something else (such as a derived adjective), and (b) as to whether its relationship is one of [direct] attribution or of some other kind (such as apposition) – and indeed, whether this relationship is that of an immediate adnominal constituent or not.

As mentioned above (§2.1.2), Plank re-introduces the terms PRIMARY and SECONDARY to refer to the two nominal members of the construction, which he symbolizes as X and Y, a practice I shall follow below.

Disregarding the word order of the two elements, Plank opts for an elaborate head vs. dependent marking typology, in which he differentiates between pure relational markers and pronominal markers, which he calls RELATEDNESS-INDICATORS.[16]

> The relations identified may be those of secondary [pure dependent marking] or of primary [pure head marking] or of both [pure double marking],

[16] I use here the term *pronominal* in the basic meaning of representing (and possibly substituting) a noun. In a similar typology proposed by Riester (2001: ch. 2), such markers are termed AGREEMENT MARKERS. Riester's typology is further elaborated in that it distinguishes between LOCAL AGREEMENT, i.e. a marker exhibiting features of its own constituent, and NON-LOCAL AGREEMENT, i.e. a marker exhibiting features of the other constituent. Only the latter would be considered RELATEDNESS-INDICATORS in Plank's system.

> with the markers normally associated, morphologically or syntactically, with the respective nominals themselves. Relatedness-indicators may occur on the secondary [pronominal dependent marker], reflecting some property of the primary that it belongs with (such as its number, gender/class, person, or case); or they may be on the primary [pronominal head marking], reflecting some property of the secondary that it belongs with, or on both [pronominal double marking]. (Plank 1995: 38)

Since each one of the 4 markers type is in principle independent of the others, this yields 16 construction types. In fact, in the case of no marking at all, Plank distinguishes between syntactic juxtaposition of the primary and secondary (X#Y), and morphological compounding of them (X+Y). However, except for this distinction, and judging from the citation above, syntactic and morphological markings are considered alike.[17] Plank acknowledges, however, the possibility of a third locus of marking, namely "markers of the entire construction, linking primary and secondary without forming a morphological co-constituent of either [...] ('associative' markers or lexical items such as 'thing', 'possession/belong', 'place')" (Plank 1995: 39). He dubs these items "links". The elements may themselves carry pronominal markers of the primary, the secondary or both, adding 4 more construction types.[18]

Prima facie, one would expect such "links" to form a syntactic co-constituent with the secondary (see §2.3.4), so it is not clear what distinguishes them from normal secondary marking in Plank's typology.[19] Examining the accompanying examples does not clarify this point. Notwithstanding this possible confusion, Plank's typology is important in that it raises the question of distinguishing morphological marking vs. syntactic marking, and more importantly, it makes a clear difference between pronominal markers and pure relational markers. The typology adopted in this study is based to a large extent on Plank's typology.

2.2.3 Rießler's typology of attribution marking

As a last point of reference, I shall examine a recent typology of attribution marking elaborated by Rießler (2016: Ch. 4). While Rießler focuses on adjectival attri-

[17]Thus Koptjevskaja-Tamm (2003: 656) commenting on Plank's work, writes: "[this] taxonomy does not distinguish morphological boundedness and syntactic association."

[18]He does not list construction types where both the link and the primary or secondary are marked. If all these combinations would be marked, there would be 64 construction types.

[19]Indeed, later on Plank acknowledges this difficulty: "No 7. [X Y-sec-x], [is] not always easily distinguished from No. 17, X Link-x Y" (Plank 1995: 51).

Table 2.1: Rießler's typology of attributive marking

Juxtaposition	$X\ Y$
Incorporation	$X + Y$
Linker	X LNK Y
Anti-construct state	$X\ Y_{\text{ANTI-CST}}$
Anti-construct state agreement	$X\ Y_{\text{ANTI-CST+AGR}}$
Construct state	$X_{\text{CST}}\ Y$
Double construct	$X_{\text{CST}}\ Y_{\text{ANTI-CST}}$
Head-driven agreement	$X\ Y_{\text{AGR}}$
Possessor agreement	$X - y_{\text{POSS}}\ Y$

bution, his typology covers larger ground, and is thus relevant for this study. In many respects, Rießler's typology is equivalent to Plank's typology discussed above, except that he uses a more technical, and to some extent obscure, terminology.[20] I discuss it here, nonetheless, in order to compare the current framework (derived by and large from Plank's) to another recent typological framework of the same domain.

Rießler (2016: 62) considers three main dimensions which characterize attributive markers, quoted hereby:

- *Syntactic source*, i.e., the central syntactic operation which constitutes attribution and belongs either to *agreement marking* or *government.* [...]
- *Syntactic pattern*, i.e., devices projecting adjective phrases versus devices projecting full noun phrases [...]
- *Syntactic locus* of the respective formatives.

By *syntactic source*, Rießler refers to the same distinction which Plank made between relational markers and (pronominal) relatedness markers. Pure relational markers are qualified by him as being issued by "government" of the entire construction ([+ GOV] in his terminology), while relatedness markers are exponents of agreement ([+ AGR]). In cases where both marker types accumulate on one

[20]Judging by the lack of citation of Plank (1995) in Rießler's work, it seems his typology was elaborated independently of Plank's work.

member, such as Plank's [X Y-sec-x] construction, he sees the agreement as being "secondary".[21]

The second dimension, *syntactic pattern*, is a novelty of this typology. Note, however, that it is specific to adjectival attribution, and moreover, it assumes that there is a clear distinction between adjective phrases and (full) noun phrases. As we shall see in §2.3.5 below such an assertion is not evident for the Semitic languages which are the object of the current study.

The third dimension, *syntactic locus*, refers to the position of the marker: either on the head or the dependent. Just as Plank (and following Nichols 1986), Rießler (2016: 59f.) recognizes a third "floating" locus of marking, not associated with any member of the construction. He terms such markers "linkers" and brings the Tagalog *na/-ng* attributive marker as an example.[22] Interestingly, he notes that such true "linkers" are not found within his survey of the languages of northern Eurasia (see in this respect footnote 19 on page 27).

Rießler does not in general classify the markers according to their binding nature (syntactic or morphological), though interestingly, just as Plank he distinguishes between syntactic juxtaposition (Plank's X#Y) and morphological incorporation (Plank's X+Y) (Rießler 2016: 29–32).

Using these different criteria, Rießler elaborates a typology of 11 different attributive construction types (not counting double marking). Disregarding those which are specific for adjectival attribution, the remaining constructions are presented in Table 2.1 on the preceding page, alongside with an adaptation of Plank's notation for these constructions. This table can be compared to Table 2.3 on page 42 which presents the attributive construction labels used in this study.

2.3 Attributive constructions from a Semitic perspective

In the Semitic language family, the typical attributive construction is the ANNEXATION construction, or CONSTRUCT STATE CONSTRUCTION (=CSC), in which

[21]In a quite unfortunate terminological decision, Rießler terms the pure relational markers "construct state" markers, whether they appear on the head or on the dependent (in which he calls it "anti-construct state"). As we shall see in the next section, the construct state category is better reserved for use as a head-marking device, while the notion of CASE should be used for dependent-marking. It seems that Rießler is reluctant to use the term "genitive case" to term the dependent-marking relational marker since he associates it with possessive semantics and his work focuses on adjectival attribution (see Rießler 2016: 43).

[22]This marker appears in the second position of the NP, irrespectively whether the NP has the order attribute+head or head+attribute.

the primary is marked by a special morphological form, the CONSTRUCT STATE.[23] In Semitic grammars, the primary in this construction is normally called NOMEN REGENS, and the secondary NOMEN RECTUM, but I will stick to the terms primary and secondary.

2.3.1 Relational nouns and the category of state

In Semitic languages, nouns (as well as other nominals) are inflected not only for the familiar categories of NUMBER, GENDER and possibly CASE, but also for the category of STATE (cf. for Hebrew Van Hecke 2013: 579; Doron & Meir 2013: 581). In contrast to the other categories, the category of state is not PROJECTING, i.e. it is invisible for elements outside the NP in which it occurs. It may be for this reason that it has often been ignored in linguistic studies as a fundamental morpho-syntactic category of language, although it is in fact not restricted to Semitic languages.[24]

Basically, the category of state encodes the SYNTACTIC VALENCY of a noun, i.e. whether it must be followed by a complement or not.[25]

It is instructive to contrast this phenomenon with the notion of SEMANTIC VALENCY of nouns, i.e. the number of argument they have in their semantic structure. It is a well known fact of language that some nouns (like *man*) can appear by themselves, while others (e.g. *son*) conceptually require some specification. Barker (1995: 8) calls the second group RELATIONAL NOUNS and the first NON-RELATIONAL NOUNS. The relational nouns are particular in that they denote relations over pairs of referents, while the non-relational denote simple referents (see also Nikolaeva & Spencer 2013: 216f.). In terms of valency, the relational nouns are semantically bi-valent, while the non-relational are semantically mono-valent (counting the referent of the noun itself as one argument). In many languages, this semantic difference is not related to any morpho-syntactic category. Other languages do mark the difference. One common possibility cross-

[23]The use of the term CONSTRUCT STATE alone to name the construction is thus misleading. Unfortunately, such a usage is prevalent in certain formal schools of linguistics, and even made it way to the Encyclopedia of Arabic Language and Linguistics (Benmamoun 2005).

[24]But see Retsö (1984–1986: 344; 1997: 268, especially fn. 3), who treats the notion of state as a morphological category in Semitic languages, albeit as representing "allomorphic variation", as he relies on the notion of structural paradigms (see §2.1). The converse position, denying the validity of the category of state, is advocated by Faust (2014: 318), who claims that the construct state is "not a primary linguistic notion".

[25]Semantically, this complement may be conceived as a mandatory argument of some sort of the noun, or as an adjunct qualifying the noun, but this distinction is neutralised syntactically. Of course, from a syntactic view point, a mandatory adjunct is *de facto* an argument.

linguistically is to encode the difference of valency by distinguishing two classes of nouns, namely alienable vs. inalienable nouns, the latter representing relational nouns mandatory complemented by a possessor. For instance, in the American Navajo language the root *-beʾ* 'milk' cannot appear by its own, but must be possessed: *bi-beʾ* 'her milk (from her breasts)' or *ʾa-beʾ* 'something's milk' (Bickel & Nichols 2013).

In contrast to languages which mark semantic valency, which is inherent to the nominal lexeme, state morphology, marking syntactic valency, encodes *ad-hoc* whether in a given context a noun should be understood as relational (i.e. requiring a complement) or as potentially non-relational (self-sufficient).[26] The former is marked by the CONSTRUCT STATE, while the latter is marked by the FREE STATE,[27] which is typically also the citation form of a noun.[28] By way of analogy, the construct state is the nominal parallel of causative morphology in verbs: both add one syntactic argument to the argument structure of their host.

In light of the above, it is clear why the state category is non-projecting. In contrast to case, which signals what kind of dependent a noun is, and therefore should be accessible by constituents outside the NP, the state morphology determines whether a nominal governs another nominal NP-internally, and therefore is invisible outside the domain of the NP. Intrinsically, state morphology is a head-marking device.

Thus defined, it is clear that the construct state, or rather state morphology, is not a phenomenon restricted to Semitic languages. In this vein, Creissels (2009: 74) proposes to use the notion of CONSTRUCT FORM "as a general label for noun forms that are obligatory in combination with certain types of noun dependents

[26] As the non-relational form is the unmarked form it does not exclude the possibility for a noun to receive a complement. Indeed, inherently relational nouns, such as kinship terms, may still appear in the non-relational form in languages with state morphology. Note also that in Semitic languages the construct state applies as well to other nominal elements (such as adjectives or numerals) when they are mandatory accompanied by a complement. It is important to stress that in such a system inherently relational nouns (inalienable nouns) are not distinguishable morpho-semantically from non-relational nouns. This is clearly stated by Pat-El (2013b) for Biblical Hebrew. The claim to the contrary of Meltzer-Asscher & Siloni (2013) regarding the existence of a syntactic class of inalienable nouns in Modern Hebrew is factually wrong, as their alluded ungrammatical or infelicitous examples are neither ungrammatical nor infelicitous.

[27] Some authors use the traditional term ABSOLUTE STATE as opposed to construct state. Apart from being less self-explanatory, this term is problematic in the context of Aramaic, as will be explained below.

[28] A similar proposal, cast in a more formal apparatus, is given by Heller (2002). Heller sees construct state nouns as denoting functions from individuals to individuals, in contrast to free state nouns which denotes individuals.

and cannot be analyzed as instances of cross-referencing in the genitive construction".[29] Such a definition equates the construct state with the primary relation marker of Plank (1995).[30] Creissels goes on to identify construct state forms in a variety of African languages, ranging from Nilotic languages in the east to Wolof in the west.

A terminological word of caution is appropriate here. Notwithstanding the above conception of the construct state notion, it should be noted that in grammars of pre-modern Aramaic a three-way state distinction is given, opposing ABSOLUTE STATE, EMPHATIC STATE and CONSTRUCT STATE. Both the absolute state and the emphatic state are in fact instances of the free state, as defined above, and the opposition between them is related to the domain of determination: In the earliest stage of Aramaic, the emphatic state was used to mark nouns as definite (as early forms of Aramaic lack a syntactic definite article; see §1.3),[31] while the absolute state was in general used to mark nouns as indefinite. In this setting, the three-way state distinction is justified, in that a construct state noun is by itself not determined, but rather the entire CSC inherits its determination feature from its secondary (see §2.3.3). With time, the definite value of the emphatic state was eroded, and it became the default form of the free noun, the absolute state being restricted to specific syntactic contexts (Jastrow 2005; Muraoka 1997: 22, §18).

2.3.2 The construct state construction across Semitic languages

From the above discussion it should be clear that the CSC is essentially a head-marking construction,[32] as in the following Hebrew example (contrast with בַּיִת *bayiṯ* 'house.FREE'):

[29]Creissels prefers the term CONSTRUCT FORM over construct state due to the confusion arising from the use of the former as a construction label. I shall stick to the traditional term, but note that the notion of CONSTRUCT STATE can relate both to the morphological marking, and to the syntactic position of a primary (not necessarily marked as such). When in doubt, I will use the term "construct state marking" or "construct state form".

[30]An alternative term, proposed by Dixon (2010: 268) is PERTENSIVE "based on the Latin verb *pertinēre* 'to belong'". The term has not gained wide usage, as far as I am aware of. Dixon uses this term, moreover, as designating both simple markers and pronominal markers. It may be for this reason that he does not simply adopt the notion of construct state, although he is aware of the partial equivalence between the two (Dixon 2010: 310, fn. 16.2). I am grateful to Adam Pospíšil, who drew my attention to this term.

[31]For possible origins of the emphatic state, unique to Aramaic among Semitic languages, see König (1901).

[32]In the Semitic languages which mark case, namely Akkadian and Classical Arabic, it is a double-marked construction; see discussion further down in this section.

(2) Biblical Hebrew: **Noun–Noun (Head-marked AC)**
בֵּית הַמֶּלֶךְ
bēṯ ham-mɛlɛḵ
house.CST DEF-king
'the house of the king'

In Hebrew the construct state nominals are characterized by "lighter vocalisation" in comparison with their corresponding free state. Sometimes they are marked by specific suffixes, namely *-aṯ* for feminine singular nouns (in contrast to free form *-ā*) and *-ē* (Modern Hebrew *-ey*) for masculine plural nouns (in contrast with *-īm*). All these changes can be explained by the primary losing word stress, and forming one phonological word with the secondary (Van Hecke 2013: 580). This explanation, however, is diachronic, as in Modern Hebrew these forms prevail even when the primary gets its own stress, as is evident from cases where two construct state primaries are conjoined:[33]

(3) Modern Hebrew: **Conjoined Nouns–Noun Phrase**
מורֵי ותלמידֵי בֵּית הספר
[mor-ey ve= talmid-ey] [bet ha-sefer]
teacher-M.PL.CST and= pupil-M.PL.CST house.CST DEF-book
'teachers and pupils of the school'

Biblical Hebrew allows not only nouns as secondaries, but also other elements, such as prepositional phrases and clauses (Cohen 2013: 236).

The CSC of Pre-modern Aramaic is similar in essence to Hebrew. The AC system of Syriac shall be treated in detail in Chapter 3.

In Akkadian and Classical Arabic, which manifest the old Semitic case system, the secondary is further marked by the genitive case, giving effectively rise to a doubly marked construction. In Akkadian, the construct state is created by removing the MIMATION, i.e. an *-m* ~ *-n* suffix, typical of free state nouns. In some texts, the singular construct state forms are further characterized by losing the case endings, though they may surface before pronominal secondaries (Goldenberg 2013a: 144).

[33] In Biblical Hebrew it is generally accepted that only one nominal can occur as primary, as the counter-examples are extremely rare (Verhej 1989: 210): Gesenius (1909: 433, §128a, note 1) lists 4 such tentative cases, of which only one is really clear (Ezekiel 31:16): מִבְחַר וְטוֹב־לְבָנוֹן *[miḇḥar wə ṭōḇ] ləḇānōn* 'the choice and best of Lebanon' (King James translation). Yet one finds other cases of intervening material between a construct state primary and its secondary; see Freedman (1972). In Syriac too there is a rare occurrence of conjoined primaries; see example (11) on page 52. Similar examples are attested in Standard Arabic (Badawi et al. 2004: 138f.).

(4) Akkadian: **Noun–Noun (Double-marked AC)**
bīt-∅ *awīl-i-m*
house-CST man-GEN-FREE
'man's house' (Goldenberg 2013a: 232)

Clausal secondaries in Akkadian are marked by a special verbal form, the SUBJUNCTIVE:

(5) Akkadian: **Noun–Clause (Double-marked AC)**
bīt-∅ *īpuš-u*
house-CST made.3MS-SBJV
'house (which) he made' (Cohen 2010: 80)

The situation in Classical Arabic is similar to Akkadian, in that the NUNATION (from Arabic تنوين *tanwīn*), or *-n* suffix, disappears, while case endings, however, are retained.[34] In Arabic, the nunation occurs in complementary distribution with definite article, and therefore is normally seen as an exponent of the indefinite. This analysis, however, is challenged by Lyons (1999: 91–94). He argues that the nunation (in a variant form), can co-occur with the definite article in plural and dual nouns, and thus cannot mark indefiniteness. While he analyses it as "a semantically empty marker of nominality" (Lyons 1999: 93f.), he notes that it is always dropped in the construct state. Thus, it seems reasonable to conclude that the nunation is a marker of the free state.[35] The lack of nunation of definite singular nouns may be then tentatively explained as resulting from the principle of ECONOMY, as the primary of the CSC cannot in general be determined by a definite article.[36] Conversely, the absence of nunation coupled with the absence of a definite article is a clear indicator of the construct state, as in the following example:[37]

[34]I refer here to the functional similarity between Arabic and Akkadian. Whether the two are historically related is of course a separate question. It is worthwhile noting, in this respect, that also Hebrew FREE.M.PL suffix *-im*, as well as Aramaic ABS.M.PL suffix *-in* lose the */m/* or */n/* segments respectively in construct state. *Prima facie*, it seems reasonable to assume that all these functionally and phonetically elements share a common origin.

[35]A similar position is maintained by Retsö (1997), who investigates also the origin of this system.

[36]The exception for this is the CSC headed by adjectives, a construction termed in Arabic Grammar IMPURE ANNEXATION. See Goldenberg (2002: 204ff.) for further details and analysis.

[37]The situation, however, is complicated by the fact that a certain class of nouns is never marked by the nunation.

(6) Arabic: **Noun–Noun (Double-marked AC)**
بيتُ الملكِ
bayt-u-∅ *l-malik-i*
house-NOM-CST DEF-king-GEN
'The house of the king.'

In Modern Arabic dialects, both the case endings and the nunation are gone, giving rise to pure juxtaposition of the primary and secondary, the only indicator of the CSC being the lack of definiteness marking on the primary:

(7) Iraqi Arabic: **Noun–Noun (Juxtaposition)**
bēt *ʿali*
house A.
'Ali's house' (Erwin 2004 [1963]: 370)

(8) Maltese: **Noun–Noun (Juxtaposition)**
omm *Pawlu*
mother P.
'Paul's mother' (Fabri 1996: 230)

A remnant of the construct state marking is however found in feminine nouns, which in Classical Arabic are written with a *tāʾ marbūṭa* letter (ة) word-finally. This letter represents a /t/ phoneme, which is however not pronounced at the edge of a phonological word. In the CSC, such a primary forms one phonological word with the secondary, and ends therefore with an *-(a)t* segment, effectively marking the construct state in opposition to the free state ending *-a*.

(9) Iraqi Arabic: **Noun–Noun (Head-marked AC)**
sayyār-at *ʿali*
car-FS.CST A.
'Ali's car' (Erwin 2004 [1963]: 370)

(10) Maltese: **Noun–Noun (Head-marked AC)**
nann-t *Pawlu*
grandmother-FS.CST P.
'Paul's grandmother'' (Fabri 1996: 232)

(11) Moroccan Arabic: **Noun–Noun (Head-marked AC)**
mədras-t *Nadya*
school-FS.CST N.
'Nadia's school'' (Benmamoun 2005: 479)

2.3.3 The construct state construction and determination

From the above examples, an important characterisation of the classical CSC is apparent, namely the impossibility to mark the definiteness feature on the primary. Instead, the entire NP represented by the CSC acquires its definiteness feature from the marking on the secondary (see Doron & Meir 2013: 587f.). If a CSC is embedded within another one, only the very last secondary can be marked for definiteness, implying definiteness for the entire CSC:

(12) Modern Hebrew: **Noun–Noun Phrase (embedded CSC)**
לשכת נְשיא המדינה
liška-t *nəsiʾ* *ha-mədina*
office-FS.CST president.CST DEF-state
'the office of the president of the state'

In formal linguistic literature, this phenomenon is referred to using the term (IN)DEFINITENESS SPREADING, as if the definiteness marking "spreads" from the secondary to the entire CSC (cf. Danon 2008). From a constructionist point of view one can argue that the CSC has only one available slot for marking the definiteness, this slot being tied to the secondary. The marking, however, bears on the entire CSC and not on the secondary directly. Such a view is especially fortunate for cases where a marking of definiteness on the secondary entails definiteness of the entire construction, but not of the secondary itself. This is particularly the case when the secondary is understood non-referentially, as in the following example, where *kala* 'bride' does not refer to any particular bride, while the entire expression may refer to a specific wedding gown:[38]

[38]Danon (2008) brings further converse examples where a definite-marked secondary entails definiteness *only* on the secondary. In such cases, the definiteness marking may be assumed to be local to the secondary, the CSC being ambiguous between full-scope and secondary only definiteness. Note, however, that syntactically, any definiteness marking on the secondary triggers definite agreement of adjectives with the CSC.

(13) Modern Hebrew: **Noun–Noun**
שמלת הכלה
simla-t ha-kala
gown-FS.CST DEF-bride
'the wedding gown'

As Verhej (1989) notes, whenever several conjoined nouns appear as the secondary, they must agree in definiteness in order to produce a felicitous CSC.[39] This again shows that the marking of definiteness on the secondary is rather mechanical, and it relates to the marking of definiteness of the entire construction.

From the discussion in §2.3.1, we see that there is nothing in definition of the construct state given there that entails the lack of definiteness marking on the same noun. Rather, the situation of the CSC is comparable to the complementary distribution of determiners and genitives in other languages (such as English: *[the president]'s office*). A possible explanation of this cross-linguistic phenomenon, based upon the linguistic principle of economy, is given by Haspelmath (1999).

In some modern Semitic languages the situation is somewhat different: While generally there is still only one slot for marking definiteness, its position is sometimes changed. This is especially clear in colloquial Modern Hebrew, where the definiteness marking of the CSC appears regularly before the primary, especially when the secondary is non referential. In such cases, one may see the CSC as comparable to morphological compounding (Borer 2008; see also Gutman 2014). Thus, example (14) below has the same meaning as example (13) above, the difference being mainly in register. Note, however, that while the 'bride' of example (13) could be understood as referential to a specific bride, this is impossible in the following example.

(14) Modern Hebrew: **Noun–Noun**
השמלת כלה
ha-simla-t kala
DEF-gown-FS.CST bride
'the wedding gown'

In NENA as well, one finds sporadic cases where the determiner appears before the primary, but without implying a compound reading.

[39]Verhej's observation regards Biblical Hebrew, but it is by and large valid for Modern Hebrew as well.

(15) JZakho: **Noun–Noun**
ʾō šūl nāṭōr-e
DEF.MS affair.CST guard(s)-POSS.3MS
'the affair of his guards' (Cohen 2012: 121 (134))

In modern Arabic vernaculars, on the other hand, the definiteness marking is still regularly maintained on the secondary:

(16) Iraqi Arabic: **Noun–Noun**
wuṣḷ-at l-iqmaaš
piece-FS.CST DEF-cloth
'the piece of cloth' (Erwin 2004 [1963]: 371)

2.3.4 The analytic linker construction

As an alternative to the CSC, virtually all Semitic languages allow for an alternative attributive construction, which I shall term the ANALYTIC LINKER CONSTRUCTION (=ALC) or simply the LINKER CONSTRUCTION.[40] The essence of this construction is that the primary is in the free state, while the secondary is following a third element with which it forms a syntactic (but not morphological) co-constituent. I shall term this element LINKER (glossed LNK), in resonance with Plank's "link", with some reserves regarding this terminology below.

Thus, in Modern Hebrew, the analytic alternative to example (13) on the preceding page is the following:

(17) Modern Hebrew: **Noun–Noun**
הבַּיִת של המלך
ha-bayit [šel ha-melek̠]
DEF-house.FREE LNK DEF-king.FREE
'the house of the king'

The linker is treated in the literature as a preposition or as a genitive marker (a.k.a. *nota genitivi*, see Bulakh 2009), or sometimes both (cf. the *genitive preposition* of Doron & Meir 2013: 582). In fact, as Goldenberg (1995: 3–6) claims, it is best treated cross-Semitically as a pronominal element being notionally in construct

[40]In the literature, this construction is sometimes termed ANALYTIC GENITIVE CONSTRUCTION (see *inter alia* Grassi 2013; Bulakh 2009). The term GENITIVE CONSTRUCTION should be understood in this context as equivalent to the term ATTRIBUTIVE CONSTRUCTION, as no genitive case marking is necessary implied.

state, and capable of standing in apposition with an optional explicit nominal antecedent being in free state.[41] This is represented schematically as follows:

$$[\{X_{\text{FREE}}\} \leftrightarrow [\text{LNK} \mapsto Y]_{\text{CSC}}]_{\text{ALC}}$$

Note that the linker, being a pronoun heading a CSC, is quite special in that it acts as a head of a complex NP, in contrast to most pronouns which replace an entire NP.

From a diachronic view point, the linkers of many Semitic languages are in fact cognate with the Akkadian construct state pronoun *ša*:[42]

(18) Akkadian: **Pronoun–Noun**
ša *šarr-i-m*
PRO.CST king-GEN-FREE
'that of the king' (Goldenberg 2013a: 232)

The term LINKER may seem unfortunate for an element which can serve as an independent syntactic head. Note, however, that even when no primary is explicitly present, the linker mediates between an understood primary and a necessarily present secondary. Moreover, from the point of view of discourse frequency, more often than not it does link between two explicit nominal elements, bleaching its pronominal value and rendering it rather a construction marker. When necessary, I shall differentiate between a PRONOMINAL LINKER, capable of standing by its own without a primary, akin to example (18) on the current page, and a PURE LINKER, necessarily standing between two elements, being effectively a simple secondary marker, similarly to the English preposition 'of' used in the possessive sense.

The question of the different semantics of the ALC and the CSC has been much researched in the literature of Semitic languages (for Modern Hebrew see for instance Shelzinger & Ravid 1998 and bibliography there). The exact functional difference is outside the scope of this work, and I shall only briefly touch this question regarding the languages under study.

[41] As we shall see, there are exceptions to this rule, such as the rare Syriac example (35) on page 61 or more systematically in JUrmi; see §7.3.2.

[42] The Hebrew linker *šel*, present in example (17) on the facing page is in fact particular in that it has incorporated the preposition *l-* 'to' (Goldenberg 2013a: 240).

2.3.5 Goldenberg's typology of attributive constructions in Semitic

Goldenberg (2013a: Ch. 14) presents an elaborate typology of ACs in Semitic languages. Following his previous works (Goldenberg 1995), he sees the CSC (the GENITIVE CONSTRUCTION in his terminology) as the basic exponent of the attributive relationship in Semitic languages. His classification is based first and foremost on the important observation that the attributive relationship is not restricted to nouns, but can in fact hold also between other phrasal categories. Thus, the secondary (attribute) can be a noun, a pronoun, a prepositional phrase (PP) or a clause, while the primary (head) can be a noun or a pronoun (and in fact also adverbial elements, namely prepositions or conjunctions). The various combinations yield 8 different patterns, presented in Table 2.2.

Table 2.2: Members of the attributive relationship (Goldenberg 2013a: Ch. 14)

	Head	Attribute
A	Noun	Noun
B	Noun	Pronoun
C	Pronoun	Noun
E	Pronoun	Pronoun
G	Noun	PP
H	Pronoun	PP
I	Noun	Clause
J	Pronoun	Clause

Syntactically, all these patterns can in principle be expressed by the CSC. Yet, when a pronoun is involved, they may (or sometimes must) be expressed morphologically. For instance, Pattern B is normally expressed by attaching a possessive pronominal suffix to the head noun, yielding a morphological construction somewhat different from the CSC. Moreover, adjectives, according to Goldenberg, are simply morphological realisations of pattern C, where a pronoun, denoting a referent, and a nominal attribute denoting a quality, are fused together into one word.

Pronominal elements play a further important role in Goldenberg's classification, since they permit the extension of the basic AC, be it the syntactic CSC or a morphological construction, into more elaborate periphrastic constructions. This is possible, since the pronominal elements can stand in *apposition* (in the sense defined in §2.1.1) with other NPs. For instance, example (18) on page 39, being an instance of Goldenberg's Pattern C, can be extended by adding a nominal primary appositional to the pronominal head of the CSC, yielding the ALC.

(19) Akkadian: **Noun↔Pronoun–Noun**
mārum [ša šarr-i-m]
son PRO.CST king-GEN-FREE
'the king's son' (Goldenberg 2013a: 232)

Goldenberg's analysis of the ALC in Syriac is given in §3.5, while a more elaborate extension, the Double Annexation Construction, involving two appositions, is presented in §3.6 in the context of Syriac.

Goldenberg's pronominal elements are quite similar to Plank's relatedness-indicators. Yet their definitory property is that they are pronouns, i.e. they substitute a noun in an AC, and as such they can form an independent NP constituent together with their antipodal locus. Inflectional properties reflecting number, gender, person, or case of a co-referenced noun are incidental and do not need to appear. For instance, the Akkadian construct state pronoun *ša*, shown in example (19) on this page, does not inflect.

2.4 Typology of attributive constructions used in this study

The typology of attributive constructions used in this study is informed both by Plank's typology (see §2.2.2) and Goldenberg's typology (see §2.3.5), while being adapted to the languages studied, namely the NENA dialects.

The classification of ACs undertaken in this study is based, on the one hand, on the morphemic make-up of the constructions (syntagmatic axis) and, on the other hand, on the categorical variation available for the primaries and secondaries (paradigmatic axis). The two axes are detailed in the two sections below.

2.4.1 Syntagmatic axis

I distinguish between two LOCI of marking (primary and secondary) and two types of marking: simple relation markers and pronominal markers (the latter named relatedness-indicators in Plank's terminology). Ignoring the possible accumulation of markers on one locus, and leaving aside the question of the ordering of the elements, this leads to 7 principal constructions, summarized in Table 2.3.

Following Plank (1995: 39), X represents the primary, Y the secondary, while x and y are co-referential pronominal markers. Subscripts represent morphological marking. Curly brackets indicate optional elements, while square brackets delimit independent NPs.

Further comments about each construction and their usage in the NENA group are given below. The terminology and the relevant glossing conventions used f or each construction are introduced here as well.

Table 2.3: Principal Attributive Constructions

Juxtaposition	$X\ Y$
Genitive case marking	$X\ Y_{\text{GEN}}$
Construct state construction	$X_{\text{CST}}\ Y_{\{\text{GEN}\}}$
Juxtaposition-cum-agreement	$X\ Y_{\text{AGR}}$
Analytic linker construction	$\{X_{\{\text{CST}\}}\}[x_{\text{LNK}}\ Y_{\{\text{GEN}\}}]$
Possessive suffix marking	$[X - y_{\text{POSS}}]\ \{Y_{\{\text{GEN}\}}\}$
Double annexation construction	$[X - y_{\text{POSS}}]\ [x_{\text{LNK}}\ Y_{\{\text{GEN}\}}]$

Juxtaposition The ∅-marking strategy: the two members of the construction are merely juxtaposed to each other.

Simple primary marking The primary is marked morphologically by the construct state (glossed CST), yielding the CONSTRUCT STATE CONSTRUCTION (CSC). In the NENA dialects, I shall differentiate between three types of construct state: a "classical" construct state characterized by phonological reduction of the corresponding free state, typically apocope of the last vowel; a suffixed marker *-əd*, typically replacing the last vowel; and a suffixed marker originating in the Iranic Ezafe.[43]

Simple secondary marking The secondary is marked morphologically by means of GENITIVE CASE (glossed GEN). In NENA dialects only some determiners can be marked by genitive case. Alternatively, in Syriac one finds a dative preposition (glossed DAT) marking the secondary (see §3.7). A clausal secondary can be marked as such by means of a relativizer (glossed REL).

[43]In the interlinear glossing of examples the two first types shall be differentiated as .CST vs. -CST, while the Ezafe shall be glossed as -EZ. In abstract representations of constructions, however, I shall use the gloss .CST to encompass all three types.

(Simple) double marking Both the primary and the secondary are marked with the above markers. As in the NENA dialects genitive marking is normally only possible with some secondaries, I treat this as a variant of the CSC.

Pronominal secondary marking A pronominal linker (glossed LNK, representing the primary, intervenes between the two construction members, bonding syntactically with the secondary (see §2.3.4), yielding the ANALYTIC LINKER CONSTRUCTION (ALC). Note that the secondary may additionally be marked by genitive case. In this construction, an explicit nominal primary may appear in free state, or more rarely in construct state (see §7.3.2). If the pronominal element is not an overt linker but is rather fused morphologically with the secondary, as is the case of adjectives according to Goldenberg's analysis, then the secondary exhibits agreement features (marked as AGR); in this case I shall speak of the JUXTAPOSITION-CUM-AGREEMENT construction (although it is assimilated with the pure juxtaposition construction, as agreement features can be neutralised).

Pronominal primary marking The head noun is marked by a pronominal suffix representing the secondary. Following the traditional terminology in Semitic studies, I call these suffixes POSSESSIVE SUFFIXES (glossed POSS), although their usage is wider than denoting possession only.[44] In NENA this construction occurs without an explicit nominal secondary, the suffix effectively representing the secondary. In other languages, such as Turkish, one finds this marking co-occurring with an explicit nominal secondary (which may or may not be marked by genitive case; see example (1) on page 25).

Pronominal double marking In this construction both the primary and the secondary are marked with the above pronominal markers, yielding the DOUBLE ANNEXATION CONSTRUCTION (DAC).[45] Such a construction is very rare in NENA, but is found in Syriac (see §3.6).

In addition to these terms, I shall use occasionally the more general terms HEAD MARKING, DEPENDENT MARKING and DOUBLE MARKING, as explained above in §2.2.1.

---

[44] Cf. Ornan (1964: ch. 2) who uses the Hebrew term כינוי קניין *kinuy qinyan* 'possessive pronoun'.

[45] In the usage of this term I follow Goldenberg (2013a: 234, fn. 15), who credits Ornan (1964: 124 [2011: 85]) for introducing this term in Hebrew as סמיכות כפולה *smixut kfula*. In descriptive grammars of Hebrew (e.g. Glinert 1989: 34) as well as in typological works referring to Hebrew (e.g. Comrie & Thompson 2007: 366) it is often translated as DOUBLE GENITIVE. For the use of the term GENITIVE in this respect see footnote 40 on page 38.

2.4.2 Paradigmatic axis

For a fine-grained classification of the ACs, it is profitable to examine the question of which elements can appear as primaries and as secondaries apart from nouns. The classification of these elements is a necessary methodological choice, and does not reflect any cross-linguistic claims regarding the universality of the proposed categories.

My classification is based on the traditional distinction between the Parts-of-Speech (Nouns, Pronouns, Adjectives, Participles, Infinitives, Adverbs). Additionally, I make a distinction between one-word elements and phrasal, multi-word, constituents.[46] I distinguish CP NOUNS [=Complex Predicate Nouns] as a special functional sub-category of nouns which participate, together with a light verb, in complex predication structures. Complex predication is quite common in Iranic languages such as Persian (see for instance Samvelian 2012), and has been borrowed to some extent into some NENA dialects. On the other hand, I conflate into one category of ADVERBIALS all elements which head phrases of adverbial function, be they prepositions, conjunctions or adverbs, following Cohen (2010).[47] In the case of the analytic linker construction, where no explicit primary appears besides the pronominal linker, I shall treat this absence as a ZERO (∅) primary.

In the secondary position I observe two further categories: ordinal numerals ('first', 'second', etc.) and clauses. Thus, as possible primaries or secondaries I distinguish between the following categories:

1. Noun {Phrase}
2. Pronoun
3. CP Noun
4. Infinitive {Phrase}
5. Participle {Phrase}
6. Adjective {Phrase}

[46] This distinction permits us to distinguish between constructions which are morphological in nature and require a single-word host, from those which are syntactic. It should not be understood as implying that single-word constituents can not act as phrasal constituents.

[47] The rationale for this choice is that often one and the same element can take all three functions, depending on its complements, such as the English word 'before'. In the example titles, however, I shall give more precise labels (Preposition, Conjunction, Adverb), unless I wish to emphasize the general adverbial nature of the element in question.

7. Ordinal
8. Clause
9. Adverbial
10. Zero (∅)

2.4.3 Synopsis

Table 2.4: Parameters of an AC structure, disregarding order variation

Primary (X)	CST [± POSS]	LNK	GEN	Secondary (Y)
				Noun
Noun				Pronoun
Pronoun				CP Noun
CP Noun	Ap. [± POSS]			Infinitive
Infinitive	*-əd*	+	+	Participle
Participle	-EZ	∅	∅	Adjective [± AGR]
Adjective	∅			Ordinal [± AGR]
Adverbial				Adverbial
Zero (∅)				[± REL] Clause

The different syntagmatic and paradigmatic possibilities for ACs in NENA, as analysed in the current work, are summarised in Table 2.4. Each column shows the variation available at each morphemic slot. To this one should add the two ordering possibilities: typically the primary precedes the secondary (X Y), but also the inverse order can be found.

The primary may be marked by construct state morphemes of various types: APOCOPE (=Ap.), the native suffix *-əd*, or Ezafe marking, or it may stay unmarked (∅). Following the apocopate construct state (or a variant thereof) one may find a POSSESSIVE SUFFIX, which functions as a pronominal secondary.

As for the secondary marking, there are two main markers: a pronominal linker and/or a genitive case. These may independently be present (+) or absent (∅). Adjectives and ordinals may show additionally agreement features (AGR), while a relativizer may precede a clausal secondary.

3 Attributive constructions in Syriac

3.1 Introduction

The point of departure of this study is Syriac, taken to be an approximation of the precursor(s) of the NENA dialects of the Classical Aramaic period. While it is sometimes assumed that all NENA dialects developed from a unique undocumented Proto-NENA dialect (cf. Hoberman 1988), such an assumption is uncertain at the current state of our knowledge. A plausible alternative assumption is that the dialectal continuum observed in NENA existed also in the Classical Aramaic period (cf. Kim 2008: 512). Be that as it may, only a few Eastern dialects of that period left traces as literary languages. Arguably, among these Syriac is the best documented. Thus, in the absence of contrary evidence, I assume that any constructions extant in Syriac existed as well in the pre-NENA dialects. This assumption is supported by the fact that the constructions surveyed in this chapter are by and large extant also in two other documented Eastern Classical Aramaic languages, namely Jewish Babylonian Aramaic and Classical Mandaic. Where relevant, some comparative notes regarding these two languages are given as well.

The research into ACs in Syriac, often termed "genitive" in the literature, is of course old and vast, and in the following I cannot expect to innovate much. Rather, the aim of the current section is to position the data about the Syriac attributive system in the framework described in §2.4, to facilitate comparison with the NENA dialects and contact languages.

My point of departure is the seminal article of Goldenberg (1995), "Attribution in Semitic Languages", in which he masterfully analyses the basic constructions available in Syriac. A further extension of these ideas is given in Goldenberg (2013a: Ch. 14), particularly in pp. 236ff. regarding Syriac.

The data in this survey are drawn from two types of sources: On the one hand, I have consulted Syriac grammars, notably the classical grammars of Nöldeke (1898), Duval (1881) and the pedagogical grammars of Muraoka (1997; 2013). On the other hand, I have drawn extensively on textual studies of various Syriac texts of the *Peshiṭta – The book of 1 Kings* (Williams 2001), *The Gospel of Matthew*

(Joosten 1996), *Sirach (The Wisdom of Ben-Sira)* (Van Peursen 2007) and *The Prayer of Manasseh* (Gutman & Van Peursen 2011) – as well as *The Book of the Laws of the Countries* of Bardaisan (Bakker 2011). In all cited examples I have indicated both the primary source (if given) and the secondary source in which I have found the example. Whenever possible, I have tried to verify the correctness of the example in the primary source.[1] To round off the picture, I have also gathered numerous examples directly from the first part of the *Acts of Thomas* published by Wright (1871: ܩܦܪ–ܩܒܒ)[2], as well as some examples from the Syriac dictionary of Payne Smith (1903).[3] Some further examples were taken from specialized articles cited below.

The chapter is organised as follows: The next section gives a brief reminder regarding the three morphological states present in Syriac. Section §3.3 discusses the use of possessive pronominal suffixes, while the three subsequent sections deal with the three main attributive constructions of Syriac, namely the construct state construction (§3.4), the analytic linker construction (§3.5), and the double annexation construction (§3.6). Section §3.7 deals with the marginal dative linker construction, while §3.8 presents the juxtaposition-cum-agreement construction used by adjectival secondaries. Section §3.9 concludes this chapter with some general remarks.

3.2 The three states in Syriac

Following the discussion in §2.3.1, recall that Syriac, like other Aramaic varieties of antiquity, possesses a 3-way state distinction in nouns, namely the CONSTRUCT STATE, and two free states: the ABSOLUTE STATE and the EMPHATIC STATE, the latter being the citation form of nouns and adjectives. In Syriac, the absolute state is used only in specific syntactic environments (especially with adjectives used predicatively), while the emphatic state is the commonly used form of the (free) noun (Muraoka 1997: 22). Morphologically the emphatic state is marked

[1] I would like to thank my colleague Ralph Barczok for helping me in finding some of the more obscure primary sources.

[2] The page numbers of the Syriac section of this edition are given in Syriac letters, a convention which I have kept in the citations below. The same text is reproduced in the chrestomathy of Muraoka 1997: 30*–40*.

[3] In all cases the Syriac text is reproduced as it appears in the source cited. For the sake of consistency, however, it is always transcribed according to the East-Syriac vocalisation system, which indicates length only for the vowels /a/ and /e/. Unpronounced letters are generally not transcribed except in some suffixes and clitics in which they are printed as superscript letters. Spirantization, which is usually not phonemic, is not transcribed.

by means of an *-ā* suffix (in the singular), which is absent in the absolute and construct states. The MS absolute and construct states, moreover, are identical in form. Examples of these forms are given in Table 3.1.

Table 3.1: The three states of Syriac singular nouns, as well as their pre-suffixal forms with the 3MS possessive pronoun

	ABS	CST	EMPH	'his'
'name'	*šem*		*šm-ā*	*šm-ēh*
'king'	*mlek*		*malk-ā*	*malk-ēh*
'queen'	*malkā*	*malka-t*	*malkt-ā*	*malkt-ēh*

3.3 Possessive pronominal suffixes (X-y.POSS)

Syriac, as all Semitic languages, has a set of pronominal suffixes, which attach to nouns and prepositions (Muraoka 1997: 19; Goldenberg 2013a: 88). Following the conventional terminology, I shall call these suffixes POSSESSIVE PRONOUNS. These suffixes attach to the PRE-SUFFIXAL nominal stem (Goldenberg 2013a: xix), which can be derived from the emphatic state by dropping off the emphatic state suffix *-ā*. Consequently, the possessive pronouns, just like the MS construct state ∅ suffix (i.e. lack of suffix), stand in opposition to the emphatic state suffix *-ā* (see Table 3.1).

(1) Syriac: **Noun–Pronoun**
ܗܝܡܢܘܬܗ
haymānut-ēh
faith-POSS.3MS
'his faith' (Muraoka 1997: 70, §91e)

(2) Syriac: **Noun–Pronoun**
ܒܫܡܗ
ba= šm-ēh
in= name-POSS.3MS
'by his name' (*Peshiṭta*, Prayer of Manasseh, ed. Baars & Schneider 1972: A3; Gutman & Van Peursen 2011: 90 (3A))

The possessive pronouns are strongly bound to the head noun, and have scope over it alone. Thus, they should be seen as morphological word-level inflectional suffixes (see §4.2). Whenever two nouns are conjoined, each noun must have its own possessive suffix (contrast with example (51) on page 65):

(3) Syriac: **Conjoined Nouns–Pronoun**
ܪܘܓܙܟ ܘܚܡܬܟ
rugz-āk *w=ḥemt-āk*
rage-POSS.2MS and=fury-POSS.2MS
'your rage and your fury' (*Peshiṭta*, Prayer of Manasseh, ed. Baars & Schneider 1972: A3; Gutman & Van Peursen 2011: 90 (4A))

While syntactically the N+POSS construction is parallel to an NP, morphologically it is equivalent to a single noun.[4]

3.4 The construct state construction (X.CST Y)

The formally simplest, though not most frequent, attributive construction in Syriac is the construct state construction (CSC), in which the primary appears in the construct state.

(4) Syriac: **Noun–Noun**
ܡܠܟܘܬ ܫܡܝܐ
malkut *šmayyā*
kingdom.CST heaven
'kingdom of heaven' (*Peshiṭta*, Matthew 11:11; Muraoka 1997: 61, §73a)

Muraoka (1997: 61) notes that this construction "tends to be confined to standing phrases verging on compound nouns", citing the following examples:

(5) Syriac: **Noun–Noun**
ܓܙܪ ܕܝܢܐ
gzār *dinā*
decision.CST judgement
'verdict' (Muraoka 1997: 61, §73a)

[4]The behaviour of the suffixed noun as a single noun can be illustrated by the observation of Van Peursen (2007: 187, fn. 21), who notes that in the corpus of Sirach the maximal chain of construct state nouns consists of two construct state nouns and one final noun, irrespectively of the question whether the final noun bears a possessive suffix or not.

(6) Syriac: **Noun–Noun**

ܒܪ ܚܐܪ̈ܐ

bar ḥērē

son.CST free.PL

'a free-born man' (Muraoka 1997: 61, §73b)

In such idiomatic cases, the secondary is non-referential. Furthermore, in idiomatic usage, one finds also cases where the secondary is a PP:

(7) Syriac: **Infinitive–Prepositional Phrase**

ܡܣܡ ܒܪܝܫܐ

msām b= rišā

put.INF.CST in= head

'death penalty' (Duval 1881: 338, §357a)

(8) Syriac: **Noun–Prepositional Phrase**

ܡܦܩ ܒܪܘܚܐ

mappaq b= ruḥā

utterance.CST in= spirit

'an excuse' (Duval 1881: 338, §357a)

The compounding is sometimes reflected in the orthography when the expression is spelt as one word (with possible further phonetic reductions), such as ܡܣܡܒܪܫܐ *msām-b-rišā* 'death penalty' used as an alternative spelling of example (7) (Payne Smith 1903: 285), or the frequently occurring ܒܪܢܫܐ *bar-nāšā* 'man' (lit. son-man).

The morpho-syntactic independence of the two members of the construction is apparent, on the other hand, when they are separated by intervening material, notably second position clitics, be they certain conjunctive adverbs[5] or the enclitic personal pronoun. It should be noted, however, that such cases are not so frequent and these clitics tend to normally appear after the entire CSC (Van Peursen and Falla 2009: 69).[6]

[5] See Van Peursen and Falla (2009: 67) for the term CONJUNCTIVE ADVERB.

[6] See further Van Peursen (2007: 183) who defines the CSC as an indivisible PHRASE ATOM.

(9) Syriac: **Noun–Noun**
ܒܢܝ̈ ܕܝܢ ܒܠܗܐ
bnay =dēn Balhā
son.PL.CST =however B.
'the sons of Bala, however' (*Zachariae Episcopi Mitylenes, Anectoda Syriaca* Vol. 3, ed. Land 1870: 39, 16 *apud* Nöldeke 1898: 157, §208A)

(10) Syriac: **Noun–Noun**
ܒܢܝ̈ ܐܢܘܢ ܙܕܝܩܐ̈
bnay =ʾennon zaddiqē
son.PL.CST =3PL righteous.PL
'They are sons of the righteous.' (*S. Ephræmi Opera* vol. 2 ed. Benedictus 1740: 384 D; Nöldeke 1898: 158, §208A)

In these examples, the primaries must carry word-stress, otherwise clitics could not attach to them. Thus, following the discussion in §2.3.2, they confirm the view that construct state in Syriac as in many other Semitic languages is not merely a phonological artefact resulting from stress shift, but is rather a marker of a morpho-syntactic category. Further evidence to this is adduced by the quite rare case where two conjoined nouns appear in construct state.[7]

(11) Syriac: **Conjoined nouns–Noun**
ܟܬܒܝ ܘܩܪܝܝ ܫܡܗܝ̈ܗܘܢ
[kātbay w= qāryay] šmāhay-hon
writing.CST and= reading.CST names-POSS.3M.PL
'writing and reading their names' (*Zachariae Episcopi Mitylenes, Anectoda Syriaca* Vol. 3, ed. Land 1870: 136, 14 *apud* Nöldeke 1898: 158, §208A)

Noun phrases, including inflected possessed nouns, can regularly appear as secondaries of the CSC, whether they represent an attributive construction (leading to a chain of constructs[8]), a conjoined NP, or a combination of both.

[7]Recall that while this usage is very rare in Syriac and other classical Semitic languages, a similar construction is quite frequent in Modern Hebrew (mostly in the written style, see example (3) on page 33) and in Standard (modern) Arabic (Badawi et al. 2004: 138f.), hinting that this is in fact a natural development of the language.

[8]Van Peursen (2007: 187) notes that at most one embedded CSC occurs as the secondary of the CSC in the corpus of Sirach. See also footnote 4 on page 50.

(12) Syriac: **Noun–Possessed Noun**
ܢܐܓܪܬ ܪܘܚܟ
na'grat ruḥ-āk
prolonging.CST spirit-POSS.2MS
'your patience[9]' (*Acts of Thomas*, ed. Wright 1871: ܡܚܠ = Muraoka 1997: 37*)

(13) Syriac: **Noun–Noun Phrase**
ܠܥܝܢ ܒܢܝ ܐܢܫܐ
l= 'ayn [bnay nāšā]
to= eye son.PL.CST man
'in the eyes of men' (*Peshiṭta*, Sirach 1:29 *apud* Van Peursen 2007: 186)

(14) Syriac: **Noun–Conjoined Nouns**
ܣܘܟܝ ܬܫܒܘܚܬܐ ܘܐܝܩܪܐ
sawkay [tešbuḥtā w= 'iqārā]
branch.PL.CST praise and= honour
'branches of praise and honour' (*Peshiṭta*, Sirach 24:16 *apud* Van Peursen 2007: 210)

(15) Syriac: **Noun–Conjoined Noun Phrases**
ܘܒܝܬ ܡܣܡܟ ܬܫܒܘܚܬܐ ܘܐܝܩܪܐ ܕܠܥܠܡ
bēt [[mesmak tešboḥtā] w= [iqārā da= l= 'ālam]]
house.CST support.INF.CST praise and= honour LNK= to= eternity.ABS
'a house of support of praise and eternal honour' (*Peshiṭta*, Sirach 1:19 *apud* Van Peursen 2007: 210)

Moreover, the secondary can be determined by an attributive demonstrative:

(16) Syriac: **Noun–Determined noun**
ܪܘܡܝ ܐܢܬܬ ܗܘ ܡܠܟܐ
Rumi 'attat haw malkā
R. wife.CST DEM.MS king
'Rumi, wife of this king' (Simeon Beth-Arsamensis, *Homeritarum martyrium*, ed. J. S. Assemanus 1719: 368, 2; Duval 1881: 339, §357f[10])

---

[9]The form ܢܐܓܪܬ *na'grat*, unattested elsewhere, is understood to be a synonym of ܢܓܝܪܘܬ *naggirut* 'patience', or a corruption thereof (Muraoka 1997: 37*, fn. 62).

In the context of the ALC, such a demonstrative is arguably a definite article (Pat-El 2010: 65; see discussion in §3.5.6.

3.4.1 Adjectives and participles as primaries

The CSC can be headed by other part-of-speech categories as well, notably participles and adjectives. A CSC headed by a participle yields a nominalisation of a verbal phrase, where the secondary corresponds to an argument (not necessarily a direct one) of the primary.

(17) Syriac: **Participle–Noun Phrase**
ܡܢ ܝܬܒܝ ܟܘܪܣܘܬܐ ܕܡ̈ܠܟܐ
men yātbay [kursāwātā d= malkā]
from sit.PL.PTCP.CST thrones LNK= king
'from those who sit on royal thrones' (*Peshiṭta*, Sirach 40:3; Van Peursen 2007: 203)

A CSC composed of an adjectival primary and nominal secondary is quite peculiar in its semantics, as it is the primary (the adjective) which qualifies the secondary (the noun), yet the entire phrase acts as an adjective phrase. Thus, in the following example, *saggi ḥnānā* 'great.CST compassion' should be understood as 'bearer of great compassion'. The example shows, moreover, the equivalence of such CSCs to regular adjectives.[11]

(18) Syriac: **Adjective–Noun**
ܕܐܢܬ ܗܘ ܡܪܝܐ ܢܓܝܪ ܪܘܚܐ· ܘܡܪܚܡܢܐ ܘܣܓܝ ܚܢܢܐ
ʾat =^{h}u māryā ngir ruḥā wa= mraḥmānā w= saggi
2MS =3MS Lord long.CST spirit and= merciful and= great.CST
ḥnānā
compassion
'You are the Lord, long-suffering and merciful and of great compassion.' (*Peshiṭta*, Prayer of Manasseh, ed. Baars & Schneider 1972: A7; Gutman & Van Peursen 2011: 217 (7a))

---

[10] Duval mistakenly gives the wrong page number (365).

[11] See Goldenberg (2002) for an analysis of the phenomenon in Arabic, and Doron (2014) for a analysis of the phenomenon in Modern Hebrew, cast in formal semantics terminology. In NENA, on the other hand, such examples are very rare (see the Qaraqosh example (35) on page 161), and in most dialects virtually non-existent.

3.4.2 Adverbial secondaries

Deviating further from the typical noun+noun AC, adjectives and participles in construct state can be followed also by adverbials (PPs or adverbs), including infinitives headed by the preposition *l-* (Muraoka 1997: 76, §96b; Brock 1997: 53ff.).

Of particular interest is the usage of the secondary *b=* *kull* 'in all', which according to Brock (1997: 54f.) was used in sixth- and seventh-century translations as the equivalent of Greek superlatives.

(19) Syriac: **Adjective–Prepositional Phrase**
ܕܚܟܝܡ̈ܝ ܒܟܠ ܝܘܢ̈ܝܐ
d= *ḥakkimay* *b=* *kull (yawnāye)*
LNK= wise.M.PL.CST in= all Greek.PL
'of the most wise (the Greeks)' (Eusebius, *Theophania* ed. Lee 1842: II.ܦܐ; Brock 1997: 55[12])

A similar construction has been preserved in NENA to express superlatives, using however nominal secondaries including the pronoun *kull* 'all' itself; see examples (32)–(33) on page 123 for JZakho and example (31) on page 195 for JUrmi.

Another noteworthy usage of adverbial secondaries is the usage of infinitives headed by the preposition *l-*, which seems to have entered regular usage in Syriac in the sixth or seventh century as well (Brock 1997: 57f.):

(20) Syriac: **Participle–Infinitive**
ܘܝܕ̈ܥܝ ܠܡܒܐܫܘ
w= *yādʿay* *l=* *mabʾāšu*
and= know.PTCP.M.PL.CST to= harm.INF
'and who know how to harm' (Babai, *Commentary on Evagrius' Centuries*, Cod. Vatic. syr. N. 178, f. 8b, ed. Frankenberg 1912: 22, 2; Brock 1997: 58)

Finally, there are other examples of adverbial secondaries, headed by adjectives or participles:

(21) Syriac: **Adjective–Prepositional Phrase**
ܫܰܦܺܝܪ̈ܰܬ ܒܚܶܙܘܳܐ
šappirat *b=* *ḥezwā*
beautiful.F.PL.CST in= appearance
'beautiful in appearance' (*Peshiṭta*, Genesis 12:11; Nöldeke 1898: 158, §206)

[12]Brock mistakenly attributes the edition to Cureton. Moreover, he cites the words in wrong order, putting the appositive *yawnāye* 'Greeks' at the beginning of the phrase.

(22) Syriac: **Participle–Prepositional Phrase**
ܥ̈ܳܐܠܰܝ ܠܓܢܘܢܐ
'ā'ellay *la= gnonā*
enter.PTCP.M.PL.CST to= bridal_chamber
'those who enter the bridal chamber' (*Acts of Thomas*, ed. Wright 1871: ܩܡܒ)

(23) Syriac: **Participle–Adverb**
ܡܳܝ̈ܬܰܝ ܩܰܠܝܠܳܐܝܬ
māytay *qalilā'it*
die.PTCP.M.PL.CST quickly
'those who die quickly' (*Acta Martyrum Orientalium et Occidentalium* Vol. 1, ed. S. E. Assemanus 1748: 79, 10; Nöldeke 1898: 157, §207)

3.4.3 Adverbial primaries

As for adverbial primaries, many prepositions of Syriac can be analysed as being adverbial nouns in construct state. Thus, the preposition ܩܕܡ *qdām* 'before' is the construct state of ܩܕܡܐ *qdāmā* 'front'.

(24) Syriac: **Adverbial Noun–Noun**
ܩܕܳܡ ܝܰܘܡܳܐ
qdām *yawmā*
front.CST day
'yesterday' (Payne Smith 1903: 490)

Similarly, nouns in construct state may join basic prepositions to form adverbial expressions:

(25) Syriac: **Adverbial Phrase–Noun**
ܒܝܰܕ ܡܳܪܰܢ
[b= yad] *mār-an*
in= hand.CST master-POSS.1PL
'by our Lord' (*Acts of Thomas*, ed. Wright 1871: ܩܡܒ)

3.4.4 The proclitic *d-* as a pronominal primary

A category which is quite restricted from appearing as primary, if not completely absent, is that of pronouns. According to my survey, none of the independent personal pronouns, demonstrative pronouns or interrogative pronouns can appear as a primary of the CSC construction. This is not surprising, given that in general these elements do not show state distinctions. However, according to Goldenberg (1995) one element, namely the proclitic *d-~da-* can serve as a pronominal head. Thus, he draws a parallel between the following two cases, arguing that both instantiate an attributive relationship (a GENITIVE CONSTRUCTION in his words).

(26) Syriac: **Noun–Noun**
deḥlat ʾalāhā
fear.CST God
'fear of God' (Goldenberg 1995: 4)

(27) Syriac: **Pronoun–Noun**
d= *alāhā*
PRO= God
'that[13]of God' (Goldenberg 1995: 4)

The syntactic equivalence between the *d-* proclitic and a construct state noun is especially clear when it is used to repeat anaphorically a construct state primary, as in the following conjoined NP:[14]

(28) Syriac: **Noun–Conjoined Nouns**
ܢܒܝ̈ܝ ܒܥܠܐ ܘܕܗܘܓܒ̈ܐ
nbiyay *Baʿlā wa= d=* *hugbe*
prophets.CST B. and= PRO= shrines
'the prophets of the Baal and those of the shrines' (*Peshiṭta*, 1 Kings 19:1; Williams 2001: 21)

While the proclitic *d-* certainly qualifies as being pronominal by virtue of replacing a noun, it is hardly justifiable to see it morphologically (rather than syntactically) as being in construct state, since it does not have a corresponding free

[13] Goldenberg translates this phrase as "N of God".

[14] *Pace* Williams (2001: 8) this should not be seen as a "mixed construction" (as is the case with example (35) on page 61), but rather as two conjoined ACs. This structure should furthermore be contrasted with example (14) on page 53 in which we have one AC, consisting of a primary modified by two conjoined secondaries.

state.[15] Therefore, while example (27) on the preceding page clearly represents an AC, it is not exactly an instance of the CSC.[16]

As we shall see in the following section, the most frequent function of the *d*-proclitic is to stand between an overt NP and its attribute. Therefore, as discussed in §2.3.4, we shall call it a PRONOMINAL LINKER or simply LINKER (glossed LNK). In cases such as example (27) on the previous page, we may say that it links between an implicit referent and the secondary.[17]

3.5 The analytic linker construction (X LNK Y)

Probably the most frequent AC in Syriac is the construction where the primary and the secondary are mediated by the pronominal linker *d(a)-*. This construction, which we term the ANALYTIC LINKER CONSTRUCTION (=ALC) is illustrated by the following examples:[18]

(29) Syriac: **Noun–Noun**
deḥltā d= alāhā
fear.EMPH LNK God
'fear of God[19]' (Goldenberg 1995: 4)

[15]It can be traced back to the Northwest Semitic pronominal **ðū*, of which Aramaic retained the fossilized genitive form **ðī* which evolved into *d-* (Gzella 2011: 437). As such, it is etymologically related to the demonstrative pronouns, as is evident from the FS demonstrative pronoun *hāḏē*, but synchronically it is hard to see it as the construct state form of the former. See also Duval (1881: 297, §316):"Le pronom ܕ [*d-*] est un ancien démonstratif, qui se subordonne un mot ou une phrase, comme un nom à l'état construit".

[16]Bar-Asher Siegal (2013a) presents a competing analysis, according to which *d-* is in essence a subordinating particle, introducing always clausal secondaries (cf. §3.5.2). A noun following *d-* should be understood, according to this idea, as a clause representing a *predicative possessive construction*, in which only the possessor is overtly expressed as a *topic*. While this idea is thought provoking, it suffers from some shortcomings: first, it requires the postulation of a null existential particle in each such case. More importantly, the expression of possessors as topics is unknown in Aramaic outside this context.

[17]Goldenberg calls this element a PRONOMINAL HEAD, a term which may raise some confusion since every pronoun serves as a head of its phrase. Another term found in the Semitic literature, following the work of Pennacchietti (1968) is DETERMINATIVE PRONOUN. Wertheimer (2001), using a somewhat different perspective, analyses the *d-* as a *translatif*, a term due to Tesnière denoting a conversion morpheme, as the *d-* can convert a noun to an an attribute, a clause to a noun, etc.

[18]See footnote 40 on page 38 for the use of the term ANALYTIC GENITIVE CONSTRUCTION. The very same construction with the linker *d-* is attested in other Eastern Classical Aramaic languages, such as Classical Mandaic (Häberl 2007), and Jewish Babylonian Aramaic (Bar-Asher Siegal 2013b: 93, §4.3).

[19]Goldenberg translates this example as "fear [N]of God", emphasizing the nominal nature of the linker, which is not apparent in the English translation otherwise.

(30) Syriac: **Noun–Noun**
ܡܠܟܘܬܐ ܕܫܡܝܐ
malkutā da= šmayyā
kingdom.EMPH LNK= heaven
'kingdom of heaven' (*Peshiṭta*, Matthew 11:21; Muraoka 1997: 61, §73a)

(31) Syriac: **Noun–Noun**
ܫܠܝܚܐ ܕܐܠܗܐ
šliḥā d= alāhā
apostle LNK= God
'apostle of God' (*Acts of Thomas*, ed. Wright 1871: ܩܚܚ)

Goldenberg (1995) analyses this construction as two constituents standing in apposition to each other, only the latter being a GENITIVE CONSTRUCTION. In the terminology used here, however, the entire construction qualifies as being an AC, the primary and secondary standing in INDIRECT ATTRIBUTIVE RELATIONSHIP.[20] Goldenberg's analysis, contrasted with this study's terminology, is presented in the Table 3.2:

Table 3.2: Goldenberg's analysis of the ALC, contrasted with terminology used in this study

Goldenberg's terminology		
Apposition	Genitive Construction Head	Attribute
deḥltā	d-	alāhā
malkutā	da-	šmayyā
Primary	Linker	Secondary
Attributive Construction		
Terminology used in this study		

[20] Compare with the formulation of Goldenberg (2000: 79) discussing this construction: "We may call 'indirect annexion' a construction in which the head noun is represented by a formal head substitute [...] and the full noun which is replaced by that formal substitute precedes the kernel annexion as in ܪܘܚܐ ܕ-ܩܘܕܫܐ [*rūḥa* [*d-qudša*]]". The bracketing of the example clearly shows the unity of the whole construction.

The pronominal nature of the linker *d-* becomes evident when it appears without an immediate nominal antecedent, such as in examples (27)–(28) on page 57. In this work such cases are treated as having a zero (∅) primary, and we shall indicate the position where a nominal primary could have appeared by the symbol ∅.[21] The following famous quotations illustrate this (and see also example (61) on page 68):

(32) Syriac: ∅–**Noun**
ܠܐ ܡܬܪܥܐ ܐܢܬ ܕܐܠܗܐ ܐܠܐ ܕܒܢܝ̈ ܐܢܫܐ
lā metraʿē =ʾat ∅ d= alāhā ʾellā ∅ da= bnay= nāšā
NEG think =2SG ∅ LNK= God but ∅ LNK= son.PL.CST= man
'You are not thinking of things of God but of things of men.' (*Peshiṭta*, Matthew 16:23; Muraoka 1997: 71)

(33) Syriac: ∅–**Noun**
ܗܒܘ ܗܟܝܠ ܕܩܣܪ ܠܩܣܪ ܘܕܐܠܗܐ ܠܐܠܗܐ
habaw hākēl ∅ d= qesar l= qesar w= ∅ d= alāhā l= alāhā
give.IMP.PL then ∅ LNK= Caesar to= Caesar and= ∅ LNK= God to= God
'Give then that which is of Caesar to Caesar and that which is of God to God.' (*Peshiṭta*, Matthew 22:21; Muraoka 1997: 71)

An intervening clitic can easily be attached to the primary in this constriction:

(34) Syriac: **Noun–Noun**
ܣܘܓܐ ܓܝܪ ܕܒܢܝܐ
sogā =gēr da= bnayā
multitude =indeed LNK= sons
'many children, indeed' (*Acts of Thomas*, ed. Wright 1871: ܡܦܐ)

Since the primary does not directly govern the secondary, but rather stands in apposition with the linker, it must appear in the free state, typically being the emphatic state in Syriac. There are, however, some rare exceptions to this rule:[22]

[21]This ∅ is thus a paradigmatic zero. In Saussurian terms it relates *in absentia* to a possible antecedent. Cf. Muraoka (1997: 70): "At times the nucleus noun phrase to be qualified by the following Dalath [=*d-* linker] phrase is wanting".

[22]Nöldeke (1898: 155, §205B, fn. 1), however, sees such cases as textual errors. Similarly, Hopkins (1997: 25, fn. 6) comments: "The correctness of this construction is not well established and most of the examples alleged in the literature are plain blunders occurring in unreliable sources or the result of mistaken analysis of the text." In the context of the JUrmi NENA dialect, where such constructions are regular, I shall analyse this phenomenon as AGREEMENT IN STATE (see §7.3.2).

(35) Syriac: **Noun–Possessed Noun**
ܝܰܘܡܰܝ̈ ܕܛܠܝܘܬܝ
yawmay d= ṭaliut-^{i}
day.PL.CST LNK= youth-POSS.1SG
'the days of my youth' (*S. Ephræmi Opera* vol. 3 ed. S. E. Assemanus 1743: 429; Duval 1881: 339, §357g)

As Duval (1881) notes, this construction should be kept apart from the similar-looking sequence of morphemes corresponding to a simple CSC, in which the linker is an integral part of the secondary, lacking an explicit primary (here noted as ∅).

(36) Syriac: **Noun–Noun Phrase**
ܝܰܘܡܰܝ̈ ܕܒܶܝܬ ܕܘܩܠܛܝܢܘܣ
yawmay [∅ d= bēt Dokletiyanos]
day.PL.CST ∅ LNK= house.CST D.
'the days of those of the house of D.' (*Julianos der Abtrünnige*, ed. Hoffmann 1880: 24, 9 *apud* Duval 1881: 339, §357g)

Whenever two conjoined nouns appear as secondaries, the linker is normally repeated:

(37) Syriac: **Noun–Conjoined Nouns**
ܩܠܐ ܕܨܦܘܢܘ̈ܬܐ ܘܕܗܕܪܘ̈ܠܐ
qālā d= ṣepunwātā w= d= hadrulē
voice LNK= bagpipes.PL and= LNK= water_organ.PL
'sound of pipes and organs' (*Acts of Thomas*, ed. Wright 1871: ܡܓ)

Cases without the repetition of the linker appear as well, especially if the conjoined nouns form an idiomatic expression, as in the first of the following two examples:

(38) Syriac: **Noun–Conjoined Nouns**
ܕܪ̈ܐ ܕܒܣܪܐ ܘܕܡܐ
dārē d= [besrā wa= dmā]
generation.PL LNK= flesh and= blood
'the generations of flesh and blood' (*Peshiṭta*, Sirach 14:18 *apud* Van Peursen 2007: 209)

(39) Syriac: **Noun–Conjoined Nouns**
ܢ̈ܡܘܣܐ ܕܪ̈ܩܡܝܐ ܘܐܘܪ̈ܗܝܐ ܘܥܪ̈ܒܝܐ
nāmusē d= [rāqāmāyē w= ursāyē w= ʿarbāyē]
laws LNK= Rakamaens and= Edessans and= Arabs
'the laws of the Rakamaens, the Edessans and the Arabs' (Bardaisan, *Book of the Laws of the Countries* ed. Drijvers 1965: 46:13 *apud* Bakker 2011: 125)

In contrast to the CSC, both the primary and the secondary can be expanded to multi-word NPs, as in the following example:

(40) Syriac: **Noun Phrase–Noun Phrase**
ܒܪܐ ܡܫܠܡܢܐ ܕܪ̈ܚܡܐ ܡ̈ܫܠܡܢܐ
[brā mšalmānā] d= [raḥmē mšalmānē]
son perfect.MS LNK= mercy(PL) perfect.M.PL
'perfect son of perfect mercy' (*Acts of Thomas*, ed. Wright 1871: ܡܚܠ)

The secondary itself can be a CSC:

(41) Syriac: **Noun–Noun Phrase**
ܘܬܪܥܐ ܕܒܝܬ ܓܢܘܢܐ
tarʿā d= [bēt gnonā]
door LNK= house.CST bridal_bed
'the door of the bridal chamber' (*Acts of Thomas*, ed. Wright 1871: ܡܗ)

Similarly, a noun inflected with a possessive pronominal suffix can act as a primary or as a secondary of the ALC. Its usage as a primary should not be confused with the DAC discussed in §3.6.

(42) Syriac: **Possessed Noun–Noun**
ܐܝܕܗ ܕܝܡܝܢܐ
ʾid-ēh d= yamminā
hand-POSS.3MS LNK= right(FS)
'his right hand' (*Acts of Thomas*, ed. Wright 1871: ܡܢܝ)

(43) Syriac: **Noun–Possessed Noun**
ܠܘܝܐ ܕܥ̈ܒܕܘܗܝ
lewyā d= ʿabd-aw
companion LNK= servant-PL.POSS.3MS
'companion of His servants' (*Acts of Thomas*, ed. Wright 1871: ܡܚܠ)

It is difficult to come across cases where two conjoined nouns act as a single primary of the analytic linker construction. Van Peursen (2007: 204) notes that in the book of *Ben-Sira* such potential constructions are rendered instead by a conjunction of two ACs, the first being the ALC and the second the possessive suffix construction:

(44) Syriac: **Conjoined Nouns–Noun**
ܟܠ ܡܬܠܐ ܕܚܟܝܡܐ ܘܐܘܚܕܬܗܘܢ
[kol matlē d= ḥakkimē] w= [ʾuḥdātat-hon]
all proverbs LNK= wise.PL and= riddles-POSS.3PL
'all the proverbs of the wise and their riddles' (*Peshiṭta*, Sirach 50:27; Van Peursen 2007: 204)

This may, however, be an artefact of this text being translated from Hebrew. In the source text this construction would have been rendered by a CSC which prohibits (in classical Hebrew) conjoined primaries. Indeed, in other sources one finds such cases regularly:

(45) Syriac: **Conjoined Nouns–Noun**
ܬܪܒܝܬܐ ܘܫܘܡܠܝܐ ܕܦܓܪܐ
[tarbitā w= šumlāyā] d= pagrā
growth and= perfection LNK= body
'the growth and perfection of the body' (Bardaisan, *Book of the Laws of the Countries* ed. Drijvers 1965: 34:14 *apud* Bakker 2011: 123)

(46) Syriac: **Conjoined Noun–Noun Phrase**
ܘܗܕܝܐ ܘܡܕܒܪܢܐ ܕܐܝܠܝܢ ܕܡܗܝܡܢܝܢ ܒܗ
w= [hadāyā wa= mdabrānā] d= [aylēn da= [mhaymēnin
and= guide and= conductor LNK= who.PL LNK= believe.PTCP.M.PL.ABS
b-ēh]]
in-3MS
'and guide and conductor of those who believe in Him' (*Acts of Thomas*, ed. Wright 1871: ܡܚܠ)

(47) Syriac: **Conjouned NPs–Participle**
ܘܒܝܬ ܓܘܣܐ ܘܢܝܚܐ ܕܐܠܝܨܐ
[[bēt gawsā] wa= nyāḥā] d= ʾaliṣē
house.CST refuge and= rest LNK= afflict.PASS.PTCP.EMPH.M.PL
'refuge and repose of the afflicted' (*Acts of Thomas*, ed. Wright 1871: ܡܚܠ)

A somewhat unusual usage of the linker construction is to introduce a secondary noun which is appositive to the primary. It could tentatively be assimilated with cases of adjectival secondaries in the ALC, which are normally analysed as reduced relative clauses (see §3.5.3), but in contrast to those cases, the secondary is in the emphatic state.

(48) Syriac: **Noun–Noun**
ܓܒܪ̈ܝܗܝܢ ܕܓ̈ܠܝܐܐ
gabrey-hen *d=* *gelyāʾē*
man.PL-POSS.3F.PL LNK= G.M.PL
'their men, (who are) the Gelians' (Bardaisan, *Book of the Laws of the Countries* ed. Drijvers 1965: 44:17 *apud* Bakker 2011: 121)

In this case, the linker stands not only in apposition with the primary, as is always the case in the analytic linker construction, but also with the secondary, as all nominal expressions in this example – the primary, the linker and the secondary, have the same referent.

3.5.1 Pronominal secondaries

Pronominal secondaries are realized in the ALC by means of the possessive pronominal suffixes (see §3.3) attached to an allomorph of the linker, namely *dil-*. Diachronically *dil-* can be analysed as a combination of the linker *d-* with the dative preposition *l-* but synchronically it is simply the allo-form the linker takes when it attaches to the pronominal suffixes.[23]

As Gutman & Van Peursen (2011: 90) note, it is difficult to establish a functional difference between this construction and the possessive suffix construction, as different manuscripts of the same text may use one or the other construction. Muraoka (1997: 71), on the other hand, states that this construction puts some EMPHASIS on the secondary. This may be related to the fact that unlike the pronominal suffixes, the base *dil-* can bear stress. Contrast examples (1)–(3) on page 49 with the following:

[23] The same form is found in Classical Mandaic (Macuch 1965: 404, §260). In Jewish Babylonian Aramaic, on the other hand, the form is normally *dīd-* (Bar-Asher Siegal 2013b: 108), though one finds the form *dīl-* as well in "rare and dialectal use" (Sokoloff 2002: 331). Nöldeke (1875: 332, fn. 2) proposes to analyse the form *dīd-* as originating in *d* + *yād* 'LNK+hand.CST' (cf. Garbell 1965b: 60), but it seems more plausible to explain it as a cognate of *dil-* mutated by assimilation (Bar-Asher Siegal 2013b: 108). The earliest attested form, from the Early Aramaic period, is *ðīl-*.

(49) Syriac: **Noun–Pronoun**
ܗܝܡܢܘܬܐ ܕܝܠܗ
haymānutā dil-ēh
faith.EMPH LNK-POSS.3MS
'his faith' (Muraoka 1997: 70, §93e)

(50) Syriac: **Noun–Pronoun**
ܒܫܡܐ ܕܝܠܟ
ba= šmā dil-āk
in= name.EMPH LNK-POSS.2MS
'by your name' (*Peshiṭta*, Prayer of Manasseh, ed. Baars & Schneider 1972: B3; Gutman & Van Peursen 2011: 90 (3B))

(51) Syriac: **Noun Phrase–Pronoun**
ܚܡܬܐ ܘܪܘܓܙܐ ܕܝܠܟ
ḥemtā w= rugzā dil-āk
fury.EMPH and= rage.EMPH LNK-POSS.2MS
'your fury and rage' (*Peshiṭta*, Prayer of Manasseh, ed. Baars & Schneider 1972: B5, Gutman & Van Peursen 2011: 90 (4B))

As the last example shows, in contrast to the possessive suffix construction, when the linker construction is used, one pronominal secondary is enough for a conjoined NP primary, as the linker can be appositive to an entire NP (compare also with examples (44)–(45) on page 63).

Moreover, the syntactic autonomy of the linker permits it to precede the primary:

(52) Syriac: **Noun–Pronoun**
ܕܝܠܗ ܣܦܪܐ
dil-ēh seprā
LNK-POSS.3MS book
'his book' (Muraoka 1997: 71, §91f)

3.5.2 Clausal secondaries

Relative clauses in Syriac cannot be introduced by the CSC; Rather, the ALC is obligatory used (Goldenberg 2013a: 236f.).[24] For this reason, the linker *d-* is referred by some authors also as RELATIVE PRONOUN (Muraoka 1997: 21, §15). It can be co-referent with any argument (or adjunct) of the relative clause.[25]

(53) Syriac: **Noun (subject)–Clause**
ܢܒܝܐ ܕܐܬܐ ܠܘܬܢ
nabyā d= etā lwāt-an
prophet LNK= came to-POSS.1PL
'the prophet who came to us' (Muraoka 1997: 63, §77)

(54) Syriac: **Noun (object)–Clause**
ܢܒܝܐ ܕܫܕܪܬܗ ܠܘܬܟ
nabyā d= šaddar-t-ēh lwāt-āk
prophet LNK= sent-A1SG-P3MS to-POSS.2MS
'the prophet whom I sent to you' (Muraoka 1997: 63, §77)

While I agree with Goldenberg (1995) that *d-* represents one and the same morpheme regardless of the material that follows it, it is worthwhile noting that the distribution of *d*+Clause is somewhat different from *d*+Noun, implying that these combinations are not equivalent (Van Peursen 2007: 245f.). This can be illustrated by cases in which the same primary is expanded both by a nominal and a clausal secondary. In such cases, the two *d-* phrases are not conjoined (contrast with example (37) on page 61):[26]

(55) Syriac: **Noun–Noun+Clause**
ܒܫܘܥܝܬܐ ܕܣܒܐ ܕܫܡܥܘ ܡܢ ܐܒܗܝܗܘܢ
b= [šoʿitē d= sābē] da= [šmaʿ-u men ʾabāh-ayhon]
in= tales LNK= elders LNK= heard-3PL from fathers-POSS.3PL
'the discourse of the elders, which they have heard from their fathers' (*Peshiṭta*, Sirach 8:9 *apud* Van Peursen 2007: 232)

[24] Other classical Semitic languages allow the usage of the CSC with clausal secondaries, notably Akkadian, but also Classical Hebrew, Arabic and Ge'ez (Goldenberg 2013a: Ch. 14).

[25] The term CLAUSE is used here to cover verbal clauses with finite verbs. Nominal clauses, and in particular clauses with participial predicates are treated in the next section.

[26] One may argue that the NP *šoʿitē d=sābē* 'discourse of the elders' is the primary of the relative clause, rather than the noun *šoʿitē*. Yet in the dependency model I use, as well as from the semantic point of view, the relative clause is an expansion of *šoʿitē* 'discourse' alone.

Notwithstanding the pronominal nature of the linker *d-*, in its usage as a relative pronoun it does not co-occur with a zero primary, according to my survey. Instead, an explicit pronominal primary can occur in this construction, yielding either a FREE RELATIVE, or, less frequently, a non-restrictive relative clause.

(56) Syriac: **Pronoun–Clause**
ܡܢ ܕܠܝ ܡܩܒܠ ܠܡܢ ܕܫܠܚܢܝ ܡܩܒܠ
man d= [l-i mqabbel] l-man d= [šalḥa-n^{i}] mqabbel
who LNK= to-1SG receive.PTCP.MS to-who LNK= sent-P1SG receive.PTCP.MS
'he who receives me receives him who has sent me[27]' (*Peshiṭta*, Matthew 10:40; Muraoka 1997: 87, §111)

(57) Syriac: **Pronoun–Clause**
ܐܢܬ ܕܐܣܪܬܝܗܝ ܠܝܡܐ
ʾat d= esar-t-āy l-yammā
2MS LNK= bound-A2MS-P3MS ACC-sea
'You, who bound the sea' (*Peshiṭta*, Prayer of Manasseh, ed. Baars & Schneider 1972: B3; Gutman & Van Peursen 2011: 221 (3a))

As Gutman & Van Peursen (2011: 87) note, the interrogative pronoun *man* 'who', which typically introduces non-specific free relatives as in example (56), can in fact also introduce free relatives referring to specific referents, as in the following example:[28]

(58) Syriac: **Pronoun–Clause**
ܡܢ ܕܐܚܕܬ ܠܬܗܘܡܐ
man d= eḥad-t la-thomā
who LNK= held-A2MS ACC-abyss
'Who held[29] the abyss' (*Peshiṭta*, Prayer of Manasseh, ed. Baars & Schneider 1972: B3; Gutman & Van Peursen 2011: 221 (3b))

A quite distinct usage of the *d*+Clause pattern occurs when *d-* serves as a complementizer. This is the case when *d-* introduces complements of verbs, be

[27] Note that the first relative clause is in fact a participial clause, treated in the next section.

[28] Peripherally to this, note that in Modern Hebrew the pronouns introducing free relatives are frequently preceded by the definite accusative marker את *ʾet*, rendering them syntactically (but not necessarily semantically) definite.

[29] In the Syriac text, the verb appears in the 2nd person, yet the grammatical context seems to require a 3rd person. Indeed, in another version of the same text, the verb appears in the 3rd person; see discussion of Gutman & Van Peursen (2011: 87f.).

they direct object or adverbial complements. These constructions are arguably not ACs at all, as their function is not to modify an implied referent. Indeed, in these cases, no nominal antecedent appears before the *d-*, and one could argue that no nominal primary is possible at all in this position. Nonetheless, I list these examples for the sake of completeness, but I gloss the *d-* in this function as COMP.[30]

(59) Syriac: **Verb–Clause**
ܫܰܪܺܝ ܕܢܡܰܠܶܠ
šarri *da=* *nmalel*
begin.PRF.3MS COMP= speak.IMPF.3MS
'He began to speak.' (*Peshiṭta*, Mark 12:1; Muraoka 1997: 65, §82)

(60) Syriac: **Verb–Clause**
ܐܳܙܶܠ ܐ̱ܢܳܐ ܕܶܐܛܰܝܶܒ ܠܟܽܘܢ ܐܰܬ݂ܪܳܐ
ʾāzel *=nā* *d=* *eṭayyeb* *l-kon* *ʾatrā*
go.PTCP =1SG COMP= prepare.IMPF.1SG to-POSS.2M.PL place
'I go to prepare a place for you.' (*Peshiṭta*, John 14:2; Muraoka 1997: 65, §82)

The distinct functions of *d-* serving either as a complementizer or as pronominal linker are especially clear in the rare cases where two *d-* morphemes follow, each with another function, as in the following example:[31]

(61) Syriac: **∅–Noun**
ܐܶܫܬܰܟ݂ܚܰܬ ܐܺܝܕܳܐ ܕܕܫܳܩܝܳܐ ܗ̱ܝ
ʾeštakḥat *ʾidā* *d=* *∅ d=* *šāqyā* *=^{h}i*
was_found.3FS hand(FS) COMP= ∅ LNK= cupbearer =3FS
'the hand was found to be that of the cupbearer' (*Acts of Thomas*, ed. Wright 1871: ܩܟܚ)

The *d-* morpheme functions likewise as a complementizer when it follows an adverbial acting as a conjunction. Note that in such cases the attributive rela-

[30] Wertheimer (2001: 275) argues that both functions of *d-*, introducing relative clauses or complement clauses, stem from its more general function as a conversion morpheme (*translatif* in her terms), and indeed both uses are in fact nominalizations: as a relativizer *d-* nominalizes clauses into adjectives, while as a complementizer it nominalizes clauses into nouns (or *substantives* in her terms).

[31] The ∅ primary refers to the noun *ʾidā* 'hand', which can be analysed as having been raised out of the CP to serve as the subject of the matrix-clause. See also Muraoka (1997: 35*, fn. 51). The continuation of this sentence is given in example (79) on page 74.

tionship is already marked by the construct state of the adverbial. Compare the following with example (24) on page 56:

(62) Syriac: **Adverbial Noun–Clause**
ܩܕܡ ܕܢܩܪܐ ܬܪܢܓܠܐ
qdām [d= neqrē tarnāglā]
front.CST COMP= call.IMPF.3MS cock
'before a cock crows' (Payne Smith 1903: 490)

The structure of this example is superficially parallel to that of examples (35)–(36) on page 61, in that the *d-* follows an element in construct state. The fine difference is that here it acts as a complementizer (nominalizing an event), and thus does not designate any implied referent. Note also that the construct state marking is needed in order to transform the noun ܩܕܡܐ *qdāmā* 'front', which can by itself be used adverbially, into a conjunction requiring a complement phrase.

3.5.3 Adjectives and participles as secondaries

Adjectives and participles are closely related in Syriac. Both show nominal inflection, and are characterised by the fact that in predicative position they commonly appear in absolute state. Moreover, with a 3rd person subject, they can dispense with the enclitic personal pronoun (e.p.p.) which normally appears after predicative nominals. In the following examples, the two categories are kept separate, but in some cases it is difficult to tease them apart.

As explained in §3.8, adjectives used attributively stand in apposition with their head noun and thus agree with it in state, being most commonly the emphatic state. The usage of absolute state, on the other hand, is typical of the predicative use of adjectives and participles.[32] Moreover, in absolute state they can appear as secondaries in the ALC. As the absolute state is typical of predicative function, these secondaries are often considered in Syriac grammars as elliptical relative clauses, lacking an explicit subject argument (Muraoka 2013: 66, §94; Van Peursen 2007: 211ff.).[33]

It is quite difficult to find cases of single-word adjectival secondaries following a nominal primary in this construction. Van Peursen (2007) gives the following example as a case of *d*+Adjective:

[32] This distinction is also true in Jewish Babylonian Aramaic; see Bar-Asher Siegal (2013b: 63).

[33] Alternatively, Goldenberg (1983: 115, §§9–10) analyses these elements as being quasi-verbal conjugated predicates, of which the 3rd person marker is a ∅. Yet appositive nominal secondaries in emphatic state can also appear in a similar syntactic structure, as example (48) on page 64 shows.

(63) Syriac: **Noun–Participle**
ܢܫܐ ܕܣܐܒ
nāšā d= sāb
man LNK= old.ABS.MS
'an old person' (*Peshiṭta*, Sirach 8:6 *apud* Van Peursen 2007: 211)

Yet most cases of adjectival secondaries introduced in this construction are multi-word expressions:

(64) Syriac: **Noun–Adjective Phrase**
ܡܣܟܢܐ ܕܚܝ ܘܥܙܝܙ ܒܓܘܫܡܗ
meskēnā d= [ḥay w= ʿazziz b= gušm-ēh]
miserable LNK= alive.ABS and= vigorous.ABS in= body-POSS.3MS
'a poor man who is alive and sound in his body' (*Peshiṭta*, Sirach 30:14 *apud* Van Peursen 2007: 212)

(65) Syriac: **Noun–Adjective Phrase**
ܠܥܒܘܬܐ ܘܐܣܘܛܘܬܐ ܕܠܐ ܡܬܒܥܝܐ
laʿbutā w= āsoṭutā d= [lā metbaʿāyā]
avidity(FS) and= intemperance(FS) LNK= NEG necessary.ABS.FS
'intemperance and unnecessary luxury[34]' (Bardaisan, *Book of the Laws of the Countries* ed. Drijvers 1965: 34:25 *apud* Bakker 2011: 129)

This tendency is inverted whenever there is no overt primary. In such cases, one can easily find single-word adjectives following the linker. The adjective in these cases is effectively nominalized, as the following example demonstrates:

(66) Syriac: ∅–**Adjective**
ܥܒܶܕܘ ܕܫܰܦܺܝܪ
ʿbed-ᵘ ∅ d= šappir
do.IMP-PL ∅ LNK= beautiful.MS.ABS
'Do what is good' (*Peshiṭta*, Matthew 5:44; Muraoka 1997: 87, §111)

According to Wertheimer (2001: 271), who discusses similar cases with clausal secondaries, the nominalisation is achieved exactly due to the lack of an overt primary.

[34] Bakker (2011: 129, fn. 117) argues that the secondary modifies only the second noun, arguing that "it would seem superfluous to specify *intemperance* with the notion of not being necessary". Note, however, that it is the second noun that means "intemperance". Nonetheless, given that the adjective has a singular form, it is probably correct that it modifies only one of the nouns.

One finds similar expressions with the pronominal primary ܡܕܡ *meddem* 'something':

(67) Syriac: **Pronoun–Adjective**
ܡܕܡ ܕܫܦܝܪ
meddem d= šappir
something LNK= beautiful.MS.ABS
'something (that is) beautiful' (*Peshiṭta*, Sirach 23:5; Van Peursen 2007: 211)

Longer, phrasal adjectival secondaries can also follow ∅ or pronominal primaries:

(68) Syriac: ∅**–Adjective Phrase**
ܘܕܩܠܝܠ ܛܒ
w= d= [qalil tāb]
and= LNK= light.MS.ABS very
'and what is very light' (*Peshiṭta*, Sirach 22:18 *apud* Van Peursen 2007: 199)

Participial phrases following pronominal primaries are quite regular. See the participial secondaries in example (56) on page 67 or example (46) on page 63, or the following example:

(69) Syriac: **Pronoun–Participial Phrase**
ܗܠܝܢ ܕܥܒܪ̈ܢ ... ܘܗܠܝܢ ܕܠܐ ܥܒܪ̈ܢ
hālēn d= [{lā} ʿābr-ān]
DEM.PL LNK= {NEG} pass.PTCP-ABS.F.PL
'those that are {not} transitory' (*Acts of Thomas*, ed. Wright 1871: ܩܡܚ)

In contrast to the case of clausal secondaries with finite verbs (see §3.5.2), participial secondaries can co-occur with ∅ primaries, though this does not happen very frequently:

(70) Syriac: ∅**–Participial Phrase**
ܘܶܐܡܰܪ ܠܕܳܐܬܶܝܢ ܥܰܡܶܗ
(w= emar l=) ∅ d= [ātēn ʿamm-ēh]
and= said to= ∅ LNK= come.PTCP.ABS.M.PL with-POSS.3MS
'and he said to those who were coming with him' (*Peshiṭta*, Matthew 8:10; Muraoka 1997: 87, §111)

(71) Syriac: ∅–**Participial Phrase**
ܕܫܠܝܛ ܓܝܪ ܒܟܠ ܚܕ ܗܘ
∅ d= [šalliṭ gēr b= kol] (ḥad =^{h}u)
∅ LNK= rule.PTCP.MS.ABS however in= all one =3MS
'He who controls all (is one).' (Muraoka 1997: 87, §111)

For discussion of the factors motivating the appearance of adjectives in the ALC versus simple apposition, see §3.8.2.

3.5.4 Adverbial secondaries

Similarly to adjectival secondaries, adverbial secondaries are usually considered to be reduced clauses. Being in fact PPs, they always consist of multiple words (considering the preposition itself, being a proclitic, as a separate syntactic word):

(72) Syriac: **Noun–Prepositional Phrase**
ܐܝܠܢܐ ܕܒܦܪܕܝܣܐ
ʾilānē da= b= pardaysā
tree.PL LNK= in= garden
'the trees in the garden' (*Peshiṭta*, Genesis 3:2; Muraoka 1997: 72)

The preposition ܐܝܟ *ʾak* 'as' is also found followed by *d*+PP. If the PP is seen as a reduced clause, such cases should be treated as similar in structure to example (62) on page 69, where the *d*- serves as a complementizer.

(73) Syriac: **Conjunction–Prepositional Phrase**
ܐܝܟ ܕܒܫܡܝܐ
ʾak d= ba= šmayyā
as COMP= in= heaven
'as in heaven' (Muraoka 1997: 64, §78)

(74) Syriac: **Conjunction–Prepositional Phrase**
ܐܝܟ ܕܒܐܟܣܢܝܐ
ʾak d= b= aksnāyā
as COMP= in= stranger
'as upon a stranger' (*Acts of Thomas*, ed. Wright 1871: ܩܠܗ)

3.5.5 Numerals as ordinal secondaries

An noteworthy usage of this construction is to form ordinal numerals out of the cardinal numerals. The construction is especially interesting, since the secondary, i.e. the numeral, agrees in gender with the primary.[35] Example (75) can be directly contrasted with example (105) on page 85.[36]

(75) Syriac: **Noun–Ordinal**
ܝܘܡܐ ܕܬܪܝܢ
yawmā da= trēn
day(MS) LNK= two.M
'the second day' (Nöldeke 1898: 178, §239)

(76) Syriac: **Noun–Ordinal**
ܒܫܢܬܐ ܕܬܠܬ
b= šattā da= tlāt
in= year(FS) LNK= three.F
'in the third year' (*Peshiṭta*, Deuteronomy 26:12; Muraoka 1997: 38, §44b)

This construction too can be used without an explicit primary:

(77) Syriac: **∅–Ordinal**
ܕܬܠܬܐ
da= tlātā
LNK= third.M
'a third one' (*Peshiṭta*, Sirach 23:16 *apud* Van Peursen 2007: 258)

3.5.6 The analytic linker construction with a correlative

[35] This construction is preserved in many NENA dialects, although the gender distinction is lost in some; see §11.5.2.

[36] When a numeral functions as a cardinal, it typically precedes the quantified noun without any marking of an attributive relation:

(i) Syriac: **Noun–Cardinal**
ܚܕܐ ܠܬܠܬܐ ܝܘܡܝܢ
xdā la= tlātā yawmēn
one.F to= three.M day.PL.ABS
'once in three days' (Payne Smith 1903: 614)

Similarly to an ordinal numeral, a cardinal numeral agrees in gender with the modified noun. The linker *d-* appears only sometimes following the cardinal ܐܠܦ *ʾālef* 'thousand', but in this construction the cardinal acts syntactically as a primary (see Nöldeke 1898: 177, §239).

The ALC exhibits a variant construction in which the linker is preceded by a demonstrative or interrogative pronoun, traditionally termed "correlative" (Nöldeke 1898: 175f., §236). This happens especially frequently with clausal secondaries. Pat-El (2010) discusses this construction, bringing *inter alia*, the following example:

(78) Syriac: **Noun Phrase–Clause**
ܐܝܕܗ ܕܝܡܝܢܐ܆ ܗܝ ܕܐܪܝܡ ܥܠ ܝܗܘܕܐ
[ʾid-ēh d= yamminā] hāy d= [arim ʿal Yhudā]
hand-POSS.3MS LNK= right(FS) DEM.FS LNK= struck.3MS on Judas
'his right hand with which he had struck Judas' (*Acts of Thomas*, ed. Wright 1871: ܡܚܝ)

In the same textual source there is another such example, but with an enclitic personal pronoun intervening between the primary and the demonstrative pronoun. This example is the continuation of example (61) on page 68:

(79) Syriac: **Noun–Clause**
ܕܫܩܝܐ ܗܝ܂ ܗܘ ܕܡܚܐܝ ܗܘܐ ܠܝܗܘܕܐ
d= šāqyā =^{h}i haw da= mḥā-y =^{h}wa l-Yhudā
LNK= cupbearer =3.FS DEM.MS LNK= struck-P.3MS =PST ACC-J.
'it was that of the cupbearer who had smitten Judas' (*Acts of Thomas*, ed. Wright 1871: ܡܚܝ)

While structurally the pronoun may be analysed as a pronominal primary (see the analysis of Wertheimer 2001: 274), functionally Pat-El argues that it should be seen as a definite article, marking the attribute, and thus the entire AC, as definite.[37]. Indeed, such a demonstrative, acting as a definite article, can precede nominal primaries as well (see also examples of Pat-El 2010: 67):

(80) Syriac: **Noun–Noun**
ܪܘܡܐ ܗܘ ܕܫܡܝܐ
rawmā haw da= šmayyā
height DEM.MS LNK= heaven
'the height of heaven' (*Peshiṭta*, Prayer of Manasseh, ed. Baars & Schneider 1972: A10; Gutman & Van Peursen 2011: 91 (7A))

[37]It is interesting to note the parallelism between this construction and the classical Semitic CSC, in which the definite article is attached to the secondary, as discussed in §2.3.3. See in this context also example (16) on page 53

This last example is parallel functionally to example (85) on the next page, which uses instead a proleptic pronoun to render the AC definite. This is discussed in the following section.

3.6 The double annexation construction (X-y.POSS LNK Y)

3.6.1 Plain construction

Another frequent AC used in Syriac is a variant of the ALC with a proleptic (i.e. cataphoric) possessive pronominal suffix attached to the primary, indexing the secondary. Following Goldenberg (2013a: 234, fn. 15) I shall term this construction the DOUBLE ANNEXATION CONSTRUCTION (=DAC).[38]

(81) Syriac: **Noun–Noun**
ܪ̈ܓܠܘܗܝ ܕܫܠܝܚܐ
regl-aw^hi *da=* *šliḥā*
foot-PL.POSS.3MS LNK= apostle
'the feet of the apostle' (*Acts of Thomas*, ed. Wright 1871: ܦܣܒ)

(82) Syriac: **Noun–Noun**
ܡ̈ܠܘܗܝ ܕܡܪܝܐ
mell-aw *d=* *māryā*
word-PL.POSS.3MS LNK= Lord
'the words of the Lord' (Muraoka 1997: 88, §112d)

(83) Syriac: **Noun–Noun**
šm-āh *d=* *attətā*
name-POSS.3FS LNK= woman
'the name of the woman' (Goldenberg 2013a: 236)

Goldenberg (2013a: 234) analyses this construction as "a complex construction made of a sequence of two correlated annexions $\text{N}^1\text{–PRON}^2$ ~ $\text{PRON}^1\text{–N}^2$, identical indices indicateting coreferentiality". Schematically, he represents the construction as if there were two appositions involved:[39]

The syntactic independence of the two phrases is demonstrated by cases where an intervening clitic appears:

[38] See footnote 45 on page 43 for further information on this term.

[39] The apposition between the two attributes must be understood as an indirect apposition, or merely co-reference, since each attribute is governed by another head.

Table 3.3: Goldenberg's representation of the Double Annexation Construction

Head	Attribute
šm-	-āh
↕	↕
d-	attetā

(84) Syriac: **Noun–Noun**
ܐܚܘܗܝ ܐܢܐ ܕܝܗܘܕܐ
ʾaḥ-aw =na d= Yhudā
brother-POSS.3MS =1SG LNK= Judas
'I'm the brother of Judas' (*Acts of Thomas*, ed. Wright 1871: ܡܦܐ)

According to Muraoka (1997: 61f.) the DAC is used "when both nouns ... are logically determined". Indeed, this construction is used as an alternative to marking definite determination by means of a "correlative" demonstrative pronoun (contrast with example (80) on page 74):

(85) Syriac: **Noun–Noun**
ܪܘܡܗ ܕܫܡܝܐ
rawm-āh da= šmayyā
height-POSS.3FS LNK= heaven(FS)
'the height of heaven' (*Peshiṭta*, Prayer of Manasseh, ed. Baars & Schneider 1972: B9; Gutman & Van Peursen 2011: 90 (7B))

It is not accurate, however, to claim that both constituent nouns are determined. Rather, it is the AC as a whole which is determined. Thus, we can find cases where the secondary is indefinite, albeit with a generic reading.

(86) Syriac: **Noun–Noun**
ܢܦܫܗ ܕܡܣܟܢܐ
napš-ēh d= meskēnā
soul-POSS.3MS LNK= poor
'the soul of a poor man' (*Peshiṭta*, Sirach 35:20 *apud* Van Peursen 2007: 207)

(87) Syriac: **Noun–Noun**
ܥܒܕܗ ܕܢܓܪܐ
ʿbād-ēh d= naggārā
work-POSS.3MS LNK= carpenter
'the business of a carpenter' (*Acts of Thomas*, ed. Wright 1871: ܨܕ)

The secondary may be expanded into a multi-word noun phrase or a possessed noun:

(88) Syriac: **Noun–Noun Phrase**
ܒܪܗ ܕܐܠܗܐ ܚܝܐ
br-ēh d= [alāhā ḥayyā]
son-POSS.3MS LNK= God alive.MS
'the son of the living God' (*Peshiṭta*, Matthew 16:16; Muraoka 1997: 62, §73f)

(89) Syriac: **Noun–Possessed Noun**
ܒܩܢܘܡܗ ܕܐܠܗܘܬܟ
ba= qnom-āh d= alāhut-āk
in= nature-POSS.3FS LNK= divinity(FS)-POSS.2MS
'in the nature of Your Godhead' (*Acts of Thomas*, ed. Wright 1871: ܨܦ)

The primary, on the other hand, cannot be a possessed noun, as the possessive suffix is a marker of the construction itself (contrast with example (42) on page 62). Whenever the primary is expanded to a multi-word NP, the possessive suffix, being a nominal suffix, must be attached to the head noun itself, or if some head nouns are conjoined, to each of them (cf. Duval 1881: 340, §359b):

(90) Syriac: **Noun Phrase–Noun**
ܚܝܠܗ ܪܒܐ ܕܐܠܗܐ
[ḥayl-ēh rabbā] d= alāhā
power-POSS.3MS great.MS LNK= God
'the great power of God' (*Peshiṭta*, Acts 8:10; Muraoka 1997: 89, §112j)

(91) Syriac: **Conjoined Nouns–Noun**
ܙܒܢ̈ܘܗܝ ܘܙܢ̈ܘܗܝ ܕܟܝܢܐ
zabn-aw *wa=* *zn-aw* *da=* *kyānā*
time-PL.POSS.3MS and= manner-PL.POSS.3MS LNK= nature
'the periods and modes of nature' (Bardaisan, *Book of the Laws of the Countries* ed. Drijvers 1965: 34:10–11, Bakker 2011: 123)

The DAC can also be embedded in a larger AC. This is the case of example (86) on page 76, which is embedded in the following example. Note that the definite value of the DAC is propagated to the entire AC:

(92) Syriac: **Noun–Noun Phrase**
ܡܪܪܐ ܕܢܦܫܗ ܕܡܣܟܢܐ
mrārā *d=* *[napš-ēh* *d=* *meskēnā]*
bitterness LNK= soul-POSS.3MS LNK= poor
'the bitterness of the soul of a poor man' (*Peshiṭta*, Sirach 35:20 *apud* Van Peursen 2007: 207)

The secondary can itself be pronominal, leaning on the linker *dil-*:

(93) Syriac: **Noun–Pronoun**
ܣܶܦܪܶܗ ܕܺܝܠܶܗ
sepr-ēh *dil-ēh*
book-POSS.3MS LNK-POSS.3MS
'his book' (Muraoka 1997: 71, §91f)

Only in such cases can we find a possessive pronoun on the primary which is not of the 3rd person:

(94) Syriac: **Noun–Pronoun**
ܙܥܘܪܘܬܝ ܕܝܠܝ
zʿorut-ⁱ *dil-ⁱ*
littleness-POSS.1SG LNK-POSS.1SG
'my littleness' (*Acts of Thomas*, ed. Wright 1871: ܨܟ)

The DAC is found also with adverbial heads, serving to mark the secondary as definite (Mengozzi 2005a: 371). Pat-El (2013a: 324) suggests that it spread from nominal primaries to prepositional primaries due to the fact that most of the prepositions in Semitic languages are derived from nominal forms.

(95) Syriac: **Preposition–Noun**
ܥܰܡܗܶܝܢ ܕ݁ܒ݂ܢܳܬ݂ܶܗ
ʿamm-hēn da= bnāt-ēh
with-POSS.F.PL LNK= daughters-POSS.3MS
'together with his daughters' (Muraoka 1997: 88, §111e)

(96) Syriac: **Preposition–Noun**
ʿamm-ēh d= malkā
with-POSS.MS LNK= king
'with the king' (Mengozzi 2005a: 377)

In such cases, one may question whether the linker can be analysed as standing in apposition with the prepositional primary, as it does with nominal primaries. Mengozzi (2005a: 372), drawing a parallel between the cases of nominal primaries and prepositional primaries, suggests that the answer is positive:

> The construction [with a prepositional primary] is a variant of the genitive phrase with proleptic pronoun [= DAC with nominal primary]. The determinative pronoun [= *d-*] functions in [the former case] as a "pro-preposition", in that it resumes the head of the prepositional phrase, i.e. the preposition itself.

Cohen (2015: 118), on the other hand, writing on a similar construction occurring in the NENA JZakho dialect, suggests that such an analysis is implausible: "In this position, there is no motivation for the pronoun *d-* to occur, since there is no sense in pronominally representing the preposition (as there is, e.g. between two nouns, where *d-* perfectly represents the first noun)."

Indeed, Mengozzi's position is somewhat contradictory: A pronoun cannot become a "pro-preposition" without losing its pronominal status. Thus, his analysis in fact implies that the *d-* morpheme in this position is no more pronominal, but rather serves as a pure linker connecting the preposition to its complement. An alternative solution reveals itself if we observe carefully the linguistic facts: In Syriac, a *d*+Noun combination never occurs directly after a bare preposition, but only after a preposition followed by a proleptic pronoun.[40] Thus, it seems reasonable to postulate that the *d-* represents not the proposition but rather the referent introduced by the proleptic pronoun. As for the secondary, it could be analysed as a reduced equational relative clause, specifying the referent of these

[40] This is also true of Jewish Babylonian Aramaic (Bar-Asher Siegal 2013b: 95).

pronouns, somewhat similarly to example (48) on page 64.[41] Thus, example (96) on the previous page should be literally translated as 'with him, who is the king', but, of course, the heavy pragmatic markedness that is associated with such an English translation is not present in the Syriac original (except for the marking of the secondary as definite).[42]

As the *d-* linker is co-referential both with the possessive suffix and the secondary, we get schematically a skewed picture of the grammatical relations in this construction, as compared to Table 3.3 on page 76:

Table 3.4: Relations within a DAC headed by a preposition

Head	Attr.		
ʿamm-	-ēh		
	↕		
	d-	⟺	malkā
	Head		Attr.

3.6.2 Variants of the double annexation construction (X-{y.POSS} LNK-y.POSS LNK Y)

A variant of the DAC is a construction in which the possessive suffix is not attached to the primary noun, but rather to the linker *dil-*, yielding a quite elaborate structure:

(97) Syriac: **Noun–Noun**
ܡܫܡܫܢܐ ܕܝܠܗ ܕܡܠܬܐ
mšamsānē dil-āh d= meltā
ministers LNK-POSS.3FS LNK= word(FS)
'ministers of the word' (*Peshiṭta*, Luke 1:2; Muraoka 1997: 88, §112h)

As the linker is syntactically independent it can precede, together with the secondary, the primary (compare with example (52) on page 65):

[41]But note that in this example the secondary specifies the nominal primary, and not the possessive suffix.

[42]This analysis is in some respects similar to the analysis of Bar-Asher Siegal (2013a) of *d-* followed by nouns (see footnote 16 on page 58), in that both assume that *d*+Noun can be interpreted as a clause. However, the type of clause involved, and the scope of this analysis (which is in our case quite limited) marks a clear difference between the two approaches.

(98) Syriac: **Noun–Noun Phrase**
ܕܝܠܗܘܢ ܕܬܪܥܣܪ ܫܠܝܚܐ ܫܡܗܐ
[dil-hon da= tre'sar šliḥē] šmāhē
LNK-POSS.3M.PL LNK= twelve apostles names
'the names of the twelve apostles' (*Peshiṭta*, Matthew 10:2; Muraoka 1997: 88, §112h)

This construction can even appear without a primary (i.e. with a ∅ primary) in predicative position. This is the case in the following example, in which the inflected *dil-* linker is separated from the *d-* linker by an enclitic personal pronoun, which serves to mark the AC as being predicative:[43]

(99) Syriac: ∅–**Noun**
ܘܩܠܐ ܗܢܐ ܕܚܕܘܬܐ ܕܝܠܗ̇ ܗܘ ܕܡܫܬܘܬܐ
(w= qālā hānā d= ḥadutā) ∅ dil-āh =ʰu d= meštutā
and= sound DEM.MS LNK= joy ∅ LNK-POSS.3FS =3MS LNK= feast(FS)
'and this sound of rejoicing is that of the wedding-feast' (*Acts of Thomas*, ed. Wright 1871: ܨܕ)

A highly elaborate variant of this construction occurs when the possessive suffix is attached both to the primary noun and to a linker. If not for its rareness, one might term this a TRIPLE ANNEXATION CONSTRUCTION:

(100) Syriac: **Noun–Noun**
ܡܗܝܡܢܝܗ̇ ܕܝܠܗ̇ ܕܐܣܬܝܪ
mhaymanay-āh dil-āh d= Estēr
eunuchs-POSS.3FS LNK-POSS.3FS LNK= E.
'the eunuchs of Esther' (*Peshiṭta*, Esther 4:4; Williams 2001: 8)

At the other extreme, a variant of the DAC in which the linker is completely lacking does not exist in Syriac as such, although it is attested in the contemporary Galilean Aramaic, a western Classical Aramaic language (Hopkins 1997: 25). Only the word ܟܘܠ *kul* 'all', which could be analysed as standing in attributive relation to its complement, shows this syntax regularly:[44]

[43]Cf. Muraoka (1997: 33*, fn. 24).

[44]It is interesting to note that this peculiar syntax of the word *kul* is conserved in many NENA dialects. A survey of different Syriac constructions involving *kul* can be found in Williams (2001: Ch. 3).

(101) Syriac: **All–Noun**
ܒܟܠܗܝܢ ܒܪܝܬܟ
b= kul-hin beryāt-āk
in= all-POSS.3F.PL creature.F.PL-POSS.2MS
'in all Your creatures' (*Acts of Thomas*, ed. Wright 1871: ܡܘ)

3.7 The dative linker construction (X-{y.POSS} DAT Y)

As an alternative to the usage of the *d-* pronominal linker, one finds cases where the dative/allative preposition ܠ *l-* 'to' (glossed here DAT) is used (Duval 1881: §362).[45]

(102) Syriac: **Noun–Noun Phrase**
ܒܢܫ̈ܐ ܠܡܠܟܐ ܕܗܘܢܝ̈ܐ
b= nešē l= [malkā d= hunāyē]
in= women DAT= king LNK= Huns
'amongst the women of the king of Huns' (*Chronique de Josué le Stylite* ed. Martin 1876: 18, 1; Duval 1881: 342, §362)

Such cases are, however, quite rare, and often it is difficult to say whether the preposition is a pure marker of the AC, or rather contributes some semantic content.[46]

The above construction can be seen as a parallel of the ALC, but with a dative linker instead of a pronominal one. Similarly, a rare alternative to the DAC exists as well. In this construction the secondary is indexed by a possessive pronoun on the primary, followed by the preposition *l-*:

[45] As for the usage of prepositional linkers, Williams (2001: 8) lists also the "the partitive construction with ܡܢ [=*men* 'from']" as a "genitive construction". In this case, however, the preposition contributes semantically to the partitive reading, and should therefore be analysed as a contentful head of a PP, rather than an AC marker. See Joosten (1996: 56) for more examples of the partitive construction.

[46] Thus, in the second example cited by Duval (1881: 342, §362), ܟܘܒܫܐ ܠܪ̈ܓܠܝܟܝ *qubšā l-reglayk* 'a footstool for your feet' (*Peshiṭta*, Acts 2:35), the *l-* seems to fulfil its ordinary function as a contentful preposition rather than a marker of an AC. This phrase, moreover, is a literal translation of the Biblical Hebrew הֲדֹם לְרַגְלֶיךָ *hădom lə-raglēkā* (Psalms 110:1). One may speculate that such Biblical Hebrew constructions may indeed be the source for the Syriac construction. The Biblical Hebrew construction is said to be used especially when a definite secondary follows an indefinite primary (Waltke & O'Connor 1990: 157; Jenni 2003: 63). Given the rarity of the Syriac construction, it is difficult to tell whether this is true in Syriac as well. As for the colloquial Arabic usage of a similar construction, see below.

(103) Syriac: **Noun–Noun**
ܫܡܗ ܠܐܡܗ
šm-āh *l=* *emm-ēh*
name-POSS.3FS DAT= mother-POSS.3MS
'the name of his mother' (Matthew 13:55, Curetonian (ed. Burkitt 1904) and Sinaitic (ed. A. S. Lewis 1910) manuscripts *apud* Joosten 1996: 56)

(104) Syriac: **Noun–Noun**
ܐܡܗ ܠܟܠܬܐ
ʾemm-āh *l=* *kaltā*
mother-POSS.3FS DAT= bride
'the mother of the bride' (*Acts of Thomas*, ed. Wright 1871: ܩܡܒ)

This construction is discussed in length by Hopkins (1997), who gives credit to Goldenberg (1979: 324) for being the first to note it, as only three examples of it are attested in the standard version of the *Peshiṭta* (Ruth 1:2; 2:19; Luke 1:27). In all of these cases, as in example (103) on the current page, the primary is the noun ܫܡܐ *šmā* 'name'.

The prepositional linker *l-* differs from the pronominal linker *d-*, in that it does not represent a noun. In this sense, it is a truly a pure marker of the AC. In this respect one can cite Polotsky (1961: 254), who writes regarding a similar construction in Ge'ez:

> The complement introduced by *la-* therefore lacks the ability, which an apposition ought to possess, of leading a separate syntactic existence; and this accounts for the fact the analytical construction really makes the impression of a unified whole, rather than of two separable elements in apposition.

Hopkins (1997: 30ff.) suggests that the origin of this construction belongs to a colloquial register of Aramaic, and for this reason it is nearly absent from literary sources. He attributes the existence of a similar construction in the vernacular Eastern Arabic dialects to an Aramaic substratum.[47] Moreover, he shows that this

[47] Erwin (2004 [1963]: 380) notes that in Iraqi Arabic this construction (with the possessive suffix) has always a definite secondary. See for instance the following example:

(i) Iraqi Arabic: **Noun–Noun**
ṣadīq-a *l=* *ʿali*
friend-POSS.3MS DAT= A.
'Ali's friend' (Erwin 2004 [1963]: 380)

construction gave rise to the "normal possessive construction" of Western Neo-Aramaic, in which the *l-* preposition has been encliticized to the head, yielding an *-il* suffix functioning as a construct state marker (see example (23) on page 320), parallel to the NENA *-əd* suffix (see §4.4).

3.8 Adjectival attribution by apposition (X Y.AGR)

3.8.1 The juxtaposition-cum-agreement construction

Goldenberg (1995: 8) qualifies adjectives as follows:

> If we admit that adjectives have to do both with the carrier of the quality etc. and with the attributed quality itself, then the form "adjective" is recognized as an attributive complex with pronominal reference and attribute as distinguishable components, the former represented by the inflectional markers and the latter given in the lexeme involved. The implied attributive relation marks the adjective as the morphological exponent of that relation, and consequently as the morphological correlate of the genitive complex.

Goldenberg's "pronominal reference" is our pronominal linker, while his "attribute" is our secondary. Thus, using the current terminology, he equates an adjective to a LNK+secondary phrase. Indeed, just as the linker stands in apposition with the primary to be qualified, the adjective stands in apposition with the noun it qualifies, giving raise effectively to a juxtaposition-cum-agreement construction. Nonetheless, for simplicity I shall refer to adjectives as being simple secondaries.[48]

The equivalence between the adjective and the linker phrase is especially clear in the case of ordinal secondaries. These can be realised using the linker construc-

[48]While Goldenberg's conception of the adjective is appealing in its structural elegance, it does not provide us with any operational criterion to distinguish between adjectives and inflecting nouns (e.g. those which designate animate beings). The key difficulty lies in the fact that are no clear criteria to demarcate words which designate a "carrier of quality" (=adjectives) from those which designate directly a "substance" or "entity" (=nouns). For example, if the Hebrew adjective שָׂב *śāb* 'aged man' can be analysed as אִישׁ שֵׂיבָה *ʾīš śebā* 'a man of old age' (Goldenberg 1995: 9), shouldn't also the noun יֶלֶד *yeled* 'child' be analysable along similar lines as אִישׁ יַלְדוּת *ʾīš yaldūt* 'a man of childhood'? Note also that *yeled*, denoting an animate noun, can inflect for gender and number just as the adjective *śāb*. Indeed, the apparent difference between the two lies not in their structure but rather in their distribution, as *yeled* is rarely used as a modifier of another noun.

tion (see §3.5.5 and especially example (75) on page 73), or by adjectival derivation of the ordinal:

(105) Syriac: **Noun–Ordinal**
ܝܘܡܐ ܬܪܝܢܐ
yawmā trayānā
day(MS) second.MS
'the second day' (Nöldeke 1898: 178, §239)

The equivalence is schematized in Table 3.5, to be contrasted with Table 3.2 on page 59 (cf. Goldenberg 2013a: 236).

Table 3.5: Adjectival attribution according to Goldenberg, contrasted with the terminology used in this study

Apposition	Head	Attr.
yawmā	da-	trēn
yawmā	tarayānā	
Primary	Secondary	

Notwithstanding the constitutional equivalence between adjectives and the linker phrase, in Syriac, as in other Semitic languages, there is a morphological difference between the two: while the *d-* linker is an uninflecting particle, the "pronominal reference" within the adjective is made overt by the very inflecting character of the adjective, which agrees with its primary in gender, number and determination.[49]

(106) Syriac: **Noun–Adjective**
ܡܠܟܐ ܛܒܐ . ܡܠܟܬܐ ܛܒܬܐ
malk-ā ṭāb-ā malk-ātā ṭāb-ātā
monarch-MS.EMPH good-MS.EMPH monarch-F.PL.EMPH good-F.PL.EMPH
'a good king / good queens' (Muraoka 1997: 72, §92.1)

On the other hand, adjectives and linker phrases show many similar syntactic properties. Just as the linker phrase can stand alone without any explicit primary,

[49]In Syriac, the agreement in determination is apparent by the agreement in state (absolute or emphatic). This is also true in principal in Jewish Babylonian Aramaic, although some examples seem to indicate that attributive adjectives are always in emphatic state, irrespective of the state of the primary (Bar-Asher Siegal 2013b: 64).

so too can an adjective be used independently without any antecedent, as in the following example (the adjectives are marked as **bold**):

(107) Syriac: ∅–**Adjective**
ܗܘ ܕܡܕܢܚ ܫܡܫܗ ܥܠ ܛܒܐ ܘܥܠ ܒܝܫܐ
haw d= madnaḥ šemš-ēh ʿal ***ṭāb-ē*** *w=*
DEM.MS LNK= rise.CAUS.PTCP.MS sun-POSS.3MS on good-M.PL.EMPH and=
ʿal ***biš-ē***
on bad.M.PL.EMPH
'He who makes his sun rise above the good ones and the evil ones' (*Peshiṭta*, Matthew 5:45; Muraoka 1997: 76, §96d)

Similarly, the adjective can sometimes precede its primary, just as the linker can (see example (98) on page 81):

(108) Syriac: **Noun–Adjective**
ܩܕܡܝܬܐ ܫܬܐܣܬܐ
qadmāytā šetestā
first.FS foundation(FS)
'the first foundation' (Muraoka 1997: 69, §91a)

Finally, in parallel to cases where the ALC has a demonstrative preceding the linker phrase, thus rendering it definite (see §3.5.6), the same pattern occurs with adjectival secondaries, as Pat-El (2010: 66–67) notes.

(109) Syriac: **Noun–Conjoined adjectives**
ܠܨܒܝܢܐ ܓܝܪ ܗܘ ܪܒܐ ܘܩܕܝܫܐ
l= ṣebyānā =gēr haw [rabbā w= qaddišā]
to= will(MS) =indeed DEM.MS big.MS and= holy.MS
'to that great and holy will' (Bardaisan, *Book of the Laws of the Countries* ed. Drijvers 1965: 62:2–3 *apud* Bakker 2011: 137; Pat-El 2010: 67)

In spite of all these similarities, it is worth noting that the adjective itself can appear as part of a linker phrase, i.e. as the secondary of the ALC. The conditions governing this usage are briefly discussed in the next section.

3.8.2 Juxtaposition vs. the analytic linker construction

The usage of the juxtaposition-cum-agreement construction (in either order), as well as the independent usage of adjectives, should be regarded as the default

AC for adjectival secondaries. But, as we saw in §3.5.3, adjectives can also appear as secondaries of the ALC, with or without overt primaries. For example, Van Peursen (2007: 211) states that ܚܟܝܡܐ *hakkimā* 'wise.EMPH' alternates freely with ܕܚܟܝܡ *d=hakkim* 'LNK=wise.ABS', both corresponding to Hebrew חכם *ḥak̲am* 'a wise person'.

Van Peursen (2007: 212) also notes that it is difficult to establish a "functional difference" between the two constructions, but rather the linker construction is more frequent in certain contexts. In my interpretation, these contexts are (a) the occurrence of a (multi-word) AdjP as secondary or (b) the occurrence of a pronominal primary, ∅ included.[50]

The usage of the linker construction in cases like (a) may be motivated by the speaker's desire to delineate the phrasal nature of the secondary, and thus avoid any ambiguity as for the scope of modifiers of the adjective. The motivation for (b) may lie in her desire to clearly express the pronominal head extant in the adjective. This is achieved by attaching to the adjective an explicit pronominal head, namely the linker.[51]

3.9 Conclusions

This chapter gave a survey of the various ACs of Syriac. Three main construction are used in this domain: the construct state construction, the analytic linker construction and the double annexation construction. The former is the least productive of the three, being used mostly with fixed expressions or specific primaries, while the latter two are used more frequently. The alternation between these two seems to be chiefly related to questions of determination. The latter two constitute the source for the Neo-CSC present in NENA dialects, as is discussed in §10.4.1.

Some marginal attributive constructions of Syriac are variants of the DAC as well as the dative linker construction. The latter may be the source of Neo-CSC in Western Neo-Aramaic.

Beyond these constructions one finds the juxtaposition-cum-agreement construction used with attributive adjectives, a construction which is extant in all strata of Aramaic.

[50] If no explicitly primary appears, the linker fully assumes its pronominal role.

[51] One may tentatively analyse an adjective appearing in absolute state as expressing the adjectival lexeme alone without a pronominal head, in contrast to the emphatic state of the adjective, which is "the formal expression of its structure as a nomen adiectivum, which includes an inherent pronominal reference to the qualified substantival entity" (Goldenberg 1991: 718). If this is true, the linker is effectively an extraction of the pronominal head from the adjective.

4 The D-markers in NENA dialects

4.1 Introduction

In all NENA dialects one finds AC markers which are cognate with the Syriac linker *d(a)-* (discussed in §3.5), which must have existed also in the NENA precursors of the Classical Aramaic period. These are easily identifiable by virtue of containing a segment */d/* or */t/*, accompanied optionally by a schwa before or after it. The probable unified historical origin of these markers has led many scholars to analyse them synchronically as variants of one and the same particle, termed in general "the annexation/genitive particle *d*". For example, Jastrow (1988: 25) writes in his description of Hertevin: "Die Annexion eines Nomens an ein vorangehendes Leitwort (Genetivverbindung) erfolgt durch die Genetivpartikel *d*, die zwischen die beiden Nomina tritt." This particle is assumed to have different allomorphs, varying both regarding its voice feature (*/d/* vs. */t/*), and – more importantly – regarding its attachment as an enclitic to the primary or as a proclitic to the secondary.[1] This is most clearly stated by Fassberg (2010: 44): "The Cl[assical] Aram[aic] relative pronoun דִּי/דְּ [=di-/d-] has allomorphs in J[ewish] Challa: *-əd*, *-d*, *d-*, *ʾəd-*." Other scholars use in general the same practice, including Khan in his detailed descriptions of various NENA dialects.

While I agree that these elements must all be ultimately derived from a common ancestor morpheme *d-* (see the diachronic treatment in Chapter 10), one of the claims advanced in this study is that these forms, which I subsume under the name *D-markers*, represent in fact different morphemes, differing in their morpho-syntactic distribution and, to a finer degree, in their pragmatic implication. More precisely, I distinguish between 1) a head-marking (phrasal) suffix *-əd*, equivalent functionally to construct state marking, 2) a dependent-marking pronominal proclitic *d-*,[2] and 3) a dependent-marking genitive (phrasal) prefix

[1] The phonological attachment is not always clearly stated in the descriptions, as sometimes one finds the *d* written as a separate word standing between the two. This is the usual practice in Jastrow's description cited above.

[2] Note that the = symbol, marking clitic boundaries, is only used in glossed examples. For aesthetic and typographic reasons, in the running text I use the hyphen as marking a general morpheme boundary.

d-. In this I follow Cohen (2010; 2012) in his description of JZakho, although his terminology is somewhat different. In the view advocated here, the separate existence of these morphemes can be observed in most NENA dialects, albeit with differing levels of clarity.

As distinct morphemes, one would expect their semantic-pragmatic (their SIGNIFIÉ or MEANING in a broad sense) to differ as well. This is indeed the case, but as this difference is very fine, I shall not use it as a decisive criteria. Instead, I shall establish their separate linguistic existence relying chiefly on their distributional properties. Accordingly, as written above, two shall be characterized as AFFIXES and one as a CLITIC.

Needless to say, these terms are hotly debated in recent linguistic literature, and their relevance to typology, or linguistics in general, has been cast in doubt (cf. most recently Haspelmath 2015). Therefore, in the first section of this chapter, I discuss my understanding of these terms, and why they should be relevant for this study. In the second section, I present the usage of these terms in a similar and highly relevant linguistic debate, namely the analysis of a Persian AC marker, the so-called Ezafe. This debate is interesting not only due to the similar analytical and methodological problems posed by this marker, but also due to the similar properties shared by the Ezafe and the NENA AC markers, bearing in mind the contact situation between the Iranic languages using the Ezafe (chiefly Kurdish and Persian) and NENA dialects. Finally, in the last two sections, I use the concepts discussed in the former sections to affirm the distinction between the three above-mentioned NENA morphemes.

The claims put forward in this chapter bear a general character, claiming validity for all NENA dialects. Yet, as these dialects are quite different (some could be considered to be different languages), it is clear that not all the details of my claims would be true for each and every dialect. Some dialects, moreover, are not well enough documented at this stage in order to test these claims. To overcome this methodological difficulty, I establish the claims with examples of Barwar, possibly the best documented dialect so far (Khan 2008c), with sporadic examples from other dialects. Given that Cohen (2010) has put forward a similar analysis for JZakho, I hope in this way to show that the three morphemes are differentiable at least in principle across NENA, opening the way for further research on this question. Moreover, as I posit a clitic-affix continuum, I have a certain methodological leeway: The three morphemes may be diverging to different degrees in each dialect, yet still show the same general pattern. While in this chapter I take a bird's-eye view perspective, recall that in the subsequent chapters four dialects (JZakho, Qaraqosh, JSanandaj and JUrmi) are examined in further detail.

4.2 Clitics, affixes, and phrasal affixes

In this study, I use the notions *clitics* and *affixes* to designate different types of bound morphemes, i.e. morphemes which cannot stand by themselves, but have to attach to other morphemes in order to form a self-standing phonological word, i.e. a stress-unit.[3] While these terms are commonplace in current linguistic analysis, they are not always used alike by different linguists, and thus I find it necessary to clarify my understanding of these terms in the context of this study.[4]

In current linguistic thinking, the most common distinction between the two types is related to their syntactic status: While affixes are considered to be building blocks of words, clitics have the syntactic and distributional properties of full-fledged words, but happen to be phonologically deficient in that they are typically devoid of stress. Thus, in a recent characterisation of clitics the framework of Canonical Typology, Spencer & Luís (2013: 140) write: "the canonical clitic is an element which has the form of a canonical affix [i.e. it is phonologically bound] and the distribution of a canonical function word".

Indeed, the distinction between affixes and clitics lies to a large extent on a modular view of language, differentiating two sub-systems: One, MORPHOLOGY, has to do with the *make-up* of words, while the second, SYNTAX, has to do with *arrangement* of words in discourse. In the last century, this distinction has received various formalisations (and at times denied altogether), but the core insight justifying this distinction remained the same: While words can combine together to form sentences in a seemingly limitless fashion, the building blocks of words combine in a much more limited and regular fashion. In this view, affixes fall under the domain of morphology while clitics are treated syntactically. Thus, the bond between a host and an affix is stronger than the one holding with a clitic.[5] A corollary of this is that clitics can attach phonologically to a certain word while forming a syntactic constituent with another word (cf. Klavans 1985).

Yet the keystone of this partition, the notion of the WORD, or more precisely the morpho-syntactic word, has remained an elusive concept and defied any attempt

[3]In the scope of this research, dealing exclusively with stress-accent languages, I equate the notion of phonological word with the notion of stress unit: a sequence of morphemes carrying exactly one stress-accent. Cf. Garbell (1965b: 39): "A minimal free form constituting a stress unit is a word."

[4]Needless to say, I use the terms *suffixes* and *enclitics* to denote those bound morphemes which attach backwards, and *prefixes* respectively *proclitics* to denote those which attach forwards.

[5]This notion can be formalised as a transition probability: The probability of an affix following a prosodic (and syntactic) host should be higher than the probability of a clitic following its prosodic host. In the scope of this study I leave this notion at an intuitive level.

to define it cross-linguistically. This has recently led Haspelmath (2011) to reject the validity of this notion and subsequently the dichotomy between morphology and syntax (see more references there). In a follow-up article, Haspelmath (2015) claims that the notion of clitic cannot be defined consistently cross-linguistically, and therefore he suggests to dispense with it altogether.

While Haspelmath's argumentation is compelling, his suggestion to abolish this terminology is not helpful. He suggests to replace these terms with the terms PLENIMORPH and MINIMORPH. Not only would this add to the terminological inflation in linguistics, but these terms do not address the issue at hand: Plenimorphs are simply lexical bases, while minimorphs are functional morphemes, covering both affixes and clitics. Indeed, it may be that the notion of clitic is not useful in a large scale typological survey where clearly defined comparative concepts are needed. However, in a smaller study, covering typologically or genealogically related languages, these notions can be proven useful, as they permit to discern between different levels of attachment of morphemes to their hosts, on the one hand, and distinguish distributional classes on the other hand. Moreover, in the field of language change and grammaticalisation, it is a well known fact that independent morphemes can become more and more bound to their hosts, finally becoming grammatical affixes. As this is a gradual process, it is convenient to use the label CLITIC to designate intermediate stages of such processes.[6]

Thus, my suggestion is to understand the notions of AFFIX and CLITIC not as absolute terms, but rather as relative terms, which can be fully appreciated only in the context of a study of a specific language, or a group of related languages. Hence, one can use different criteria proposed in the literature, such as those famously proposed by Zwicky & Pullum (1983), to gauge the proximity of a morpheme to its host, and not as categorical distinctions. Needless to say, MORPHOLOGY and SYNTAX are not considered in such a view as distinct modules of language, but rather as *end points* on a continuum which permit us to classify different types of linguistic signs.[7]

Of special importance for us is the SELECTIVITY CRITERION proposed by Zwicky & Pullum (1983). Since inflection is normally associated with a specific word-class (nominal inflection, verbal inflection, etc.), morphemes which attach only to a specific word-class are typically affixes, especially if they stand in grammatical opposition with other such morphemes, encoding different values of a specific

[6]A neat analysis of such a process, showing that the same source morpheme may be grammaticalised differently as a clitic and as an affix, is given by Lahiri (2003) treating the TAM system of Bengali.

[7]In this respect, my approach is similar to that of Canonical Typology, which defines grammatical notions in terms of "ideals" with possible deviations; see Brown & Chumakina (2013).

grammatical feature associated with the stem.[8] From a cognitive point of view, this probably means that these morphemes are associated mentally with this word-class. From a language change perspective, if they originated in free forms, it means that their usage has been maximally restricted to a sub-part of the lexicon, reaching the endpoint of a grammaticalisation process. Bound morphemes which have a freer distribution, on the other hand, are typically CLITICS, as they conserve better the distributional freedom associated with phonologically independent forms, i.e. words.

Of course, in the process of becoming an affix, an element may become more selective but still keep some features of free forms. In this study, one such important feature is PHRASAL SCOPE. An affix, attaching to a single base, has typically scope only over that base. Conversely, a free word, or a clitic, can have scope over a syntactic phrase. To designate the intermediate state of affairs, I shall use the term PHRASAL AFFIX for bound morphemes which are selective with respect to their hosts, but exhibit phrasal scope. This term can be conveniently contrasted with the term WORD-LEVEL AFFIXES, to denote the typical affixes.

To conclude, in the realm of phonologically bound morphemes, I shall distinguish three types of morphemes, on the basis of the above criteria:[9]

Clitics Phonologically bound morphemes showing syntactic distribution and scope of free morphemes (i.e. words).

Phrasal affixes Bound morphemes tied to the inflectional system of a specific grammatical category (part-of-speech), but exhibiting wide scope over phrases.

Word-level affixes Bound morphemes tied to the inflectional system of a specific grammatical category, and having narrow scope over the inflected word alone.

This is schematically presented in Table 4.1 on the next page.

[8]In this respect, note that while Zwicky & Pullum (1983: 511) observe that "special cliticization and inflection can look much alike", they still keep the two notions strictly apart. In applying this logic they show that the English ending *n't* (as in *can't, won't* etc.), which seemingly is a reduced clitic form of the English negator *not*, is in fact not a clitic but rather an inflectional affix of certain English verbs. Thus, INFLECTION in my terminology should be understood as word-internal (morphological) marking, which is typically realised by means of affixes, and is opposed to marking by clitics.

[9]While these criteria are sufficient for concise definitory purposes, more criteria will be examined in the following discussions.

Table 4.1: The Affix–Clitic Continuum

	Word affixes	Phrasal affixes	Clitics	
More bound	⟵		⟶	Less bound
Phon. dependent	+	+	+	
Phrasal Scope	-	+	+	
Selective	+	+	-	

4.3 The Persian Ezafe: Clitic or phrasal affix?

In several Iranic languages, ACs are marked by a morpheme known as Ezafe (the Persian adaptation of the Arabic term إضافة *iḍāfa* 'annexation'), which is typically attached phonologically to the primary. A detailed description of the usage patterns of the Ezafe in Kurdish dialects is given in Chapter 9. Here, I shall consider the case of the Persian Ezafe, and briefly survey the controversy accompanying its grammatical analysis. A more detailed discussion can be found in Haig (2011: §3.1), as well as in the papers cited below.

In Persian, the Ezafe is a *-(y)e* morpheme attaching to the primary of an AC, whether the primary is phrasal or not, as in the following illustrative example of Samvelian (2007a):

(1) Persian: **Noun Phrase–Noun**
این کتابِ کهنه‌یِ بی ارزشِ مریم
in [[ketâb-e kohne]-y̯e bi arzeš]-e maryam
DEM book-EZ ancient-EZ without value-EZ M.
'This ancient worthless book of Maryam.' (Samvelian 2007a: 606)

Analyses of the Ezafe provide two competing accounts of the syntactic status of the Ezafe. The basic question is whether the Ezafe forms a morpho-syntactic constituent with the primary (to which it attaches phonologically) or with the secondary. In the latter case, it must be a clitic, since there is a mismatch between its phonological attachment and syntactical attachment, while in the former case it could be seen as an inflectional affix, encoding construct state.[10] The earliest

[10]Of course, in contrast to the Semitic construct state the Ezafe must mark nouns modified by adjectives as well. This difference has to do with the nature of adjectives in Persian. In contrast to Semitic adjectives which denote *bearers of qualities* and thus embody within them an attributive relation (see §2.3.5), the Persian adjectives denote *qualities* alone and thus must stand in explicit attributive relation with the noun referring to the bearer of the quality.

formulation of this debate, which I am aware of, is given by Fairbanks (1979: 41), who treats the Ezafe as a preposition associated syntactically with the secondary, but gives the following remark in an endnote:

> In conversation with Charles A. Ferguson he has pointed out to me that the *izafe* may be considered an inflection of the preceding noun, an inflection that would mark the noun as one that is determined. This is another indication of the tenuousness of the distinction between inflections and prepositions or postpositions. I would prefer to consider the immediate constituents of *kitab e buzurg* [book EZ big] 'the big book' as *kitab / e buzurg*, although *e* is enclitic to *kitab*. This is the equivalent to considering *I'll go* to have the immediate constituents *I / ll go* although *ll* is enclitic to *I*. (Fairbanks 1979: 43, note 1)

These two competing analyses may affect our understanding of the Ezafe as head-marking or dependent-marking (see §2.2.1), if these concepts are understood as indicating syntactic association. Indeed, some authors associate the Ezafe with the notion of CASE, which is typically understood as a dependent-marking device. Samiian (1994), working within X-bar theory, sees the Ezafe as a "dummy case assigner", while Larson & Yamakido (2006) treat it as a genitive case-marker. In both accounts, the Ezafe is syntactically associated with the secondary.[11] A similar position, in the framework of LFG, is advocated by Bögel & Butt (2013); Bögel et al. (2008), who analyse the Urdu Ezafe (which is borrowed from Persian) as forming a constituent with the secondary, notwithstanding its phonological attachment with the primary.[12]

It is not my intention to discuss these proposals in detail, but they raise an interesting methodological question: given that the Ezafe in Persian is *always* phonologically attached to the primary, why do these authors prefer to analyse it as a clitic syntactically attached to the secondary, thus implying a phonology-syntax mismatch?[13]

One answer is that the Ezafe is marked not on the head of the phrase it modifies, but rather phrase-finally. For example, in case of a conjoined phrase acting as a primary, the Ezafe appears only once phrase-finally:

[11] Larson & Yamakido (2006) discuss mostly data from Kurdish Zazaki, but they apply their analysis to Persian as well.

[12] To be exact, they allow for two possible analyses: X [EZ Y] or [X EZ Y] but they rule out the structure [X EZ] Y.

[13] In Kurmanji Kurdish such an analysis may be more plausible, as an independent Ezafe can appear without an overt primary, thus forming a constituent with the secondary. The situation in Kurdish is discussed in more detail in Chapter 9.

(2) Persian: **Cojoined NPs–Noun**
کلاهِ سفید و لباسِ زردِ مریم
[kolâh-e sefid va [lebâs-e zard]]-e maryam
hat-EZ white and dress-EZ yellow-EZ M.
'Maryam's white hat and yellow dress' (Samvelian 2007a: 630)

Yet, as Samvelian (2007a: 624) notes, wide scope over coordination does not necessarily entail clitic status. Indeed, the unique marking of conjoined nouns by one affix is a phenomenon known in the literature by the name of SUSPENDED AFFIXATION, coined by G. L. Lewis (1967) in the context of Turkish (for more recent studies, see Kabak 2007 or Broadwell 2008). The similar phenomenon where a suffix belonging to a head is marked phrase-finally on a complement is known in the literature under the name SUFFIXHÄUFUNG (Plank 1995: 50).

Another, meta-linguistic reason may lie in the fact that the *architecture* of formal grammars have been geared toward the syntax of major European languages, which are mostly dependent-marking. Therefore, they do not provide easy provisions for head-marking morphemes. Thus Haig (2011) comments: "all the proposals [...] are faced with the same dilemma: how to fit the Ezafe particle into a theoretical framework which provides no category that readily accommodates it."[14]

If, on the other hand, the notion of construct state is seen as part of the STATE grammatical category, as advocated in §2.3.1, then the phonological attachment of the Ezafe to the primary can be easily accounted to in terms of head-marking state inflection. Such an approach (using different terminology) is advanced by Samvelian (2007a; 2008), who treats the Ezafe as a "head-marking inflectional affix".[15]

In her view, the Ezafe can be seen as part of nominal morphology in Persian. With the exception of some lexically determined prepositions (which may be of nominal origin), it can only follow nominal elements, and it is barred from

[14]The difficulty to admit an analysis in which the Ezafe is head-marking is explicitly stated by Bögel & Butt (2013: 317): "This is problematic because the head is difficult to access for agreement purposes and it is also difficult to state a constraint that just when the XP+*ezafe* is initial, the XP is restricted to be nominal (or a PP). The licensing of the modifying XP also becomes a matter of stating a long distance dependency between the *ezafe* and the modifying constituent that must be propagated up and down through various levels of the tree." Note that these are technical difficulties related to the grammatical framework, rather than conceptual difficulties.

[15]See also Thackston (2006a: 11–17) who treats the Kurmanji Ezafe as "construct case". The term "construct" is appropriate, but not so the term "case", which should be reserved for dependent-marking morphology.

appearing after finite verbs. Moreover, as a nominal inflectional affix, it stands in opposition with other similar affixes, namely the indefinite marker *-i* and the so-called pronominal enclitics (which are in fact affixes, according to this view), i.e. they are in paradigmatic complementary distribution.[16] All these affixes are special in that they do not attach to the head-noun of the phrase they modify, but rather phrase-finally, though always after a nominal element.[17] Similarly, they all have wide scope over coordination.

Such an approach is preferable in my opinion, as it does not stipulate a mismatch between phonology and syntax, which, by the principle of scientific simplicity (OCKHAM'S RAZOR) should only be called upon as a last resort.

4.4 The *d-* proclitic vs. the *-əd* suffix

4.4.1 Introduction

Cohen (2010) is the first to clearly state the different syntactic status of the *d-* proclitic and the *-əd* suffix. Cohen's analysis relies on the assumption that the proclitic *d-* retains the pronominal function of the Syriac pronominal linker *d-*, in that it can head an NP.[18] This possibility is clearly illustrated in the following poetic Qaraqosh example (=example (84) on page 174):[19]

(3) Qaraqosh: **d**$_{\text{LNK}}$**–Noun**
kə-mzámri　də=　ʾurxàṯa.ˈ
IND-sing.3PL LNK= roads
'(The people) of the roads sing.' (Khan 2002a: 279 [Poetry 29])

In Barwar *d-* headed NPs are found in predicative positions:[20]

[16] A similar conclusion is reached by Kahnemuyipour (2003: 338f.), working within the Phrasal Phonology framework, who sees the Ezafe as well as the other post-nominal morphemes discussed above as inflectional in nature, and thus prefers to call them "suffixes".

[17] The pronominal enclitics can also occur after finite verbs to designate their complements, but in this position they exhibit different paradigmatic oppositions, and should arguably be treated differently. This is somewhat reminiscent of the situation in Semitic languages, where the pronominal suffixes can appear as complements both after verbs and nouns.

[18] Recall that unlike most pronouns which replace an entire NP, the pronominal linker heads a complex NP. This is due to the fact that it replaces a construct state noun, which must be followed by a complement. See also §2.3.4.

[19] In JZakho the regular form of the linker is in fact *dīd*. The form *d-* is almost exclusively restricted to clausal secondaries, except in the context of possessive pronominal suffixes, where the two forms are allomorphs. See §5.4.

[20] This example is complicated by the fact that one would expect here a genitive marking of the demonstrative pronoun as well. See footnote 46 on page 110 for a possible solution.

(4) Barwar: **d$_{\text{LNK}}$–Determined Noun**
lɛ́wət d= áwwa ʾàθṛaʾ
NEG.COP-2MS LNK= DEM.PROX.MS country
'You are not one of this country.' (Khan 2008c: 112 [A25:82])

Cohen argues that if the *-əd* form is equivalent to the *d-* proclitic, it must also be a pronominal linker (a PRONOMINAL NUCLEUS in his terminology), representing pronominally the primary to which it is attached. He notes, however, that the suffixed form *-əd* attaches not only to nominal primaries but also to prepositional primaries, as in the examples below. Since a preposition is not a noun, it cannot be said to be represented pronominally by a pronominal element, and thus one must conclude that the *-əd* form is not a pronominal element, but rather a pure primary marker (NUCLEUS MARKER in his terminology), different from the pronominal proclitic *d-*.[21]

(5) JZakho: **Preposition–Noun**
ʾəmm-əd gōra
with-CST man
'with the man' (Cohen 2010: 82)

(6) Barwar: **Preposition–Noun**
qám-ət gə̀ppa
before-CST cave
'before the cave' (Khan 2008c: 442 [A8:28])

Cohen's argument is convincing but it may be undermined by inverting it, claiming that a possible conclusion is rather that the *d-* proclitic is a pure relational marker rather than a pronominal one (explaining away the cases where it heads an NP as a kind of primary ellipsis). Alternatively, one may claim that the *-əd* attaching to some prepositions is a lexicalised element, which should be kept apart from the *-əd* suffix following a nominal primary. Instead of trying to refute such attacks, I shall substantiate Cohen's claim on different grounds, showing that the distribution of the *d-* morph is different from the *-əd* morph. In essence, I shall argue that while the *d-* morph is indeed a proclitic, the *-əd* morph is better seen as a nominal suffix, since it stands in paradigmatic opposition to other nominal suffixes. In this claim, I reproduce the line of argumentation of Samvelian (2008; 2007a), who argues that the Persian and Kurmanji Ezafe morphemes should be analysed as inflectional affixes.

[21] See also the discussion following the Syriac examples (95)–(96) on page 79.

It is important to stress that *-əd* and *d-* cannot be considered allomorphs: Their presence is normally not conditioned by any grammatical or phonological factors, but is rather a deliberate choice of the speaker (reflecting some stylistic or pragmatic choice; see below §4.4.2.7). For example, given the Barwar primary *kθawa* 'book' and secondary *qaša* 'priest', both *kθaw-ət qaša* and *kθawa t-qaša* are grammatical expressions meaning 'the book of the priest' (Khan 2008c: 488). On the other hand, the two morphs cannot be considered as free variants either (disregarding for the sake of argument the fine difference in function), as in some grammatical environments, detailed below, their distribution is different.

Let us first consider the forms attaching to the secondary, namely *d-* and its variant forms *də-* ~*ʾəd-* ~*t-*.[22] These elements are phonologically bound forms, as they normally lack stress, forming instead a stress-unit together with the first word of the secondary. In doing so, they show very low selectivity of their host (if any at all), and can attach to nouns, adjectives, verbs (being part of an attributive clause), the negator *la* and various adverbs.[23] In this respect, it seems reasonable to treat them as proclitics.

Similarly, these elements show no sensitivity to the morpho-syntactic structure of the primary, as long as it is nominal in nature (i.e. it has a nominal head). They can, moreover, be separated from the primary by intervening material, and stand in a separate intonation group. This is expected under the analysis of *d-* as a pronominal head, separate from its antecedent (the primary), and forming an NP together with the secondary. Given that a syntactic head is typically conceived of as a syntactic word (i.e., not an inflectional element) this fact too establishes it as a proclitic.

What about the form *-əd*? At first sight, in accordance with the quotes given at the beginning of the chapter, one may consider *-əd* to be an enclitic version of the same morpheme. Evidence for this includes the fact that *-əd* can appear phrase-finally, having wide scope over the entire phrase, such as in the following examples:[24]

[22] The exact form depends on the dialect as well as some syllabic constraints, which are immaterial to the current discussion. For Barwar, Khan (2008c: 396) claims the unvoiced *t-* form to be the basic one.

[23] Note this is true only of dialects which make use of *d-* as a general linker. Some dialects, such as JZakho, use it principally before clausal secondaries, in which case it attaches normally to verbs. See Table 10.1 on page 297.

[24] The dialects of Arbel, Sulemaniyya and Qaraqosh exhibit also examples of phrase-final *-əd* marking, but only after NPs consisting of conjoined nouns (see §4.4.2.5).

(7) Barwar: **Noun Phrase–Noun**
[ʾo= bɛ́θ-a zór]-ət yə̀mm-i.
DEF.MS= house-FREE.SG small-CST mother-POSS.1SG
'the small house of my mother' (Khan 2009a: 76)

(8) JZakho: **Noun Phrase–Noun**
[gōra qamāy]-ət [d-anya baxt-āsa]
man first.MS-CST GEN-DEM.PL woman-PL
'The first husband of these women' (Cohen 2012: 101 (49))

A closer look, however, reveals some differences that distinguish it from the *d-* proclitic, rendering it rather a phrasal suffix. Following Samvelian (2007a), I apply some of the different criteria of Zwicky & Pullum (1983) to show that the *-əd* morph is rather inflectional in nature, while the *d-* morph is (as anticipated) a clitic.

4.4.2 Distinguishing factors

4.4.2.1 Selectivity with respect to the host

As stated above, the *d-* proclitic is not selective at all. The *-əd* morph, on the other hand, is rather selective: With the exception of some lexically determined adverbials (mostly prepositions but also some conjunctions; see examples (5)–(6) on page 98), it can only occur directly after nominals (nouns, pronouns and adjectives). Indeed, NP-finally, it can only attach to nominals.[25]

4.4.2.2 Arbitrary gaps

The *d-* proclitic does not show any arbitrary gaps in its distribution. The *-əd* morph, on the other hand, shows idiosyncratic gaps in its attachment to prepositions. While some prepositions require the *-əd* suffix before full nominal complements, other prepositions cannot occur with it. Yet another class of prepositions can co-occur optionally with the *-əd* suffix. Before pronominal complements, realized as possessive suffixes, the *-əd* suffix is typically absent.

The exact distribution of the *-əd* suffix with different prepositions is different from dialect to dialect. As an example, the distribution of *-əd* with Barwar prepo-

[25]Note that in principle an NP containing a relative clause may end in a verb or an adverb, but the *-əd* morph does not attach to such NPs.

sitions is given in Table 4.2 (Khan 2008c: 432–445).[26] Note that the forms that do not take an *-əd* suffix generally lack stress, and pro-cliticize to their complement, while those that take the *-əd* suffix are phonologically independent.

Table 4.2: Distribution of *-əd* suffix with Barwar prepositions before a full nominal

No suffix	Optional
ax- 'like'	*bahs-/báhsət* 'about'
b- 'in, at'	*bar-/báθər/báθrət* 'about'
bēn-/bēl- 'between'	*qam-/qámət* 'before'
gu- 'in'	*xo-/xót* 'under'
hal- 'until'	
kəs- 'by'	**Mandatory**
l- 'to'	
mən-/m- 'from'	*barqúlət/barqúlət* 'opposite'
qa- 'for'	*ç̌ənnəḵérət* 'around'
reš- 'upon'	*qámθət* 'in front of'
t-la- 'without' [<LNK+NEG]	*šáwpət* 'instead'
ṭla-/ta- 'for'	

4.4.2.3 Morpho-phonological idiosyncrasies

The *d-* proclitic does not show any major morpho-phonological idiosyncrasies, although it presents variant forms which may be motivated phonologically. The same is true in general for the *-əd* suffix as well. In Amədya, however, there is one exceptional form discussed by Greenblatt (2011: 71, fn. 27): the Arabic loanword *jamaʿa* 'community' takes the construct state form *jamaʿa-t* rather than the expected **jamaʿ-əd*. Whether this is a true morphological idiosyncrasy replicating the Arabic construct state morphology or a phonetic artefact related to the presence of the pharyngeal /ʿ/ is hard to tell without further investigation.

[26] I disregard cases of /*d*/ segments appearing before demonstrative pronouns following prepositions, as this is considered to be the genitive *d-* discussed in §4.5.

4.4.2.4 Morphological paradigm

The most important criterion according to Samvelian (2007a: 627) to distinguish an affix from a clitic is the criterion of HAPLOLOGY, devised by Miller (1992) following Zwicky (1987). In fact, this criterion boils down to showing that a morpheme stands paradigmatically IN OPPOSITION (i.e., in a paradigmatic complementary distribution) with other morphemes, forming in essence a morphological paradigm, and thus revealing its affixal nature (see also §2.1). Indeed, this is spelt out in greater clarity, from a structural perspective, in Samvelian (2008). These arguments are in essence repeated here for the case of NENA dialects.

The *-əd* morpheme does not simply attach to its host, but rather stands IN OPPOSITION with a set of other nominal-final morphemes, most conspicuously the Aramaic nominal inflectional endings *-a~-e*, but also the possessive pronominal suffixes.[27] Indeed, one never finds an *-əd* morph attaching to a noun or a preposition ending in a possessive suffix, even if their scope is different. In such cases the *d-* proclitic must be used, as stated explicitly by Khan (2008c: 490), who gives the following example:

(9) Barwar: **Noun–Noun**
jull-éy *t=* *yáwne*
clothes-POSS.3PL LNK= doves
'their clothes of doves' (Khan 2008c: 490 [A14:80])

The nominal endings *-a~-e* are clearly inflectional suffixes as they have single-word scope, as is the case with the possessive pronominal suffixes in most dialects.[28] Since the *-əd* morph stands in opposition to these suffixes, it forms part of the same inflectional system. Thus, most naturally it should also be treated as an inflectional suffix.[29]

[27] The *-əd* morpheme stands also in opposition with definite suffix *-ake*, borrowed from Sorani, in the dialects which have it, such as Koy Sanjaq or Sulemaniyya (Mutzafi 2004a: 62; Khan 2004: 232).

[28] Quite exceptional are the dialects of JSanandaj and Sulemaniyya, in which the possessive pronominal suffixes may be phrase-final, such as in the example *[ʾaxon-a ruw]-i* 'my elder brother' (brother-FREE big-POSS.1SG) (Khan 2009b: 251; 2004: 262). This may very well be under influence of Sorani, which allows similar constructions, such as *[bira gewr]-ek-em* 'brother big-DEF-POSS.1SG' (Wârmâwa, MacKenzie 1961: 81).

[29] One may argue that there is no principal restriction disallowing a clitic to stand in opposition with an affix. I'm unaware of such analyses in the literature, but in any case, such an analysis goes against the very spirit of the notion of paradigmatic opposition. In the structuralist tradition, which I follow here, the fact that two elements stand in opposition is an evidence that they share the same privilege of occurrence and thus the same grammatical status, for instance

It should be noted, that even if one maintains the enclitic status of *-əd*, the fact that it cannot follow these suffixes differentiates it from the proclitic *d-*, which has no such restriction. Formally, I oppose the licit construction [X-POSS d_{LNK}=Y] to the illicit combination *[X-POSS-*əd* Y]. This alone should suffice in showing that these are two different linguistic units, which cannot merely by analysed as phonological variants of one and the same entity.[30] Since the functional load of the two elements is different (as shall be examined below), I take this difference to be morphemic.

As a suffix, the *-əd* morph marks construct state, while the *-a~-e* ending marks free state combined with number. This permits us to recognize three potential morphemic slots following the NENA nominal stem (with optional marking of pronominal secondaries): Gender + Number + State. The actual realisation of these slots, however, is subject to much fusion and idiosyncrasy (especially regarding the marking of gender), so that very often only one or two distinct suffixes are discernible on top of the stem. Some typical examples, reoccurring in many dialects, are given in Table 4.3 on the following page.[31]

4.4.2.5 The conjunction criterion

Samvelian (2007a: 630) shows that the Ezafe has wide scope over a conjoint NP (see example (2) on page 96). This is true also for the *-əd* suffix, as in the following examples:

(10) Barwar: **Conjoined Nouns–Noun**
[bab-a =w yəmm]-ət yala
father-FREE =and mother-CST child
'the father and the mother of the boy' (Khan 2008c: 488 [A15:9])

part-of-speech category. Thus, unless other reasons are invoked, one would naturally assume that affixes and clitics should appear in different paradigmatic slots.

[30] A similar claim is made by Samvelian (2008: 357) to distinguish the Kurmanji suffixed Ezafe from the independent ("demonstrative") Ezafe (see her examples (47) and (48)). In NENA the situation is clearer than in Kurmanji, since the suffix *-əd* is typically added to a nominal stem, and not to a fully fledged noun.

[31] Note that the table is not meant to be exhaustive, given the richness of morphological patterns of NENA nouns.

Table 4.3: Some typical NENA nominals suffixes (NIL=neutralised feature)

Gender	Number	State [+ pron.]
∅ (M)		*-a* (SG.FREE)
∅ (M)		*-e* (PL.FREE)
	-an (M.PL)	*-e* (FREE)
	-t (F.SG)	*-a* (FREE)
	-aṯ (F.PL)	*-a* (FREE)
∅ (M)	NIL	*-əd* (CST)
	-an (M.PL)	*-əd* (CST)
	-t (F.SG)	*-əd* (CST)
	-aṯ (F.PL)	*-əd* (CST)
∅ (M)	NIL	*-i* (CST+POSS.1SG)

(11) Qaraqosh: **Conjoined Nouns–Noun**
[wánat= u toráθ]-əd Bağdèdə
sheep= and cows-CST B.
'the sheep and cows of Qaraqosh' (Khan 2002a: 276 [F:1])

As noted in the discussion of the Persian example, such examples are characteristic of clitic status. For example, Spencer & Luís (2013: 134) state that a "clitic canonically takes wide scope over a coordinated phrase". Yet, such cases are also accommodated by the analysis of *-əd* as a phrasal affix.[32] Moreover, one may analyse such examples as cases of SUSPENDED AFFIXATION. If such an analysis is accepted, then suspended affixation manifests itself as an areal phenomenon, as it encompasses NENA, Iranic languages, and Turkish (for which the term was coined). In another respect, the single construct state marking conserves the logic of classical Semitic languages, in which it is generally not possible to conjoin directly two nouns marked for construct state, and instead alternative formulations are used.[33] Indeed, in such a view, the first noun *baba* 'father' is in fact not under

[32]Under this analysis, the free state suffix *-a* in example (10) on the preceding page is analysed as a default nominal suffix, compatible with the phrase-final construct state suffix.

[33]Recall that in Modern Hebrew such constructions are not found; see example (3) on page 33. See also the highly unusual Syriac example (11) on page 52.

the morphological scope of the *-əd* suffix, but rather its relationship with *yala* 'child' is inferred pragmatically.

Yet, in contrast to the Persian Ezafe, the analysis of *-əd* as a suffix becomes truly clear in those dialects, Barwar and JUrmi, which show an alternative construction in which both conjoined nouns are marked by the *-əd* suffix, though no explicit conjunction appears:[34]

(12) Barwar: **Conjoined Nouns–Noun**
[ʾaql-ət iđ-əd] ay baxta
leg-CST hand-CST DEF.FS woman
'the legs and hand of that woman' (Khan 2008c: 488 [A10:10])

(13) JUrmi: **Conjoined Nouns–Noun**
[id-əd reš-əd] [gor-aw]
hand-CST head-CST man-POSS.3FS
'the hands and head of her husband' (Garbell 1965b: 86)

The possibility of repeating the *-əd* suffix on both nouns indicates that in these dialects the *-əd* marker has shifted, at least partially, from being a phrasal suffix to a word-level suffix.[35] This corroborates the idea that in all dialects *-əd* has acquired some affixal features, albeit in different degrees. Moreover, these dialects provide the clearest evidence for a distributional differentiation between the *d-* proclitic and the *-əd* suffix, as there is no motivation for the *d-* proclitic to be doubled in this environment.

4.4.2.6 Prosodic autonomy

The syntactic autonomy of the linker *d-* is corroborated by the prosodic structure, as it may stand at the beginning of a prosodic phrase, separate from the primary. This fact can be observed in the grammatical descriptions of G. Khan, who indicates prosodic phrase boundaries by a small vertical line ˈ.

[34]Example (12) on the current page from Barwar is given by Khan as *ʾaqlət iđə d-ay-baxta*, but the attachment of the *d* segment to the following demonstrative can be seen as a product of syllabification of fast speech, since clearly the head noun has a construct state ending.

[35]In JUrmi, in fact, one hardly finds any evidence of *-əd* being phrasal at all. Note, moreover, that the repetition of the *-əd* suffix on each conjoint is coupled, both in Barwar and in JUrmi, with the lack of an over coordination conjunction. The occurrence of this construction may very well be related to Turkish influence, which allows the asyndetic conjunction of possessed and non-possessed alliterative nouns. See the discussion in §7.2 regarding examples (8)–(9) on page 190.

(14) Barwar: **Noun–Noun**
*rìxa*ˈ *t=* *xa=* *kàlləš*ˈ
smell LNK= INDF= carrion
'the scent of a carrion' (Khan 2008c: 399 [C8:5])

The *-əd* suffix, on the hand cannot induce a prosodic break: It is bound to the primary serving as its host, and in general is followed immediately by the secondary in the same prosodic phrase (just as *d-* is followed immediately by the secondary). Thus, aside from some exceptional cases, the *-əd* suffix stands always in the middle of a prosodic phrase.

The difference in prosodic autonomy has implications for the semantics of the different forms (see next section), but bears also on their syntactic status, as mediated by language acquisition. According to recent language acquisition theories, functional elements standing at the edges of prosodic phrases play a special role in acquiring syntactic structure, as they serve to *tag* the prosodic phrase with a syntactic label (Christophe et al. 2008; Gutman et al. 2015). Note that the *d-* linker can serve in such a function, effectively becoming a functional head of its NP, while *-əd* cannot. This may explain the mechanism of language change as well: The encliticization of *d-* as *-əd* leads to the loss of its role as tagging the category of its phrase in the process of language acquisition. It thereby loses its status as a syntactic head and is consequently reanalysed as an inflectional suffix.

4.4.2.7 Semantic differentiation

The above criteria show that on distributional grounds the *d-* proclitic and the *-əd* suffix should be treated as two separate morphemes. As such, one would expect each to have a different semantic load. The exact semantic difference between the two constructions, however, is difficult to pinpoint and is outside the scope of this work.[36] In this respect, the comments of Khan (2008c: 489ff.), the most detailed study of a NENA dialect, may be illuminating (the emphasis is mine):

> The structural difference between the *kθawət qaša* construction [=CSC] and the *kθawa t-qaša* construction [=ALC] reflects different degrees of prosodic bonding between the nouns. The first noun in the *kθawa t-qaša* construction is prosodically more independent than the first noun in the *kθawət qaša* construction. [...] The *kθawa t-qaša* construction is a "heavier" form of

[36] A similar question arises in the field of Syriac, where the exact usage conditions of the CSC, the ALC and the DAC are compared. See for example Meyer (2012); Williams (2001: Ch. 2); Joosten (1996: Ch. 4).

> coding than the more compact *kθawət qaša* construction. This heavy coding is sometimes used to give particular **salience** to a newly introduced referent that plays an important role in the discourse [...] When these referents are mentioned subsequently in the discourse, they are typically present with the lighter coding of the *kθawət qaša* construction [...] The heavy coding of the *kθawa t-qaša* construction may be used to give **prominence** to the clause as a whole. [...] The looser prosodic connection between the two components in the *kθawa t-qaša* construction is sometimes used as a device to give **prominence** to the dependent noun rather than to the phrase as a whole.

In essence, the *-əd* suffix creates a prosodically and pragmatically tighter bond between the primary and the secondary, presenting them as one NP, while the *d-* proclitic presents the two elements as two separate NPs mediated by the pronominal linker *d-*, which stands in apposition with the first NP.[37] Formally, one can contrast [X-*əd* Y]$_{NP}$ with X$_{NP_1}$ $\leftrightarrow$ [d_{LNK}=Y]$_{NP_2}$. This, in turn, permits the speaker to assign some sort of pragmatic emphasis to one of the component NPs, both of them, or the clause as a whole.

4.5 The *d-* proclitic vs. the *d-* genitive prefix

4.5.1 Introduction

An important analytic discovery made by Cohen (2010) is the distinction between two separate *d-* shaped morphemes: One is the proclitic linker (PRONOMINAL NUCLEUS in Cohen's terms) and the other is a *d-* prefix marking genitive case on a handful of morphemes, mostly definite determiners and demonstrative pronouns[38] which begin with a glottal stop (sometimes left untranscribed or unpronounced[39]) in the non-genitive (or unmarked) case, which is replaced[40] by the *d-*

[37]A similar view is advanced by Hans J. Polotsky in his yet unpublished grammatical notes about JZakho (Eran Cohen, p.c.).

[38]This includes also the interrogative determiner *ēma* 'which'. See discussion in footnote 46 on page 320.

[39]Thus, these words can also be considered to be VOWEL-INITIAL. I leave open the question whether the initial glottal stop is merely a phonetic artefact.

[40]Note that in the description of Diyana-Zariwaw by Napiorkowska (2015: 93) the *d-* prefix precedes a glottal stop in the genitive pronouns, rather than replacing it (e.g. *d-ʾawwa* [GEN-DEM.3MS]). The initial glottal stop is in fact not a strict requirement: In JZakho Cohen (2012: 109) lists also the distal demonstratives/determiners *wā(ha)* (MS) and *yā(ha)* (FS) as having genitive forms *dwā(ha)* and *dyā(ha)* respectively. In other dialects the distal forms are *ʾawāha* and *ʾayāha*, which may be the ancestral forms of the forms in JZakho.

in the genitive case (ATTRIBUTIVE marking in Cohen's terms[41]). In other words, these morphemes (all of pronominal origin) inflect for case, as is illustrated in Table 4.4 for the definite determiners.

Table 4.4: Case-inflected definite determiners in JZakho (Cohen 2010: 88)

Case		Determiner	
-GEN	*ʔ-*	*aw*	MS
+GEN	*d-*	*ay*	FS
		an	PL

The main reason for establishing this category is that the *d-* prefix appears where a linker is not expected, namely after primaries already marked for construct state (by the *-əd* suffix or by apocope), after prepositions (whether they are marked by *-əd* or not) and after the linker itself.[42]

These possibilities are illustrated in the following JZakho and Barwar examples:

(15) JZakho: **Noun–Noun**
brāt *d-ay* *baxta*
daughter.CST GEN-DEF.FS woman
'the daughter of the woman' (Cohen 2012: 110)

(16) JZakho: **Preposition–Noun Phrase**
mən [[d-o *bəhna* *rwīxa]* *d=* *[d-o* *jwanqa]]*
from GEN-DEF.MS breath(MS) wide.MS LNK= GEN-DEF.MS youngster
'from the patience of this youngster' (Cohen 2012: 106)(71))

[41]Cohen (2010: 90) identifies the same prefix also before the subordinated present copula, to which the term GENITIVE seems inappropriate, yet the term ATTRIBUTIVE may fit. For other dialects, however, the establishment of subordinate form of the copula could not be made with certainty. On the other hand, the *d-* prefix is found sporadically before the deictic adverb *axxa* 'here' in other dialects, maybe since it contains an implicit demonstrative 'in *this* place'.

[42]Interestingly, also in Neo-Mandaic possessive pronominal suffixes attach to a *d-* base after certain prepositions and construct state loan-nouns. Häberl (2007) claims that this modern *d-* is not related to the Classical Mandaic linker but arose rather from the metathesis of the final two root consonants of Classical Mandaic *qadmia* 'to, for'. Yet, if the analysis of the NENA *d-* genitive prefix advocated here is correct, it may be tentatively suggested that the Neo-Mandaic *d-* is the very same genitive marker (with a more limited distribution), reflecting an areal phenomenon preceding the emergence of the modern Aramaic dialects.

(17) Barwar: **Noun–Noun**
ahwált-ət d-ò naša'
condition-CST GEN-DEF.MS man
'the condition of that person' (Khan 2008c: 399 [B5:8])

(18) Barwar: **Preposition–Noun**
qám [d-áyya qə̀ṣṣət]
before GEN-DEM.PROX.FS story
'before this story' (Khan 2008c: 442 [A16:5])

Analysing the apparently spurious *d-* prefixes as genitive case markers provides a clear justification for their appearance. Formally, we can distinguish between the patterns [X.CST d_{GEN}-Y]$_{\text{NP}}$ and $X_{\text{NP}_1} \leftrightarrow$ [d_{LNK}= Y]$_{\text{NP}_2}$, treating prepositions and the linker itself as being functionally in construct state.

It is worthwhile noting, that such an analysis implies a revolution in Aramaic grammar: while Proto-Semitic is supposed to have case markers (on the evidence of Akkadian and Classical Arabic), Aramaic had lost all case marking by its earliest attestations (beginning of the first millennium BCE).[43] Thus, the genitive *d-* represents a structural innovation in Aramaic.[44] Note that the *d-* segment acting as a genitive prefix is highly selective, since it attaches virtually only to demonstratives and definite determiners (but see footnote 41 on the preceding page).

A similar distinction between the two *d-* morphemes is made in the native grammar of Marogulov (1976: 41f.) treating CUrmi. He distinguishes between a pronominal *d-* (which he writes as a separate particle) and a prefix *d-* attached to demonstrative pronouns after prepositions, which in his terms has no function ("le son *d* n'ayant aucune fonction spéciale"):

(19) CUrmi: **Preposition–Noun**
qə d-o nəṣə
to GEN-DEM.MS man
'to this man' (Marogulov 1976: 41)

[43] A notable exception is found in some Aramaic inscriptions from Sam'al dating from the 8th century BCE, where M.PL nouns conserve an archaic distinction between nominative and oblique cases (Dion 1978: 117).

[44] Traditionally, the linker *d-* itself is sometimes called NOTA GENITIVI, but due to its pronominal status, it should not be assimilated with a genitive case marker; see Goldenberg (2013a: 253, fn. 27).

Note that in the genitive function, the *d-* element cannot stand at the beginning of a prosodic phrase, unlike the linker *d-* (see discussion in §4.4.2.6 about the importance of the prosodic autonomy).

Taking into account more dialectal data, further justification for their differentiation can be found, as presented below.

4.5.2 Distinguishing factors

4.5.2.1 Phonological shape

In Barwar, the *d-* linker is normally realised as *t-* (Khan 2008c: 396). If it attaches to a word beginning with a glottal stop, it is normally realised as an unaspirated *t̬-*, which is phonetically expected.[45]

(20) Barwar: **Noun–Noun**
tre= pə́nxe t̬= ə́rxe
two= grinding_stones LNK= watermill
'two stones of a watermill' (Khan 2008c: 399 [A24:13])

Appearing, however, before the demonstrative pronouns, normally beginning with a glottal stop, it takes rather the voiced form *d-*, as in examples (17)–(18) on the preceding page. This is expected, if the *d-* morph does not attach before the glottal stop, but rather replaces it, as in Table 4.4 on page 108.[46]

4.5.2.2 Dialectal distribution

Also in dialects where the *d-* linker has disappeared as such one finds the *d-* prefix before determiners. This is the case in JSanandaj, where one can find the *d-* prefix even after the Ezafe suffix:[47]

[45]This is also the case before the indicative copula appearing in subordinate clauses.

[46]In other respects, the data from Barwar sometimes obscures the presence of a genitive prefix as it marks the appearance of only one *d* segment. Thus, one finds *čádra d-ò-malka* 'the tent of that king' instead of the expected *čádra d=d-ò-malka* and *ríxə d-o-xámra* 'the smell of that wine' instead of *ríxət d-o-xámra*. Especially in the second case, it seems plausible to assume that the actual forms are subject to a process of phonetic de-gemination (cf. Cohen 2012: 122 who speaks of "phonetic simplification" in similar cases).

[47]In contrast to JZakho, however, the usage of the *d-* genitive prefix is optional in JSanandaj.

(21) JSanandaj: **Noun–Noun**
fešár-e d-o màe
pressure-EZ GEN-DEM.MS water
'the pressure of the water' (Khan 2009b: 200 [A:59])

The fact that the *d-* prefix is retained in such environments while the *d-* linker in general has disappeared is easily explained if one considers the two to be separate morphemes, subject to different language change processes.

4.5.2.3 Phrase-internal marking

Similarly to the construct state suffix *-əd*, which in most dialects is a phrasal suffix (see example (10) on page 103), the genitive *d-* prefix in JZakho must be analysed as phrasal prefix, judging by examples such as the following:

(22) JZakho: **Noun–Conjoined nouns**
ʾuz-lu xıṭbe dīd d-áw jwanqa ū= ʾáy xamsa
made-3PL wedding LNK GEN-DEF.MS youngster and= DEF.FS maiden
'they made the wedding of that youngster and that maiden' (Cohen 2012: 304 (205))

The analysis of *d-* as a genitive prefix is justified by the fact that it follows linker *dīd*, and cannot therefore assume a pronominal role. However, it marks only the initial determiner *aw*, and not the subsequent determiner *ay*. Thus, when *d-* is used as a genitive inflectional morpheme of determiners, it appears only as a phrase-initial marker, or, in other words, as a phrasal prefix.[48]

In Barwar, on the other hand, one finds cases where the genitive *d-* occurs phrase-internally. This happens in cases where a secondary noun is further modified by an adjective which is preceded by a determiner. In such cases, the internal determiner is marked as genitive.

(23) Barwar: **Noun–Noun Phrase**
gnáy-ət [táwra d-o= gòṛa]
fault-CST ox GEN-DEF.MS= big.MS
'the fault of the big ox' (Khan 2008c: 517 [D2:19])

[48] Cohen (2012) brings a case of phrase-internal *d-* marker attaching to the copula (example (86) on page 139). This *d-* is arguably different from the genitive one, as it attaches to a quasi-verbal form, although Cohen subsumes both as markers of the ATTRIBUTIVE function (see footnote 41 on page 108).

Adjectives in Barwar stand in apposition to their head-noun. Therefore, the *d-* marker is not marking a dependency relationship between the adjective *goṛa* and the noun it modifies (*tawra* 'ox'). Rather, it is induced in virtue of the entire NP being in genitive case due to its attributive relation with the primary noun *gnaya* 'fault'. Similarly to the *-əd* suffix in Barwar, it seems that also the *d-* prefix has undergone a further development to become a word-level marker, permitting it to appear phrase-internally.[49] Note that there is no motivation for a linker *d-* to appear in this position.

A similar example is found in CAradhin, where the genitive marking is induced by a prepositional head:

(24) CAradhin: **Preposition–Noun Phrase**
tla [ōǰax d-ay xēta]
for clan(FS) GEN-DEF.FS other.FS
'for the other clan' (Krotkoff 1982: 49 [113])

4.6 Conclusions

In this chapter, I have shown that on various synchronic distributional grounds, one can distinguish between three different morphemes in NENA related to the Classical Aramaic proclitic linker *d-*. One of them is simply a retention of this morpheme in NENA, conserving in essence its pronominal nature, while the two other morphemes are pure relational markers: the head-marking construct state suffix *-əd* and the dependent-marking genitive case marker *d-*.

The distinction between the three morphemes is primarily based on distributional reasons. The different environments where they can be found are summarised in Table 4.5 on the next page.

I have conceptualised this distinction in terms of the strength of the bond between these morphemes and their hosts, calling the two latter morphemes affixes, while maintaining the clitic nature of the original linker. Their affixal nature stems from the high selectivity of the hosts: the *-əd* suffix appears almost exclusively on nominal hosts, while the *d-* prefix is restricted to determiners and demonstratives (which are related historically). On the other hand, their clitic

[49]Unfortunately I could not come across any examples of conjoint genitives mirroring exactly the JZakho example.

[50]Recall that in this context the notation .CST marks any type of construct state marking, be it an *-əd* suffix, apocope or an Ezafe morpheme; see footnote 43 on page 42. Note also that prepositions need not be explicitly marked as construct state in order to induce genitive case.

Table 4.5: Distribution of D-markers: a) construct state suffix *-əd*; b) linker *d-*; c) genitive prefix *d-* (X and Y indicate any phrasal primary or secondary).

Primary	Secondary
N. stem-*əd*$_{\text{CST}}$ Prep-*əd*$_{\text{CST}}$	Y
X *d*$_{\text{LNK}}$=	*d*$_{\text{LNK}}$=Y Y
X.CST[50] Prep.{CST} {X} *d*$_{\text{LNK}}$=	*d*$_{\text{GEN}}$-DET Y *d*$_{\text{GEN}}$-DEM

origin is apparent in the fact that both these morphemes show phrasal placement: in general they appear either phrase-finally (*-əd*) or phrase-initially (*d-*), yet some dialects show a further development in that they allow these markers to appear phrase-internally, as word-level inflectional suffixes.

5 Attributive constructions in the Jewish dialect of Zakho

5.1 Introduction

The study of the AC system of JZakho[1] is made easy due to the fact that the main source on which I rely, Cohen (2012), uses a conceptual framework similar to ours. A more exact formulation would be that Cohen's framework inspired ours. Indeed, chapters 2 and 4 of his work, "The attributive relationship" and "Apposition" respectively, address directly the issues at hand. A similar and concise analysis is also presented in Cohen (2010). The present survey, therefore, repeats to some extent the claims presented in these sources. Nevertheless, the current treatment is innovative in the classification of the construction according to the typology discussed in §2.4. This permits, moreover, a transparent comparison of this dialect's system to the other dialects discussed in the following chapters.

As noted in §1.3, Cohen (2012: 20–27) identifies a system of definite and indefinite determiners in the grammar of JZakho, an analysis which I adopt here.

Cohen's examples are based mainly on Polotsky's unpublished transcribed Zakho texts, as well as some published sources (see Cohen 2012: 5–8 for details).[2] Two other sources used in this chapter are Avinery (1988), a collection of texts of JZakho, and Sabar (2002). The latter is a dictionary devoted to the Cis-Zab Jewish dialects of north-west Iraq (see §1.2.2), of which JZakho constitutes an important part. I only use examples which are clearly identifiable as JZakho examples (by virtue of their source, or being explicitly marked as such).

Cohen (2012); Sabar (2002) use the sign <*ɪ*> to denote the phonemic schwa ([ə]~[ɪ]), while Avinery (1988) uses the sign <*i*>. For consistency with other dialects, I use instead the <*ə*> symbol (see 17).

[1] I maintain the J. (=Jewish) abbreviation in the dialect name, since there exists also a Christian (Chaldean) dialect of Zakho, as reported by Hoberman (1993). Due the scarcity of information on this dialect, it is not included in the current survey.

[2] Cohen's examples refer to the page number of Polotsky's transcribed texts. As these texts are as yet unpublished, I have not reproduced this number in the citations, but rather referred to Cohen's page and example numbers.

This chapter is organised as follows: In §5.2 I discuss the usage of the possessive pronominal suffixes. Subsequently, the two main ACs of JZakho are discussed: the construct state construction is treated in §5.3 and the analytic linker construction in §5.4, the latter being the richest one in terms of paradigmatic variation. The marking of secondaries by genitive case, which is compatible with both these constructions, is treated in §5.5. A rare case of the double annexation construction is discussed in §5.6, while the juxtaposition construction is handled in §5.7. §5.8 gives some general conclusions and comparative remarks.

5.2 Possessive pronominal suffixes (X-y.POSS)

A pronominal secondary can be realised as a possessive pronominal suffix (=POSS), which attaches directly to the stem of the primary noun.

(1) JZakho: **Noun–Pronoun**
ēha brāt-i
DEM.FS daugther-POSS.1SG
'this daughter of mine' (Cohen 2012: 98 (28))

If there are any further secondaries, they follow the inflected noun:

(2) JZakho: **Noun–Pronoun**
ʾaw brōn-e rūwa
DEF.3MS son-POSS.3MS big.MS
'this older son of his' (Cohen 2012: 98 (29))

As noted in §2.4.1, the term POSSESSIVE SUFFIX is traditional; its usage is in fact wider than denoting solely possession, similarly to other ACs. For instance, it can attach to an infinitive to denote one of its arguments (here its subject):

(3) JZakho: **Infinitive–Pronoun (subject)**
u= zaʿ-li b-əd ʾīzāl-i əl knəšta
and= be_lost-1SG in-CST go.INF-1SG to synagogue
'And I got lost while going to the synagogue.' (Cohen 2012: 99 (34))

Moreover, it can attach to a preposition to denote its complement:

(4) JZakho: **Preposition–Pronoun**
əmm-i
with-POSS.1SG
'with me' (Cohen 2012: 451)

5.3 The construct state construction (X.CST Y)

JZakho has two construct state markers: the suffix *-əd~-ət* and apocope (phonological reduction).[3] Cohen (2012: 97) states: "the functional distinction between them is not clear, and for now it must be regarded as mere [free] variation". He gives the following two examples, in which the noun *xabra* 'word' (PL *xabre*) is put in construct state. Note that in this case, both markings neutralize the number distinction.

(5) JZakho: **Noun–Noun**
xabr-ət xōr-e
word-CST friend-POSS.3MS
'the words of his friend' (Cohen 2012: 97 (2))

(6) JZakho: **Noun–Noun**
(p=) xabər xōr-e
in= word.CST friend-POSS.3MS
'(by) the words of his friend' (Cohen 2012: 97 (21))

The apocopated form is constructed by removing the free state-cum-number suffixes *-a* 'FREE.SG' or *-e* 'FREE.PL'. Due to the resulting consonant cluster at the end of **xabr*, an epenthetic *ə* is inserted.

Nouns (including infinitives, see §5.3.5) as well as adjectives can appear with both construct state markers, while pronouns as well as adverbials appear only with the *-əd* suffix.[4] Primary pronouns typically appear with clausal secondaries (see §5.3.2).

Rarely, the construct state suffix appears NP finally, but only when the NP ends with an adjective, as in the following example (=example (8) on page 100):

(7) JZakho: **Noun Phrase–Noun**
[gōra qamāy]-ət [d-anya baxt-āsa]
man first.MS-CST GEN-DEM.PL woman-PL
'The first husband of these women' (Cohen 2012: 101 (49))

[3] Cohen (2012: 92) relates the apocopate form to the ancient absolute state, i.e. the Early Aramaic free indefinite form. It seems more appropriate to relate it directly to the Classical Aramaic construct state. In any case, for singular nouns the two forms were mostly identical. Some apocopate construct state forms can not be easily traced to ancient Aramaic construct state forms, and must be considered innovated, such as the form *bax*, apocopate form of *baxta* 'woman, wife' (Cohen 2010). See the discussion in §11.1.

[4] As adverbials do not have a full free form one cannot postulate an apocopate form for them, making the above statement trivial for this category.

As discussed in §4.4, such examples are accommodated under the analysis of the *-əd* suffix as a phrasal suffix.

5.3.1 Pronominal, ordinal and adverbial secondaries

There is a variety of categories which can occupy the secondary position: pronouns, ordinal or PPs (adverbial phrases). The primary in each case can be marked by both construct state markings:

(8) JZakho: **Noun–Pronoun**
šəmm-ət gyāne
name-CST REFL-POSS.3MS
'his own name' (Cohen 2012: 115 (106))

(9) JZakho: **Noun–NP headed by pronoun**
ʾaqlās [xa mənn-u]
feet.PL.CST one from-3PL
'the feet of one of them' (Cohen 2012: 115)

(10) JZakho: **Noun–Ordinal**
baxt-ət tre
wife-CST two
'the second wife' (Cohen 2012: 95 (6))

(11) JZakho: **Noun–Ordinal**
gōr tre
man.CST two
'(the) second man' (Cohen 2012: 84 (7))

(12) JZakho: **Noun–Prepositional Phrase**
rubʿ-ət mənn-u
quarter-CST from-POSS.3PL
'a quarter of them' (Cohen 2012: 117 (113))

(13) JZakho: **Noun–Prepositional Phrase**
ū= ʾan nāš ʾəmm-e
and= DEF.PL person.CST with-POSS.3MS
'and the people with him' (Cohen 2012: 117 (112))

5.3.2 Clausal and infinitival secondaries

Clausal secondaries, whether full clauses or infinitival phrases, can appear regularly in the CSC.

(14) JZakho: **Noun–Infinitival Phrase**
ṭēr-ət maḥkōye
bird-CST speak.INF
'a speaking bird' (Cohen 2012: 111 (88))

(15) JZakho: **Noun–Infinitival Phrase**
waʿd-ət [īsāya dīd-e]
time-CST come.INF LNK-POSS.3MS
'time of his coming' (Cohen 2012: 111 (87))

(16) JZakho: **Noun–Infinitival Phrase**
(mṭē-le) waʿəd [ʾīsāy-ət d-anya ṭḷāha xūr-āsa]
came-3MS time.CST come.INF-CST GEN-DEM.PL friend-PL
'The time arrived for the three friends' coming' (Cohen 2012: 98 (32))

The following example is especially interesting, since the secondary consists of two conjoined infinitives. Moreover, it is split by the occurrence of the copula *la*, marking the entire CSC as a predicate. In JZakho (as in many other NENA dialects), the copula is a second-position clitic with respect to the predicate phrase.[5] Yet as this example clearly shows, the copula cannot split the construct state primary from its secondary and thus appears instead after the first conjoined secondary.[6]

(17) JZakho: **Noun–Conjoined infinitives**
urx-ət [īzāla] =la [ū= la dʾāra]
way-CST go.INF =COP.3FS and= NEG return.INF
'It is a road of going and not returning.' (Cohen 2012: 111 (87))

As stated, full clauses can appear as well in the secondary position. The primary noun can have various functions in the relative clause (subject, object, etc.)

[5] In other words, the copula typically appears after the first minimal unit of the predicate, be it a free noun or a CSC. A similar behaviour is exhibited by the Syriac enclitic personal pronouns, which can be seen as precursors of the copula; see Gutman & Van Peursen (2011: 121ff.) for a discussion and examples.

[6] Such cases should be clearly differentiated from cases where the copula itself is part of the secondary, in which case it can appear directly after the primary in a special attributive form (see §5.5.2).

(18) JZakho: **Noun (subject)–Clause**
šaps-ət zəl-la
week-CST went-3FS
'Last week (lit. The week that passed)' (Avinery 1988: 191 (1617))

(19) JZakho: **Noun (subject)–Clause**
ʾō məṭər [kuš-le xapča]
DEF.MS rain.CST fell-3MS a-little
'This rain which fell (=rained) a little' (Avinery 1988: 171 (1274))

(20) JZakho: **Noun (object)–Clause**
xabr-ət mír-rē-la
word(s)-CST said-A3MS-DAT3FS
'the words he told her' (Cohen 2012: 97 (24))

(21) JZakho: **Noun (object)–Clause**
xabər [mxē-la baxt-e b-ət ʾarya]
word(s).CST struck-3FS wife-POSS.3MS in-CST lion
'the words his wife said about the lion' (Cohen 2012: 97 (23))

Interrogative pronouns can head the CSC with clausal secondaries. In such cases they act as a head of a FREE RELATIVE, loosely speaking. In this construction, they are always marked by the construct state suffix.[7]

(22) JZakho: **Pronoun–Clause**
(mən) mā-d mər-rī-lox
from what-CST told-A1SG-DAT2MS
'from what I told you' (Cohen 2012: 94 (4))

(23) JZakho: **Pronoun–Clause**
manī-t hāwe ḥmīla qām-ox (b-āse
who-CST SBJV.be.3MS stood.RES.MS before-2MS FUT-PASS_AUX.3MS
l-qṭāla)
to-kill.INF
'whoever is standing in front of you will be killed' (Cohen 2012: 96 (14))

[7] As Cohen (2012: 96) notes, the free forms of the interrogative pronouns are used as markers of either direct or indirect questions. No apocopate forms of the interrogative pronouns are found in JZakho.

To this group one may tentatively add the pronoun/quantifier *kud* 'each':

(24) JZakho: **Pronoun–Clause**
ku-d *[ʾāwəz-lox* *hawūsa]*
each-CST SBJV.do.3MS-DAT.2MS favor
'anyone who does you a favor' (Cohen 2012: 94 (1))

In the above example I analyse *kud* as having a base-form *ku* augmented by a construct state suffix. However, a free form of *kud* is not attested (Cohen 2012: 94, fn. 5), though historically it is very probably derived from **kull + d* (Sabar 2002: 181b).[8] Moreover, as Cohen (2018: 3) notes, disregarding its construct state marking, it can be equated with a determiner of the JZakho system. Thus, one may reasonably question whether this should be seen as a genuine instance of construct state marking, or rather a fossilized remnant of it. Interestingly, instances of *ku* are found in Nerwa (Sabar 2002: 181b), but these may be cases of back-formation.

Finally, note that the interrogative *ēma* 'which' can be complemented directly by a noun-phrase, which embeds in it a clause. In this case too, the construct state-marked interrogative pronoun functions rather as a determiner:

(25) JZakho: **Pronoun–Noun Phrase**
ēm-ət *[julle* *d=* *[ʾājəb-le* *ləbb-ox]]* *(ṭḷōb* *mən*
which-CST clothes LNK= please-3MS heart-POSS.2MS take.IMP from
d-e *kwīna)*
GEN-DEF tent
'Ask for whatever clothes which please you from that tent' (Cohen 2012: 96 (16))

5.3.3 Adverbial primaries

Many adverbials are in fact nouns used adverbially, such as the noun *waʿda* 'time' (thus example (15) on page 119 can be understood adverbially: 'when he comes'). These behave as nouns, having potentially two construct state forms: one suffixed and one apocopate, besides their free forms.

In contrast to these, there are true prepositions or conjunctions (often monosyllabic, or shorter). Some of these take a construct state suffix obligatorily when

[8]The form *kull*, meaning 'all', is used in JZakho only together with possessive pronominal suffixes. Compare this with example (43) on page 163 of Qaraqosh and see further Khan (2002a: 282f.).

complemented by a syntactic word, be it a noun or a pronoun. Such is the case of *ʾəmm-əd* [with-CST] (example (5)=example (26) on this page):

(26) JZakho: **Preposition–Noun**
ʾəmm-əd gōra
with-CST man
'with the man' (Cohen 2010: 82)

(27) JZakho: **Preposition–Pronoun**
əmm-ət gyān-e
with-CST REFL-3MS
'(together) with itself' (Cohen 2012: 115 (106))

One can nevertheless identify the base form, as it appears together with the possessive pronominal suffixes (see example (4) on page 116). Moreover, it is clear that it stems etymologically from classical Aramaic עִם *ʿīm* (Sabar 2002: 97a).

Some prepositions allow for two forms to appear before syntactic words: one with the suffix *-əd* and one without it. The shorter form should not be seen as an apocopate form, as it is not derived from a full free form (except for those prepositions derived from nouns), but should rather be seen as the SIMPLE FORM of the preposition (see also the system of Barwar in Table 4.2 on page 101). Functionally, the simple form is equivalent to a construct state marked form, yet from the point of view of the classification system used here it represents an unmarked primary. In this vein, contrast the following construct state marked example with example (102) on page 144, representing an unmarked juxtaposition construction.[9]

(28) JZakho: **Preposition–Noun**
b-əd bəllūre
in-CST flute
'with a flute' (Cohen 2010: 85 (16))

The construct state marked form can precede phrasal and clausal secondaries:

(29) JZakho: **Preposition–Infinitival Phrase**
ʾəmm-ət [maʾōre dīd-a]
with-CST transfer.INF LNK-3FS
'while transferring her' (Cohen 2012: 111 (87))

[9] The preposition *b-* 'in' should be kept apart from its homonym particle *b-*, which joins the infinitive to form a gerund (Cohen 2012: 99, fn. 9; Sabar 2002: 103a). Note, moreover, that the preposition *b-əd* can precede an infinitive (without forming a gerund), as in example (3) on page 116.

(30) JZakho: **Preposition–Participial Phrase**
(u= šqīl-a-le nunīsa) b-ət [kēf-e ʾəsya]
and= took.P3FS-A3MS fish in-CST joy-POSS.3MS came.RES
'(And he took the fish) with his joy attained (=happily).' (Cohen 2012: 122 (142))

(31) JZakho: **Adverbial–Clause**
(uz-le ōha ʾərba) māṭu-t mír-rā-le
did-3MS DEM.MS sheep how-CST said-3FS-DAT.3MS
'(The sheep did) as she told him.' (Cohen 2012: 104 (67))

5.3.4 Adjectival primaries

Adjectives heading the CSC typically yield a superlative reading, whenever the secondary is a plural noun or pronoun:

(32) JZakho: **Adjective–Noun**
rūw-ət ganāw-e
big.MS-CST thief-PL
'the biggest/head thief' (Cohen 2012: 100 (41))

(33) JZakho: **Adjective–Pronoun**
ʾaw zōr kull-u
DEF.MS small.CST all-3PL
'the smallest of them all' (Cohen 2012: 100 (42))

Note that the primary adjective exhibits the gender and number features of the referent, while the secondary has plural marking.[10]

A formally related construction, though functionally different, is the EMOTIVE GENITIVE.[11] In this construction, loaded with some emotional emphasis, the se-

[10]The superlative preceding the qualified noun is clearly an areal phenomenon: It is present in Arabic, Sorani (MacKenzie 1961: 68; Thackston 2006b: 19), and Kurmanji (Thackston 2006a: 28). In the latter, the superlative adjective is sometimes marked as construct state. Compare also to the Syriac example (19) on page 55 as well as example (108) on page 86. One reviewer suggested this is semantically motivated, as superlatives establish a unique reference similarly to determiners which are typically pre-nominal.

[11]This term was coined by Hopkins (2009), who identifies the characteristic syntactic and semantic features of the construction and exemplifies it from various Semitic languages, including NENA. Gai (2013) attempts to trace this construction back to Akkadian.

mantic head of the construction is expressed as a secondary, while the adjectival primary agrees with it:

(34) JZakho: **Adjective–Noun**
pappūk-ət xmāra
pitiful.MS-CST donkey
'the poor donkey, that poor of a donkey' (Cohen 2012: 100 (46))

Gai (1993: 270), analysing a similar construction of CUrmi, explains it as follows:

> [B]y inserting the subordinating *d* the noun is converted to *nomen rectum*, i.e., a subordinated one [=secondary of the CSC], and by lowering the status of the noun, the status of the adjective, its subordinator in the nominal phrase, rises. [...] Thus, the communicatively more important element has the more important syntactic status, while the communicatively secondary element has the secondary syntactic status.

Cohen (2012: 101) mentions a third case of an adjectival primary, namely the use of the Arabic loanword *ġēr* 'other'. However, it is not clear synchronically why it should be considered as an adjective rather than a type of quantifier or pronoun.

5.3.5 Infinitival primaries

Infinitives can be expanded by one of their arguments in the CSC. As a general rule, infinitive of transitive verbs are expanded by their object argument, while those of intransitive verbs are expanded by their subject. Most often the infinitives are marked by the construct state suffix, but also the apocopate form is available.

(35) JZakho: **Infinitive–Noun (subject)**
(mōnəx-li čūča əl) ʾīzāl-ət ʾərba
looked-1SG a_little to go.INF-CST sheep
'I looked a little at the sheep's walking.' (Cohen 2012: 99 (36))

(36) JZakho: **Infinitive–Noun (subject)**
(pəš-la waʿəd) ʾīzal jwanq-e l= nēčīr
became-3FS time.CST go.INF.CST youngster-PL to= hunt
'It was the time of the youngsters' going out for a hunt.' (Cohen 2012: 99 (35))

(37) JZakho: **Infinitive–Noun (object)**
(ū= škəl-lu b-ət) ʾwāz-ət ṣandūqa ta ḥakōma
and= began-3PL in-CST make-CST box for king
'They began preparing a box for the king.' (Cohen 2012: 99 (37))

(38) JZakho: **Infinitive–Noun Phrase (object)**
(... mən) ʾwāz [xōrūs bnās mīr-e ū= p̄āšā-ye]
... than make.INF.CST friendship.CST daughter.PL.CST emir-PL and= pasha-PL
'(Befriending you pleases me more than) befriending daughters of emirs and pashas.' (Cohen 2012: 99 (38))

Like other nouns (examples (12)–(13) on page 118), construct state marked infinitives can also be complemented by PPs, serving as indirect objects (Cohen 2012: 117):

(39) JZakho: **Infinitive–Prepositional Phrase (indirect object)**
(ʾēn nāša la= g-sōʾa m=) mēnōx-əd ʾəbb-u
eye.CST man NEG= IND-satiate.3FS from= look.INF-CST in-3MS
'The man's eye is not satiated of looking at him.' (Avinery 1988: 164 (1197))

(40) JZakho: **Infinitive–Prepositional Phrase (indirect object)**
la= g-barya hēǰ kwāš mənn-a
NEG IND-happen.3FS still descend.INF.CST from-3FS
'It is still impossible to descend from it (the plane).' (Avinery 1988: 104 (453))

5.4 The analytic linker construction (X LNK Y)

5.4.1 Introduction

The common form of the pronominal linker in JZakho is *dīd*. It may be analysed as an expansion of the Classical Aramaic linker *d-* with an overt construct state suffix yielding *də-* + *-əd* = *dīd*. Yet contrary to regular cases where a construct state suffix appears, the linker *dīd* is compatible with possessive pronominal suffixes, as in example (41) on the following page, and thus the ending *-īd* must be seen as an integral part of the linker itself.[12]

(41) JZakho: **Noun–Pronoun**
qaḥra dīd-ox
grief LNK-2MS
'your grief' (Cohen 2012: 95 (5))

In the context of a pronominal secondary realised as a possessive suffix, the linker is in syntagmatic complementary distribution with the proclitic linker *d-*: The base *did-* is used exclusively with the monosyllabic singular possessive pronouns, while *d-* is used with the bisyllabic plural ones; see Table 10.9 on page 332 (Cohen 2012: 453).

(42) JZakho: **Noun–Pronoun**
līšāna d-ēni
language LNK-POSS.1PL
'our language' (Cohen 2012: 85 (347))

In other contexts, the proclitic *d-* is restricted almost exclusively to clausal secondaries, thus functioning similarly to a relativizer (see §5.4.3, but see also the rare exceptions in example (64) on page 132, example (83) on page 138 and example (65) on page 133).

The basic use of the linker is to create an indirect attributive relationship between a primary noun (whether explicit or implicit) and a secondary noun. This relationship is indirect, since it is the pronominal linker that stands in DIRECT ATTRIBUTIVE RELATIONSHIP with the secondary. The primary noun, which is most frequently explicit, stands syntactically in apposition with the linking pronoun, and is never marked for construct state in JZakho:

(43) JZakho: **Noun–Noun**
xa ṭēra dīd ḥukūm
INDF bird LNK sovereignty
'a royal bird' (Cohen 2012: 96 (18))

Pronouns which are realised as independent words, such as the reflexive pronouns, are treated in the same way as nouns:

[12]Diachronically, one finds the same form before possessive pronominal suffixes in Jewish Babylonian Aramaic, and it may be related as well to the Syriac *dil-*. See §10.6.2 for a discussion of its development.

(44) JZakho: **Noun–Pronoun**
(sē-le əl) bāžer dīd gyān-e
came-3MS to city LNK REFL-3MS
'(he came to) his own town' (Cohen 2012: 132 (176))

Whenever the secondary consists both of a pronominal suffix and a full noun, the linker is repeated:

(45) JZakho: **Conjoined Nouns–Pronoun+Noun**
[ḥāl ū= quṣta] dīd-i ū= dīd xa ṭēra
situation and= story LNK-1SG and= LNK INDF bird
'the story of me and a bird' (Cohen 2012: 106 (74))

Note, *in passim*, that in the last example the primary itself consists of a conjunction of two nouns (being in this case an idiomatic expression). Noun phrases are quite common as primaries of the ALC, especially those consisting of a noun modified by an adjective:

(46) JZakho: **Noun Phrase–Noun**
[ʾáy ʾasəqsa turta] dīd ḥakōma
DEF.FS ring(FS) broken.FS LNK king
'the broken ring of the king' (Cohen 2012: 102 (51))

Compare the last example to the less common construction exhibited in example (7) on page 117.

Semantically, it is noteworthy that in some cases the adjective seems to have a wide scope over the entire AC, notwithstanding its syntactic position:[13]

(47) JZakho: **Noun Phrase–Noun**
(āna ...) [brōna yakāna] dīd yəmm-i
1SG ... son only LNK mother-POSS.1SG
'(I am [...]) my mother's only son.' (Cohen 2012: 102 (52))

[13]This is not related specifically to JZakho, but it is interesting to note the phenomenon. An alternative analytic possibility is to see the adjective as a primary of an embedded ALC: [Noun [Adj. LNK Noun]].

5.4.2 Verbal nouns as members of the analytic linker construction

The notion of VERBAL NOUNS should be understood here as nominal elements which can participate in a verbal construction. In JZakho, these can be infinitives or certain participles.

Infinitives can appear both as primaries and as secondaries of the ALC. As secondaries, they are analogous to nouns:

(48) JZakho: **Noun–Infinitive**
narʾa dīd [qṭāʾ-ət dār-e]
axe LNK cut-CST tree-PL
'an axe to cut trees' (Cohen 2012: 132 (177))

When an infinitive is the primary of the ALC, the secondary is an argument of the infinitive, either its subject or object. In the latter case, if the infinitive is part of a verbal periphrastic expression, one could argue that the relation to its nominal complement is a completive relation rather than an attributive one (see §2.1.1 and cf. Cohen 2012: 100). However, it is interesting to see that formally this relation is expressed by the same construction.

Thus, in the following example the infinitive *mēsōye* 'to bring' functions both as the primary of an ALC with its objective argument as a secondary, and as a secondary of a wider ALC. Note that in the contrast to the object *nāše* 'people', the locative adverbial *qam məšpaṭ* 'before the court' is not marked by a linker.

(49) JZakho: **Infinitive–Noun (object)**
(húl-lē-lu šūla dīd) mēsōye dīd nāše qam məšpaṭ
gave-A3MS-DAT3PL task LNK bring.INF LNK people before court
'(He gave them) the task of bringing the people in front of court.' (Cohen 2012: 111 (87))

Pronominal arguments are also linked by means of the same construction, as can be seen in examples (15) on page 119 and (80) on page 137.

Parallel to example (45) on the preceding page, whenever both a pronominal and a nominal argument are expressed, the linker is repeated:

(50) JZakho: **Infinitive–Pronoun+Noun (subjects)**
ʾīxāla[14] *dīd-a u= dīd gōr-a*
eat.INF LNK-POSS-3FS and= LNK man-POSS.3FS
'her and her husband's food (eating)' (Cohen 2012: 106 (73))

[14]The infinitive *ʾīxāla* functions here practically as a normal noun, denoting 'food'. Yet in general

Of special interest are cases in which the object of an infinitive is expressed pronominally on a linker, while it appears in immediate apposition to an explicit nominal object. These are in fact cases of PROLEPSIS, discussed by Cohen (2012: 142–4). Note that there are two possible realisations of the full object: First, it may be a secondary of an ALC standing in apposition to the first linker. In this case the nominal may be marked by genitive case (on which see §5.5).

(51) JZakho: **Infinitive–Pronoun/Noun (object)**
u= pəš-la mahōye dīd-a, dəd d-ē baxta
and= became-3FS assist_delivery.INF LNK-3FS LNK GEN-DEM.FS woman
sməx-ta
pregnant-FS
'She started to assist her in delivery, this pregnant woman.' (Avinery 1988: 53 (3))

Alternatively (and more frequently), only the explicit object appears, standing in apposition with the pronominal secondary. In this case it is not marked as genitive, since it does not stand in direct attributive relation with a linker. This is shown in the following example, taken from the same story as the previous one.

(52) JZakho: **Infinitive–Pronoun/Noun (object)**
pəš-la mandōye dīd-e ʾaw tūma
became-3FS throw.INF LNK-3MS DEF.MS garlic
'She started to throw it, the garlic.' (Avinery 1988: 53 (6))

It is important to note that the object of an infinitive may also be introduced by the accusative/locative preposition *ʾəl* (see Sabar 2002: 96), in which case an AC is not used. The functional equivalence of the two constructions, as apparent in the following example, suggests indeed that the AC serves in such cases to instantiate a completive relation. The following example illustrates the two possibilities:

(53) JZakho: **Infinitive–Pronoun (object)**
(ū= pəš-la ṭāl-a maṛaq) nḥāqa ʾəll-e ū xpāqa
and= became-3FS for-3FS desire touch.INF ACC-3MS and hug.INF
dīd-e
LNK-3MS
'(and it became her desire) to touch him and hug him' (Cohen 2012: (40))

---

it still functions as an infinitive (see Sabar 2002: 93), and thus deserves its place here.

Not only infinitives can act as primaries of this construction, but also resultative participles, which form part of the analytic perfect tense. Here again, functionally this is a completive relation, which is formally realised as an AC. The following example is analogous to example (52) on the previous page.

(54) JZakho: **Participle–Pronoun (object)**
ṭamāha wē-lu mukīm-e dīd-a ʾay bāžər
why COP.PST-3PL blackened.RES-PL LNK-3FS DEF.FS city
'why had they blackened the town' (Cohen 2012: 144 (7))

5.4.3 Clausal secondaries

Clausal secondaries (i.e., relative clauses) can follow both the linker *dīd* and the shorter form *d-*, apparently in free variation. Note that the form *d-* is typically reserved in JZakho for clausal secondaries. In both cases, the clausal secondary stands in direct attributive relation with the linker, which represents the modified primary. In this respect it is similar to a relative pronoun, except that it is external to the relative clause; indeed, inside the relative clause one normally finds a second pronominal index representing the primary.

(55) JZakho: **Noun (subject)–Clause**
(ta) [d-aw gōra] dīd [wḗ-wa-le faqīr]
for GEN-DEF.MS man LNK COP.PST-PST-3MS poor
'(to) the man who was poor' (Cohen 2012: 120 (121))

(56) JZakho: **Noun–Clause**
(rīš) kursi d= wē-la tūta rēš-e
on chair(MS) LNK= COP.PST-3FS sat.RES.FS on-3MS
'(on) the chair on which she was sitting' (Cohen 2012: 134 (189))

(57) JZakho: **Noun Phrase–Clause**
u= [trḗ sūsə-wāsa dīd-i] dīd [ʾāna g-rakw-en ʾəll-u]
and= two horse-PL LNK-1SG LNK 1SG IND-ride-1SG on-3PL
'and two of my horses which I ride' (Cohen 2012: 135 (190))

Pronouns may also act as primaries of the ALC with clausal secondaries. Such is the case of the interrogative pronoun *mani* 'who' in the following example. Note that in this example *mani* itself acts as a secondary of a CSC headed by the pronoun *kud* 'every':

(58) JZakho: **Pronoun–Clause**
ku-d *[mani dīd [yāwəl* *pāre* *ta ṣədāqa]]*
every-CST who LNK SBJV.give.3MS money for charity
'each one who gives money for charity…' (Cohen 2012: 96 (13))

Contrast this example with examples (23) and (24) on page 121, in which both *mani* and *kud* are primaries of a construct state-marked AC with a clausal secondary. Note that *kud* cannot act as the primary of the ALC due to its inherent construct state marking.

5.4.4 Numerals as ordinal secondaries

Numerals serving as ordinal secondaries occur frequently in this construction:

(59) JZakho: **Noun–Ordinal**
ʾō *gabāra dīd tre*
DEM.MS hero LNK two
'the second hero' (Cohen 2012: 95 (11))

(60) JZakho: **Noun–Ordinal**
ē *baxta* *dīd ṭḷāha*
DEM.FS woman LNK three
'the third wife' (Cohen 2010: 85 (12))

As Cohen (2010: 85) points out, a phrase headed by a pronominal linker is the syntactic counterpart of an adjective. This is especially clear in the case of ordinal numerals, since the ordinal 'first' is always expressed as a morphological adjective:

(61) JZakho: **Noun–Ordinal**
ē *baxta* *qamē-sa*
DEM.FS woman first-FS
'the first wife' (Cohen 2010: 85 (11))

For an elaboration of this point in the context of Syriac, see the discussion in §3.8.

5.4.5 Adverbials as secondaries

Adverbials, whether true adverbs, or PPs, can occur following a linking pronoun:

(62) JZakho: **Noun–Adverb**
ku-d žaġīl dīd tam
every-CST worker LNK there
'any worker (who was) there' (Cohen 2012: 116 (109))

(63) JZakho: **Noun–Prepositional Phrase**
aw gōra dīd go māya
DEF.MS man LNK in water
'the man in the water' (Cohen 2012: 132 (175))

(64) JZakho: **Noun–Adverbial Phrase**
xabra d= [la l= dūk-e]
word LNK= NEG to= place-POSS.3MS
'inappropriate word (lit. word not in its place)' (Cohen 2012: 217 (11))

Given that the linker *d-* typically precedes clausal secondaries, the last example's secondary may be understood as a reduced clause, lacking a copula.

Note that adverbials (prepositions or conjunctions) cannot serve as primaries of the ALC. This is not surprising, since a pronominal element cannot in general represent a preposition. Moreover, adverbials by virtue of their function are equivalents of construct state nouns which require a complement, and are as such incompatible with the linker. When a linker occurs after a preposition, it refers anaphorically to an implicit primary (see example (71) on page 134).

5.4.6 Linkers without an explicit primary

As explained in §2.3.4, the linker is seen as pronominal since it is capable of heading an AC without any explicit nominal preceding it, functioning analogously to a construct state noun. Yet in JZakho at least, the linker is different from fully fledged pronouns in that it does not in general replace an entire determined noun-phrase, but rather only the head noun of a bare noun-phrase (see Table 1.2 on page 13). Thus, whereas a normal pronoun would not typically follow a determiner, the pronominal linker usually requires a determiner to precede it, as the following examples show. In the majority of cases the determiner is definite, but not always, as example (70) on page 134 shows.[15] For clarity of exposition, I put a ∅ symbol in the examples, where an overt primary could have occurred.

[15]Following the terminology presented in Table 1.2 on page 13, the normal pronouns represent a determined NP (or DP), while the linker represents a bare NP.

(65) JZakho: ∅–**Ordinal**
ʾay ∅ *d=* *treʾ*
DEF.FS ∅ LNK= two
'the second (one$_{FS}$)' (Cohen 2012: 95 (7))

(66) JZakho: ∅–**Ordinal**
ʾaw ∅ *dīd* *tre*
DEF.MS ∅ LNK two
'the second (one$_{MS}$)' (Cohen 2010: 84 (8))

This construction is also common with clausal secondaries, yielding a kind of FREE RELATIVE:

(67) JZakho: ∅–**Clause**
ʾay ∅ *d=* *g-əbá-wā-le*
DEF.FS ∅ LNK= IND-want.A3FS-PST-P3MS
'the one$_{FS}$ who wanted him' (Cohen 2012: 134 (183))

(68) JZakho: ∅–**Clause**
ʾaw ∅ *dīd* *hāyē* *=b-e* *əll-i*
DEF.MS ∅ LNK SBJV.be.3MS =in-3MS ACC-1SG
'the one$_{MS}$ who can defeat me' (Cohen 2010: 84 (9))

In some cases, as in the following example, the linker is seemingly coalesced with the genitive marking of the copula (see the discussion of example (91) on page 140). Alternatively, such cases could be analysed as case of asyndetic free relative clauses (see example (110) on page 146) with an attributive marked copula.

(69) JZakho: ∅–**Clause**
ʾan ∅ *d-īlu* *ʾəsye* *m=* *qabəl* *mənn-an*
DEF.PL ∅ {LNK}.GEN-COP.PL came.RES.PL from= before from-1PL
'those who came before us' (Cohen 2012: 122 (141))

One may wonder whether the determiners themselves should not be simply analysed as pronouns in the primary position of an AC. To this Cohen (2012: 134) answers: "The DETS *ay*, *aw* and *an* are neither pronouns nor do they function as such, and hence cannot be suspected to be antecedents. In all these examples, what we have are in effect determined complex nominal syntagms." Other cases, however, do cause an analytical ambiguity. Such is the case of *xa* 'one' in the following example, where it can be analysed both as a indefinite determiner or as an indefinite pronoun. Cohen (2012: 111f.) seems to imply that *xa* in this position is a determiner.[16] Note, moreover, that the noun phrase introduced by *xa* is itself the secondary of CSC headed by *pumma* 'mouth'.

(70) JZakho: **Pronoun/∅–Clause**
(mən pumm-ət) xā {∅} d= [la ʾāwəz gāzənda
from mouth-CST INDF.PRO/DET {∅} LNK= NEG SBJV.do.3MS complaint
mən baxt-e]
from wife-POSS.3MS
'(from the mouth of) someone who does not complain about his wife' (Cohen 2012: 112 (89))

In some cases, however, the linker does appear without an overt determiner or nominal element immediately preceding it, and these require some further examination.[17] The first case occurs whenever the linker is complemented by a pronominal suffix, such as in the following examples (the relevant expressions are marked in **bold**):[18]

(71) JZakho: **∅–Pronoun**
mā= xulla qaḥra dīd-ox zōdan-ta =la mən ∅ ***dīd-i***
what= RHETORIC grief(FS) LNK-2MS superior-FS =COP.3FS from ∅ LNK-1SG
'Is your grief superior to mine?' (Cohen 2012: 95 (5))

[16] One may argue that the long version [xā] present in the example represents necessarily a pronoun (cf. Sabar 2002: 191). Yet the vowel-lengthening may be due to prosodic reasons, like the lack of a stress-bearing nominal following *xa*, and as such cannot be taken as a clear indication of grammatical status. See also the similar example (109) on page 146 where *xa* does not have a long vowel.

[17] I dismiss cases where *dīd* forms part of a conjoint attributive complex, such as in examples (45) on page 127 or (50) on page 128, as in such cases one can argue that both *dīd* phrases are leaning on the same primary noun.

[18] Cohen (2012: 138) writes on the complex LNK-POSS: "The latter is a pronoun, rather than an adjective", but at the same time *dīd/d-* is considered to be on its own a "construct-state pronoun" (Cohen 2012: 452).

(72) JZakho: ∅–**Pronoun**
ha= wē-la šasəqsa dīd-a ʾəmm-i ū= kaffīya dīd-a ū= ∅
here= COP-3FS ring LNK-3FS with-1SG and= scarf LNK-3FS and= ∅
dīd-i *lēw-u kəs-li*
LNK-1SG NEG.COP-3PL at-1SG
'Here is her ring with me and her scarf, but mine are not with me' (Cohen 2010: 84, fn. 7)

Such cases call for two analyses: either the combination LNK+POSS has been grammaticalised as an independent genitive pronoun (possibly due to the inherent definiteness of the pronominal suffix[19]), or it simply forms a bare NP that has a ∅ determiner (which is defined by Cohen (2012: 454) to be "±definite; generic"). The latter option may be more adequate, since a similar example of a linker followed by a possessive pronoun is found with an overt determiner (but note the somewhat unexpected non-definite meaning):

(73) JZakho: ∅–**Pronoun**
ay ∅ d-ōhun (mərta =la)
DEF.FS ∅ LNK-3PL said.RES.FS =COP.FS
'One$_{fem}$ of them (has said).' (Cohen 2012: 138, fn. 36)

Another case where a linker construction appears without an overt determiner is in predicative position. In this position it may well be a bare NP, as the predicate position is quite flexible syntactically (it can accommodate as well bare adjectives or adverbial phrases). The following two examples constitute a question/answer pair, both having a predicative *dīd*.

(74) JZakho: ∅–**pronoun**
∅ dīd mani =le ōqadda māl?
∅ LNK who =COP.3MS so_much property
'Whose is so much property?' (Cohen 2012: 95 (12))

(75) JZakho: ∅–**noun**
g-əmr-i: ∅ dīd flāna nāša =le
IND-say-3PL ∅ LNK certain man =COP.3MS
'They say: it is of a certain man.' (Cohen 2012: 95 (12))

[19] Recall that the definiteness of the Semitic CSC is typically determined by the secondary; see §2.3.3.

Finally, there is a quite different usage of the *d-* morpheme without a nominal primary, namely its usage as a complementizer, such as in the following examples:

(76) JZakho: **Verb–Clause**
(u= xa lá= k-ī'ē-wa) d= 'anya trē' baxt-ā́s
and= one NEG= IND-know-PST COMP= DEM.PL two woman-PL.CST
d-ō gōra =lu
GEN-DEM.MS man =COP.3PL
'(But nobody knew) that these two are wives of the same man.' (Cohen 2012: 121 (136))

(77) JZakho: **Verb–Clause**
(la r'əš-le) d= d-īla ḥməl-ta məl'él mənn-e
NEG felt-3MS COMP= GEN-COP.3FS stood.RES-FS above from-3SG
'He didn't feel she is standing above him.' (Cohen 2012: 124 (143))

One may reasonably argue that when used as a complementizer, *dīd/d-* is not part of an AC, and is thus distinct from the linker.[20] Further evidence to this is adduced by the fact that in some cases, such as in example (76) the copula does not appear in its genitive form, as expected in an AC.

5.5 Genitive marking of secondaries

As discussed in §4.5, all determiners and demonstratives of JZakho which start with a glottal-stop or a vowel have a special genitive allomorph, formed by removing the glottal stop and prefixing the genitive *d-* marker. These include the definite articles (see Table 4.4 on page 108), some demonstratives and the interrogative determiner *ēma* 'which'. As mentioned there, the discovery and analysis of this phenomenon in JZakho is due to Cohen (2010), but it occurs in other dialects as well. As the facts motivating this analysis are the clearest in JZakho, I repeat them here briefly.

First, as stated above, the *d-* prefix appears only before a closed set of determiners and demonstratives, and not before other any ' or vowel-initial word (compare (17) on page 119), thus excluding a simple phonological conditioning of its appearance.[21]

[20]Paradigmatically, it can be replaced by other complementizing particles, such as *'ənnu* 'that' or *hakan* 'whether', attesting to its different status. See also the discussion regarding the similar Syriac examples (59)–(62) on page 68.

[21]Clearly, such a phonological conditioning took part in the diachronic emergence of the marker,

Second, note that the *d-* prefix appears after primaries with a suffixed construct state marker, primaries marked by apocopate construct state, as well as unmarked invariable primaries:

(78) JZakho: **Noun–Noun**
pumm-əd d-aw nāša
mouth-CST GEN-DEF.MS man
'the mouth of the man' (Cohen 2012: 107 (76))

(79) JZakho: **Noun–Noun**
bēs d-aw gōra
house.CST GEN-DEF.MS man
'the house of the man' (Cohen 2012: 107 (75))

(80) JZakho: **Noun–Infinitival Phrase**
sabab [d-o ʾīzāla dīd-ax]
reason(INV) GEN-DEF go.INF LNK-2FS
'the reason of your going' (Cohen 2012: 111 (87))

The first example proves that the *d-* prefix is distinct from the construct state marker, while the second and third examples show that it occurs also when no /d/ segment is called for by a construct state marking.

The last point can also be exemplified when the genitive marking follows an adverbial which normally do not get the *-əd* suffix:

(81) JZakho: **Preposition–Noun**
mən d-ay xzēna
from GEN-DEF treasure
'from the treasure' (Cohen 2012: 108 (77))

In contrast to other dialects, the genitive marking is obligatory whenever its appearance conditions are met. The very few exceptions listed by Cohen (2012: 108, fn. 15) can probably be explained by speech *lapsi* (or transcription errors), rather than a systematic optionality.

As we will see below, the genitive marker is also distinct from the linking pronoun, with which it can co-occur.

---

but it is no longer operative. In Nerwa (texts from the 17th century) one finds examples like *šəmm-əd d-ʾəlāha* 'name of God' (Sabar 2002: 38, §2).

5.5.1 Genitive marking following the linker

Since the linker stands in direct attributive relationship with its complement (the secondary), the latter is marked by genitive case whenever possible:

(82) JZakho: **Noun–Noun**
ʾōda dīd d-aw gōra
room LNK GEN-DEF.masc man
'the room of the man' (Cohen 2012: 106 (72))

A genitive marker following the short linker *d-* is also found, as in the following example (=example (16) on page 108). In the original source it is written as a separate word, but very likely it procliticizes to the following word. Given that *d-* typically comes before clausal secondaries (see §5.4.3), it is possible that it appears here as a phonetic simplification of the sequence *dīd d-o* > *d= d-o.*

(83) JZakho: **Noun Phrase–Noun**
(mən) [d-o bəhna rwīxa] d= [d-o jwanqa]
from GEN-DEM.MS breath(MS) wide.MS LNK= GEN-DEM.masc youngster
'(from) the patience of this youngster' (Cohen 2012: 106 (71))

5.5.2 Genitive marking of clauses

As we have seen above (§5.3.2), clauses may act as secondaries. In some cases, their secondary status is marked by the very same prefix *d-*. Indeed, JZakho has developed a special series of *genitivally* marked copulas, which consist of the normal (indicative present) copula preceded by *d-*. While the copula is the marked element, the scope of the marking should be understood as the entire secondary clause. As Cohen (2010) notes, this innovation of JZakho is similar to an Akkadian construction, but no direct influence can be adduced.[22]

[22] It should be noted that the genitive marking of clauses is different from the SUBJUNCTIVE MOOD (i.e. *šaqəl* forms without a pre-verbal particle) which exists in JZakho and other dialects. While the subjunctive mood is frequently found with embedded clauses, it adds a semantic mood value to the utterance, in contrast to the genitive marker, which is a pure grammatical mark of secondary position. Moreover, the subjunctive form can appear in matrix clauses, as example (92) on page 140 shows.

(84) JZakho: **Noun–Clause**
(b-əd) ḥaqq-əd d-īlu ʾəsye mən mōṣəl
in-CST price-CST GEN-COP.3PL came.RES from M.
'at the price which they had come to you from Mosul' (Cohen 2012: 119 (116))

(85) JZakho: **Noun–Clause**
(psōx) xā sandŭ́q [d-īle mutwa go qurnīs-ət čappe]
open.IMP INDF chest GEN-COP.3MS placed.RES in corner-CST left
'open a chest that is placed in the left corner' (Cohen 2012: 119 (119))

Thus, the genitive marking appears both after nouns with suffixed CST marker or in apocopate CST form. It is worthwhile noting that the *d-* prefix occurs even when the copula is not the first element of the attributive clause, though this must occur quite rarely, as the following example is unique in my survey:

(86) JZakho: **Noun–Clause**
(qam mesē-li ʾəl) d-ay qaṣər [maṭməryam
PST brought.A3PL-P1SG to GEN-DEF castle.CST VM.
d-īla ʾəll-e]
GEN-COP.3FS on-3MS
'(They brought me to) the castle, on which (the statue of) Virgin Mary is.[23]' (Cohen 2012: 119 (117))

The genitive marking appears also in ACs headed by adverbial conjunctions, whether they are invariable or construct state marked:

(87) JZakho: **Conjunction–Clause**
mən hīng-əd d-īla hwīsa
from then-CST GEN-COP.3FS born.RES.FS
'from the time she was born' (Cohen 2012: 120 (127))

(88) JZakho: **Conjunction–Clause**
čukūn d-īw-ət qarīwa l= ləbb-i
since GEN-COP-2MS close.MS to= heart-POSS.1SG
'since you are close to my heart' (Cohen 2012: 121 (130))

[23]If *dīla* is assumed to open the relative clause, it yields the quite odd interpretation "the castle of Virgin Mary, whose (statue) is on it".

The same genitive copula is used also for clausal secondaries of the ALC, i.e. following the linker:

(89) JZakho: **Noun (subject)–Clause**
ō gōra dīd d-ī-le go namūsīy-e
DEM.MS man LNK GEN-COP-3MS in bed-POSS.3MS
'the man who is in his bed' (Cohen 2012: 119 (120))

(90) JZakho: **Noun (subject)–Clause**
ʾē baxta d= d-ī-la baxt-e
DEM.FS woman LNK= GEN-COP.3FS woman-POSS.3MS
'that woman who is his wife' (Cohen 2012: 122)

In the last example the *d-* linker cliticizes to the *d-* genitive marker. This resulting *d=d* cluster is sometimes simplified to a de-geminated /*d*/, serving in both functions (cf. Cohen 2012: 122):

(91) JZakho: **Noun (subject)–Clause**
ay ʾurxa d-īl-a msukar-ta mən qam mšalxāne ū= ganāwe
DEF.FS road LNK.GEN-COP-3FS closed.RES-FS from before robbers and= thieves
'the road which is closed because of robbers and thieves' (Cohen 2012: 121 (137))

The genitive marking of clauses, on the other hand, is possible only whenever the secondary clause uses the indicative copula. When no such copula is present, such as when a form of the verb 'to be' is used, no genitive marking is apparent. This is exemplified by example (23) on page 120 and possibly also by example (109) on page 146. Similarly the existential particle (glossed EX), combined here with the preposition *b-* 'in' to denote ability, has no genitive marking:

(92) JZakho: **Pronoun–Clause**
(šaql-axni) mā-t [ʾī-b-an mṭāš-ax go jēbē-ni]
SBJV.take-1PL what-CST EX-in-1PL SBJV.hide-1PL in pocket.PL-POSS1PL
'Let's take whatever we can hide in our pockets.' (Cohen 2012: 96 (20))

5.6 The double annexation construction (X-y.POSS LNK-y)

In general the DAC is not used in JZakho. A rare usage of it occurs when the secondary is pronominal, in which case a possessive pronoun can be suffixed both to the primary noun and to a linker. This yields some added pragmatic emphasis.

(93) JZakho: **Noun–Pronoun**
baxt-i *dīd-i*
woman-POSS.1SG LNK-1SG
'my own wife' (Cohen 2012: 113, fn. 19)

5.7 Juxtaposition (X Y.{AGR})

By JUXTAPOSITION I mean a construction in which the two members of the AC are put adjacent to each other, without any further marking (except for the possibility of agreement, in which case it is juxtaposition-cum-agreement). This type of construction is reserved in JZakho for several quite distinct cases, which are detailed below.

5.7.1 Adjectival attribution

Adjectives are normally directly juxtaposed after the primary noun. Syntactically, they stand in apposition with the primary noun; the attributive relationship itself is expressed indirectly by agreement of the adjective with the head noun. Such cases are termed here accordingly JUXTAPOSITION-CUM-AGREEMENT. The inflection of adjectives, however, is mostly restricted to adjectives of Aramaic origin, especially with regard to the gender feature.

(94) JZakho: **Noun–Adjective**
xa *jwanqa* *sqīl-a*
INDF youth(MS) beautiful-MS
'a beautiful youth' (Cohen 2012: 214)

(95) JZakho: **Noun–Adjective**
xa *xamsa* *sqəl-ta*
INDF maiden(FS) beautiful-FS
'a beautiful maiden' (Cohen 2012: 214)

The ordinal *qamāya* 'first' acts as an adjective, as is seen in example (61) on page 131.

Borrowed adjectives sometimes do not inflect (or inflect only for number). This is the case of the adjective *ʿāqəl* 'wise', borrowed from Arabic (Sabar 2002: 246a). Such cases are truly zero-marked ACs:

(96) JZakho: **Noun–Adjective**
ʾaxōna ʿāqəl
brother wise(INV)
'(the) wise brother' (Cohen 2012: 214)

Occasionally an inflecting definite determiner precedes the adjective, instead of the primary noun (Cohen 2012: 215). The reasons for this are unclear, and may be related to some unknown semantic or stylistic factors. One syntactic possibility is that it marks the grammatical features of a non-inflecting (or partially inflecting) adjective, as in the following example (=example (4) on page 12):

(97) JZakho: **Noun–Adjective**
axōna aw rūwa
brother DEF.MS big.SG[24]
'the older brother' (Cohen 2012: 214)

Another motivation might be the occurrence of a possessed noun as the primary, which normally is not marked by a determiner preceding it:

(98) JZakho: **Noun Phrase–Adjective**
axōn-e aw ʿāqəl
brother-POSS.3MS DEF.MS wise(INV)
'his wise brother' (Cohen 2012: 214)

Recall, however, that similar examples occur also in Syriac (see example (109) on page 86).[25]

[24]Note that *rūwa* 'big' inflects only for number in JZakho (Sabar 2002: 288b).

[25]Another possibility suggested by Eran Cohen (p.c.) is that the determiner imitates the position of the Kurmanji linker Ezafe, which precedes the adjective (see §9.5.2 as well §10.4.2.2.5 on page 316). For possible relationship to the Semitic heritage see footnote 15 on page 11.

5.7.1.1 Inverse order juxtaposition (Y X)

Cohen (2012: 214, fn. 2) mentions that "in a small number of cases", the adjective precedes the noun, creating an inverse juxtaposition construction:[26]

(99) JZakho: **Noun–Adjective**
aw fīta ṭūra
DEF.MS huge(INV) rock(MS)
'the huge rock[27]' (Cohen 2012: 214, fn. 2)

(100) JZakho: **Noun–Adjective**
ʾē fīta brāta
DEM.FS huge daughter
'this grown-up girl' (Avinery 1988: 124 (680))

Interestingly, Sabar (2002) mentions a variant of this construction with the construct state suffix, which is very similar to the EMOTIVE GENITIVE construction presented in example (34) on page 124.

(101) JZakho: **Noun–Adjective**
xa fīt-a/əd gōra
INDF huge-FREE/CST man
'a huge person' (Sabar 2002: 263a)

Thus, it may be that inverse juxtapositioninverse juxtaposition construction of adjectives has some emotive value as well, but this question has not been investigated in the scope of this work.

5.7.2 Adverbial primaries

As mentioned in §5.3.3, prepositions which are not explicitly marked with a construct state *-əd* suffix cannot be considered to be marked by apocope, since they do not have a free form (unless they are derived from nouns). In these cases they are merely juxtaposed before their complement, as in the following example (contrast with example (28) on page 122):

[26]Recall that the title of examples follows always the order Primary-Secondary.

[27]Sabar (2002: 172a) lists *ṭūra* as 'mountain', but I follow here the translation given by Cohen.

(102) JZakho: **Preposition–Noun**
b= bəllūre
in= flute
'with a flute' (Cohen 2010: 85 (15))

Nonetheless, most prepositions induce an attributive relationship, as is clear from the occurrence of genitive marked secondaries following them, such as in example (81) on page 137.

Cohen (2012: 104) does mention, however, one preposition, *bēb* 'with', which does not induce genitive case, and thus formally always realises a juxtaposition pattern:[28]

(103) JZakho: **Preposition–Pronoun**
bēb ʾāwa
with 3MS
'with him' (Cohen 2012: 104 (70))

It is interesting to note that a preposition can be diachronically derived from an apocopate construct state noun, without being any more synchronically connected to it. Such is the case of the preposition *rəš* 'on', derived from the noun *rēša* 'head', still present in the dialect. The former is a phonologically reduced form of the construct state of the latter, *rēš*.[29] While synchronically the noun can also occur as *rēšəd*, the preposition is invariable. The contrast is neatly shown in the following example (continuing example (43) on page 126):

(104) JZakho: **Preposition–Noun Phrase**
rəš [rēš-ət manī-t yātū-wa]
on head-CST who-CST SBJV.sit-PST
'on the head of whomever it would sit' (Cohen 2012: 96 (18))

[28]Sabar (2002: 108) lists this preposition as being possibly from Kurdish origin, while Mutzafi (2008a: 121) gives a possible Aramaic etymology *b-ēh b-* consisting of the preposition *b-* 'in' repeated with a proleptic pronoun. Given that Kurdish Kurmanji prepositions induce oblique case, the Aramaic etymology may be the correct one.

[29]The derivation of the preposition 'on' from the noun 'head' is probably a pattern borrowing from Kurdish, where the word *ser* has the same two meanings (Noorlander 2014: 206).

5.7.3 Adverbial secondaries

Nouns, as well as pronouns, can be modified by at least some adverbial secondaries without any AC marking, neither on the primary nor on the secondary:

(105) JZakho: **Noun–Prepositional Phrase**
xá quṭeʾfa mux quṭeʾf-ət ʾədyo ġzē-li
INDF cluster like cluster-CST today saw-1SG
'a cluster like the cluster I saw today' (Cohen 2012: 217 (12))

(106) JZakho: **Pronoun–Prepositional Phrase**
xá mənn-ēni
one from-1PL
'one of us' (Cohen 2012: 217 (14))

5.7.4 Clausal secondaries

Clausal secondaries can follow an indefinite primary noun asyndetically, i.e. without any particular marking. Cohen (2012: 138) tentatively relates this pattern to Arabic influence, whether direct or indirect, as in Arabic too the construction is confined to indefinite primaries.[30]

(107) JZakho: **Noun–Clause**
(u= ʾāna gəb-ēn ṭāʾ-ət-tə) [xa xamsa] [hōya
and= 1SG IND.want-1SG look-A2MS-DAT.1SG INDF maid SBJV.be.3MS
mən məšpāḥá bāš]
from family good
'I want you to look for a maid (who) is from a good family.' (Cohen 2012: 137 (214))

Such asyndetic clauses may be related to examples like the following:

(108) JZakho: **Noun–Clause(?)**
(mpəq-le mən xá= ʾāl) [xa ʾarya] [ʾēn-e smōq-e]
came_out-3MS from one= side INDF lion eye-POSS.3MS red-PL
'From one side came out a lion, his eyes red' (Cohen 2012: 225 (63))

[30] "Most asyndetic adjective clauses [... are] perhaps modeled after the Arabic ([but] this phenomenon also occurs in NENA dialects that are clearly outside the Arabic speaking area)." (Cohen 2012: 137f.). See discussion in §11.3.1.

Cohen (2012: 225) classifies such cases as NON-CLAUSAL ADJECTIVAL NEXUS. In his view, while these are expressions of a predicative relation (a NEXUS, see §2.1.1), they are not clausal, since they lack a copula.[31] Nevertheless, since nominal clauses lacking a copula do occur (albeit rarely) in NENA dialects, one may relax the usage of the term CLAUSE to include such cases as well.

The morpheme *xa*, followed by an asyndetic attributive clause, presents the same analytical difficulty found in example (70) on page 134. Either one analyses it as an indefinite pronoun ('someone'), which is followed directly by an attributive clause, and is not marked as construct state (contrast with the construct state pronouns in examples (22)–(25) on page 120), or one analyses it as an indefinite determiner, followed by a ∅ primary noun + relative clause, which renders the structure parallel to the above examples:

(109) JZakho: **Pronoun/∅–Clause**
(la ġzē-lu) xa {∅} [šəmm-e hāwe qaramấn]
NEG saw-3PL INDF.PRO/DET {∅} name-POSS.3MS SBJV.be.3MS Q.
'They did not find anyone whose name is Qaraman.' (Cohen 2012: 137 (216))

Note that in either analysis, *xa* introduces a discourse referent, which is referred to in the secondary clause by the 3MS pronominal indices.

The latter analysis may also be preferred due to the rare occurrence of a similar structure introduced by a *definite* determiner. In such examples, as the following, I also posit the occurrence of a ∅ primary.[32]

(110) JZakho: ∅**–Clause**
an ∅ k-sēm-i mənn-an
DEF.PL ∅ IND-hate-3PL from-1PL
'those who hate us' (Cohen 2012: 138 (217))

[31] Cf. Goldenberg (2013a: 257) who writes: "such syntagms are not conceived as asyndetically embedded sentences, which in Neo-Aramaic would require a copula [...] In other words, such syntagms might be said to incorporate the cohesive or relational, but not the assertive, constituent of the nexus."

[32] Note though that such cases are unusual, in that a definite primary would normally not allow an asyndetic relative clause. Cohen (2012: 138) mentions that such examples are only found in one source (Sabar 2007), which is a unique genre of autobiographical account.

5.7.5 Infinitival primaries

As shown in §5.3.5, infinitives can be marked by construct state morphology. This marking, however, is not obligatory, probably due to the verbal nature of infinitives: When followed by an object argument, the infinitive can induce a completive relation, which is manifested by the unmarked juxtaposition construction, rather than a marked attributive relation. Contrast the following example with example (38) on page 125 (which is the continuation of this example):

(111) JZakho: **Infinitive–Noun**
(bəš xlē-la ʾəll-i) ʾwāza xōrūs-ax (mən ...)
more pleased-3FS to-1SG make.INF friendship-POSS.2FS than ...
'Befriending you (pleases me more than befriending emirs' and pashas' daughters.)' (Cohen 2012: 99 (38))

5.8 Conclusions

JZakho has three types of AC markers (construct state marking, the linker, and genitive case), but only two can co-occur at the same time, as the CST and LNK marking are in complementary distribution. In other words, JZakho has two slots of marking the AC, presented in Table 5.1. Note that these slots do not correspond directly to head-marking vs. dependent marking, as the first slot opposes the head-marking construct state markers attaching to the primary with the dependent marking linker, which attaches syntactically and phonologically to the secondary.

Table 5.1: AC markers in JZakho

	1	2	
X	CST (*-əd*, Ap.) LNK (*d-*, *dīd*)	± GEN(*d-*)	Y

The dialect presents both innovative and conservative aspects of the AC system, as compared to Classical Aramaic (of which I take Syriac as the main point of comparison). First and foremost, it conserves the classical Semitic logic of the attributive relation marking: this relation must be marked either directly on the primary noun (by means of construct state marking), or indirectly by means of a pronominal linker. Moreover, the distinction between nominal/clausal attribution, in which the attributive relationship is overt, and adjectival attribution, in which it is covert (formally realised only by agreement) is strictly kept. On the other hand, JZakho innovated the morphological material available for marking the construct state, most notably the suffixed construct state *-əd* marker, and to a lesser degree novel apocopate forms. Cohen (2015: 121ff.) suggests that the development of the *-əd* suffix is related to pattern replication from the coterritorial Kurmanji, yet an internal development stemming from encliticization of the Classical Aramaic *d-* linker to the primary is possible as well (see discussion in §10.4.2).

Another related morphological innovation is the introduction of the variant form *dīd* as an independent linker, in contrast to a base appearing only with possessive pronominal suffixes as in Jewish Babylonian Aramaic. This may be explained by the resemblance of the *dīd* linker to a *d-* linker augmented by the construct state *-əd* suffix; see §10.6.2 for a discussion. Note that all the above discussed innovations do not change the basic logic of the system, but rather affect only the forms involved.

Structurally more innovative is the introduction of genitive marking in certain morphological environments (certain determiners, and the indicative copula). While genitive marking existed in ancient Semitic languages, it is unknown in prior strata of Aramaic,[33] and must be considered as an innovation. It is clearly innovative in that it constitutes an additional marker of ACs (on top of the construct state marking or the linker). Moreover, in some cases, such as ACs headed by simple prepositions, it reveals the existence of an attributive relation which could in earlier strata only be posited abstractly. In this respect, the innovation of genitive marking is more important structurally than the innovation of new construct state forms, although it affects only a restricted number of grammatical items. Nonetheless, the overall effect of this innovation on the attributive system is small, as it only adds morphological marking in restricted cases, without restructuring any AC.

Another point which can be considered innovative is the usage of the linker in marking completive relations, following infinitives as well as resultative participles (see §5.4.2). This phenomenon, however, is situated at the periphery of the attributive system, and is in fact related to the development of periphrastic verbal constructions.

Another innovation, as compared to earlier strata of Aramaic, is the possibility of introducing relative clauses directly after primaries marked for construct state, irrespective of the type of marking (apocope or the *-əd* suffix). While this

[33]But see footnote 43 on page 109.

possibility existed in ancient Semitic languages (such as Biblical Hebrew), it must have been reintroduced in NENA. Indeed, the usage of clausal secondaries after apocopate construct state primaries is specific to the J. Cis-Zab group, as it is only clearly attested there.[34] To be sure, it does not appear in Syriac. This innovation can be understood as filling a syntactic gap (or asymmetry) in the system which existed in previous Aramaic dialects, including Syriac, since it extends the possibility of marking ACs with nominal secondaries either by the linking pronoun or by the construct state marking to clausal secondaries as well. As such, it can be said to be an internally motivated development (due to the general force of ANALOGY), but see again Cohen (2015: 123) who suggests that this possibility is due to pattern replication from Kurmanji. In the realm of relative clauses, one finds also the innovation of asyndetic relative clauses (see §5.7.4), which is known in other Semitic languages, but not in Aramaic. Here, the suggestion of borrowing from Arabic (Cohen 2012: 138) seems plausible; see further discussion in §11.3.1.

As for the phonological material, JZakho is clearly conservative, as it recycles the same material for the new morphological devices. The D-markers derive from the Classical Aramaic linker *d-*, which by various cliticization and re-analysis processes yielded the construct state suffix *-əd* (see §10.4) and the genitive prefix *d-* (§10.5). The linker *dīd* existed already in Classical Aramaic (in particular in Jewish Babylonian Aramaic) as a pronominal base of the independent genitive pronouns, but it has been reanalysed in JZakho as an independent linker, capable of introducing full nominal secondaries (see §10.6.2). Thus, no morphemes are borrowed from contact languages.

In summary, notwithstanding the possibility of language contact, it seems that most of the JZakho features regarding the AC system can be explained, at least in principle, by processes of internal development. These processes "shuffle around" morphemic material (making essentially analytical forms synthetic), but keep the essential logic of the system intact.

[34] See Table 11.1 on page 349 and the following Amədya example for another J. Cis-Zab dialect showing this construction:

(i) Amədya: **Noun–Clause**
ḥil yom gawər-wa-la
until day.CST marry.A3MS-PST-P3FS
'until the day he married her' (Greenblatt 2011: 73)

6 Attributive constructions in the Christian dialect of Qaraqosh

The data of the Qaraqosh dialect is based on Khan (2002a). Note that the town name Qaraqosh is referred to as *Bağdedə* in the dialect itself, as will be apparent in some of the examples below.[1]

Compared to JZakho, Qaraqosh presents a more conservative system of ACs, as we shall see below. With respect to the AC system, the dialect is quite similar to the neighbouring dialect of Alqosh (=Alqosh), described by Coghill (2003), but still somewhat more conservative.

The main ACs in Qaraqosh are the suffixed CSC (see §6.2) and the ALC (see §6.3). Due to the frequent resyllabification of the */d/* segment, however, it is not always easy to distinguish between the two. This fuzzy situation may be related to the conservative nature of the dialect. Moreover, in contrast to JZakho, there is no regular genitive *d*- marking, although some cases may resemble it (see example (76) on page 172). In Gospel translations one finds also the DAC (see §6.4.2).

The chapter discusses also some other constructions found in Qaraqosh: the use of the possessive pronominal suffixes, in which Qaraqosh has some particularities, is discussed in the next section. Double marking due to hesitation is discussed in §6.4.1. Juxtaposition constructions, on the periphery of the AC system of Qaraqosh, are discussed in §6.5.

6.1 Possessive pronominal suffixes (X-y.POSS)

Qaraqosh, like all NENA dialects, has a series of pronominal possessive suffixes, that can attach freely to nouns. The possessive pronouns replace the last vowel

[1]The examples are cited referring to the page in the grammar in which they are treated. Examples which are part of the texts collected by Khan are furthermore indicated by a textual reference, using Khan's notation system in square brackets. The single letters refer to informants' free speech, while the labels *Proverbs, Play, Poetry* and *Gospel* refer to recordings of a collection of proverbs, a theatre play, poetry recitation, and a Gospel translation. Note that the recordings of informant K (including the proverbs) are publicly available (see link under Khan 2002a in the Bibliography).

of the noun, which corresponds to the free state and number marking. As a consequence, when the number distinction is expressed solely by this vowel, it is lost. Such is the case of the noun *tora* 'ox' with the plural form *torə*:

(1) Qaraqosh: **Noun–Pronoun**
tór-əḥ
ox(en)-POSS.3MS
'his ox(en)' (Khan 2002a: 76)

Qaraqosh, however, exhibits a special feature, in that the plural possessive pronominal suffixes retain the number distinction of the noun to which they attach: these suffixes transform a plural /-ə/ suffix to an /-e/ suffix, instead of suppressing it. As Khan (2002a: 77) notes, this is an archaism of the dialect, which conserves the reflex of an original **ay*:

(2) Qaraqosh: **Noun–Pronoun**
tór-∅-hən
ox(en)-SG-POSS.3PL
'their ox' (Khan 2002a: 77)

(3) Qaraqosh: **Noun–Pronoun**
tor-é-hən
ox(en)-PL-POSS.3PL
'their oxen' (Khan 2002a: 77)

The possessive suffix attaches strictly to the primary noun. A modifying adjective appears after this complex (contrast with example (59) on page 167):

(4) Qaraqosh: **Noun Phrase–Pronoun**
sús-əḥ kóma
horse-POSS.3MS black
'his black horse' (Khan 2002a: 280)

An interesting phenomenon particular to this dialect is the insertion of an -*ətt* suffix (glossed below as FS) before the possessive pronoun in some feminine nouns, such as *ʾarnúwa* 'rabbit':

(5) Qaraqosh: **Noun–Pronoun**
ʾarnuw-ə́tt-əḥ
rabbit-FS-POSS.3MS
'his rabbit' (Khan 2002a: 204)

As most of the nouns which behave in this way are of Arabic origin, Khan (2002a: 206) relates this phenomenon to the retention of the Arabic *tāʾ marbūṭa*, which is an *-ət* suffix appearing in construct state feminine nouns.[2] In this account, the gemination of the /t/ segment may be explained by a merger with the Aramaic feminine suffix *-ta*, yielding *-ət* + *-ta* = *-ətta*, noting that the final *-a* vowel is dropped before the possessive suffixes. The gemination could also be explained on phonological grounds, as a mean to conserve the short [ə] vowel in a closed syllable. Either way, in contrast to the Arabic *tāʾ marbūṭa*, the Qaraqosh *-ətt* is not a generalized feminine construct state marker, as it appears only before possessive pronouns, and not before full nominal secondaries.

Another possibility which Khan raises is that the *-ətt* segment may be related to the linker *did*, akin to the NWNA HEAVY POSSESSIVE SUFFIXES which contain the linker *d-*,[3] but this seems less plausible due to the restricted distribution of this suffix with feminine nouns only.

Infinitives, as well as particles, take the same possessive suffixes as nouns. These suffixes mark then the complements of the verbal lexeme (see also §6.2.7):

(6) Qaraqosh: **Infinitive–Pronoun**
(xálṣa) lyàš-əḥˈ
finish.3FS knead.INF-POSS.3MS
'(She finishes) kneading it.' (Khan 2002a: 364 [B:132])

(7) Qaraqosh: **Participle–Pronoun**
k-ína šqíl-əḥ Maṣlàyəˈ
IND-COP.3PL taken.RES-POSS.3MS M._inhabitants
'The people of Mosul have taken it.' (Khan 2002a: 363 [S:49])

Some prepositions may also take the possessive pronominal suffixes:

[2] Khan (2002a: 204) notes that the final /a/ of Arabic loanwords, which corresponds to *tāʾ marbūṭa* (in its free state form), is often pronounced as [ə].

[3] See footnote 11 on page 302 for an example.

(8) Qaraqosh: **Preposition–Pronoun**
txíθ-əḥ
under-POSS.3MS
'under it' (Khan 2002a: 80)

Other prepositions, which cannot take this suffix, have a suppletive form which appears only with the possessive suffixes. Such is the case of *ʾeka~gib-* 'at' or *da~ġdal-* 'for':

(9) Qaraqosh: **Preposition–Pronoun**
gíb-an
at-POSS.1PL
'at our place' (Khan 2002a: 234 [B:138])

(10) Qaraqosh: **Preposition–Pronoun**
ġdál-əḥ
for-POSS.3MS
'for him' (Khan 2002a: 233)

As for the plural possessive suffixes, some prepositions take the plain variant, while others take the variant used after plural primaries, probably due to their nominal origin.

(11) Qaraqosh: **Preposition–Pronoun**
txəθ-hən
under-POSS.3PL
'under them' (Khan 2002a: 80)

(12) Qaraqosh: **Preposition–Pronoun**
baθr-e-hən
after-'PL'-POSS.3PL
'after them' (Khan 2002a: 80)

6.2 The construct state construction (X.CST Y)

The marking of the primary by the construct state suffix *-əd* is the most common type of AC in Qaraqosh, but its identification is not always easy, due to phonological considerations. Indeed, very often the construct state suffix syllabifies with the subsequent secondary, rendering it similar to the linker construction, discussed in §6.3. At the same time, the historical apocopate construct state is only retained in a handful of expressions, discussed below.

6.2.1 The historical construct state marking

The historical construct state marking, characterized synchronically by an apocope of the primary noun (minimally the removal of the free state suffix), is found only in a handful of "closely knit-phrases" (Khan 2002a: 209), i.e. proper nouns or fixed expressions (compounds), with either opaque semantics (see example (13) on the current page) or transparent semantics (see example (14) on this page). Additionally, one finds the primary *bi* 'house.CST' in the meaning of 'family/house of' used productively with a referential secondary (see example (15) on the current page).[4] Note that in example (14) the word *bǎxət* 'wife.CST' is formed from *baxta* 'wife.FREE' by the removal of the free state suffix *-a* and the insertion of an epenthetic *ə*.

(13) Qaraqosh: **Noun–Noun (opaque semantics)**
bi= guba; bi= yəlda; bar= zarʾa
house.CST= hole house.CST= birth; son.CST= field
'tunnel', 'Christmas', 'seed' (Khan 2002a: 209)

(14) Qaraqosh: **Noun–Noun (transparent semantics)**
bǎxət bába; syam= íḏa
wife.CST father laying.CST= hand
'step-mother, ordination' (Khan 2002a: 209)

(15) Qaraqosh: **Noun–Noun (productive expressions)**
bí xə́θna; bi= Šə̀rḥa; bi= ʿàmm-i
house.CST groom house.CST= S. house.CST= uncle-POSS.1SG
'family of the groom, of S., of my paternal uncle' (Khan 2002a: 209 [S:93])

In this respect, Qaraqosh differs from JZakho, in which the apocopate construct state is entirely productive (see example (6) on page 117 among others).

[4]For a discussion of the various types of compounds in NENA, see Gutman (2014).

6.2.2 The suffixed construct state formation

The productive formation of the construct state is made with the help of the *-(ə)d* suffix, which originates in the encliticization of the linker *d-*.[5] The suffix replaces the final vowel of the primary (if it ends in a vowel), leading often to a neutralisation of the number distinction of the primary noun:

(16) Qaraqosh: **Noun–Noun**
kθáw-əd qáša
book-CST priest
'the book of the priest' (Khan 2002a: 276)

In some cases, especially after liquid consonants following a vowel, the [ə] segment is not present, alluding to its epenthetic status.

(17) Qaraqosh: **Noun–Noun**
gúr-d máθa
men-CST town
'the men of the town' (Khan 2002a: 208 [F:96])

Some specific nouns seem to combine a historical apocopate construct state form with an *-əd* suffix. Such is the case of the nouns *ʾəbra* 'son' and *brata* 'daughter':

(18) Qaraqosh: **Noun–Noun**
bə́rd axón-i
son.CST brother-POSS.1SG
'the son of my brother' (Khan 2002a: 207)

(19) Qaraqosh: **Noun–Noun**
bə́rtəd ʿàmma
daughter.CST paternal_uncle
'the daughter of a paternal uncle' (Khan 2002a: 207 [S:40])

As Khan (2002a: 208) mentions, in some cases the /*d*/ segment is phonetically syllabified with the secondary. This happens predominantly when the secondary starts with a vowel (often preceded by an epenthetic glottal stop) or a consonant

[5] Khan treats the construct state marker and the linker as two manifestations of the same annexation particle *d*; see Chapter 4 for similar opinions of other scholars. For the development of the construct state suffix see discussion in §10.4.

cluster, in which case an epenthetic [ə] is added after the /*d*/. These cases are still in principle differentiable from the linker *d-* (treated in §6.3), thanks to the replacement of the final (free state) vowel of the primary (typically an *-a* for singular nouns) by an [ə] (glossed in such cases as schwa), or its complete elision in some cases (typically when the last consonant of the primary is a liquid).[6]

(20) Qaraqosh: **Noun–Noun**
yál -d= axòna
child(ren) -CST= brother
'children of the brother' (Khan 2002a: 208 [F:3])

(21) Qaraqosh: **Noun–Noun**
ʾít-ə -də= Šmòni[7]
church-
isischwa -CST= S.
'the church of Shmoni' (Khan 2002a: 208 [K:21])

The syllabification of the construct state suffix with a vowel-initial secondary is not automatic however, as example (18) on the preceding page and the following example show (contrast with example (20) on this page):

(22) Qaraqosh: **Noun–Noun**
báb-əd ʾaxón-əd ʾə́mm-i
father-CST brother-CST mother-POSS.1SG
'the father of the brother of my mother' (Khan 2002a: 276 [B:25])

Conversely, the suffix may syllabify with the secondary even when the above mentioned phonological conditions are not fulfilled:

[6]The elision of a final schwa in a CVCə CV environment seems to be a regular phonological process in Qaraqosh and the neighbouring Alqosh dialect (cf. Coghill 2003: 73). Since only a schwa is thus elided (and not the vowel [a]), the lack of a final vowel is a clear indication of an underlying *-əd* suffix. On the other hand, when a schwa is present, it is often difficult in normally paced speech to tell it apart from an /*-a*/ suffix, which is often realised as [æ]. When the primary noun ends in the free state with an [ə] (such as some plural nouns or infinitives) it is impossible to tell the difference between the two constructions in normal speech. Indeed, Coghill (2003: 298), describing the neighbouring Alqosh dialect, notices that it is often impossible to tell whether the /*d*/ segment is associated with the primary or the secondary, as in *nāšə-d-jéš* 'men of the army'.

[7]This is the text as it appears in the corpus. In the grammar, it is cited erroneously as *ʾitə d-Ašmoni.*

(23) Qaraqosh: **Noun–Noun**
kθayáθ-ə -də= Bağdèdə
chickens-
isischwa -CST= B.
'the chickens of Qaraqosh.' (Khan 2002a: 208 [B:105])

In some cases, the /*d*/ segment is assimilated to the following segment. In Khan's transcription the assimilated segment is written as a proclitic of the secondary:

(24) Qaraqosh: **Noun–Noun**
ʾilan-ə -z= záʾθa
tree-
isischwa -CST= olive
'olive tree' (Khan 2002a: 208 [K:56])

In cases where the resulting geminate is de-geminated, the only indicator of the construct state is the lack of the final free state vowel on the primary, and its replacement by an [ə] (in which cases it fully assumes the role of construct state marking, and is thus glossed CST):

(25) Qaraqosh: **Noun–Noun**
ʾár-ə Bağdèdə
land-CST B.
'the land of Qaraqosh' (Khan 2002a: 208 [S:48])

When the primary consists of conjoined nouns, one construct state suffix is sufficient for the entire phrase, as in the following example (=example (11) on page 104; compare to the other examples there):[8]

(26) Qaraqosh: **Conjoined nouns–Noun**
[wánat= u toráθ]-əd Bağdèdə
sheep= and cows-CST B.
'the sheep and cows of Qaraqosh' (Khan 2002a: 276 [F:1])

[8]Note that *wanat* is the plural form of *ʾuwana, wana* 'female sheep' and not an apocopate form (Khan 2002a: 727).

6.2.3 Adverbial primaries

Recall that the term ADVERBIAL is used here as a cover term for both conjunctions and prepositions, as these often assume an adverbial function (see footnote 47 on page 44). However, the CSC of Qaraqosh admits only prepositions (taking nominal complements) as primaries:

(27) Qaraqosh: **Preposition–Noun**
ríš-əd kàlθa
on-CST bride
'on the bride' (Khan 2002a: 239 [K:41])

(28) Qaraqosh: **Preposition–Noun Phrase**
txíθ-əd [dә́nw-əd ḥaywằn]
under-CST tail-CST animal
'under the tail of the animal' (Khan 2002a: 240 [B:75])

In some cases, only the /-ə/ segment remains of the construct state suffix (compare with example (25) on the preceding page):

(29) Qaraqosh: **Preposition–Noun**
txíθ-ə sùdya' ʾu= txíθ-ə làḥma
under-CST warp and= under-CST weft
'under the warp and under the weft' (Khan 2002a: 240 [B:22])

(30) Qaraqosh: **Preposition–Noun**
báθr-ə báb-əḥ
behind-CST father-POSS.3MS
'behind his father' (Khan 2002a: 233)

Conversely, when the secondary is vowel-initial the /d/ segment tends to syllabify with the secondary (compare with example (20) on page 157). In such cases, the /ə/ segment tends to fall.

(31) Qaraqosh: **Preposition–Noun**
txiθ -d= àql-əḥ
under -CST= foot-POSS.3MS
'under his foot' (Khan 2002a: 240 [F:38])

The same analysis holds for the prepositions *mən* 'from' and *max* 'like', though their construct state forms appear only before vowel-initial secondaries:[9]

(32) Qaraqosh: **Preposition–Noun**
mən -d= áḏa gdíša
from -CST= DEM.PROX.MS pile
'from this pile' (Khan 2002a: 238 [B:94])

(33) Qaraqosh: **Preposition–Adverb**
mən -d= àxa
from -CST= here
'from here' (Khan 2002a: 238 [F:11])

(34) Qaraqosh: **Preposition–Noun**
max -d= aḏa gora
like CST= DEM.PROX.MS man
'like this man' (Khan 2002a: 238)

As the above examples show, in many of these cases the vowel-initial element opening the secondary is a demonstrative pronoun. The attachment of the /d/ segment to it may be the first step in the path of its reanalysis as a genitive case marker conditioned morphologically by the presence of a demonstrative pronoun (see §10.5). This reanalysis has not taken place in Qaraqosh (or at least, not completely), as the attachment of the /d/ segment to the secondary is still conditioned by a vowel-initial phonological environment (as example (31) on the previous page shows), rather than being morphologically conditioned by the presence of certain demonstratives. Moreover, as example (115) on page 182 shows, the /d/ segment does not appear consistently before demonstrative pronouns where a

[9]The simple forms of the preposition (without a /d/ segment) are used preceding consonant-initial secondaries, giving rise to the juxtaposition construction (see §6.5.2 and examples (114) and (117) there). This restriction does not hold in other dialects, where the construct state form *mənn-əd* is found preceding such secondaries, including Nerwa (see example (59) on page 377), JUrmi (see example (18) on page 193) and Bohtan, as illustrated by the following example:

(i) Bohtan: **Preposition–Noun**
mənn-ət karačüke
from-CST gypsies
'from the Gypsies' (Fox 2009: 99)

genitive marking would be expected. See, however, example (76) on page 172 for a case where positing a genitive prefix seems to be the best analytical possibility.

6.2.4 Adjectival primaries

There are two distinct types of cases in which adjectives appear in the primary slot of the construct state construction. In the first case, akin to the IMPURE ANNEXATION in Arabic, the adjectival lexeme is modified syntactically by a secondary noun (which semantically is qualified by the adjective). The resulting AC is an adjectival phrase which modifies another noun (compare with the ALC in example (77) on page 172):[10]

(35) Qaraqosh: **Adjective–Noun**
(góra) xwár-əd kósa
man white-CST hair
'a white-haired (man)' (Khan 2002a: 281)

The second case represents an EMOTIVE GENITIVE, in which the noun posing as a secondary is in fact the semantic head, and the use of the adjective as a primary (and subsequently as a syntactic head) adds emotional value to the phrase (compare with the JZakho example (34) on page 124 and see footnote 11 there.)

(36) Qaraqosh: **Adjective–Noun**
mḥúsy-əd xəmyàn-i'
absolved.MS-CST father_in_law-POSS.1SG
'my late father-in-law' (Khan 2002a: 281 [Play 13])

(37) Qaraqosh: **Adjective–Noun**
b= áḏa həjím-əd màʕraḏ̣'
in= DEM.PROX.MS collapsed-CST showroom
'in this accursed showroom' (Khan 2002a: 281 [Play 107])

6.2.5 The primary *nafs* 'the same'

An interesting example of borrowing a construct state construction together with its primary (a matter-cum-pattern replication in the sense of Sakel 2007), is the borrowing of the Arabic function word نفس *nafs*. This word, originally meaning

[10]Compare this with the Classical Arabic example *ḥasanu l-waǧh-i* 'beautiful.CST DEF-face-GEN' (Goldenberg 2013a: 277). See Goldenberg (2002: 204ff.) for a discussion.

'soul', has been grammaticalised in Arabic into a reflexive pronoun, and as head of the CSC into a determiner meaning 'the same':

(38) Arabic: ***nafs*–noun**
نفس الأكل
nafs-u *l-ʾakl-i*
soul-NOM DEF-food-GEN
'the same food'

In Qaraqosh, the reflexive pronoun is *roxa*, a native Aramaic word meaning 'soul' (see Khan 2002a: 84).[11] The morpheme *nafs* has been borrowed, however, in its determinative function with the meaning *the same*. Moreover, its syntactic position as the head of a CSC is replicated, albeit being marked with NENA morphology, namely the construct state *-əd* suffix.

(39) Qaraqosh: ***nafs*–Noun**
náfs-əd *ʾəxàla*
same-CST food
'the same food' (Khan 2002a: 642 [F:77])

6.2.6 Clausal secondaries

The suffixal CSC can also introduce a clausal secondary:

(40) Qaraqosh: **Noun–Clause**
sókə-d *k-maθéhə*
sprigs-CST IND-bring.3PL
'the sprigs that they bring' (Khan 2002a: 209 [K:56])

(41) Qaraqosh: **Noun–Clause**
(nā́dir xáz-ət) béθ-əd *lé-bə* *tawə̀rta.'*
rarely see-2MS house-CST NEG.EX-in.3MS cow
'(You rarely see) a house that doesn't have a cow in it.' (Khan 2002a: 477 (4) [B:100])

[11]This need not be a pattern replication, as this meaning is a common source for reflexive pronouns cross-linguistically. A single example of matter replication of this sense is attested in Qaraqosh as *nafə̀ssə* 'themselves' (Khan 2002a: 739).

In the following examples, the construct state suffix syllabifies with the clause, which starts either with a vowel-initial copula, or a consonant cluster (contrast with example (40) on the facing page):

(42) Qaraqosh: **Noun–Clause**
maθwáθ -d= ina= xə̀d̲ran Bag̊dèdə
villages -CST= COP.PL= around B.
'the villages that are around Qaraqosh' (Khan 2002a: 209 [F:22])

(43) Qaraqosh: **Pronoun–Clause**
kúll mán də= g-nápəl b= idàθ-θə'
all who -CST= IND-fall in= hands-POSS.3PL
'anybody who falls into their hands' (Khan 2002a: 480 (4) [Play 135])

Note that in the last example the pronoun *mani* 'who' loses its final /i/ vowel in presence of the construct state suffix.

6.2.7 Infinitives in the construct state construction

Infinitives of transitive verbs can appear as primaries of the CSC, having their objective complement as the secondary. Infinitives of intransitive verbs are not found in this position, in contrast to JZakho, where infinitives can take their verbal subject as secondaries (see examples (35)–(36) on page 124).

(44) Qaraqosh: **Infinitive–Noun (object)**
('əm-mólpi susawáθa) štáy-əd 'əràq' u= xál-əd
FUT-teach.3PL horses drink.INF-CST araq and= eat.INF-CST
bšála d= nàšə.'
cooked_food LNK= people
'(They would teach the horses) to drink arak and eat the food of people.' (Khan 2002a: 369 (1) [F:66])

(45) Qaraqosh: **Infinitive–Pronoun (object)**
qṭál -də= g̊d̲ád̲ə
fight.INF.CST -CST= each_other
'fighting each other' (Khan 2002a: 275 (21))

(46) Qaraqosh: **Infinitive–Noun (object)**
(dúkθ-əd) ḥfāḏ-əd làxma
place-CST store.INF-CST bread
'(the place of) the storage of the bread' (Khan 2002a: 276 [B:15])

As the last example shows, an infinitive can also appear as a secondary of a CSC. In this case, it is akin to a regular noun, as the following example shows:

(47) Qaraqosh: **Noun–Infinitive**
yóm -də= gwàra
day.CST -CST= marry.INF
'wedding day' (Khan 2002a: 208 [K:40])

6.3 The analytic linker construction (X LNK Y)

6.3.1 Introduction

Qaraqosh has retained the usage of the linker as an important element of its AC system. However, due to the phonological considerations explained above regarding the construct state suffix, it is not always clear whether a specific occurrence of a proclitic *d-* should be analysed as a linker or rather as re-syllabified construct state suffix. As a general rule, if a free state suffix can be identified on the primary (SG: *-a*; PL: *-ə*), I assume a proclitic *d-* is indeed the linker. Note, however, that the plural free state suffix is ambiguous since an [ə] is also part of the construct state suffix.

In most cases, the linker can be analysed as being pronominal, i.e. representing a noun. In some cases, however, this analysis is not tenable, as we shall see below.

In Khan's transcription, the linker can occur in a variety of phonological shapes, be it *d-*, *də-*, *ʾəd-*. In many cases, this variation can be explained by the realisation of an epenthetic [ə] which breaks up a consonant cluster (cf. Khan 2002a: 64–65). A truly different morphemic shape is found in the rare form *dəd-*.[12]

(48) Qaraqosh: **Noun–Noun**
bšála d= nàšə
cooked_food LNK= people
'the food of people' (Khan 2002a: 207 [F:66])

[12]Khan analyses the form *dəd-* as a repetition of the "annexation particle" *d-*, and classifies its occurrence together with examples (102)–(103) on page 178.

(49) Qaraqosh: **Noun–Noun**
xəlxálə də= sə̀hma
bangles LNK= silver
'bangles of silver' (Khan 2002a: 207 [Poetry 29])

(50) Qaraqosh: **Noun–Noun**
zòna' dəd= roxáθa xəškanə'
time LNK= souls dark.PL
'the time of dark souls' (Khan 2002a: 209 [Poetry 8])

In principle the linker may assimilate to the first consonant of the secondary. One such example may be the following:

(51) Qaraqosh: **Noun–Noun**
ʾén-ə n= náša
eye-FREE.PL LNK= man
'the eyes of a man' (Khan 2002a: 208 [B:127])

This analysis relies on the possible identification of the suffix *-ə* as a plural free state ending. Yet as this kind of assimilation normally happens in "fast speech" (Khan 2002a: 208), it is rather more probable that such examples should be understood as cases of the CSC, with a re-syllabified suffix *-əd*, similarly to example (24) on page 158 .

When the secondary is a pronoun realised as a pronominal suffix, the linker takes the form *did-~dəd-*.[13] These forms are mostly used with those Arabic loanwords which cannot be inflected directly with the possessive pronominal suffixes (for which see §6.1):[14]

(52) Qaraqosh: **Noun–Pronoun**
tarkíz dìd-əḥ'
concentration LNK-POSS.3MS
'his concentration' (Khan 2002a: 271 [F:47])

[13] The vowels [i] and [ə] are in allophonic complementary distribution, depending on the syllable structure. The latter is used in closed syllables.

[14] From a typological point of view, the linker qualifies as being a POSSESSIVE NOUN in the sense of Bickel & Nichols (2013), which is an "abstract or generic noun [that] is put in apposition to the semantically possessed non-possessible [primary noun]". Thus, one could add Qaraqosh to the very short list of languages having exactly one possessive noun. It would moreover be the first identified possessive noun in Eurasia.

(53) Qaraqosh: **Noun–Pronoun**
ʾaṭfāl= dìd-əḥ
children= LNK-POSS.3MS
'his children' (Khan 2002a: 271 [B:22])

In one case, the linker is doubled before a possessive suffix. This may be due to an ad-hoc re-analysis of the LNK+POSS construction as a genitive pronoun, which is compatible with a preceding linker (see general discussion in §10.6.1):

(54) Qaraqosh: **Noun–Pronoun**
šúrṭa də= də̀d-xu'
police LNK= LNK-POSS.2PL
'your police' (Khan 2002a: 271 [F:77])

As expected from a *pronominal* linker, the linker phrase has a certain prosodic and syntactic autonomy vis-à-vis the primary. The primary and secondary can be separated prosodically (see example (50) on the preceding page) and by intervening material:

(55) Qaraqosh: **Noun–Noun**
(ʾu= ʾə́t-lə) bàlṭat k-ămí-hə,' ʾəd= xàšab'
and= EX-3MS knives IND-call.A3PL-P3MS LNK= wood
'It has "knives" – so they call it – of wood.' (Khan 2002a: 278 (14) [K:28])

Of interest is also the possibility to negate the linker, thus denying the existence of the specified primary. Note also in this case the repetition of the linker before each conjoint secondary:

(56) Qaraqosh: **Negated noun–Conjoined nouns**
(lá pəšlí= b-ə) qàtta,' lá d= xəṭṭíθa= w lá d= sʾə̀rta.'
NEG remain= in-3MS stick NEG LNK= wheat= and NEG LNK= barley
'No stick remains in it, neither of wheat nor of barley.' (Khan 2002a: 277 (4) [B:62])

In the following poetic example, two linker phrases are topicalised before their primaries. For clarity, the secondaries and primaries are marked with corresponding subscripts in the glosses, while the translation follows the normal English word-order:

(57) Qaraqosh: **Noun–Noun**
də= rəxmúθa k-ó̱da ʾìḏa,ˈ màθ-an,ˈ ʾu= də= šláma
LNK= love$_Y$ IND-do festival$_X$ village-POSS.1PL and= LNK= peace$_Y$
k-péša yawə̀ntaˈ
IND-become dove$_X$
'It makes a festival of love, our town, and becomes a dove of peace' (Khan 2002a: 278 (11) [Poetry 18])

Finally, whenever the primary consists of a noun qualified by an adjective, the ALC is regularly used. This can be contrasted with the situation in JZakho, in which the CSC is available in such cases; see example (7) on page 117.

(58) Qaraqosh: **Noun Phrase–Noun**
[qála ṣə́pya] də= zamìraˈ
sound pure LNK= pipe
'with the pure sound of the pipe' (Khan 2002a: 278 (9) [Poetry 2])

(59) Qaraqosh: **Noun Phrase–Pronoun**
[béθa rába] díd-əḥ
house big LNK-POSS.3MS
'his big house' (Khan 2002a: 271)

With a pronominal secondary, an alternative formulation is possible, with the adjective following the possessive suffix; see example (4) on page 152.[15]

6.3.2 Verbal nouns as primaries

Recall that verbal nouns are nouns which can form a verbal construction, typically infinitives and participles.

As the following examples show, infinitives as well as active participles can be complemented by their object by means of the ALC:

[15] In CAradhin one finds a similar alternative construction, making use additionally of the linker:

(i) CAradhin: **Noun Phrase–Adjective**
qalp-e dīy-e aw zȧra
hull-POSS.3MS LNK-POSS.3MS DEF yellow
'Its yellow hull' (Krotkoff 1982: 22 [19])

(60) Qaraqosh: **Infinitive–Noun (object)**
(ʾu= k-óḏi) palóʾə d= əxàlaʾ
and= IND-do.3PL share.INF LNK= food
'They make a division of food.[16]' (Khan 2002a: 369 (10) [K:10])

(61) Qaraqosh: **Participle–Noun (object)**
mšadr-an-íθa də= šlìḥəʾ
send-PTCP-FS LNK= apostles
'the sender of the apostles' (Khan 2002a: 368 (1) [Play 111])

6.3.3 Clausal secondaries

The ALC is also compatible with clausal secondaries:

(62) Qaraqosh: **Noun–Clause**
léša də= k-óḏ-ax áxni làxma mə́nn-əḥ
dough LNK= IND-do-1PL 1PL bread from-3MS
'dough from which we make bread' (Khan 2002a: 209 [K:22])

(63) Qaraqosh: **Noun–Clause**
ʾəb= máya ʾəd= iyéwa sə̀ryəʾ
in= water LNK= COP.PST dirty
'in water that was dirty' (Khan 2002a: 476 (11) [K:12])

As these examples show, the linker is often followed directly by a verb or a copula.

In case of conjoined attributive clauses, the linker can be repeated:

(64) Qaraqosh: **Noun–Conjoined Clauses**
súsə d= àxəlʾ gúrgur= u maràqa =wʾ d= sátə ʿəràqʾ
horse LNK= eat burghul= and soup =and LNK= drink araq
'a horse that eats burghul and soup and drinks arak' (Khan 2002a: 475 (8) [F:79])

[16]This example appears as such in the transcribed corpus, but in the recording the speaker is saying *muqāsam-əd əxala* 'division.CST food', using the Arabic loanword *muqāsama*. Indeed, the apparent usage in the transcription of an Aramaic infinitive as a complement of a light verb is quite odd.

As we have seen above in the context of nominal secondaries, the linker phrase can be separated from its primary, in line with the pronominal nature of the linker.

(65) Qaraqosh: **Noun–Clause**
ʾu= nášə makìx= iyewa d= g-ʿéši bgáw-aḥ'
and= people simple= COP.PST LNK= ind-live.3PL in-3FS
'and the people were simple, those who lived in it' (Khan 2002a: 475)

In some cases a pronoun, either interrogative or demonstrative, is inserted between the primary noun and the linker. This pronoun should be understood as standing in apposition to both elements.

(66) Qaraqosh: **Noun Phrase–Clause**
fa= ʾáwwal mə́ndi ma= də= k-òḏi'
and= first thing what= LNK= IND-do.3PL
'the first thing they do' (Khan 2002a: 482 (21) [S:52])

(67) Qaraqosh: **Noun–Clause**
há dúkθa ʾéka d= íwa də́rya gàw-aḥ.'
behold place where LNK= COP.PST laid.RES in-3FS
'Behold the place where he was laid.' (Khan 2002a: 482 (22) [Gospel 25 = Mark 16:6])

When a demonstrative pronoun is used, it usually follows a prosodic break:

(68) Qaraqosh: **Noun–Clause**
ʾu= ʾə́tlan biráθa Bağdédə,' ʾán də= k-maʾtəmdì-wa'
and= EX-1PL wells B. DEM.PL LNK= IND-depend.3PL-PST
ġdedàyə'
B._inhabitants
'And we have wells in Qaraqosh, upon which the inhabitants depended.' (Khan 2002a: 369 (5) [K:87])

As in Syriac (see §3.5.2), the particle *d-* is used also as a complementizer. While such a usage may resemble formally an AC without a primary (see §6.3.7), the syntactic function of this *d-* is different, as it introduces a clausal complement of a verb (but see footnote 30 on page 68).

(69) Qaraqosh: **Verb–Clause**
*ʾáxni g-báʾax d= šákxax l= àne*ˈ
1PL IND-want.1PL COMP= complain.1PL about= DEM.DIST.PL
'We want to complain concerning those people.' (Khan 2002a: 505 (1) [F:73])

As a complementizer, *d-* can also introduce an adverbial purpose clause.

(70) Qaraqosh: **Verb–Clause**
*daré-wa-l tàma,*ˈ *ʾəd= yàwəš*ˈ
put.A3PL-PST-P3MS there COMP= dry.3MS
'They used to put it there to dry.' (Khan 2002a: 494 (8) [K:52])

6.3.4 Adverbial primaries

The *d-* morpheme is used following adverbials serving as conjunctions, i.e. complemented by a clause. Superficially, these constructions may be assimilated to the ALC with clausal secondaries discussed above. Yet as the *d-* in such cases cannot be said to represent pronominally the conjunction, I prefer to analyse the *d-* morpheme in this position as a complementizer, as in examples (69)–(70) on this page.

(71) Qaraqosh: **Conjunction–Clause**
*hál də= mṭíhə lə́= ġḏa dúka (ʿamùqt= ela)*ˈ
until COMP= arrived.3PL to= INDF.FS place deep= COP
'until they arrived at a place (that was deep).' (Khan 2002a: 477 (10) [S:26])

(72) Qaraqosh: **Conjunction–Clause**
*hál dəd= ʾáθə ʾìḏa*ˈ
until COMP= SBJV.come festival
'until the festival came' (Khan 2002a: 494 (8) [K:52])

The principal difference between a linker and a complementizer in the current framework is that a linker stands in apposition to its primary, while the complementizer is governed by the conjunction. This is represented schematically in Table 6.1.

In some respects, however, the complementizer *d-* is quite similar to the linker *d-*. For instance, with conjoined complement clauses, it can be repeated before

Table 6.1: Complementizer and linker constructions

Conj.	↦	[COMP	↦	Clause]
Noun	↔	[LNK	↦	Clause]

each conjoint (compare the structure to example (64) on page 168). Note also the variation between the forms *dəd* and *d-*.

(73) Qaraqosh: **Conjunction–Conjoined Clauses**
ʾə́mma dəd= k-oḏí-la b= idàθθə' wa= də= g-dáre tùma
when COMP= IND-do.A3PL-P3FS in= hands and= COMP= ind-put garlic
bgáw-aḥ'
in-3FS
'when they make it with their hands and put garlic in it' (Khan 2002a: 488 (5) [S:77])

Other data also support the idea that the difference between the complementizer *d-* and the linker *d-* is not so great. This is the case when the interrogative pronoun *ma* 'what' is inserted between the conjunction and the *d-* morpheme.[17] In such cases, it is possible to analyse the *d-* as a linker whose antecedent is the interrogative pronoun:

(74) Qaraqosh: **Pronoun–Clause**
ʾəm= qámə má d= yadə̀ʾ-la'
from= before what LNK= know-P3FS
'before he knew her' (Khan 2002a: 492 (3) [Gospel 1 = Matthew 1:18])

In such cases the conjunction governs the interrogative pronoun, which in turn stands in apposition to the linker. The apposition between the interrogative pronoun and the linker can be deduced from cases in which the linker is absent:

(75) Qaraqosh: **Pronoun–Clause**
m= qámə ma= máṭax ʾəl=[18] *Már Qurṭàya*
from= before what= reach.1PL to= M. Q.
'before we reach (the monastery) of Saint Q.' (Khan 2002a: 492 (2) [K:79])

[17]Functionally, *ma* does not serve here as an interrogative pronoun, but rather as a kind of indefinite pronoun, representing the event described in the complement clause.

[18]The preposition *ʾəl*, absent in the original transcript, can be heard in the recording. This is immaterial to the current discussion.

The two possibilities are represented schematically in Table 6.2:.

Table 6.2: Combinations of conjunctions and interrogative pronouns

Conj. $\mapsto$ Intrg.	$\leftrightarrow$	[LNK	$\mapsto$ Clause]
Conj. $\mapsto$ Intrg.		$\mapsto$	Clause

In contrast to conjunctions, prepositions cannot in general be followed by a *d-* morpheme, neither as a linker nor as a complementizer. Examples where this seems to be the case were analysed above as CST-marked prepositions where the *-d* suffix was resyllabified with the secondary; see examples (31)–(34) on page 159. There is, however, one case which cannot be explained in this way, due to the conservation of the final /*-a*/ vowel at the end of the preposition, which excludes the occurrence of an *-əd* suffix. This is the case of the preposition *eka* 'at':

(76) Qaraqosh: **Preposition–Noun**
ʾeka= d= áwa xána xə̀nna
at= GEN(?)= DEM.DIST.MS square(FS) other.MS
'in the other square' (Khan 2002a: 234 [B:186])

Such cases may arise by analogy to the above mentioned examples, and may represent the first signs of an emerging genitive marker.

6.3.5 Adjectival primaries

In one instance, an adjectival primary is modified by a noun with the aid of the linker. The construction is similar to the IMPURE ANNEXATION of Arabic, except for the fact that linker replaces the construct state marking of the primary present in Arabic (contrast with example (35) on page 161, and the Arabic example given there).

(77) Qaraqosh: **Adjective–Noun**
xlíθ-i smóqta də= pàθa'
sweet.FS-POSS.1SG red.FS LNK= face
'my rosy-faced sweet-heart' (Khan 2002a: 281 [Poetry 3])

6.3.6 Pronominal primaries

There are some cases of pronominal primaries in the ALC. According to my survey, in such cases the secondary is always clausal. The analysis of these cases as representing the ALC rather than the CSC relies on the fact the final vowel of the primary noun is not altered, and moreover the /*d*/ marker cannot be said to replace a free state suffix. Yet from a prosodic point of view the distinction is quite fuzzy, as the /*d*/ segment is often syllabified with the pronominal primary.

Different types of pronouns can act as primaries. Among these are personal pronouns, as in the following example:

(78) Qaraqosh: **Pronoun–Clause**
w= áhu d= là g-laqə́m-wa'
and= 3MS LNK= NEG IND-catch-PST
'anyone who did not catch it' (Khan 2002a: 479 (1) [B:172])

Interrogative pronouns are quite common:

(79) Qaraqosh: **Pronoun–Clause**
ʾu= šqə́lhə ma= d= šqə́lhə m= Baġdèdə.'
and= took.3PL what= LNK= took.3PL from= B.
'And they took what they took from Qaraqosh.' (Khan 2002a: 480 (1) [F:4])

(80) Qaraqosh: **Pronoun–Clause**
w= éma d= g-laqə́m-wa ʾá̱di qátta zùrta'
and= which LNK= IND-catch-PST DEM stick small
'whichever (person) caught the small stick' (Khan 2002a: 480 (7) [B:172])

When the initial pronoun is a demonstrative pronoun, two analyses are possible. Either the demonstrative is seen as the primary element, as in the preceding examples, or it is analysed as determiner, in which case there is no primary (its absence is marked by a ∅below). The latter analysis is possible since the linker acts as a syntactic head, due to its pronominal nature. Recall that such an analysis was suggested for JZakho, in which phonologically reduced demonstratives serve as determiners (see §5.4.6).

(81) Qaraqosh: **Pronoun/∅–Clause**
ʾá̱da {∅} d= ilə mənn-àḥ'
DEM.MS {∅} LNK= COP with-3FS
'The one who is with her' (Khan 2002a: 479 (3) [Play 17])

Interesting to note is a short version of the plural demonstrative *anə*, which resembles the determiner of JZakho (see also example (68) on page 169):[19]

(82) Qaraqosh: **Pronoun/∅–Clause**
ʾan {∅} də= g-náṭri xə̀θna'
DEM.PL {∅} LNK= IND-guard.PL groom
'Those who look after the groom' (Khan 2002a: 479 (7) [K:44])

Similar analytical difficulty is present in the case of the element *xa*, which can be interpreted either as an indefinite pronoun or an indefinite determiner. Yet in the following example, the fact that *xa* follows the quantifier *ay* 'any' (borrowed from Arabic) renders the pronominal interpretation more plausible (compare with JZakho example (70) on page 134). Be it as it may, both possibilities are given in the glossing below:

(83) Qaraqosh: **Pronoun/∅–Clause**
ʾáy= xa {∅} d= ílə márʾa ḥabábə'
any= INDF.PRO/DET {∅} LNK= COP ill pustules
'anyone who is ill with pustules' (Khan 2002a: 479 (1) [S:16])

It should be noted, moreover, that a determiner category has not been posited by Khan for Qaraqosh. The analysis required to establish the existence of such a category is outside the scope of the work, and therefore I leave the two possibilities open.

6.3.7 Linkers without an explicit primary

In subject position, cases of the ALC without a preceding primary are quite rare, and seem to be restricted to formal genres. Such are example (57) on page 167, where the (semantic) primary appears after the construction, as well as the following example, where no primary appears at all (=example (3) on page 97). For convenience, the place of the absent primary is marked by the symbol ∅, without implying the existence of a ∅ morpheme there.

(84) Qaraqosh: **∅–Noun**
kə-mzámri ∅ də= ʾurxàθa.'
IND-sing.3PL ∅ LNK= roads
'(The people) of the roads sing.' (Khan 2002a: 279 (21) [Poetry 29])

[19]Khan (2002a: 82) explains that "[t]he final /ə/ may be elided altogether when the pronoun is closely connected to what follows by the relative particle *d-*". See also footnote 64 on page 324.

A similar example is attested in the Gospels translation, with a clausal secondary:

(85) Qaraqosh: ∅–**Clause**
(əmbùrx =elə) ∅ d= áte b= šə́mm-əḥ əd= rább-i.'
blessed =COP ∅ LNK= come.3MS in= name-POSS.3MS LNK= lord-POSS.1SG
'Blessed is he who comes in the name of the Lord.' (Khan 2002a: 482 (1) [Gospel 19 = Matthew 23:29])

Clausal secondaries following a linker without an immediate primary occur rarely also in cleft sentences.

(86) Qaraqosh: ∅–**Clause**
ʾu= ʾàḏe =l ∅ d= k-oḏí-la da= gùpta.'
and= DEM.PROX.MS =COP ∅ LNK= IND-make.A3PL-P3FS into= cheese
'It is this that they make into cheese.' (Khan 2002a: 508 (2) [S:73])

As a predicate, on the other hand, a linker phrase can easily appear without an immediate primary (as the latter is typically mentioned in the subject position). The predicate position is easily recognized as it is normally marked by a following copula.

(87) Qaraqosh: ∅–**Noun**
fá ʾáḏa pàšmaʾ ∅ ʾəs= sáw-i =iwa.'
and DEM.PROX.MS garment ∅ LNK= grandfather-POSS.1SG =COP.PST
'This *pašma* belonged to my grandfather.' (Khan 2002a: 279 (16) [F:112])

(88) Qaraqosh: ∅–**Noun**
ʾáhi ʾiyáwa ∅ d= ʾə̀zla.'
3FS 3FS.COP.PST ∅ LNK= wool
'It was of wool.' (Khan 2002a: 279 (18) [K:29])

(89) Qaraqosh: ∅–**Pronoun**
ʾəxála lélə ∅ dìd-ux.' kása lélə ∅ dìd-ux?'
food NEG.COP ∅ LNK-POSS.2MS stomach NEG.COP ∅ LNK-POSS.2MS
'The food is not yours, but the stomach is indeed yours!' (Khan 2002a: 273 (10) [Proverbs 11])

Occasionally a nominal subject acting as primary is lacking altogether in the sentence, though it appears in the textual context. Such are the following examples, the first one being poetic:

(90) Qaraqosh: ∅–**Noun**
bəd-péša ∅ *d=* *rəxmùθa'* *'u=* ∅ *d=* *bəsmúθa* *'u=* *bənyànə.'*
FUT-become.FS ∅ LNK= love and= ∅ LNK= delight and= buildings
'It will become (a town) of love, delight and buildings.' (Khan 2002a: 279 (20) [Poetry 4])

(91) Qaraqosh: ∅–**Pronoun**
∅ *dìd-an* *=ina'*
∅ LNK-POSS.1PL =COP.3PL
'They are ours.' (Khan 2002a: 273 (9) [S:49])

6.3.8 Ordinal secondaries

Ordinals are regularly formed by placing cardinal numerals as secondaries of the ALC. These agree with the primary noun, possibly by analogy with adjectives (see example (108) on page 180), though morphologically the agreement pattern is different:

(92) Qaraqosh: **Noun–Ordinal**
góra d= *tré*
man LNK= second.MS
'the second man' (Khan 2002a: 225)

(93) Qaraqosh: **Noun–Ordinal**
báxta *d=* *tə́ttə*
woman LNK= second.FS
'the second woman' (Khan 2002a: 225)

This construction, however, is often avoided in favour of the construction using borrowed Arabic numerals, as in examples (110)–(111) on page 181.

6.4 Double-marking constructions

6.4.1 Simple double-marking (X.CST LNK Y)

The occurrence of an AC marked both by a construct state suffix and a linker happens mostly due to hesitation according to Khan (2002a: 208). The following examples illustrate this (the ... sign signals the hesitation):

(94) Qaraqosh: **Noun–Noun**
šə́kl-əd ... d= fàrwa
form-CST ... LNK= fur
'the form of a fur' (Khan 2002a: 208 [K:17])

(95) Qaraqosh: **Noun–Noun**
ʾarút-əd ... də-ḥàša
Friday-CST ... LNK= suffering
'Good Friday' (Khan 2002a: 208 [K:77])

(96) Qaraqosh: **Infinitive–Noun (object)**
(ʾáhu kə-mšaġə́l-wa bə=) raqóʾ-əd ... ʾəd qòndarat'
3MS IND-work-PST in= sew.INF ... LNK shoes
'He used to work at the making of shoes.' (Khan 2002a: 369 (4) [K:50])

(97) Qaraqosh: **Infinitive–Noun (object)**
ʾəl= ʾastòy-əd' ... də= [wánat də́t-te ʾu= nàšə']
to= drink.CAUS.INF-CST ... LNK= sheep LNK-POSS.3PL and= people
'to provide drinks for their sheep and for people' (Khan 2002a: 369 (5) [K:87])

(98) Qaraqosh: **Pronoun–Noun**
(ʾu= k-zálan əg-máṭax) hál ékəd ... ʾəd= ʾàrʾa'
and= IND-go.1PL IND-reach.1PL until where-CST ... LNK= land
'We go until we reach the land.' (Khan 2002a: 390 (19) [K:78])

Indeed, even when there is no hesitation sign in the transcribed corpus, listening to the examples reveals a hesitation, which I have marked in the following examples:[20]

(99) Qaraqosh: **Noun–Clause**
əl= ʾén-əd ... də= kə- ... masxé-wa-la qadə́šta Sàra
to= spring-CST ... LNK= IND- ... make_swim.3PL-PST-3FS St. S.
'to the spring in which they made Saint Sarah swim' (Khan 2002a: 209 [K:12])

[20] Recall that only the recordings of informant K are publicly available.

(100) Qaraqosh: **Adverbial–Pronoun**
(yəʾə̀l-wa-la káθlaka ʾə̀ll-aḥ') ... ʿan= ṭarìq-əd[21] *... ʿan= ʾùrx-əd*
entered-PST-3FS Catholicism to-3FS ... by= way-CST ... by= way-CST
...' də̀= xxa' (šə̀mm-əḥ' ... Már Yoḥánna Dilèmi.')
... LNK= one name-POSS.3MS ... M. Y. D.
'(Catholicism entered it) by means of one (whose name is Mar Yoḥanna Dilemi.)' (Khan 2002a: 479 (2) [K:1])

Of special interest are cases where the primary noun is the reflex of an historical construct state form, i.e. without a /-d/ suffix. This shows that it is not a simple repetition of the /d/ segment:

(101) Qaraqosh: **Noun–Noun**
ʾu= bí ... d= Aqlìmus.'
and= house.CST ... LNK= A.
'and the family of Aqlimus.' (Khan 2002a: 544 [K:18])

All these cases can be analysed as instances of two appositive ACs, in which the first one is lacking a secondary, due to a difficulty of the speaker.

Table 6.3: Appositive repetition of an AC due to hesitation

Primary		Secondary
X	↦	...
↕		↕
LNK	↦	Y

However, the same construction is used "sporadically", according to Khan, also where no hesitation is present (I could not verify this by listening to these examples):

(102) Qaraqosh: **Noun–Noun**
b= paqárt-əd d= áne ḥawāwìn
in= neck-CST LNK= DEM.DIST.PL animals
'on the neck of those animals' (Khan 2002a: 208 [B:72])

[21]The words *ʿan ṭarìq-əd* are not present in the transcript, but are clearly audible in the recording. Indeed, the speaker first uses the Arabic loan-expression *ʿan ṭarīq* with an Aramaic construct state suffix, before correcting to the native Aramaic word *ʾurxa* (but still employing the Arabic preposition *ʿan*).

(103) Qaraqosh: **Infinitive–Noun**
dyáq-t-ət *də=* *ləbbawàθa*
beat.INF-FS-CST LNK= hearts
'the beating of hearts' (Khan 2002a: 208 [Poetry 14])

The first case may be explained by the emergence of a GENITIVE marker before a demonstrative pronoun (see examples (32)–(34) on page 160 for a discussion, as well as example (76) on page 172), while the second one is taken from a poetic text, which may explain its peculiar syntax.[22] Two other cases which Khan (2002a: 209) mentions as repetition of the /*d*/ particle are simply cases where the /*dəd*/ allomorph of the linker is used (see example (50) on page 165).

Another exceptional case of seemingly double marking is the following example, in which the primary is marked by a /*-ə*/ suffix, while the secondary is marked by the /*ʾəd*/ allomorph of the linker. Although it resembles cases of a re-syllabified construct state suffix (see examples (20)–(24) on page 157), it differs from them by the intervening glottal stop. Again, the poetic origin of this example may explain its peculiar morpho-phonology.[23]

(104) Qaraqosh: **Noun–Noun**
máθ-ə *ʾəd=* *dérə* *ʾu=* *ʾitàθa*
town-CST LNK= monasteries and= churches
'town of monasteries and churches' (Khan 2002a: 208 [Poetry 17])

To summarize, the cases of double marking which are not motivated by difficulties in production (i.e. hesitation) are highly exceptional.

6.4.2 The double annexation construction (X-y.POSS LNK Y)

Another type of double marking, which occurs only in the Gospel translations, arises from a direct translation of the Syriac double annexation construction (see §3.6).

[22]It is also possible that the linker is in fact a resyllabified construct state suffix. If this is true, the doubling of the /*d*/ segment may be explained by the phonological constraint of conserving the short [ə] vowel in a closed syllable. Note that the schwa cannot be elided (as is sometimes the case), since it follows a consonant cluster in both cases.

[23]The sources marked as Poetry are transcriptions of recitations of poems, which may obey specific metrical rules, on the one hand, or try to imitate a classical syntax, on the other hand.

(105) Qaraqosh: **Noun–Noun**
Yósəf ʾə́br-əḥ əd= Dawìd'
Y. son-POSS.3MS LNK= D.
'Joseph, the son of David' (Khan 2002a: 279 (22) [Gospel 3 = Matthew 1:20)

6.5 Juxtaposition (X Y.{AGR})

Juxtaposition in principle does not serve as an AC in Qaraqosh, as it cannot be used to modify a noun by a noun.[24] However, it is used in some tangential cases:

6.5.1 Adjectival modification: Juxtaposition-cum-agreement

Adjectives follow their primary, and – if inflecting – agree in number (and possibly in gender) with it, forming effectively a juxtaposition-cum-agreement construction:

(106) Qaraqosh: **Noun–Adjective**
'ənšə surayə
women Christian.PL
'Christian women' (Khan 2002a: 212)

(107) Qaraqosh: **Noun–Adjective**
baxta bāš
woman good(INV)
'a good woman' (Khan 2002a: 220)

The ordinal 'first' behaves as an adjective:

(108) Qaraqosh: **Noun–Ordinal (first)**
báxta qaméθa
woman first.FS
'the first woman' (Khan 2002a: 225)

[24] A possible exception is the phrase *ḥǔkum Qaraqòš* 'the governance of Qaraqosh' (Khan 2002a: 3; 643 (83)), but the usage of the Arabic name of Qaraqosh indicates that the entire expression is borrowed from Arabic.

In some cases an adjective can precede the primary.[25] This is the case for the Kurdish-borrowed adjective *xoš* 'good' which occurs regularly before the noun, as in the following example:[26]

(109) Qaraqosh: **Noun–Adjective**
*xóš ʾəmmàθa*ˈ
good(INV) mothers
'good mothers' (Khan 2002a: 281 [Play 120])

Arabic ordinals, used often instead of the Aramaic equivalents, are regularly placed before their nominal primaries, mirroring the Arabic construction (contrast with examples (92)–(93) on page 176 as well as (108) on the facing page):[27]

(110) Qaraqosh: **Noun–Ordinal (first)**
ʾawwal yoma
first day
'the first day' (Khan 2002a: 516)

(111) Qaraqosh: **Noun–Ordinal**
ʾu= θáləθ yóma
and= third day
'the third day' (Khan 2002a: 640 [F:72])

The word *xənna* 'other', although semantically not a typical adjective[28] behaves syntactically as one insofar it agrees with the modified noun in number and gender. Unlike typical adjectives, however, it may variably appear before or after the noun (compare to example (39) on page 162).

(112) Qaraqosh: **Noun–Adjective**
(ʾə́t-lan) xə́rta ṭaʿólta
EX-1PL other.FS game
'(We have) another game.' (Khan 2002a: 285 [K:35])

[25]Recall that the titles of the examples always follow the order **Primary-Secondary**.

[26]This adjective shows also exceptional order in Kurdish, which normally has post-nominal adjectives. Its irregular syntax is due to the fact that it originates in Turkic languages (Turkish *hoş*, Azeri *xoş*), which regularly have pre-nominal adjectives.

[27]In Arabic, the numeral is formally in construct state, but this is no longer apparent in the borrowed expression.

[28]Unlike a typical adjective, it does not refer to an attribute (i.e., quality) of the referent, but rather signals that it is different from a similar previously-mentioned referent. Indeed, Khan (2002a: 285) classifies it as a "non-attributive modifier".

Finally, "emotionally charged" adjectives may appear before their noun. This is possible related to the emotive genitive construction shown in examples (36)–(37) on page 161:

(113) Qaraqosh: **Noun–Adjective**
məskín-ə ġdedáy-ə
poor-PL inhabitants-PL
'the poor inhabitants of Qaraqosh' (Khan 2002a: 281 [B:68])

6.5.2 Adverbial primaries

Most adverbials attach to their complements without any special marking. Compare the following example to example (34) on page 160:

(114) Qaraqosh: **Preposition–Noun**
máx [tóbba zùrta]
like ball(FS) small.FS
'like a small ball [K:31]' (Khan 2002a: 238)

Note also the following example, in which the preposition is directly followed by a vowel-initial demonstrative pronoun (with an epenthetic glottal stop), without any special marking (unlike in JZakho, where it would take genitive marking):

(115) Qaraqosh: **Preposition–Noun**
(zə́l-le) hál ʾáya máθa
went-3MS until DEM.DIST.FS village
'He went as far as that village' (Khan 2002a: 235)

A preposition may appear unstressed and cliticize to its complement:

(116) Qaraqosh: **Preposition–Noun**
ʾeka= nəšwàθa
at= relatives
'at the home of relatives' (Khan 2002a: 234 [K:5])

(117) Qaraqosh: **Preposition–Adverb**
mən= táma
from= there
'from there' (Khan 2002a: 238 [F:86])

(118) Qaraqosh: **Preposition–Adverb**
hal= daha
until= now
'until now' (Khan 2002a: 235 [K:87])

Conjunctions can also precede their clausal complement without any special marking. Such cases may be assimilated to asyndetic attributive clauses (see §6.5.4), but have a wider distribution (contrast with example (73) on page 171):

(119) Qaraqosh: **Conjunction–Clause**
fa= ʾə́mma zálh= ắmi da= sàw-i'
and= when go.3PL= say.3PL to= grandfather-POSS.1SG
'and, when they go and tell my grandfather' (Khan 2002a: 489 (12) [F:25])

6.5.3 Infinitival primaries

The complement of an infinitive may be attached to it without any marking (contrast with examples (44)–(46) on page 163 showing the CSC and example (60) on page 168 exhibiting the ALC, as well as the doubly-marked examples (96)–(97) on page 177):

(120) Qaraqosh: **Infinitive–Noun (object)**
(xálṣi) wáḏa ay= ràqqə'
finish.3PL do.INF DEM.PROX= dish
'They finish making those *raqqe*.' (Khan 2002a: 369 (6) [B:134])

6.5.4 Clausal secondaries

Certain restrictive clausal secondaries may follow their primary without any marking. This occurs exclusively with indefinite primary nouns. It may allude to Arabic influence, which has a similar distribution of asyndetic relative clauses only after indefinite primaries. Judging by the examples given by Khan (2002a: 477) such examples occur most frequently when the matrix-clause is an existential clause.

(121) Qaraqosh: **Noun–Clause**
ʾə́t-lan ʾəxálta k-amáx-la harìsa.'
EX-1PL dish IND-say.A1PL-P3FS harisa
'We have a dish called *harisa*.' (Khan 2002a: 477 (9) [K:62])

One exceptional case is the following (the second half of example (71) on page 170):

(122) Qaraqosh: **Preposition–Clause**
lə́= ġḏa dúka ʿamùqt= ela'
to= INDF.FS place deep= COP
'to a place that is deep' (Khan 2002a: 477 (10) [S:26])

Cases of attributive nominal clauses which lack a copula (similar to the NON-CLAUSAL ADJECTIVAL NEXUS of JZakho example (108) on page 145) also occur. Note that the subject of such attributive clauses is always definite by virtue of a possessive pronoun.

(123) Qaraqosh: **Noun–Clause**
ʾíθə náša lə́bb-əḥ níxa b= áḏa yòma?'
EX man heart-POSS.3MS content in= DEM.PROX.MS day
'Is there a person whose heart is content nowadays?' (Khan 2002a: 478 (14) [Play 96])

A similar example occurs with an indefinite pronominal primary *xa* (=end of example (100) on page 178):

(124) Qaraqosh: **Adverbial–Pronoun**
xa' šə̀mm-əḥ' Már Yoḥánna Dilèmi.'
one name-POSS.3MS M. Y. D.
'one whose name is Mar Y.D.' (Khan 2002a: 479 (2) [K:1])

6.6 Conclusions

The dialect of Qaraqosh has in principle two loci of marking: the primary (by the construct state *-əd* suffix) and the secondary (by the *d-* linker). The two strategies are in principle mutually exclusive, but in some peripheral cases they are used simultaneously, as explained in §6.4. The distinction, however, between the two types of marking is not always so clear, due to the frequent re-syllabification of the /*d*/ segment of the construct state suffix with vowel-initial secondaries. Since the emergence of the construct state suffix is related (at least partly) to the re-syllabification of the linker with the primary (see §10.4), the flux between the two constructions in Qaraqosh may be related to its conservative nature (Khan 2002a: 10).

An important source of impact on Qaraqosh is Arabic. Geographically, the town of Qaraqosh is located near the Arabic speaking regions of Iraq (only 32 km away from Mosul), and as such it is influenced by Arabic more than other dialects. While Khan (2002a: 9) claims that the Arabic influence is relatively recent, judging by the lexical material, we see that the dialect possess many constructions which are similar to Arabic ones. These include the replication of the Arabic *tāʾ marbūṭa* (example (5) on page 153), the Arabic adjectival AC (IMPURE ANNEXATION; example (35) on page 161 and example (77) on page 172), the integration of the Arabic nominal modifier *nafs* (see §6.2.5) and ordinal numbers (examples (110)–(111) on page 181) and possibly also asyndetic clausal secondaries (see §6.5.4). On the other hand, direct Kurdish influence is harder to pinpoint, except for the pre-nominal use of the Kurdish (originally Azeri) loan-adjective *xoš* 'good' (example (109) on page 181).

7 Attributive constructions in the Jewish dialect of Urmi

The data for JUrmi is based on two different sources: Garbell (1965b)[1] and Khan (2008b).[2] For consistency, I use the transcription system of Khan.[3] In citations of examples from Khan, the reference to the section number in the corpus is given in square brackets, when available.

The richest and most prominent attributive construction strategy of JUrmi is head-marking. Pronominal head marking is covered in §7.1 while the construct state construction is addressed at §7.2. There are reasons to believe that in JUrmi, unlike in JZakho and Qaraqosh, the construct state *-əd* suffix is a word-level inflectional suffix rather than a phrasal suffix.

Alongside the CSC one finds in JUrmi the analytic linker construction using an alternative linker form *ay* (see §7.3). Moreover, it differs from the typical ALC in that the primary is normally marked as construct state, making it a double-marked construction. Another additional marking is the usage of genitive marking, covered in §7.4, yielding triple-marked constructions. The classical double annexation construction, occurring rarely in JUrmi, is covered in §7.5.

The usage of the borrowed relativizer *ki* before clausal secondaries is discussed in §7.6. Finally, the use of juxtaposition is presented in §7.7. The usage of inverse juxtapositioninverse juxtaposition construction (where the secondary precedes

---

[1] Garbell's description covers several dialects of Iranian Azerbaijan as well as the neighbouring Turkish territory, which she divides into a northern group (JUrmi and neighbouring dialects) and a southern group (J. Solduz and Šĭno). The data used here is based on her description of the northern group, of which JUrmi is considered to be representative.

[2] I have also conducted fieldwork with Rabbi Ḥaim Yeshurun, a speaker of JUrmi currently living in Israel, and have consulted the corpus of Ben-Rahamim (2006). Though no examples from these sources are presented here, both Yeshurun and Ben-Rahamim's texts are in accordance, according to my examination, with the descriptions of Garbell and Khan, especially in what regards the AC system.

[3] Note especially the marking of velarized words by an initial ⁺ sign. In some examples I have added a missing velarization mark between parenthesis ⁽⁺⁾, when such a mark was justified according to the sources' lexica. Note that in Garbell's work, the lack of velarization may be due to dialectal variation, as her work describes several related dialects, as explained in footnote 1.

the primary) is presented in §7.8, together with the claim that it arose due to language contact.

7.1 Possessive pronominal suffixes (X-y.POSS)

In JUrmi, as in other North-Eastern Neo-Aramaic dialects, a possessive pronominal suffix can attach directly to a noun or to a preposition:

(1) JUrmi: **Noun–Pronoun**
bel-ew
house-POSS.3MS
'his house' (Khan 2008b: 56)

(2) JUrmi: **Preposition–Pronoun**
mənn-ew
from-POSS.3MS
'from him' (Khan 2008b: 196)

Two possessed nouns can sometimes be conjoined asyndetically, with the repetition of the possessive pronoun:

(3) JUrmi: **Asyndetically Conjoined Nouns–Pronoun**
da-ew dad-ew
mother-POSS.3MS father-POSS.3MS
'his parents' (Garbell 1965a: 171)

Garbell (1965a: 171, §2.32.11) attributes the availability of this constrution to Azeri influence: "On the border between syntactical and stylistical interference of T[urkish Azeri] with the dialect is the extremely frequent occurrence of two asyndetic heads in a nominal phrase, more often than not alliterative". She compares the above example to the following Azeri example:[4]

(4) Azeri: **Asyndetically Conjoined Nouns–Pronoun**
anna-si baba-si
mother-POSS.3SG father-POSS.3SG
'his parents' (Garbell 1965a: 171)

[4]The asyndetic construction is not limited to possessed nouns. Garbell (1965a: 171) gives also the Azeri example *gille glale* 'grasses strings, vegetation'.

7.2 The construct state construction (X.CST Y)

7.2.1 Introduction

JUrmi, like the NENA dialects surveyed in the previous chapters, has a suffixed construct state marker *-əd*, related to the Classical Aramaic linker *d-*. Garbell (1965a: 171) claims this "is clearly due to the impact of the K[urdish] relation suffix *-i* [=Ezafe]", an idea which is discussed in §10.4.2. The exact form of the suffix varies: Normally it is realised as */əd/*~*/ət/*, but following stems whose last vowel is */a/* it is optionally realised as */at/*~*/ad/* as in example (6) on the current page (Khan 2008b: 174), a phenomenon which may be attributed to local vowel harmony.[5]

(5) JUrmi: **Noun–Noun**
tar-əd bela
door-CST house
'the door of the house' (Khan 2008b: 174)

(6) JUrmi: **Noun–Noun**
⁺dá-ət/-at brona
mother-CST son
'the mother of the boy' (Khan 2008b: 174)

(7) JUrmi: **Noun–Noun**
gor-ət tre reše
man-CST two heads
'the man of two heads' (Garbell 1965b: 86)

In contrast to JZakho (example (7) on page 117) and Qaraqosh (example (26) on page 158), I could not find in my survey of JUrmi cases where an NP is marked phrase-finally by a single *-əd* suffix. Such cases seem to require the ALC (see §7.3). An apparent exception is example (32) on page 196, where a participial phrase is marked by a final *-əd* suffix. Yet this apparent phrasal-final marking is only possible since the participle itself is the last element of the phrase.[6] Another possible

[5]In this it may reflect some influence of Turkish, in which vowel harmony is abundant.

[6]In this I disagree with Khan (2008b: 230), who draws from this example the quite general conclusion that "[i]f the head of the annexation [the primary] consists of a phrase in which one noun is dependent on another, the annexation inflection is placed only on the head of this phrase".

deviation is shown in example (87) on page 211. There an optional construct state suffix appears phrase-finally on a noun itself serving as secondary of a CSC (thus not being the head of the NP). This may be explained as a product of a wrong bracketing of the expression, in analogy to an [x-*əd* [y-*əd* z]] expression (instead of the actual [[x-*əd* y] z] required by the semantics).

Notwithstanding these exceptional cases, in JUrmi it seems safe to analyse -*əd* as a word-level inflectional marker, rather than a phrasal suffix.[7] Such an analysis is corroborated by cases where two asyndetically conjoined nouns occur in the primary slot, and each is marked by an -*əd* suffix ((8)=example (13) on page 105):

(8) JUrmi: **Asyndetically Conjoined Nouns–Noun**
[id-əd reš-əd] gor-aw
hand-CST head-CST man-POSS.3FS
'the hands and head of her husband' (Garbell 1965b: 86)

(9) JUrmi: **Asyndetically Conjoined Nouns–Noun**
[naš-ət xəzmaw-ət] ⁺hatān
people-CST relatives-CST groom
'the family and relations of the bridegroom' (Garbell 1965b: 86)

From a language contact angle, one may relate such cases to the availability of asyndetic conjunction in JUrmi, which Garbell (1965a: 171) attributes to Azeri influence (see discussion of example (3) on page 188). While the asyndetic conjunction of nouns is not restricted to ACs, the repetition of the -*əd* suffix may facilitate the asyndetic conjunction, as the conjoined nouns are often alliterative in this construction. Note, moreover, that the -*əd* suffix seems to block the occurrence a coordinating conjunction following it.[8]

One finds asyndetic conjunction of nouns also in secondary position, as in the following example. Khan (2008b: 235) restricts the occurrence of asyndetic conjunction (whether in an AC or not) mainly to a "few sets of tightly-knit nouns".

(10) JUrmi: **Noun–Asyndetically Conjoined Nouns**
šúl-ət [góra baxtá]
affair-CST man woman
'the affairs of a husband and wife' (Khan 2008b: 230 [48])

[7] Cf. Garbell (1965b: 54, §2.12.2), who treats the construct state markers, both the -*əd* suffix and apocope, as "inflection in relation" of nouns.

[8] Judging by the few examples I have, the conjoined possessed nouns appear to be semantically inalienable nouns, but it is not clear whether this a real restriction of the construction.

7.2.2 Apocopate construct state marking

Alongside the suffixed construct state *-əd* morpheme, JUrmi can mark construct state nouns by means of apocope. In these nouns, the final free state vowel, typical of words of native Aramaic origin, is elided (see §11.1 for a discussion of the development of these forms).

(11) JUrmi: **Noun–Noun**
bron əčči šənne
son.CST sixty years
'a man 60 years old' (Garbell 1965b: 86)

In feminine nouns, except *brata* 'daughter', the feminine-gender marker *-t-*, is elided as well (Garbell 1965b: 55), unlike in the apocopate construct of Classical Aramaic. Contrast the following two examples:

(12) JUrmi: **Noun–Noun**
pqar ay d-o gora
neck.CST LNK GEN-DEM.DIST.MS man
'the neck of that man' (Garbell 1965b: 87)

(13) JUrmi: **Noun–Noun**
brā̆t ⁺šultanà
daughter.CST king
'the daughter of the king' (Khan 2008b: 175 [29])

Khan (2008b: 175) qualifies the occurrence of the apocopate CSC as happening "occasionally", and gives no semantic or functional qualifications of it. Garbell (1965b: 55) sees the apocope as a zero suffix being in free variation with the *-əd* suffix (the only restriction being that the stem should not end in a consonant cluster). Indeed, judging by the examples, the two types of marking are functionally equivalent, though the suffixed marking seems to be more frequent.

Prosodically, when the primary is marked by apocope, it is sometimes devoid of stress, and cliticizes to the secondary, as in the following example:

(14) JUrmi: **Noun–Noun**
tār= šəmmé
door.CST= heavens
'the door of heaven' (Khan 2008b: 175 [52])

Some nouns have an apocopate form which is not restricted to the contexts where one would expect a construct state noun (i.e., head of a CSC). Khan (2008b: 161) lists the nouns *naša* 'person' and *gaba* 'side' as having short variants *naš* and *gab* respectively, used "predominantly when they are indefinite". Diachronically, these apocopate forms may be derived from the absolute state, which was used in indefinite contexts (see §2.3.1). As it is hard to establish whether such forms should be analysed as marked for construct state when they serve as primaries, I have in general not analysed them as being marked for construct state.

7.2.3 Adjectival primaries

An adjective modified by a noun can appear as a primary of the CSC:

(15) JUrmi: **Adjective–Noun**
ó *⁺torbá* *⁺mlit-ə́t* *fəssé* *dehwé'*
DEM.DIST bag full.FS-CST money gold_piece.PL
'the bag full of gold coins' (Khan 2008b: 219 [60])

An adjective appearing in the primary position of the CSC followed by a plural noun yields a superlative meaning. The grammatical information regarding the referent (gender and number) is marked inflectionally on the adjective, which is the syntactic head. A similar construction is found JZakho (see example (32) on page 123).

(16) JUrmi: **Adjective–Noun**
sqəl-t-ət *niše*
beautiful-FS-CST women(PL)
'The most beautiful woman' (Garbell 1965b: 55)

7.2.4 Adverbial primaries

Some prepositions may be marked by the construct state suffix when they are complemented by a noun. Mostly this is optional (see §7.7.4 for examples), but for some prepositions it seems to be obligatory. Thus, the preposition *bod* 'because', adapted from the Kurdish preposition *bo* 'because', always appears with a construct state suffix *-d* (Garbell 1965a: 166).

(17) JUrmi: **Preposition–Noun**
gá-at Urmì
in-CST U.
'in Urmi' (Khan 2008b: 194 [136])

(18) JUrmi: **Preposition–Noun**
mənn-ət bela
from-CST house
'from the house' (Khan 2008b: 196)

(19) JUrmi: **Preposition–Asyndetically Conjoined Nouns**
bá-at [⁺kalo ⁺hatàn]
for-CST bride groom
'to the bride and groom' (Khan 2008b: 193 [93])

(20) JUrmi: **Preposition–Pronoun**
bo-d= ma
because-CST= what
'Why?' (Khan 2008b: 191)

Similarly, some conjunctions are in fact interrogative adverbs augmented with the construct state suffix (cf. examples (37)–(38) on page 197).

(21) JUrmi: **Conjunction–Clause**
kəmm-ə̀t ⁺məss-étun
how_much-CST can-2PL
'as much as you can' (Khan 2008b: 371 [67])

(22) JUrmi: **Conjunction–Clause**
imǎ̆n-ət àd-e
when-CST SBJV[9].come-3MS
'whenever he comes' (Khan 2008b: 372)

[9]The SBJV is marked by the lack of an indicative prefix *ad-* attached to the stem.

7.2.5 The pronominal primary *od*

In rare cases, the distal singular demonstrative pronoun *o* appears in the construct state form *od* after some prepositions, such as *bod* 'because' (itself marked obligatorily by the construct state suffix; see example (20) on the preceding page).[10] This pronoun allows the introduction of a clausal complement of the preposition (yielding an apparent composite conjunction *bod od*).

(23) JUrmi: **Pronoun–Clause**
bo-d= *ó-d* *hála zùrt* *=ela*
because-CST= DEM-CST still young =COP.FS
'because of the fact that she is still young' (Khan 2008b: 374 [74])

The construct state pronoun *od* is compatible with the relativizer, as is shown in examples (101)–(102) on page 215.

7.2.6 Pronominal, ordinal and adverbial secondaries

A pronoun can occupy the secondary slot. The following two examples present both the use of an indefinite (interrogative) pronoun and a definite (reflexive) pronoun in this position:

(24) JUrmi: **Noun–Pronoun**
bel-ət *mâni*
house-CST who
'whose house' (Garbell 1965b: 86)

(25) JUrmi: **Noun–Pronoun**
(g=) bel= *nòš-u*
in= house.CST= REFL-3PL
'(in) their own house' (Khan 2008b: 215 [158])

Modification by ordinal numerals uses the same construction, whether the numeral is marked by the ordinal suffix *-minji*,[11] or not:

[10] In this I agree with Khan (2008b: 374), but disagree with Garbell (1965b: 61) who sees the */od/* segment as an allomorph of the construct state ending.

[11] Garbell (1965a: 166, §1.22.3) explains this suffix is a combination of the Sorani (originally Persian) ordinal suffix *-emîn* and the Azeri ordinal suffix *-ji*.

(26) JUrmi: **Noun–Ordinal**
baxt-ət awwal
woman-CST first
'the first woman' (Khan 2008b: 187)

(27) JUrmi: **Noun–Ordinal**
yom-ət tre-mənji
day-CST two-ORD
'the second day' (Garbell 1965b: 86)

(28) JUrmi: **Noun–Ordinal**
bel-əd arbi =w xa
house-CST forty =and one
'the forty-first house' (Garbell 1965b: 86)

Adverbial modification (either by a PP or by an adverb) can also occur within this construction. While this is attested also in other dialects (see §5.3.1 on page 118 for JZakho examples), it seems to be more widespread in JUrmi:

(29) JUrmi: **Noun–Prepositional Phrase**
ktab-ət b= id-ew
book-CST in= hand-POSS.3MS
'the book in his hands' (Garbell 1965b: 87)

(30) JUrmi: **Noun–Adverb**
⁺qətt-ət təxya
piece-CST below
'lower piece' (Khan 2008b: 600)

(31) JUrmi: **Participle–Adverb**
⁺samx-an-ət tə́xya
stand-PTCP-CST below
'the one/those standing below' (Garbell 1965b: 84)

Note that the last example has a participle as its primary. Khan (2008b: 78) notes that normally the participle is used "as a noun or adjective describing a characteristic, time-stable property of a referent". This nominal character is retained also when participles are complemented by an object, as in the following example, which has a participial phrase as its primary (regarding the initial position of the complement, see §7.8.2).

(32) JUrmi: **Participial Phrase–Noun**
[ixala bašl-an-ət] *⁺sultana*
food cook-PTCP-CST king
'the king's cook (lit. "food cooker")' (Garbell 1965b: 86)

7.2.7 Clausal secondaries

Nouns in construct state may be followed by participial or infinitival phrases, which can be seen as reduced relative clauses (for the order of elements inside these phrases, see §7.8):

(33) JUrmi: **Noun–Participial phrase**
naš-ət *[bar-ew* *yarq-an-e]*
people-CST after-POSS.3MS run-PTCP-PL
'people that run after him' (Garbell 1965b: 87)

(34) JUrmi: **Noun–Infinitival Phrase**
bel-ət *[ixala bašole]*
house-CST food cook.INF
'house of food cooking, kitchen' (Garbell 1965b: 86)

A noun may also be complemented like this by a clause, but, according to Garbell (1965b: 88), only when the clause has no NP functioning as a subject argument (i.e., it has only the obligatory pronominal subject marking on the verb).[12]

(35) JUrmi: **Noun–Clause**
šat-ət *adya*
year-CST SBJV.come.3FS
'the coming year' (Garbell 1965b: 88)

[12] Garbell qualifies this type of clause as a VP, which implies that the subject suffix on the verb is merely an agreement marker. Note, however, that the subject of the embedded clause may be different than the primary noun, as in example (36) on the next page. The only restriction is that the subject must be expressed pronominally as a verbal suffix. See, however, example (39) on the facing page for a possible counter-example of Garbell's assertion.

(36) JUrmi: **Noun–Clause**
gor-ət [bron-ew ⁺qtə́l-wa-le]
man-CST son-POSS.3MS killed-PST-A3MS
'the man whose son he had killed' (Garbell 1965b: 88)

Note that in the last example, *bronew* 'his son' cannot be the subject of the clause due to the above-mentioned restriction on appearance of subject NPs in secondary clauses.

The interrogative pronouns *ma* 'what' and *măni* 'who' can also be complemented by a clause in this construction:

(37) JUrmi: **Pronoun–Clause**
má-t abyát
what-CST SBJV.want.2FS
'whatever you want' (Khan 2008b: 358 [10])

(38) JUrmi: **Pronoun–Clause**
mắni-t áde
who-CST SBJV.come.3MS
'whoever comes' (Khan 2008b: 357 [32])

Exhibiting such a primary, the following example shows that Garbell's above-mentioned restriction does not hold. This may be due to the fact that the construct state suffix has been grammaticalised into the primary pronoun, and is not felt any more as such. As the counter-example comes from Khan's description (about 40 years after Garbell's) it may reflect, moreover, a subtle language change.

(39) JUrmi: **Pronoun–Clause**
má-t nắš m= əlhá abè'
what-CST man from= God SBJV.want.3MS
'whatever a person wants from God' (Khan 2008b: 358 [109])

For the alternative strategy of using a relativizer, see §7.6.

7.3 The analytic linker construction (X LNK Y)

7.3.1 Introduction

JUrmi uses the morpheme *ay* as a linker, and not the inherited *d-* as do JZakho and Qaraqosh. It is identical in form to the singular proximal demonstrative *ay* (which Garbell 1965b: 58 qualifies as an "archaic" form), and very probably related to it diachronically, but, contrary to the latter, it does not inflect according to number. Nonetheless, in some cases it is difficult to decide between the two possible analyses (as example (73) on page 207 shows).

Garbell (1965a: 171) relates the linker *ay* to the "relational morpheme of [Kurdish, which] is likewise demonstrative in its origin". She notes moreover that in the related dialects of Southern Persian Azerbaijan, J. Solduz and Šĭno, the Sorani marker *i* is used in the same position. A similar suggestion is made by Khan (2008b: 176):

> It is likely to have developed under the influence of the *izafe* construction in Iranian languages. It appears not to be a direct loan from Iranian, in which the *izafe* is in principle monosyllabic (*e, i, a*), but rather an imitation of the *izafe* using Aramaic morphological material.

For an evaluation of these proposals see §10.6.4.

In general *ay* is an independent phonological word, as it carries stress. Quite often, however, it is found cliticized forward with the secondary or, sporadically, backward with the primary.[13] The latter possibility is especially frequent with adverbial primaries, which tend to cliticize forward on their own account (but see example (47) on page 200).

The pronominal origin of *ay*, and – more importantly – the fact that it can form an AC without an explicit primary (see §7.3.7), are the main motivations to analyse it as a pronominal linker, rather than a simple secondary marker. As such, it forms an independent syntactic (and sometimes prosodic) constituent with the secondary. From a comparative perspective, it may be seen as the functional equivalent of the *d-* or *did* linkers of other dialects. Yet in contrast to the dialects surveyed in the previous chapters, in JUrmi, the linker regularly occurs with CST-marked primaries, as examined in §7.3.2. In fact, cases where the primary is marked by the free state (i.e., the default form) are only found sporadically according to Khan (2008b: 175).

[13] Information about stress and cliticization is given only in Khan (2008b), where clitic boundaries are marked by a hyphen.

(40) JUrmi: **Noun–Noun**
o aġa ay ašqalon
DEM.DIST.SG lord LNK A.
'that lord of Ascalon' (Garbell 1965b: 87)

(41) JUrmi: **Noun–Noun**
gora ay tre reše
man LNK two heads
'the man of two heads' (Garbell 1965b: 87)

Yet, as noted in §7.2, whenever the primary is a noun phrase, rather than a simple noun, the CSC is generally not available, and the ALC becomes the sole option (ignoring possible circumlocutions). Since the construct state marking in JUrmi is not phrasal, the primary NP cannot be marked as construct state:

(42) JUrmi: **Noun Phrase–Noun**
[tq-ət aqla] ay naš
place-CST foot LNK man
'human footprints (lit. place of foot of man)' (Garbell 1965b: 87)

(43) JUrmi: **Noun Phrase–Noun Phrase**
[zóra broná] áy [tmánya ⁺əčča šənnè]
small son LNK eight nine years
'the young boy of eight or nine years' (Khan 2008b: 175 [141])

In such cases the linker may form an independent prosodic constituent with the secondary:

(44) JUrmi: **Noun Phrase–Noun**
[xa= danká ⁺torbà]ˈ ay= ixalàˈ
one= unit bag LNK= food
'a bag of food' (Khan 2008b: 176 [22])

(45) JUrmi: **Noun Phrase–Noun**
kúl-lu ⁺ktabèˈ ay= dunyèˈ
all-3PL books LNK= world
'all the books of the world' (Khan 2008b: 176 [29])

There is one case where two separate secondaries appear, each in its own prosodic phrase. Note that the linker phrase *áy awuršúm* 'of silk' is adjacent to the adjective *sqilè* 'beautiful.PL' which refers semantically to the primary *gory-ə́t awuršùm* 'silk stockings'. Yet syntactically the adjective can be analysed as being an attribute of the pronominal linker itself:

(46) JUrmi: **Noun Phrase–Asyndetically Conjoined Nouns**
xá= zoa gory-ə́t awuršùm' áy šušà,' áy awuršúm sqil-è'
one= pair stockings.CST silk LNK nylon LNK silk beautiful-PL
goryé mabruq-é mdità' bá-at ⁺kalò.'
stockings shining-PL brought.RES.FS for-CST bride
'She has brought a beautiful pair of silk stockings, of nylon, of silk, shining stockings for the bride' (Khan 2008b: 219 [94])

There may also be rare cases where the linker forms a prosodic constituent with the primary. Yet, such cases may be analysed differently. For instance, in following example the primary and the secondary are co-referential, atypically for an AC. In this case, the *ay* element may equally well be analysed as a demonstrative pronoun, followed by a prosodic stress due to hesitation:[14]

(47) JUrmi: **Noun–Noun**
brona =ày' ⁺hatā́n
son =LNK/DEM.SG groom
'the son (who is) the groom' (Khan 2008b: 219 [79])

7.3.2 Linker following a construct state (X-CST LNK Y)

The typical usage of the linker is following a CST-marked primary:

(48) JUrmi: **Noun–Noun**
o aġá-ad ay ašqalon
DEM.DIST.SG lord-CST LNK A.
'that lord of Ascalon' (Garbell 1965b: 87)

[14] According to Khan's transcription it is the noun that loses the stress and apparently "procliticizes" to the stressed linker. Yet, since in JUrmi the default stress placement is on the ultimate syllable, especially before intonation boundaries (Khan 2008b: 46), it is more plausible to analyse this case as an encliticization of the linker to the primary, with a default stress placement on the resulting phonological word.

(49) JUrmi: **Noun–Noun**
gor-ət ay tre reše
man-CST LNK two heads
'the man of two heads' (Garbell 1965b: 87)

This construction can easily be iterated:

(50) JUrmi: **Noun–Noun Phrase**
ó raís-ət áy [komsér-ət áy Urmì]
DEM.DIST.SG head-CST LNK police-CST LNK U.
'the head of police of Urmi' (Khan 2008b: 230 [134])

Note that the primary can also be marked by the apocopated construct state, as in the following example (=example (12) on page 191; cf. *pqarta* 'neck' in free state):[15]

(51) JUrmi: **Noun–Noun**
pqar ay d-o gora
neck.CST LNK GEN-DEM.DIST.MS man
'the neck of that man' (Garbell 1965b: 87)

These cases, appearing regularly, pose a problem to the analysis of *ay* as a classical pronominal linker. As outlined in §2.3.4, the essence of the classical Semitic ALC, is that the linker stands in apposition with a nominal in free state, being outside the scope of the attributive relation, strictly speaking. Yet this analysis is not tenable with regard to those cases in which the primary is explicitly marked by the construct state. One possible solution is to argue that the linker and the primary are still in apposition, yet the primary shows AGREEMENT IN STATE with the linker, which is syntactically in construct state. This means that both the primary and *ay* head this type of construction, similarly to cases where two construct state nouns head a CSC, as in examples (8)–(9) on page 190. The resulting construction, moreover, is one cohesive NP, as is clear from the fact that the primary in construct state cannot be separated from the following linker.

Yet this analysis is challenged by cases where the linker intervenes between a construct state marked preposition and its complement:

[15]Regarding the genitive marking, see §7.4.4.

(52) JUrmi: **Preposition–Noun Phrase**
(zə́l-lu) géb-əd ay= [⁺rəww-ət ay= komsèr]
went-3PL at-CST LNK= chief-CST LNK= police
'They went to the chief of police' (Khan 2008b: 198 [127])

(53) JUrmi: **Preposition–Noun**
gá-at ay= daxlà
in-CST LNK= agriculture
'in agriculture' (Khan 2008b: 198 [152])

It is not possible to argue that a pronominal element stands in apposition with a preposition, as the latter is not nominal. Thus, at least in the latter cases, *ay* must have lost its pronominal force (i.e. the necessity of representing a noun), and has become a simple marker of the prepositional phrase, a PURE LINKER. As such, it approaches the status of a phrasal genitive marker.

7.3.3 Syllabification of the construct state suffix with the linker

Some analytic confusion arises from cases in which the linker *ay* is preceded by /*d-*/ segment. While it is tempting to simply analyse this segment as the genitive prefix, which can occur before vowel-initial pronominal elements (see discussion in §7.4), this analysis is inconsistent with the view advocated here that the linker is not governed by the primary, but rather stands in apposition with it.[16]

The solution to this difficulty is to analyse the /*d-*/ segment as part of the construct state suffix *-əd*, which has been resyllabified with the linker due to phonological reasons, in particular the fact that the linker is vowel-initial.[17]

In some cases, a vestige of the vocalic nucleus of the construct state suffix (/*ə*/ or /*a*/, glossed in both cases
isischwa) remains attached to the primary, while in other cases the vowel is elided.

[16]In other words, while the linker marks the secondary, it stands outside it. This is true even if one sees *ay* as a pure marker of the AC, as suggested in the previous section. Of course, this is only the case if the particle under consideration is not in fact the homophonous demonstrative pronoun *ay* in genitive case.

[17]As Khan (2008b: 175) in fact suggests: "The consonant of the genitive enclitic [-d] may be syllabified with the *ay* particle."

(54) JUrmi: **Noun–Noun**
bél-ə -d= áy ⁺flankás
house-
isischwa -CST= LNK so_and_so
'the familly of so-and-so' (Khan 2008b: 175 [72])

(55) JUrmi: **Noun–Proper Noun**
yá ⁺šultán-a -d= áy Pahlawì'
DEM.PROX.SG king-
isischwa -CST= LNK P.
'that king (Reza Shah) Pahlavi' (Khan 2008b: 370 [169])

A similar resyllabification occurs with prepositional primaries. In these cases it is further motivated by the fact that the prepositions themselves cliticize to the linker as a whole.

(56) JUrmi: **Preposition–Noun**
əl-d= áy ⁺amart-èw
ACC-CST= LNK palace-POSS.3MS
'his palace[18]' (Khan 2008b: 198 [45])

(57) JUrmi: **Preposition–Noun**
ba-d= áy elčyè
for-CST= LNK messengers
'for the messengers' (Khan 2008b: 198 [77])

Note that in the last examples the construct state morpheme is realized as a sole /*d*/ without a vocalic nucleus: Contrast this example with example (19) on page 193, where it is realized with a vocalic nucleus as /*-at*/.

7.3.4 Adjectival secondaries following an apparent linker

There are sporadic cases where an adjective follows an *ay* morpheme, which *a priori* could be analysed as a linker. Such an analysis would reinforce the idea that the JUrmi ALC is a pattern replication from Kurmanji, where adjectives follow the Ezafe (see §9.5.2). Closer scrutiny nevertheless suggests that, given the

[18] The preposition *əl* 'to' serves in this case as an accusative preposition, i.e. marking an object of a phrase. It is thus not rendered in the translation.

rarity of such occurrences, the *ay* in these cases is actually the demonstrative pronoun. Thus, in the following example, *ay* can be analysed as a definite determiner attached to the adjective rather than the possessed noun (compare with JZakho example (97) on page 142):[19]

(58) JUrmi: **Noun–Adjective**
[kpan-aw] ay ⁺rast
shoulder-POSS.3FS DEF.SG right(INV)
'her right shoulder' (Garbell 1965b: 87)

In the following example *ay* is also a definite determiner, serving to nominalize the adjective:

(59) JUrmi: **Preposition–Adjective**
gáll-ə -d= áy smoqà,' idá smoqà'
with-
isischwa CST= DEF.SG red.MS hand(MS) red.MS
'with red, a red hand' (Khan 2008b: 198 [173])

7.3.5 Infinitival phrases as secondaries

Infinitive phrases as well can appear as secondaries in the JUrmi ALC.

(60) JUrmi: **Noun–Infinitive**
(gə=) tkán-ə -d= áy [ləxmá zabonè]'
in shop-
isischwa -CST= LNK bread sell.INF
'in the shop of bread selling' (Khan 2008b: 291 [174])

(61) JUrmi: **Noun–Infinitive**
léle -d= áy [pardìn šaroé]
night -CST= LNK curtain untie.INF
'the night of the releasing of the curtain' (Khan 2008b: 291 [84])

[19] As discussed in footnote 25 on page 142, Eran Cohen has suggested that this very placement of a determiner in the pre-adjectival position may itself represent pattern replication of the Ezafe construction. If this is true, this development may be regarded as a pre-cursor to the re-analysis of the demonstrative pronoun as a linker. Yet the rarity of this construction could argue against such a scenario, at least in the context of JUrmi. An alternative possibility is to consider ⁺*rast* as a noun meaning 'the right side'; see discussion of the Kurmanji example (62) on page 276.

7.3.6 Ordinal and adverbial secondaries

Also ordinals and adverbs can serve as secondaries in the ALC:

(62) JUrmi: **Noun–Ordinal**
o *gor-ət* *ay* *tre-mənji*
DEM.DIST.MS man-CST LNK two-ORD
'that second man' (Garbell 1965b: 87)

Compare the above example to (27) on page 195.

(63) JUrmi: **Noun–Adverb**
⁺qayd-ət *ay=* *lòka'*
custom-CST LNK=[20] there
'the custom of the place' (Khan 2008b: 230 [151])

7.3.7 Linkers without an explicit primary

As explained in §2.3.4, the ALC is analysed as a construction in which the linker is standing in an attributive relationship with the secondary and in apposition with the primary. As such, the linker is expected to be able to occur without an explicit primary. This expectation is indeed borne out, but only when the linker phrase acts as the predicate of the clause.

(64) JUrmi: **∅–Noun**
ay *šabbat*
LNK Sabbath
'belonging to the Sabbath' (Garbell 1965b: 88)

(65) JUrmi: **∅–Ordinal**
ay *arbi*
LNK forty
'the fortieth' (Garbell 1965b: 88)

[20] Arguably, the *ay* element here could be an instance of the demonstrative *ay* serving to nominalize the adverb. Indeed, Khan translates this example as 'the custom of *that* place'. Compare with example (86) on page 211 and see also example (70) on the next page and the discussion following it.

(66) JUrmi: ∅–**Pronoun**
(kalò') ay= noš-èw (=ila.')
bride LNK= REFL-3MS =COP.FS
'The bride belongs to him.' (Khan 2008b: 233 [81])

(67) JUrmi: ∅–**Infinitive**
áy šaqolè (=le)
LNK buy.INF =COP.MS
'It is worth buying.' (Khan 2008b: 292)

(68) JUrmi: ∅–**Infinitival Phrase**
áy [ləbbá qyalà] (=we-la)
LNK heart burn.INF =COP.PST-FS
'It was liable to burn the heart, it was pitiable.' (Khan 2008b: 293 [121])

(69) JUrmi: ∅–**Asyndetically conjoined infinitives**
bǎle fkár wad-én ki= did-àn' ⁺rába ⁺rába ∅ ay= xazoè' rába ∅
but thought do-1MS REL= GEN-1PL much much ∅ LNK= see.INF much ∅
ay= šamoè ilá.'
LNK= hear COP.3FS
'but I think that our (wedding) is very much something to see and something to hear about' (Khan 2008b: 233 [71])

One case where a linker phrase is found in a non-predicative position is after the adverbial *magon* 'like', itself appearing in predicative position:

(70) JUrmi: ∅–**Adverb**
magón ∅ ay= láxxa là k-awyá-wa'
like ∅ LNK= here NEG IND-be.FS-PST
'It was not like (the situation) here' (Khan 2008b: 198 [106])

In this case, one may reasonably interpret the *ay* as referring pronominally to an implicit situation, in essence nominalizing the adverb *laxxa* 'here'. An alternative analysis would be to see *ay* as a pure linker standing between *magon* and its complement, but in this case one would expect *magon* to be marked with the construct state suffix, as in examples (52)–(53) on page 202.

7.4 Genitive marking of secondaries

7.4.1 Introduction

Demonstrative and interrogative pronouns, which are normally vowel-initial,[21] are marked by a genitive prefix *d-* when they appear as secondaries, either as determiners of NPs or as full NPs in their own right. The motivation to analyse this segment as a genitive marker, rather than a phonological artefact, is given in §4.5. The possible development path of this marker is discussed in §10.5.

In general, the primary is expected to be marked as construct state, either by means of the *-əd* suffix or by apocope. This exception is indeed borne out in some cases:

(71) JUrmi: **Noun–Noun**
dád-ət d-ò broná
father-CST GEN-DEM.DIST.SG son
'the father of that son' (Khan 2008b: 175 [70])

(72) JUrmi: **Noun–Pronoun**
baxt-əd d-ay
wife-CST GEN-DEM.PROX.MS
'the wife of this (man)' (Garbell 1965b: 86)

(73) JUrmi: **Noun–Noun**
bel d-ay gora
house.CST GEN-DEM.PROX.MS man
'the house of this man' (Khan 2008b: 175)

Khan (2008b: 175) brings some cases in which the primary is apparently left unmarked:[22]

[21]JUrmi does not have initial glottal stops (Khan 2008b: 35).

[22]In Khan's analysis this is the default case. For him, there is only one *d* morpheme, which is a particle that can attach either to the primary as an "annexation enclitic" or to the secondary's determiner as a prefix. Moreover, he does not consider reduced nouns, such as *bel* 'house' in example (73), to be in construct state, but rather as lacking the enclitic, which is attached to the following demonstrative (Khan 2008b: 174–175). See §4.4 for arguments against such an analysis.

(74) JUrmi: **Noun–Noun**
ni⁺šā́n d-o pardá
sign.(CST?) GEN-DEM.DIST.SG curtain
'the symbolic meaning of that curtain' (Khan 2008b: 175 [88])

(75) JUrmi: **Noun–Noun**
áy xabúša d-émnu yalè =le?
DEM.PROX.SG apple GEN-which child =COP.3MS
'This apple belongs to which child?' (Khan 2008b: 175)

Both these examples may be explained differently, however: In example (74), the primary *ni⁺šā́n* 'sign' can be analysed as being an instance of apocopated construct state, since there exists a long variant *ni⁺šā́na*.

As for the example (75) on this page, judging by Khan's translation ('This is the apple of which child?'), it seems that he analyses *xabúša d-émnu yalè* as one NP. Yet it seems more reasonable to analyse *áy xabúša* as the subject NP and *d-émnu yalè* as a predicate NP, in which case *d-émnu* is an independent genitive pronoun, lacking an explicit primary. Functionally, the genitive marking without an explicit primary is somewhat similar to the pronominal linker *d-*, otherwise absent in JUrmi, as it can be said to assume a pronominal role of representing the primary.

7.4.2 Genitive marking following adverbials

Prepositions stand in a direct attributive relation with their complement and thus induce a genitive marking on it, irrespective of the question whether the preposition itself is marked as construct state or not.

(76) JUrmi: **Preposition–Noun**
dowr-ət d-o bela
around-CST GEN-DEM.DIST.SG house
'around that house' (Khan 2008b: 194)

(77) JUrmi: **Preposition–Pronoun**
dowr-ət d-o
around-CST GEN-DEM.DIST.SG
'around that one' (Khan 2008b: 194)

(78) JUrmi: **Preposition–Noun**
bar d-o gora
behind GEN-DEM.DIST.SG man
'behind that man' (Khan 2008b: 192)

(79) JUrmi: **Preposition–Pronoun**
bar= d-o
behind= GEN-DEM.DIST.SG
'behind that one, behind him' (Khan 2008b: 192)

Of interest are cases in which the adverbial has a part of the construct state suffix, namely the vowel /ə/, followed by a genitive marked pronoun. Such cases are akin to those in which the /-*d*/ segment of the construct state suffix has resyllabified with the following element (compare with §7.3.3). Given, however, that pronominal determiners are normally marked by the genitive, one must conclude that the *d-* prefix does double duty in these cases, serving both to the construct state suffix and to the genitive prefix. In other words, while phonologically it is a simple /*d*/ segment, syntactically it is understood as geminated.[23]

(80) JUrmi: **Preposition–Noun**
⁺g=aralġ-ə -d-emnu naše
in=between-
isischwa -CST.GEN-which people
'between which people?' (Khan 2008b: 196)

(81) JUrmi: **Preposition–Noun**
⁺mqulb-ə[24] *-d-o gora*
instead-
isischwa -CST.GEN-DEM.DIST.SG man
'instead of that man' (Khan 2008b: 196)

[23]This analysis is independent of the question whether diachronically there was a geminated /*d-d*/ in this position. In fact, the resyllabification of the construct state *-əd* suffix may have been the trigger for the innovation of the *d-* genitive prefix, prior to any gemination. See discussion in §10.5.

[24]Khan analyses *⁺mqulb* as consisting of the prefix *m-* 'from' and a Kurdish (originally Arabic) element *qulb* (Khan 2008b: 569).

7.4.3 Independent genitive pronouns

All personal pronouns have a genitive allomorph, which takes the general form of *did*+POSS (Khan 2008b: 58). These forms appear whenever one expects a pronoun in an attributive position and this pronoun cannot be expressed as a pronominal suffix for morphological reasons (Khan 2008b: 233; contrast with examples (1)–(2) on page 188).

(82) JUrmi: **Noun–Pronoun**
kalo did-ew
bride GEN-POSS.3MS
'his bride' (Khan 2008b: 233)

(83) JUrmi: **Preposition–Pronoun**
bo-d= did-ew
because-CST= GEN-POSS.3MS
'because of him' (Khan 2008b: 192)

The first example has a primary noun *kalo* 'bride' which does not end in an /*a*/ vowel, and thus cannot take a regular pronominal suffix. Similarly, the preposition *bod* 'because' cannot take a pronominal suffix, since it ends obligatory with the construct state marker.

Note that semantically there is a certain overlap between the 3rd person genitive pronouns (MS: *didew*; FS: *didaw*; PL: *didu*) and the independent demonstratives with genitive marking (SG: *do*; PL: *dune*; see examples (77) and (79) on the preceding page). This is expected, as the same overlap appears in the non-genitive case. Indeed, without the genitive marking, the distal demonstratives *o* 'that' and *une* 'those' are identical to the independent pronouns (Khan 2008b: 55–56).

In JUrmi, the *did-* base is bound to the pronominal suffixes, and cannot occur before free standing nominals. Consequently I analyse it as a genitive base, and not as a pronominal linker, in contrast to JZakho (see §5.4) and Qaraqosh (examples (52)–(54) on page 165). This point will be discussed in more detail in §10.6.1. Unlike the *d-* genitive marker, however, in some cases it has a certain pronominal value, especially when it acts as the head of an NP in predicative position (but see example (75) on page 208 for a similar analysis of the *d-* prefix). Formally, I analyse such cases as having a ∅ primary, as an explicit noun could appear in the primary position.

(84) JUrmi: **∅–Pronoun**
ma-t ə́t-ti l-ə́t-ti kúll-u ∅ did-àx =ilu.'
what-CST exist-1SG NEG-exist-1SG all-3MS ∅ GEN-2FS =COP.3MS
'Whatever I have is all yours.' (Khan 2008b: 233 [8])

7.4.4 Genitive case following the linker *ay*

A demonstrative or interrogative pronoun appearing after the linker will also be marked by the genitive prefix *d-*. Together with the construct state marking, this yields a triple-marked construction (see also example (12) on page 191):

(85) JUrmi: **Noun–Noun**
tre be-ət ay d-ay gora
two eggs-CST LNK GEN-DEM.PROX.SG man
'the two eggs of this man' (Garbell 1965b: 87)

(86) JUrmi: **Noun–Noun**
⁺qayd-ət áy d-ò= tka
custom-CST LNK GEN-DEM.DIST.SG= place
'the custom of that place' (Khan 2008b: 176 [144])

Example (85) neatly shows the difference in both function and in marking of the linker *ay* and the demonstrative *ay*.

An independent genitive pronoun can also occur as a secondary following the linker. This seems to further indicate that the genitive base *did-* should not be confounded with the linker. Note also the optionality of the construct state marking at the end of the primary NP.

(87) JUrmi: **Noun Phrase–Pronoun**
[ǰull-ət ⁺šultanul-a/ət] ay did-ew
clothes-CST royalty-FREE/CST LNK GEN-3MS
'his royal clothes' (Garbell 1965b: 87)

7.5 The double annexation construction (X-y.POSS LNK Y)

Garbell (1965b: 87) mentions that "in rare cases" a double genitive construction can occur. In such cases, the apposition between the primary noun and the linker is quite clear:

(88) JUrmi: **Noun–Noun**
tar-ew ay d-o gora
gate-POSS.3MS LNK GEN-DEM.DIST.MS man
'that man's gate' (Garbell 1965b: 87)

7.6 Usage of the relativizer (X REL Y)

7.6.1 Introduction

The linker *ay* is in complementary distribution with the relativizer *ki*, which appears only before clausal secondaries.[25]

(89) JUrmi: **Noun–Clause**
qúš ki= [baxtà =ila]
bird REL= wife =COP.3FS
'the bird who is the wife' (Khan 2008b: 353 [46])

(90) JUrmi: **Noun Phrase–Clause**
[xa ⁺jahəl jwanqa], ki [atta ⁺matóy-le]
INDF young youth REL now arrive.INF-3MS
'a young man who has just reached maturity' (Garbell 1965b: 88)

With the use of *ki*, there is clearly no restriction as for the appearance of an explicit subject NP in the relative clause, in contrast to clausal secondaries following the construct state marking, which may have such a restriction according to Garbell. Contrast the following example with examples (35)–(36) on page 196:

(91) JUrmi: **Noun–Clause**
xa xabra ki [naš la ⁺miss-e ód-le]
INDF thing REL man NEG can-3MS SBJV.do.A3MS-P3MS
'a thing that no one can do' (Garbell 1965b: 88)

The primary may moreover be a pronoun:

[25] This complementary distribution is reminiscent of the alternation between *ke* and *ya* in JSanandaj discussed in §8.6. In the latter case, however, both forms serve as relativizers. According to Garbell (1965a: 171–172) the relativizer is borrowed from Azeri Turkish, while the usage of the linker as well as the construct state suffix stems from pattern replication of Kurdish.

(92) JUrmi: **Pronoun–Clause**
ó ki= [la dhə́l-le g= qór-ət dad-éw]
3SG REL= NEG knocked-3MS in= grave-CST father-POSS.3MS
'the one who did not beat on the grave of his father' (Khan 2008b: 356 [69])

Interestingly, sometimes a clause-like complement lacking a finite verb can appear in this construction (Khan 2008b: 361).

(93) JUrmi: **Noun–Infinitive phrase**
(⁺hudaé m=) [pə́lg-ət ⁺wə́rxa] kí [knəštá izalà]' (der-í-wa
Jews from= half-CST way REL synagogue go.INF return-3PL-PST
gòlbara)
back
'(Jews turned back from halfway) along the road that they had gone to the synagogue' (Khan 2008b: 361 [157])

(94) JUrmi: **Pronoun–Noun**
ána ki= [⁽⁺⁾də́qna-xwára]
1SG REL= beard-white
'I, who am an elder' (Khan 2008b: 356 [17])

In the last two examples adding a copula to the secondaries would make them full clauses. In particular, the infinitive *izala* 'go' could combine with a copula to form the progressive tense. Thus, these cases may indicate that it is possible to omit the copula in relative clauses.

7.6.2 Adverbial primaries

Some adverbial primaries use the relativizer construction to govern clausal secondaries. This is the case with *magon* 'like' in the following example (but this is optional; see example (119) on page 220):

(95) JUrmi: **Adverbial–Clause**
magon= kì' [k-yèt]'
like= REL IND-know.2MS
'as you know' (Khan 2008b: 373 [51])

Of interest is the adverbial *hal* 'until' which uses the same construction both for clausal and nominal complements:

(96) JUrmi: **Adverbial–Clause**
⁺hal= ki= [yá ⁺šultán-a -d=áy Pahlawì' ədyè-le].'
until= REL= DEM.PROX.SG king-CST -CST=LNK P. came-3MS
'until king (Reza Shah) Pahlavi came' (Khan 2008b: 370 [169])

(97) JUrmi: **Adverbial–Noun Phrase**
⁺hal= kì [lel= xlulá]
until= REL night.CST= wedding
'until the wedding night' (Khan 2008b: 371 [73])

The latter case may be interpreted as a clausal complement in which the copula has been omitted as in examples (93)–(94). It seems more reasonable, however, to analyse the element *ki* as if it had been integrated into the adverbial *hal.* The following example, in which the whole expression *hal ki* governs a genitive case, corroborates this view:

(98) JUrmi: **Adverbial–Noun**
⁺hál ki= d-o= lelé (=š)
until REL= GEN-DEM.DIST.MS= night =also
'until that night' (Khan 2008b: 371 [82])

7.6.3 Relativizer following the construct state (X-CST REL Y)

The relativizer, like the linker, may follow a head noun which is marked by the construct state suffix. In this case, as in examples (35)–(36) on page 196, it seems that the clause cannot have an NP subject argument.

(99) JUrmi: **Noun–Clause**
naš-ət ki [lóka wé-lu]
people-CST REL there COP.PST-3PL
'the people who were there' (Garbell 1965b: 55)

(100) JUrmi: **Noun–Clause**
o brát-ət ki [midyá-wa-lu gall-ew]
DEM.DIST.SG girl-CST REL brought.P3FS-PST-A3PL with-3MS
'that girl whom they had brought along with him' (Garbell 1965b: 88)

In these cases, as those involving the linker (see §7.3.2 on page 201), the primary noun may be analysed as exhibiting AGREEMENT IN STATE with the relativizer, which is then understood to be syntactically in the construct state. Note, however, that the construct state marking is not a simple variant of the construction, as it restricts the class of secondary clauses following it to those that do not contain a subject NP. Thus, one may postulate that *ki.*CST is grammatically different from *ki*, albeit the forms are identical.

In some restricted cases, the relativizer can follow the construct state pronoun *od* (see §7.2.5). Khan (2008b: 374–5) brings examples of this construction only with the prepositions *bod* 'because' and *reš* 'on':

(101) JUrmi: **Pronoun–Clause**
bo-d= ó-d kì' xălifá kotàk dahə́l-le
because-CST= DEM-CST REL teacher blow beat.A3MS-P3MS
'because of the fact that the teacher beats him' (Khan 2008b: 374 [139])

(102) JUrmi: **Pronoun–Clause**
(mqé-lan) reš= d-ó-d kí [⁺kalò' ki= bratá
spoke-1PL on= GEN-DEM-CST REL bride REL(when)= girl
yadlà-wa' jùwe šúla =š g-od-í-wa].'
give_birth.FS-PST different work =also IND-do-3PL-PST
'(We have spoken) about the fact that a daughter-in-law, when she gave birth to a girl, people acted differently.' (Khan 2008b: 375 [120])

As for adverbial primaries, those which normally take the construct state suffix will do so also when followed by a clausal complement introduced by the relativizer *ki*.

(103) JUrmi: **Adverbial–Noun**
m=qulb-ə́t ki= [adé geb= marasxaná əl-lí xazè]
from=stead-CST REL= come.3MS at= hospital ACC-1SG see.3MS
'instead of coming to the hospital to see me' (Khan 2008b: 569 [148])

7.6.4 Relativizer in construct state (X REL-CST Y)

Above, I claimed that the relativizer *ki* may sometimes be considered to be in construct state syntactically speaking, although it is not marked as such morphologically. JUrmi seems to corroborate this claim by some cases in which the relativizer is explicitly marked by a construct state suffix: *ki-t*. This seems to happen, though, only after a handful of adverbials. Khan (2008b) gives the following three cases:

(104) JUrmi: **Adverbial–Clause**
⁺hál kí-t [idáyle léle -d= áy [pardìn šaroé]]
until REL-CST come.INF.3MS night -CST= LNK curtain untie.INF
'until the night of the releasing of the curtain came' (Khan 2008b: 291 [84])

(105) JUrmi: **Adverbial–Clause**
⁺hal kí-t ya= bronà'yá axón-i zóra ləbb-éw
until REL-CST DEM= son DEM brother-1SG small heart-POSS.3MS
zìl'
went.3MS
'until the boy, my young brother, had fainted' (Khan 2008b: 371 [142])

(106) JUrmi: **Conjunction–Clause**
bar ki-t ⁽⁺⁾dməx-lan lele
after REL-CST slept-1PL night
'after we went to bed' (Khan 2008b: 369)

The restriction of this marker to these conjunctions only may indicate, however, that *ki* is no longer felt as a relativizer in these cases, but as a part of the conjunction. Indeed, there are other occurrences of the adverbial *hal-ki* (examples (96)–(98) on page 214), which suggest the same view.

7.7 Juxtaposition (X Y.{AGR})

7.7.1 Introduction

Juxtaposition of two nouns is used only marginally in JUrmi as a means of marking an attributive relation:

(107) JUrmi: **Noun–Noun**
naša tre reše
man two heads
'the two-headed man' (Garbell 1965b: 86)

(108) JUrmi: **Noun–Noun**
⁺səmha ilane
festival trees
'Festival of the Trees (holiday of *Tu bi-Shvat*)' (Khan 2008b: 587)

The first example may be motivated by the intervention of a numeral between the primary and the secondary (but contrast with example (7) on page 189). The second example, on the other hand, is an idiom which refers to the Jewish holiday of ט"ו בשבט *Tu bi-Shvat* (15th of the month of Shvat). While the word *⁺səmha* 'festivity' is borrowed from Hebrew (Khan 2008b: 587), the expression as a whole is probably not borrowed from the Hebrew parallel שמחת אילנות *simḥa-t ʾilanot*, since in Hebrew the word *simḥa-t* is clearly marked by the FS construct state suffix *-t*.

Juxtaposition as means of marking an AC is regularly found, on the other hand, with adjectival secondaries. On the periphery of the AC system juxtaposition is used with nouns which are standing in apposition with one another, as well as in adverbial phrases. These cases are discussed in the following subsections.

7.7.2 Adjectival secondaries

Juxtaposition-cum-agreement is chiefly used in JUrmi for expressing adjectival attribution (but often the adjective precedes the head, see §7.8).

While most adjectives of Aramaic origin agree with the primary, some adjectives, mostly of foreign origin (mostly Kurdish or Azeri), are invariable in form, and thus show a pure juxtaposition pattern. Some other loan-adjectives do show agreement but only for number (Khan 2008b: 181).

(109) JUrmi: **Noun–Adjective**
gi⁺lasta smuq-ta
cherry(FS) red-FS
'the red cherry' (Garbell 1965b: 83)

(110) JUrmi: **Noun–Adjective**
tkana šušaband
shop glass-covered(INV)
'a glass-covered shop' (Garbell 1965b: 84)

7.7.3 Nominal quantification and apposition

Juxtaposition is regularly used when two nouns are in apposition with each other, but these cases do not fall normally under the definition of an AC used here. Yet some of these cases can be considered as borderline ACs, since one noun qualifies the other. This is for instance the case when the head noun is part of a quantifying expression (Q. NP), as in the following examples (see further Khan 2008b: 233–234). The following example illustrates the analytical ambiguity of such expressions: One the one hand, the primary and the secondary are co-referential[26] and share the same grammatical feature (plurality), and could thus be qualified as appositional to each other. On the other hand, the secondary 'clothes' clearly qualifies the primary, as it designates the type of 'sets'.[27]

(111) JUrmi: **Q. Noun Phrase–Noun**
[tre daste] julle
two sets clothes
'two sets of clothes' (Garbell 1965b: 85)

In this class of examples one may also include the use of the numeral classifier *danka* 'unit' (PL *danke*). The usage of a classifier, as well as the classifier itself, is a matter-cum-pattern replication from Kurdish (or possibly Azeri), in which it originally means 'grain' (Garbell 1965a: 172, §2.32.12.4(a)).

(112) JUrmi: **Q. Noun Phrase–Noun**
[xa danka] baxta
one unit woman
'one woman' (Garbell 1965a: 172)

The apposition between the two elements can be illustrated by the fact that the primary can stand alone, without an explicit secondary:

(113) JUrmi: **Q. Noun Phrase–∅**
isra danke
ten unit.PL
'ten (people or objects)' (Garbell 1965a: 172)

[26] To illustrate this, note that one may say "These are clothes" as well as "These are two sets".

[27] The syntactic ambiguity of quantification is clearly manifested in Hebrew morpho-syntax, where numerals appear in construct state when followed by a definite nominal, and in free state when followed by an indefinite one.

Other quantification examples, however, are more clear-cut in that the primary and the secondary are not co-referential, as in the following example:

(114) JUrmi: **Q. Noun Phrase–Noun**
[kəmma ⁽⁺⁾*bate] hudae*
few houses Jews
'a few Jewish houses' (Garbell 1965b: 85)

Another example of juxtaposition verging on apposition is the following one, where the secondary noun marks the biological sex of the primary noun *quš* 'bird', which by itself has no inherent grammatical gender (see glossary of Khan 2008b: 569). In this respect, the nominal secondaries of the following example are not unlike adjectives (compare to example (89) on page 212):

(115) JUrmi: **Noun–Noun**
qúš gorá (ba=) qúš baxtá (mar-è)
bird man to= bird woman say-3MS
'The male bird (says to) the female bird' (Khan 2008b: 219 [45])

7.7.4 Adverbial primaries

Adverbial primaries, which are not marked by the construct state suffix, effectively yield a juxtaposition construction.

(116) JUrmi: **Preposition–Noun**
b= šəmme
in= sky
'in the sky' (Khan 2008b: 192)

(117) JUrmi: **Preposition–Pronoun**
bá= ma
for= what
'Why?' (Khan 2008b: 191)

(118) JUrmi: **Preposition–Infinitive**
gal= rə̀qla,ˈ gal= zamòreˈ
with= dance.INF with= sing.INF
'with dancing, with singing' (Khan 2008b: 292 [77])

(119) JUrmi: **Conjunction–Clause**
magón k-yé-tun
like IND-know-2PL
'as you know' (Khan 2008b: 372 164)

Compare these examples with the CSC of examples (17)–(20) on page 193. The last example can be contrasted as well with the ALC of example (70) on page 206.

7.8 Inverse juxtaposition (Y X)

The usage of inverse constructions, in which the secondary precedes the primary, is not uncommon in JUrmi, but it is restricted to two domains: adjectival and adverbial attribution as well as complementation of verbal nouns.[28]

7.8.1 Adjectival and adverbial secondaries

Adjectives commonly precede the head noun in JUrmi. This is attributed by Garbell (1965a: 172, §2.32.12 (2)) to Azeri influence. Like post-nominal adjectives generally (see §7.7.2), adjectives of Aramaic stock normally agree in gender and number with the primary noun, while loan-adjectives are often uninfecting.

(120) JUrmi: **Noun–Adjective**
xal-ta ⁺kalo
new-FS bride
'the new bride' (Garbell 1965b: 83)

(121) JUrmi: **Noun–Adjective**
kor naš-e
blind(INV) people-PL
'blind people' (Garbell 1965a: 167)

When two adjectives modify a noun, they are generally placed around the noun (Garbell 1965b: 84). It is the adjective with larger scope which appears before the noun:

[28]Recall that in the example headings the categories of the constituents of the AC are always listed in the order **Primary–Secondary**.

(122) JUrmi: **Noun Phrase–Adjective**
zúr-ta [tkana šušaband]
small-FS shop(FS) glass-covered(INV)
'a small glass-covered shop' (Garbell 1965b: 84)

Adverbials modifying an adjective appear before it. Consequently, an adverbial may precede an adjective within an adjectival phrase preceding a head noun:

(123) JUrmi: **Adjective–Adverb**
[⁺raba xriwa] naš
much bad.MSperson
'a very bad person' (Garbell 1965b: 84)

(124) JUrmi: **Adjective–Prepositional Phrase**
[[ba= taltoe] šbir-e] naš-e
for= hang.INF good-PL person-PL
'people good for hanging' (Garbell 1965b: 84)

(125) JUrmi: **Adjective–Prepositional Phrase**
[mən-nox biš zudda] naš-e
from-2MS more brave(INV) person-PL
'men braver than you' (Garbell 1965b: 84)

One finds also the adverbial *magon* 'like' modifying directly a noun in this way:

(126) JUrmi: **Adverbial–Noun**
magon-ox ⁺hasid-e
like-2MS pious_man-PL
'pious people like you' (Garbell 1965b: 87)

Finally, ordinals may also precede a primary noun. In contrast to the post-nominal placement of ordinals (shown in examples (27)–(28) on page 195), the primary noun is not marked as construct state in this case. Note that the ordinal always has an invariable form.

(127) JUrmi: **Noun–Ordinal**
tre-mənji gora
two-ORD man
'The second man' (Khan 2008b: 187)

(128) JUrmi: **Noun Phrase–Ordinal**
tmanya-mənjì [lél-ət ay elá]'
eight-ORD night-CST LNK festival
'on the eight night of the festival' (Khan 2008b: 217 [104])

7.8.2 Verbal nouns as primaries

Verbal nouns, i.e. infinitives and participles (active or resultative), have their complements preceding them, just as normal verbs do. In the Semitic realm this is clearly an innovation. Indeed, the JUrmi OV order, available throughout the verbal system, is attributed by Garbell (1965a: 172, §2.32.22.1) to Kurmanji or Azeri influence.

(129) JUrmi: **Infinitive–Noun**
+hatān masxoe
groom wash.INF
'the washing of the groom' (Khan 2008b: 291)

(130) JUrmi: **Participle–Noun**
masy-e doq-ana
fish-PL catch-PTCP
'fish-catcher, fisherman' (Garbell 1965b: 86)

(131) JUrmi: **Participle–Adverb**
lóka hawy-an-e
here be-PTCP-PL
'those present there' (Garbell 1965b: 84)

(132) JUrmi: **Participle–Prepositional Phrase**
reš suse +rkiwa
on horse mounted.RES
'mounted upon a horse' (Garbell 1965b: 87)

Example (131) on the preceding page could be contrasted with example (31) on page 195, in which the adverb follows a participial in construct state. For a participial phrase acting as the primary of an AC see example (32) on page 196.

Of interest are also cases of definite direct objects of infinitives. These may be part of a prepositional phrase headed by the accusative-marking *əl*, and may also be indexed on the infinitive by a pronominal possessive suffix:

(133) JUrmi: **Infinitive–Noun**
əl= d-o gora +qatol-ew
ACC= GEN-DEM.DIST.MS man kill.INF-POSS.3MS
'the killing of that man' (Khan 2008b: 291)

Such cases accentuate the double nature of complements of infinitives, being both genitive (as complements of nouns) and accusative (as complements of verbs).

7.9 Conclusions

JUrmi presents an intricate and complex system of ACs, exploiting to a maximal extent the various marking possibilities. Indeed, there are examples with up to three simultaneous AC markers: a primary marked by construct state, a secondary marked by genitive case, and in between a linker (see §7.4.4)

The various AC markers of JUrmi and their possible combination are presented in Table 7.1.

Table 7.1: AC markers in JUrmi

	1	2	3	
X	± CST (*-əd*, Ap.)	± LNK (*ay*) ± REL.{CST} (*ki*, *ki-t*)	± GEN (*d-*, *did-*)	Y

Where does this complexity stem from? A possible answer is that the language has borrowed through language contact various AC marking strategies, which synchronically *co-exist* in the same system. Indeed, some elements are clearly borrowed: The *ki* relativizer is borrowed both formally and functionally from Azeri Turkish (Garbell 1965a: 172). Moreover, as Garbell (1965a: 171–172) suggests, the Kurmanji Ezafe construction may be the source of the JUrmi linker construction, relexified with native morphological material, and possibly also the source of the suffixed construct state marking. While these claims may be challenged (see §10.4 and §10.5 for a discussion), the result of the interaction of the different processes involved, be they pattern or matter replication and/or internal change, is an entangled and quite complex system.

The most striking structural innovation in JUrmi is the co-occurrence of a construct state primary with a linker in the ALC. This construction, unattested in previous strata of Aramaic (but found in some other NENA dialects in different forms; see §11.2), presents an analytic challenge to the conceptual framework used here. I have attempted to resolve this difficulty by postulating an AGREEMENT IN STATE rule or by re-analysing *ay* as a non-pronominal linker (see §7.3.2). It seems reasonable to assume that language contact must have played a certain role in the emergence of this not so typically Semitic construction.

The analytic difficulties revolving around the occurrences of the morpheme *ay* (Is it a pronominal linker? A secondary marker? Or simply a demonstrative pronoun?) as well as the /*d*/ segment (Is it part of the construct state suffix? A genitive prefix? Both?), seem moreover to be typical of a system which is still in a state of flux.

The use of the juxtaposition construction for quantification, involving the numeral classifier *danka* 'unit' (see examples (112)–(113) on page 218), must be a case of PATTERN-CUM-MATTER REPLICATION from Kurdish or Azeri. For discussion of whether this construction is in general due to language contact see §11.3.2.1.

A similar case where language contact must be in play is the usage of the inverse juxtaposition construction (described in §7.8). The positioning of adjectives before their nominal primaries is due to Azeri influence, while the positioning of complements before their verbal nouns is related either to Kurmanji or to Azeri influence (or both).

Notwithstanding these changes, JUrmi has preserved some of the typical characteristics of a classical Semitic system: First, it shows a clear demarcation between adjectival attribution (expressed by juxtaposition-cum-agreement) and nominal attribution (the CSC as well as the ALC). Second, the use of the CSC with clausal secondaries, while absent in previous strata of Aramaic, is a classical Semitic pattern. Note, however, that it has been superseded to some extent by the use of the borrowed relativizer *ki*.[29]

To conclude, compared to the dialects surveyed so far, JUrmi seems to present the most complex system, rich in its variety of constructions, and the most innovative one compared to the Classical Aramaic AC system. Yet it keeps also some conservative aspects typical of Semitic languages.

[29] The usage of a dedicated relativizer (differentiated from a more general linker) is by itself not unprecedented in the Semitic realm. For example, in Biblical Hebrew, one finds שֶׁ *šɛ*- or אֲשֶׁר *ʾăšɛr* exclusively in the role of relativizers (Waltke & O'Connor 1990: 331, §19.2).

8 Attributive constructions in the Jewish dialect of Sanandaj

8.1 Introduction

The Iranian city of Sanandaj is located at the eastern extremity of the NENA speaking zone. Compared to the three dialects surveyed so far, the grammar of the Jewish dialect of Sanandaj is the most divergent. This is certainly true for the AC system, which will be surveyed below, but can also be said about other domains of grammar, such as the verbal system. While the latter is outside the scope of this work, it is worthwhile noting two innovative features of the verbal system, which are of relevance to the current survey: First, the language exhibits an OV order (in contrast to the typical VO order found in most NENA dialects); and second, the language makes extensive use of complex predication, i.e. predicates consisting of a combination of a light verb and a noun (termed here CP noun).[1] These and other features are in all probability related to an extensive language contact with Sorani and Persian (Khan 2009b: 11f.).[2] While one may speculate that the divergence of JSanandaj is related to its peripheral location, it is worthwhile noting that the Christian dialect spoken in the same city presents a much more conservative grammar, but unfortunately it has not yet received a detailed grammatical description.[3]

The data for JSanandaj is based mainly on the grammatical description of Khan (2009b).[4] Additional examples are drawn from an elicitation session I have con-

[1]For an elaborate syntactic and semantic analysis of complex predication in Persian, see Samvelian (2012).

[2]As Khan (2009b: 11) notes, the Kurdish dialect of Sanandaj is not systematically described. Instead, I refer to standard Sorani for the sake of comparison. It should also be noted that Hawrami, a Gorani language closely related to Kurdish, is spoken in the vicinity of Sanandaj.

[3]See however Panoussi (1990); Heinrichs (2002) and the list of publications given in McPherson & Caldani (2013).

[4]Khan's examples are cited according to the page in the grammar in which they are treated. Additionally, a reference to the textual corpus, if available, is given in square brackets according to Khan's system: a letter indicating the informant (A–E) and a sentence number. I have also consulted the grammatical description of Schaller (2007), but as this description is mostly

ducted in Jerusalem with an elderly native speaker of the dialect, Ḥabib Nurani.[5] JSanandaj is in some respects similar to Sulemaniyya, of which I give some comparative examples drawn from Khan (2004). I present also some sporadic comparisons with Neo-Mandaic, another Neo-Aramaic language spoken in Iran.

The structure of the chapter is as follows:

First, I treat the usage of the possessive pronominal suffixes. In contrast to most other NENA dialects, these are phrasal suffixes, as discussed in §8.2.

A major difference in JSanandaj in comparison to the dialects discussed so far is that the main AC in JSanandaj is not the CSC, but rather the zero-marked juxtaposition construction, which is discussed in §8.3. This construction has two further variants: juxtaposition with agreement of the secondary with the primary (see §8.4), and inverse juxtapositioninverse juxtaposition construction with the secondary preceding the primary (see §8.5).

The use of borrowed Iranic relativizers with clausal secondaries is discussed in §8.6.

While JSanandaj does not make use of the Neo-CSC found in other dialects, it has a structural parallel formed by marking the primary with the Iranic Ezafe suffix. This construction, as well as the idiomatic retention of the historical CSC and the possible emergence of a new CSC related to stress retraction, is discussed in §8.7.

From the above it is clear that JSanandaj has hardly retained any reflex of the Classical Aramaic *d-* linker. Indeed, JSanandaj has only one reflex of this linker, namely the genitive marking of vowel-initial demonstratives. This is discussed in §8.8. On the other hand, JSanandaj has retained to a small extent the usage of the dative preposition *əl-* for marking secondaries, as discussed in §8.9.

Conclusions and a general discussion of the various constructions are presented in §8.10.

8.2 Possessive pronominal suffixes (X-y.POSS)

As in other NENA dialects, a pronominal secondary may be expressed by a possessive suffix. The possessive suffix replaces the inflectional suffix (*-a* or *-e*) of the nominal primary it attaches to:

devoted to the verbal system, no examples are drawn from there.

[5]In Khan's description, he is marked as informant A.

(1) JSanandaj: **Noun–Pronoun**
bel-ef
house-POSS.3MS
'his house' (Khan 2009b: 61)

A particularity of JSanandaj in comparison with most other NENA dialects is that the possessive pronoun is suffixed NP-finally, rather than directly on the primary noun, whenever the NP consists of a Noun+Adj. combination (Khan 2009b: 251).

(2) JSanandaj: **Noun Phrase–Pronoun**
[xa ʾăxóna xet]-àf
INDF brother other-POSS.3FS
'another brother of hers' (Khan 2009b: 53 [A:6])

A similar pattern is found in Sulemaniyya:

(3) Sulemaniyya: **Noun Phrase–Pronoun**
ʾaxón-a ruww-í
brother-FREE big-POSS.1SG
'my elder brother' (Khan 2004: 262 [R:94])

In the current framework, this distribution makes the possessive suffixes of JSanandaj and Sulemaniyya phrasal suffixes rather then word-level suffixes (see §4.2). The usage of the possessive suffixes NP-finally may very well be due to pattern replication from Sorani (see example (4) on page 256).

When attached to a verbal noun (such as an infinitive or a CP noun of a transitive verb), the pronoun denotes the object:

(4) JSanandaj: **Infinitive–Pronoun**
(ʾila di-li ba=) gărоš-ef[6]
hand placed-1SG in= pull.INF-POSS.3MS
'(I began) to pull him.' (Khan 2009b: 331)

[6]One may want to analyse the combination *ba*+infinitive as forming a gerund, as in JZakho (see footnote 9 on page 122). As I am unaware of a gerund category in JSanandaj, I prefer to analyse the preposition *ba* here, as well as in example (16) on page 231, as forming part of the verbal complex.

(5) JSanandaj: **CP Noun–Pronoun**
daʿwăt-ì *(k-ol-í)'*
invitation-POSS.1SG IND-do-3PL
'They will invite me.' (Khan 2009b: 482 [D:8])

When attached to a preposition, it denotes its complement. Note, however, that not all prepositions allow for a suffixed pronoun.

(6) JSanandaj: **Preposition–Pronoun**
reš-ef
on-POSS.3MS
'on it' (Khan 2009b: 224)

Interestingly, a pronoun attached to a true adverb can convert it to a noun:

(7) JSanandaj: **Adverb–Pronoun**
(gbé-wa *xa=párča* *zayrá* *dă-en* *ba=)* *lăxa-u*
IND.want.3MS-PST INDF=fabric yellow place-3PL on= here-POSS.3PL
'(They had to put a yellow patch on) their (body place) here.[7]' (Khan 2009b: 579 [A:78])

8.3 Simple juxtaposition (X Y)

The paradigmatically richest and most common construction in JSanandaj is the juxtaposition construction, devoid of any special marking. In cases where a noun is modified by another noun, the juxtaposition construction is the functional parallel in JSanandaj of the CSC or the ALC in the previously surveyed NENA dialects.

(8) JSanandaj: **Noun–Noun**
lišana *bšəlmane*
language Muslims
'the language of the Muslims' (Khan 2009b: 199)

In this JSanandaj is very similar to Sulemaniyya, which also makes extensive use of the juxtaposition construction:[8]

[7]From the context it seems that the informant pointed on a spot on his body ('here') referring to the same spot on the body of the referents.

[8]Yet, in contrast to JSanandaj, Sulemaniyya also makes use of the Neo-CST suffix *-əd*, as well as the linker *d-*:

(9) Sulemaniyya: **Noun–Noun**
šəmma brona
name son
'the name of the boy' (Khan 2004: 192)

While the above usage of the juxtaposition construction in JSanandaj and Sulemaniyya for nominal modification marks these dialects as special in comparison to the majority of NENA dialects, there are also more trivial cases of juxtaposition, such as its usage with adverbial secondaries:

(10) JSanandaj: **Noun–Prepositional Phrase**
ʾo gorá ga= lăxa (bărux-i =ye)
DEM.M man in= here friend-POSS.1SG =COP.3MS
'the man here (is my friend)' (Khan 2009b: 252)

Another use of the juxtaposition construction, which is cross-dialectally common and present also in JSanandaj, is in quantification expressions (see also example (56) on page 241):

(11) JSanandaj: **Q. Noun Phrase–Noun**
[xa lewan] rəzza
one cup rice
'one cup of rice' (own fieldwork)

Adjectival and ordinal secondaries normally appear in the juxtaposition-cum-agreement construction, discussed in the next section. Yet, when the lexical items in question are invariable, such as loan-adjectives or the loan-ordinal *ʾăwal* 'first', they necessarily appear in the simple juxtaposition construction:

(i) Sulemaniyya: **Noun–Noun**
xə́zm-əd kaldà
family-CST bride
'the family of the bride' (Khan 2004: 192 [A:8])

(ii) Sulemaniyya: **Noun–Noun**
məšxa d= zetùne
oil LNK= olives
'olive oil' (Khan 2004: 192 [R:98])

(12) JSanandaj: **Noun–Adjective**
mal-ăwae qarwa
village-PL near(INV)
'nearby villages' (Khan 2009b: 207)

(13) JSanandaj: **Noun–Ordinal**
gora ʾăwal
man first(INV)
'the first man' (Khan 2009b: 213)

Clausal secondaries are also found in this construction, yielding ASYNDETIC RELATIVE CLAUSES.

(14) JSanandaj: **Noun–Clause**
(măt-í-wa-le ga=) xá =tʷka [qărirà hăwé].ˈ
put-A.3PL-PST-P.3MS in= INDF =place cool SBJV.be
'They put it in a place that was cool.' (Khan 2009b: 381 [A:83])

Asyndetic clausal secondaries can also follow pronominal primaries, such as the indefinite pronoun *xa* 'one'. In the following example there are two asyndetic relative clauses, one embedded in the other.[9]

(15) JSanandaj: **Pronoun–Clause**
(bár kŭ̊leˈ kyà-waˈ) xa= [sawzì =ye,ˈ šaplultà
after all IND.come.3FS-PST one= vegetable =COP.3MS š.
kəmr-í-wa baq-éf].ˈ
call-A.3PL-PST for-POSS.3MS
'(After everything else there came) something that is a vegetable, which is called *šaplulta*.' (Khan 2009b: 382 [B:68])

Examples of clausal secondaries following demonstrative pronouns acting as primaries are given in §8.8.3.

Occasionally, the juxtaposition construction is used with an infinitival primary followed by a nominal secondary, corresponding to the direct object of a transitive verbal lexeme.[10]

[9]Note that the embedded relative clause is separated from its primary *sawzì* by the copula and a prosodic break. Alternatively, it could be analysed as an asyndetically conjoined relative clause governed as well by the primary *xa*.

[10]Such cases can also be analysed as exponents of the completive relation rather that the attributive one (see §2.1.1). Yet I prefer to to analyse them as attributive constructions, as discussed in §8.5.

(16) JSanandaj: **Infinitive–Conjoined Nouns (objects)**
(šerúʾ wí-lu ba=) yălopé hulaulà =u' yălopé făransà =u' ʿəbrì,'
start do-3PL in learn.INF Judaism =and learn.inf French =and Hebrew
fàrsi.'
Persian
'(They started) to learn Judaism, and to learn French, Hebrew and Persian.'
(Khan 2009b: 330 [B:12])

Similarly, prepositions or conjunctions are complemented by nouns or clauses without any special marking:

(17) JSanandaj: **Preposition–Noun**
reša mez
on table
'on the table' (Khan 2009b: 224)

(18) JSanandaj: **Conjunction–Clause**
mangól [ga= lăxa k-olí]'
as in= here IND-do.3PL
'as they do here[11]' (Khan 2009b: 393 [B:67])

An adjective can also serve as the primary of the juxtaposition construction, whenever it is further specified by a nominal secondary. While the secondary in such cases is an adverbial specification of the adjectival primary, formally it uses the same juxtaposition construction as the above examples (compare to example (47) on page 239, where the AC is explicitly marked by the Ezafe suffix):

(19) JSanandaj: **Adjective–Noun**
(tamā́m-e yomá) ḥărík ḥaštà (xirá =y)'
entire-EZ day busy work become.RES =COP.3MS
'(All day he has been) busy with work' (Khan 2009b: 570)

[11] An alternative analysis of this example is to see only the prepositional phrase *ga lăxa* as the complement of *mangól*, the verb *kolí* being the main verb. This would correspond to the translation 'They do as (it is) here'.

8.4 Juxtaposition-cum-agreement (X Y.AGR)

Similarly to other NENA dialects, inflecting adjectives (which are typically but not exclusively of Aramaic origin) formally use the juxtaposition construction, and at the same time show agreement features with the primary noun.

(20) JSanandaj: **Noun–Adjective**
bela *rŭwa*
house(MS) big.MS
'a big house' (Khan 2009b: 251)

Similarly, ordinals above one, juxtaposed to their primary, can optionally agree with it, similarly to adjectives:[12]

(21) JSanandaj: **Noun–Ordinal**
baxta *tre-min-{ta}*
woman(FS) two-ORD-{FS}
'the second woman' (Khan 2009b: 213)

8.5 Inverse juxtaposition (Y X)

inverse juxtaposition constructionOf special interest are constructions in which the order of the secondary and the primary is reversed, so that the secondary precedes the primary. There are two distinct kinds of these constructions, one which involves a verbal noun acting as a primary, and the second which involves an adjective or an ordinal as the secondary.[13]

8.5.1 Verbal nouns as primaries

The category of verbal nouns includes the infinitive and the active participle.[14] These nouns have the particularity that they can be complemented by a secondary which acts semantically as the direct object of the verbal lexeme. More-

[12]Note that ordinals are derived from the corresponding cardinals by means of the suffix *-min*, being of Persian or Sorani origin (see §9.4.5).

[13]Recall that the titles of the examples always reflect the order **Primary–Secondary**, irrespective of the order of these constituents in the example.

[14]The resultative participle, on the other hand, does not participate in ACs, as its distribution is restricted to some compound tenses (Khan 2009b: 90–96). Some resultative participles have acquired an adjectival meaning, but in this case they do not function differently from other inflecting adjectives (Khan 2009b: 204).

over, I include in the category of verbal nouns also nouns participating in complex predicate formation (CP nouns), as their secondaries are semantically the direct object of the entire complex predicate. Note that the extensive usage of complex predication in JSanandaj originates in the replication of an Iranic, probably Persian, pattern (of which see Samvelian 2012).

One may doubt whether constructions involving verbal nouns together with their complements should be regarded as ACs, rather than expressing simply a completive relation (see §2.1.1). However, since verbal nouns behave categorically as nouns (they share the privilege of occurrence of nouns), and complementation of nouns yields by definition an AC, it seems justifiable to regard these constructions as ACs, albeit of a special kind. Two observations strengthen this claim: First, nouns and their complements participate sporadically in explicitly marked ACs (see examples (71)–(72) on page 246 for verbal nouns modified by a possessive suffix). Secondly, whenever their complement is an independent pronoun it is explicitly marked as genitive (see §8.8.4).

Notwithstanding the above analysis, verbal nouns expanded by a complement exhibit a key property of the verbal phrase of JSanandaj, namely the pre-verbal position of the complement. In fact, the OV order of JSanandaj is very probably a contact feature originating in Iranic languages, as most NENA dialects have a VO order. Thus, these ACs are of the inverse juxtapositioninverse juxtaposition construction type, in which the secondary precedes the primary (and see also example (40) on page 238):

(22) JSanandaj: **Participle–Noun**
xola garš-ana
rope pull-PTCP
'rope puller' (Khan 2009b: 252)

(23) JSanandaj: **Infinitive–Noun**
(ʾila hiw-li ba=) xola garoše
hand gave-1SG in= rope pull.INF
'(I began) to pull the rope.' (Khan 2009b: 330)

8.5.2 Adjectival and ordinal secondaries

Normally an adjectival secondary follows the primary noun (see example (20) on the preceding page). However, according to Khan (2009b: 251), "[i]n some isolated cases the adjective is placed before the head [=the primary]. This is found where the adjective is evaluative, i.e. expressing the subjective evaluation by the speaker rather an objective description of the referent." The following example is given:

(24) JSanandaj: **Noun–Adjective**
ʿáyza kắsbi (hùl ta= nóš-ox).'
good.MS[15] gain(FS) take.IMP for= REFL-POSS.2MS
'Take the good earnings for yourself.' (Khan 2009b: 251 [A:103])

Ordinal secondaries can similarly appear before the primary, in this case without any evaluative semantics. In the case of the ordinal *ʾăwaḷ* 'one', borrowed ultimately from Arabic, this yields the typical Arabic order, but in JSanandaj this is only one possibility (contrast with examples (13) on page 230 and (45) on page 239):

(25) JSanandaj: **Noun–Ordinal**
ʾăwaḷ gora
first man
'the first man' (Khan 2009b: 213)

Ordinals above one can optionally agree with the primary noun, also when they precede it (compare example (21) on page 232):

(26) JSanandaj: **Noun–Ordinal**
tre-min-{ta} baxta
two-ORD-{FS} woman(FS)
'the second woman' (Khan 2009b: 213)

8.6 Usage of relativizer (X REL Y)

Clausal secondaries can be marked as such by the use of a relativizer. Two distinct relativizers are available in JSanandaj: *ya* and *ke*, both borrowed from Iranic languages. In particular, one finds *ke* as a relativizer in Persian (Balaÿ & Esmaïli 2013: 136).

The relativizer *ya* is used mostly with definite primaries, while the relativizer *ke* has no such restriction. The exact distribution of these relativizers is outside the scope of this work. Prosodically, both relativizers are part of the clausal secondary, as they often cliticize to its first word.

[15]This example is peculiar in that the adjective disagrees in gender with the head noun. It may be that some speakers treat *ʿáyza* as an invariable adjective, being probably of foreign origin.

(27) JSanandaj: **Noun–Clause**
ʾo= našé ya= [daʿwàt k-ol-í-wa-lu]ˈ
DEF= people REL= invitation IND-do-APL-PST-P3PL
'the people whom they invited' (Khan 2009b: 378 [A:42])

(28) JSanandaj: **Pronoun–Clause**
ʾonyé yá [ṭăbăqá ʾăwaḷ =ye-lù]ˈ
3PL REL class first =COP.PST-3PL
'Those who were the first class' (Khan 2009b: 379 [B:5])

(29) JSanandaj: **Noun–Clause**
xá=ʿəda našé ke= [ga=xá meydā́n smix =èn]ˈ
INDF=few people REL= in=INDF square stood.RES =COP.3PL
'a group of people who were standing in a square' (Khan 2009b: 380 [A:109])

In Sulemaniyya, one finds conversely the cognate relativizer *ga~ka* mostly with definite primaries, in restrictive relative clauses (Khan 2004: 414):[16]

(30) Sulemaniyya: **Noun–Noun**
yóma ga= gezí ta= Merònˈ mìl-a.ˈ
day REL= go-3PL to= M. died-3FS
'She died on the day that they went to Mount Meron.' (Khan 2004: 415 [R:185])

In JSanandaj, the relativizer *ke* is found following certain adverbials, notably *qǎme* 'before':

(31) JSanandaj: **Conjunction–Clause**
qǎme ké hètˈ
before REL SBJV.come.2MS
'before you came' (Khan 2009b: 391)

In this usage, it can also combine with the Ezafe marking; see example (55) on page 241.

The relativizer *ya* occurs once in the corpus of Khan (2009b) complementing a temporal adverb. In this case, the entire construction gets a temporal meaning:

[16] A similar restriction is found with the relativizer *ke* borrowed in Neo-Mandaic (Häberl 2009: 165).

(32) JSanandaj: **Adverb–Clause**
ʾăta ya= [daʿwăt-í wilà =y]ˈ
now REL= invitation-POSS.1SG done.RES =COP.MS
'now that they have invited me' (Khan 2009b: 379 [D:15])

8.7 The construct state construction (X.CST Y)

JSanandaj has 3 different morphological means which can be classified under the broad category of construct state as defined in §2.3.1:

8.7.1 The historical construct state marking

The historical Classical Aramaic construct state marking, formed by apocope of the primary noun, is not productive any more in JSanandaj, yet a reflex of it is retained in some collocations and idioms. For example, in the following example, the noun *belá* 'house' appears as a reduced form *be* with the meaning 'family of' (compare Qaraqosh example (15) on page 155):

(33) JSanandaj: **Noun–Noun**
be= kalda
house.CST= bride
'family of the bride' (Khan 2009b: 201)

Similarly, two prepositions of nominal origin have retained an apocopated form alongside their full form. These are the prepositions *reša* 'on' (derived from the noun *reša* 'head' by pattern replication of Kurdish; see footnote 29 on page 144), which also has the apocopated form *reš*, and the preposition *txela* 'under', which also has the apocopated form *txel*. While both forms require a complement, I consider only the apocopated one to be positively marked as construct state.

(34) JSanandaj: **Preposition–Noun**
reša/reš mez
on/on.CST table
'on the table' (Khan 2009b: 224)

(35) JSanandaj: **Preposition–Noun**
txela/txel mez
under/under.CST table
'under the table' (Khan 2009b: 225)

8.7.2 The Ezafe construction

The closest structural parallel of JSanandaj to the Neo-CSC present in other dialects is the borrowed Ezafe construction, in which an Ezafe suffix *-e~-y* marks the primary as such.[17] The form of the Ezafe in JSanandaj seems to indicate a Persian origin, an assumption which is corroborated by its frequent usage with Persian words (see example (42) on the following page).[18]

Indeed, the usage of the Ezafe is most frequent "when the noun is an unadapted loanword that ends in a consonant rather than in a nominal inflectional vowel" (Khan 2009b: 199). These loanwords are not necessarily of Iranic origin. For instance, in the following example the primary is the Mishnaic Hebrew loan-noun שַׁמָּשׁ *šămmaš.*

(36) JSanandaj: **Noun–Noun**
šămáš-e kništà
beadle-EZ synagogue
'the beadle of the synagogue' (Khan 2009b: 199 [A:43])

Note that a similar restriction appears in Sulemaniyya, where the Sorani borrowed Ezafe suffix *-i* is most frequently used with loanwords (Khan 2004: 192f.):

(37) Sulemaniyya: **Noun–Noun**
maktáb-i hulayè
school-EZ Jews
'school of Jews' (Khan 2004: 514 [R:141])

Khan (2009b: 199) also gives examples (possibly elicited) of native Aramaic primaries marked by the Ezafe. In these cases, the final number suffix (SG: *-a* or PL: *-e*) is normally retained, but can also be elided in "fast speech" (in which case the stress falls on the Ezafe suffix).

(38) JSanandaj: **Noun–Noun**
bel-{á}-e bărux-i
house-{SG}-EZ friend-POSS.1SG
'the house of my friend' (Khan 2009b: 199f.)

[17]The variant form *-y* is found in my fieldwork data.

[18]The Persian Ezafe is *-e*, while in Sorani, it is normally *-i* (but see §9.4 for possible variation). Note that in the nearby Hawrami dialect the plural Ezafe is realized as *-e* (Holmberg & Odden 2008: 133).

(39) JSanandaj: **Noun–Noun**
bat-{é}-e *bărux-i*
houses-{PL}-EZ friend-POSS.1SG
'the houses of my friend' (Khan 2009b: 199f.)

The plural of *bela* 'house' can be the irregular form *baté* or the regular *belé*. Therefore, one could argue that in example (38) on the previous page the primary's number distinction is lost. Yet, in my own elicitation I observed a slight phonetic difference between *belé* 'houses' and *bel-é* 'house.SG-EZ': in the latter form the Ezafe is produced as [æ] (and not as the expected [e]), which is understandable if this vowel is analysed as a coalescence of a singular suffix /-a/ and an Ezafe suffix /-e/. On the other hand, the coalescence of the Ezafe suffix with the plural suffix yields a construction identical to the juxtaposition construction, as Khan (2009b: 200) notes.

Similarly to the Neo-CSC of other NENA dialects, as well as the CSC of classical Semitic languages (such as Biblical Hebrew or Akkadian), the Ezafe construction can be used not only with nominal secondaries, but also with infinitival or clausal secondaries:

(40) JSanandaj: **Noun–Infinitival phrase**
(ʾaná) ḥawṣălá-e [ʾắra tărošè] (lít-i =u)ˈ
1SG patience-EZ land build.INF NEG.EX-1SG =and
'(I don't have) the patience to build on the land.' (Khan 2009b: 571 [C:6])

(41) JSanandaj: **Noun–Clause**
ʾo= baxtá-e [ləxm-ăkè k-ol-a-wa-le =ó]ˈ
DEF= woman-EZ bread-DEF IND-do-A3FS-PST-P3MS =open
'the woman who made (lit. opened) the bread' (Khan 2009b: 381 [B:22])

In contrast to the classical Semitic CSC, however, the Ezafe construction is also used with adjectival or ordinal secondaries. In some cases, where both the primary and the secondary are Persian words, the entire expression can be seen as a code-switch to Persian, as in the following example, where the AC corresponds to Persian لباسِ خراب *ləbā́s-e xărā́b* 'ragged clothes':

(42) JSanandaj: **Noun–Adjective**
ləbā́s-e xărā́b (lòš-wa)ˈ
clothing(MS)-EZ bad(INV) wear.3MS-PST
'(He wore) ragged clothes.' (Khan 2009b: 251 [A:108])

When used with native Aramaic adjectives as secondaries, these inflect as expected:[19]

(43) JSanandaj: **Noun–Adjective**
bel-{á}-e rŭwa
house(M)-{SG}-EZ big.MS
'a big house' (Khan 2009b: 251)

(44) JSanandaj: **Noun–Adjective**
pəstan-e ʿista
gown(F)-EZ beautiful.FS
'a beautiful gown' (own fieldwork)

Ordinals behave similarly to adjectives. The loan-ordinal *ʾăwaḷ* 'first' is invariable, while higher ordinals show optional agreement:

(45) JSanandaj: **Noun–Ordinal**
gorá-e ʾăwaḷ
man-EZ first(INV)
'the first man' (Khan 2009b: 213)

(46) JSanandaj: **Noun–Ordinal**
baxtá-e tre-min-{ta}
woman(FS)-EZ two-ORD-{FS}
'the second woman' (Khan 2009b: 213)

Note that adjectives can also serve as the primary of the Ezafe construction (compare example (19) on page 231):

(47) JSanandaj: **Adjective–Infinitive**
(ʾo= tré) ḥarik-é šyakà (=ye-lu).ˈ
DEF= two busy-EZ wrestle.INF =COP-3PL
'The two of them were busy wrestling.' (Khan 2009b: 331 (2))

[19]Optional inflection of adjectives following the Ezafe is attested sporadically also in Hawrami:

(i) Hawrami: **Noun–Adjective**
žæn-i zɪl-{æ}
woman-EZ big-{FS}
'big woman' (Holmberg & Odden 2008: 130, fn. 2)

The Ezafe construction can easily be embedded. In the following examples, the primaries are NPs consisting themselves of the Ezafe construction:

(48) JSanandaj: **Noun Phrase–Adjective**
[pəstan-e kald]-e zărif
gown-EZ bride-EZ beautiful(INV)
'a beautiful bridal gown' (own fieldwork)

(49) JSanandaj: **Noun Phrase–Noun**
[bel-e smoq]-e tat-i
house-EZ red(M)-EZ father-POSS.1SG
'the red house of my father' (own fieldwork)

In such cases the Ezafe behaves very similarly to its Persian model, and can similarly be analysed as a phrasal suffix (see §4.3). There are also cases where the secondary consists of the Ezafe construction:

(50) JSanandaj: **Noun–Noun Phrase**
bel-e [brat-e ʾamm-i]
house-EZ daughter-EZ aunt-POSS.1SG
'the house of my cousin (daughter of my aunt)[20]' (own fieldwork)

(51) JSanandaj: **Quantifier–Noun Phrase**
tamam-e [bat-e tat-i]
all-EZ houses-EZ father-POSS.1SG
'all the houses of my father' (own fieldwork)

Conspicuously missing, in contrast to the Persian model, are cases with adverbial secondaries (see example (1) on page 94). In Khan's description there is only one such case, consisting of the fixed prepositional phrase *ʿăla ḥăda* 'aside', borrowed through Persian from Arabic على حد *ʿalā ḥadd* (Khan 2009b: 569).

(52) JSanandaj: **Noun–Prepositional Phrase**
tănurá-e ʿăla-ḥădá
oven-EZ on-edge
'a separate oven' (Khan 2009b: 252 [B:18])

[20] Surprisingly, the speaker translated 'aunt' as *ʾamma* and not as the expected *ʾamta* (cf. Khan 2009b: 538).

Productive prepositional phrases are lacking from Khan's description, and did not show up in my elicitation. On the other hand, prepositions and nouns serving as adverbials can appear as primaries of the Ezafe construction. When complemented by clauses the relativizer *ke* is sometimes used as well:

(53) JSanandaj: **Preposition–Noun**
dawr-e mez
around-EZ table
'around the table' (Khan 2009b: 220)

(54) JSanandaj: **Adverbial noun–Clause**
wáxt-e [híye bel-àn]'
time-EZ came.3MS house-1PL
'when he came to our house' (Khan 2009b: 394 (4))

(55) JSanandaj: **Adverbial noun–Clause**
ta= zămān-e ke= [ʾanà xlulá wilí]
until= time-EZ REL= 1SG wedding did.1SG
'Until the time that I married' (Khan 2009b: 381 [A:4])

Another case where the Ezafe construction is not found is whenever the primary is a noun serving to quantify the secondary. In such cases the juxtaposition construction is used. Consider the following example, where the secondary itself is an Ezafe construction (compare example (11) on page 229).

(56) JSanandaj: **Q. Noun Phrase–Noun Phrase**
[xa lewan] [reza-y yarixa]
one cup rice(M)-EZ long(MS)
'one cup of long rice' (own fieldwork)

8.7.3 Stress retraction as emerging construct state marking

In JSanandaj, stress is commonly word-final. However, in non-pausal contexts, the stress of nouns and pronouns may be retracted (Khan 2009b: 53). While this phenomenon occurs more widely than just in ACs, it may be seen as an *emerging* construct-state marking.[21] Consider the following example, with attention to the stress position on the head:

[21]Recall that the historical Semitic construct state began also as a prosodic phenomenon of stress-shift; see §2.3.2.

(57) JSanandaj: **Noun–Noun**
bróna Jăhằn
son J.
'the son of Jahan' (Khan 2009b: 53 [A:17])

The same phenomenon of stress retraction occurs on the noun *ʾăxóna* 'brother' appearing before an adjective in example (2) on page 227.

8.8 Genitive marking of secondaries

A reflex of the Classical Aramaic linker *d-* is retained in JSanandaj only in one environment, namely optionally preceding vowel-initial demonstrative pronouns. As such, it has the same distribution as the genitive prefix *d-* found in other dialects, and indeed, in JSanandaj too it can be analysed as a genitive prefix, as it has no pronominal force typical of the linker *d-*.[22] The detailed argumentation for this analysis is given in §4.5, and see in particular §4.5.2.2 regarding JSanandaj.

The situation in JSanandaj can be contrasted with the situation in the closely related dialects of Kerend and Qarah Hasan, which have lost all trace of the *d-* linker and always use the unmarked independent pronouns in the secondary position (Khan 2009b: 11, and see example (62) on the facing page).

In the following, I discuss separately the occurrence of genitive marked demonstratives as determiners and conversely as independent genitive pronouns. A third subsection is devoted to genitive marked demonstratives preceding clausal secondaries.

8.8.1 Genitive determiners

Demonstrative pronouns used as determiners of secondaries take an optional genitive marking both after nominal and adverbial primaries. Since the marking is optional, in contrast to JZakho, the unmarked forms cannot be analysed as non-genitive, but must rather be seen as unspecified forms (±GEN):

[22] Cf. however Khan (2009b: 200), who assimilates it to the linker, or "genitive particle" in his terminology: "The Aramaic genitive particle *d* is used only when the dependent component of an annexation construction contains a demonstrative pronoun." Khan uses the notion "particle" but in fact it is a bound morpheme.

(58) JSanandaj: **Noun–Pronoun**
bela {d}-o naša
house {GEN}-DEM.DIST man
'the house of that man' (Khan 2009b: 200)

(59) JSanandaj: **Preposition–Pronoun**
reša/reš {d}-o mez
on/on.CST {GEN}-DEM.DIST table
'on that table' (Khan 2009b: 224)

Note that in the last example, the preposition *reša* can appear either in its full form or in its apocopate construct state form *reš*. Similarly, the genitive prefix also follows primary nouns marked as construct state by means of the Ezafe (=example (21) on page 111):

(60) JSanandaj: **Noun–Noun**
fešár-e d-o màe
pressure-EZ GEN-DEM.DIST water
'the pressure of the water' (Khan 2009b: 200 [A:59])

8.8.2 Independent genitive pronouns

The demonstrative pronouns may also appear as independent pronouns in the secondary position. In this case they are obligatorily marked by the genitive prefix.

(61) JSanandaj: **Noun–Pronoun**
bela d-o
house GEN-3SG
'his house' (Khan 2009b: 200)

This situation can be contrasted with the closely related dialects of Kerend and Qarah Ḥasan, where such marking is always absent:

(62) Kerend: **Noun–Pronoun**
bela o
house 3SG
'his house' (Khan 2009b: 11)

As with the genitive determiners, the genitive marking also appears after prepositions, including those marked by apocopate construct state (compare to example (59) on the preceding page and contrast with example (6) on page 228). Note that the prepositions often pro-cliticize to their complement, obscuring the fact that the *d-* is part of the secondary:

(63) JSanandaj: **Preposition–Pronoun**
ba= d-o
in= GEN-3SG
'in it' (Khan 2009b: 218)

(64) JSanandaj: **Preposition–Pronoun**
reša/reš d-o
on/on.CST GEN-3SG
'on it' (Khan 2009b: 224)

Here too, the genitive marking also occurs after the Ezafe, irrespective of the category of the primary (and see also example (71) on page 246):

(65) JSanandaj: **Noun–Pronoun**
belá-e d-o
house-EZ GEN-3SG
'his house' (Khan 2009b: 200)

(66) JSanandaj: **Preposition–Pronoun**
ba-dawr-e d-o
in-around-EZ GEN-3SG
'around it' (Khan 2009b: 220)

(67) JSanandaj: **Adjective–Pronoun**
(ʾắt hămešá) ḥăřík-e d-èaʾ
2SG always busy-EZ GEN-DEM.SG
'You are always busy with this.' (Khan 2009b: 570 [A:102])

8.8.3 Genitive pronouns preceding clausal secondaries

Certain prepositions can be complemented by a clausal secondary, with the help of an intervening demonstrative pronoun, itself marked by the genitive prefix.

(68) JSanandaj: **Preposition–Clause**
bar= d-èa *[ʾay ḥášta wil-à-lu]*
after= GEN-DEM.PROX.SG DEM.PROX work(FS) did-P.3FS-A.3PL
'after they had done this work' (Khan 2009b: 392 [B:17])

(69) JSanandaj: **Preposition–Clause**
qắme d-óa *[ʾána b= ʿolắm henà]*
before GEN-DEM.DIST.SG 1SG in= world come.SBJV-1MS
'before I was born' (Khan 2009b: 392 [A:50])

The genitive marking shows that the demonstrative pronoun in each example acts as the secondary, i.e. the direct complement of the preposition. As it is followed by a clause, one cannot analyse the demonstrative pronoun in this position as an NP determiner.[23] Indeed, Khan (2009b: 392) writes that "[the] demonstrative pronoun [...] is bound anaphorically to the following content clause". Yet what is the exact syntactic relation between the demonstrative and the clause? The role of the demonstrative pronoun is to provide a nominal head acting as the complement of the preposition. As a nominal head, it governs the clause and embeds it within an NP. It follows that the demonstrative pronoun and the clause stand in an attributive relation with each other. Yet this relationship is not marked, as it is instantiated by the juxtaposition construction, discussed in §8.3. Only the attributive relation between the preposition and the demonstrative pronoun is positively marked by means of a genitive case prefix. The two attributive relations are schematized in Table 8.1:

Table 8.1: Clausal complement of a preposition mediated by a demonstrative

Prep.	$\mapsto_1$	[DEM	$\mapsto_2$	Clause]$_{\text{NP.GEN}}$
	Genitive-marked		Zero-marked	

In other dialects, also the second attributive relationship is marked by means of a construct state marking of the pronominal primary. Such is the case in JUrmi, as is shown in examples (101)–(102) on page 215. In fact, also in JSanandaj there

[23]In JZakho, there are rare cases where a determiner is followed directly by a clause, as in example (110) on page 146, yet in such cases the determiner/demonstrative pronoun has referential power, quite distinct from the cases discussed here.

are examples in which this relation is marked by a relativizer which follows the demonstrative pronoun.

(70) JSanandaj: **Preposition–Clause**
bár= d-ea ke= [xostá xlulá wil-wa-lù]
after= GEN-DEM.PROX.SG REL= request marriage did-PST-3PL
'after they made the request of the wedding' (Khan 2009b: 392 [A:34])

8.8.4 Genitivally marked complements of verbal nouns and verbs

The genitive case is also used to mark complements of verbal nouns, be they infinitives, participles, or complex-predicate nouns. When this marking appears alongside another AC marking, such as the Ezafe in the following example, it is quite clear that it too marks the attributive relation.

(71) JSanandaj: **CP Noun–Pronoun**
da'wăt-e did-ăxun (wilì)'
invitation-EZ GEN-2PL (did.1SG)
'I invited you.' (Khan 2009b: 482 [D:8])

Yet, in other cases, one finds the genitive marking as the sole exponent of the attributive relation, as in the following example which instantiates the inverse juxtaposition construction (see §8.5.1):

(72) JSanandaj: **CP Noun–Pronoun**
(kŭ́le 'aṣər) did-án da'wàt (k-ol-í)
every evening GEN-1PL invitation IND-do-3PL
'They will invite us every evening.' (Khan 2009b: 480 [D:6])

Such cases pose an analytic difficulty as JSanandaj makes use of the genitive pronouns also to mark complements of finite verbs.

(73) JSanandaj: **Verb–Pronoun**
did-ox grəš-li
OBL-2MS pulled-1SG
'I pulled you.' (Khan 2009b: 159)

(74) JSanandaj: **Verb–Pronoun**
d-o grəš-le
OBL-3MS pulled-A.3MS
'He pulled him.' (Khan 2009b: 159)

In light of such examples, one may re-interpret the *d~did-* morphemes not as genitive case markers but rather as oblique case markers, fusing together accusative and genitive marking. This may be regarded as a development due to language contact, as oblique case is known in Iranic languages, notably in Kurmanji (see §9.4.2), which is however not in direct contact with JSanandaj, but also in Hawrami (MacKenzie 1966: 13), spoken in closer proximity to Sanandaj. Khan (2009b: 158) proposes an alternative cause, explaining example (73) on the preceding page as being a derivation of example (75) below, in which the accusative preposition *həl* was dropped. The genitive marking is thus justified, as the pronoun is a complement of a preposition:

(75) JSanandaj: **Verb–Pronoun**
həl= did-ox grəš-li[24]
ACC_Prep= GEN-2MS pulled-1SG
'I pulled you.' (Khan 2009b: 158 [modified])

Be that as it may, the development of *d~did-* into an oblique case marker permits us to analyse its occurrence in example (72) as marking the object of the entire verbal complex *daʿwàt k-ol-í* 'they invited' rather than marking an attributive secondary of *daʿwàt* alone. Yet, taking into consideration clear cases such as example (71), I prefer to analyse *did-* first and foremost as a genitive case marker, being an exponent of the attributive relation, whenever this is possible, and see any other grammatical functions as being secondary.

In this vein, I consider the following example to be showing a conjoined NP in the secondary position of the inverse juxtaposition construction, although only the pronominal complement is marked by genitive case.

(76) JSanandaj: **CP Noun–Pronoun+Noun**
(ʾaxtú tămà) [did-í =u daăk-í] daʿwát (lá kol-étun)'
2PL why GEN-1SG =and mother-POSS.SG invitation NEG IND.make-2PL
'Why do you not invite me and my mother?' (Khan 2009b: 482 [D:8])

[24] I took the liberty of changing the agent from 3rd to 1st person, in order to provide a clear parallel to the previous example.

Similarly, I consider pronominal complements of infinitives as being in genitive case, as in the following example, exhibiting again the inverse order of constituents typical of verbal constructions in JSanandaj:

(77) JSanandaj: **Infinitive–Pronoun**
(ʾila di-le ba=) did-i gărоše
hand placed-3MS in= GEN-1SG pull.INF
'He began to pull me.' (Khan 2009b: 331)

8.9 Dative marking of secondaries

The elicitation session revealed two examples of an elaborate construction in which the primary is marked by an Ezafe suffix and the secondary is marked by the dative preposition *əl-*.[25] In both cases, a short pause or hesitation is marked after the primary, which may explain the speaker's need to re-mark the secondary as such by means of the preposition. Note that the usage of the dative preposition to mark secondaries is not an innovation but rather a retention, as it is attested also in Syriac (see §3.7). A similar usage of this preposition is attested in Neo-Mandaic (Häberl 2009: 152).

(78) JSanandaj: **Noun Phrase–Noun**
[xa= dana bela]-e ... əl= [brata amm-i]
one= unit house-EZ DAT= daughter aunt-POSS.1SG
'one house of my cousin' (own fieldwork)

(79) JSanandaj: **Noun Phrase–Noun**
[bel-e raba ʿayza]-y ... əl= tat-i
house-EZ much beautiful(MS) DAT= father-POSS.1SG
'the very beautiful house of my father ' (own fieldwork)

Note that a similar usage of the dative preposition is found in Sulemaniyya, but without the Ezafe marking:

(80) Sulemaniyya: **Noun Phrase–Pronoun**
ʾaxonàˈ biš= zor-ăke ʾəl did-ànˈ
brother more= small-DEF DAT GEN-1PL
'the younger brother of ours' (Khan 2004: 262 [R:104])

[25] I did not find any mention of this usage in Khan (2009b).

Similarly, in predicative position one finds secondaries marked by the dative preposition. The semantic primary in such cases is the subject of the clause, but it does not form a syntactic constituent with the secondary. Therefore, I treat this construction as lacking a primary.

(81) JSanandaj: ∅–**Noun**
ay *bela* *[∅ əl=* *tat-i]* *=y*
DEM.PROX house ∅ DAT= father-POSS.1SG =COP
'This house is my father's.' (own fieldwork)

Again, there is a very similar construction in Sulemaniyya:

(82) Sulemaniyya: ∅–**Noun**
'ay= *belá* *[∅ 'əl=* *barux-ì]* *=ye.'*
DEM= house ∅ DAT= friend-POSS.1SG =COP
'This house belongs to my friend.' (Khan 2004: 262 (9))

Other dialects use the linker *d-* in the predicative position (see for instance examples (87)–(88) on page 175 on Qaraqosh). As JSanandaj has lost the linker *d-*, it uses instead the dative preposition *əl-*.

8.10 Conclusions

The AC system of JSanandaj is highly divergent in comparison to most other NENA dialects, and in particular the dialects surveyed in the previous chapters. This divergence is at least partly related to extensive language contact with Sorani and Persian.

The most important innovation of JSanandaj (and related dialects such as the dialect of Kerend) is the loss of the Classical Aramaic linker *d-*. Not only is the linker as such lost, but also its head-marking reflex, the *-əd* construct state suffix found in other dialects, is absent in JSanandaj. The loss of these markers is clearly correlated with the rise of the usage of the zero-marked juxtaposition construction in the dialect, discussed in §8.3. Yet the usage of the juxtaposition construction is not necessarily a direct consequence of the loss of the D-markers: The D-marked constructions can coexist with the juxtaposition construction, as is the case in Sulemaniyya (see examples footnote 8–footnote 8 on page 229). Rather, it is probable that the juxtaposition construction itself is contact induced, as will be discussed in §11.3.2.2.

The only remnant of the *d-* linker in JSanandaj is the genitive prefix *d-* used before vowel-initial demonstrative pronouns (see §8.8). Indeed, this very retention is one of my arguments in favour analysing the [d] segment in this position as a genitive prefix, since it follows an independent development path as compared to the linker *d-* (see §4.5.2.2). Possibly through contact with Kurdish or Hawrami, the *d-* prefix in JSanandaj shows moreover some progress towards becoming an oblique case marker (see §8.8.4). In the closely related dialects of Kerend and Qarah Ḥasan, on the other hand, even the genitive prefix is lost.

Another interesting retention shared by JSanandaj and Sulemaniyya is the sporadic usage of the dative preposition *əl-* to mark secondaries, found also in Syriac (see §8.9 and compare to §3.7). Again, it seems that this retention is correlated with the demise of the usage of the linker *d-*.

Alongside the extensive usage of the juxtaposition construction, there is another construction replacing structurally the Semitic CSC, namely the Iranic Ezafe construction, present both in Sulemaniyya and JSanandaj. The fact that this construction is still largely confined to loanwords may indicate that its introduction to these dialects is a relatively late process, not directly related to the loss of the D-markers or the usage of the juxtaposition construction. On the other hand, it may be an indication of the cyclic nature of language change: The loss of old grammatical markers (the D-markers) is subsequently compensated by adoption of new grammatical markers (the Ezafe). This reasoning has also led us to postulate the possible emergence of a new construct state marking due to stress shift (see §8.7.3).

The grammatical developments discussed above have caused an important structural change in JSanandaj: In contrast to the situation in Classical Aramaic, conserved in most NENA dialects, the distributional distinction between nominal secondaries (occurring typically after construct state nouns or the linker) and adjectival secondaries (occurring typically after free state nouns) has been levelled, as both the Ezafe construction and the juxtaposition construction treat these two types of secondaries alike, the only difference being that native adjectival secondaries agree in gender and number with the primary. On the other hand, clausal secondaries are sometimes signalled as such, as they are optionally preceded by borrowed relativizers in both these constructions (see discussion in §8.6).

Finally, another important effect of language contact is the emergence of the inverse juxtaposition construction, in which the secondary precedes the primary. When this construction occurs with verbal nouns as primaries (see §8.5.1), this can be explained as a consequence of the general shift of the language to an OV order in the verbal domain. The usage of the inverse construction with ordinal secondaries (see §8.5.2) is most probably a converging borrowing from Arabic and Sorani (see Table 11.5 on page 385). The rare usage of the inverse construction with adjectival secondaries may also be related to contact (possibly with Azeri), but this requires further investigation.

9 Attributive constructions in Kurdish dialects

9.1 Introduction

The following chapter surveys the attributive construction system of several Kurdish dialects. As it is not my intention to outline a complete grammar of these constructions in Kurdish, it is less detailed than the previous chapters devoted to NENA dialects. Moreover, the data will be presented in a cross-dialectal manner, contrasting the Kurmanji and Sorani dialectal groups. The aim of the chapter is to analyse the data of these languages and situate them in the same typological framework used for the NENA dialects in order to facilitate the comparison among the three.

The examples were drawn mainly from the data presented in MacKenzie (1961) as well as the grammars of standard Kurmanji and standard Sorani written by Thackston (2006a,b). Further Sorani examples were borrowed from Blau (1980) and to a lesser extent from Abdulla & McCarus (1967), a grammar of the Sulemaniyya dialect (in Sorani: سلێمانی *Silêmanî*). The Standard Kurmanji data was complemented by the descriptions of Bedir Khan (1960) and Bedir Khan & Lescot (1970).[1] Some further Kurmanji dialectal data was drawn from Blau (1975), a description of the dialects of Amadiya and Sinǰar. Some additional examples were drawn from Samvelian (2008).[2] The original examples appearing in the above sources (with the exception of Samvelian 2008) are not glossed. For clarity, I have added

[1] The Bedir Khan family originated in the Kurdish Bohtan principality in south-eastern Anatolia. While their grammatical descriptions present a standardized version of Kurmanji, they are likely based on the Bohtan variety.

[2] In the following, references to Sorani and Kurmanji refer either to the standardized varieties or the dialectal clusters (MacKenzie's Group I and Group II respectively), with reference to particular dialects clearly indicated, if these are available in the cited source. When citing MacKenzie (1961) the numerical reference to his corpus (MacKenzie 1962) is given in square brackets, if available. The Sorani name *Silêmanî* will be used to refer to the Sulemaniyya dialect (MacKenzie's Sul.) to differentiate it from the NENA dialect spoken in the same area. Similarly I distinguish between Kurdish *Amêdî* (MacKenzie's Am.) and NENA *Amədya*, both spoken in the surroundings of the town of Amadiya.

glosses according to my own analysis. For sake of consistency, I have opted to normalize the transcription of all varieties and from all sources to the Latin transcription of Kurdish used in Kurmanji.[3] The examples from Thackston (2006b) and Blau (1980) are also cited in the standard Sorani orthography using Arabic script, as is the case in these sources.

For the geographical span of the Kurdish dialect clusters and the related languages (Gorani and Zazaki), I relied chiefly on the map of Izady (1992: 171).[4] For the benefit of the reader, a map of the Kurdish dialects discussed in the book is presented in Figure 9.1. It is based on the maps of Haig & Öpengin (2014: 111) as well as MacKenzie (1961: xvi).[5] This map can be compared with the NENA map presented on page 15.

The chapter is organised as follows: In §9.2 I treat the possessive pronominal enclitics, present only in Sorani dialects. The most prominent AC markers in Kurdish are the various Ezafe morphemes. Section §9.3 gives an overview of the different forms found in standard Kurmanji and Sorani and motivates the differentiation of three distinct types of Ezafe morphemes, discussed in the following sections. Section §9.4 discusses the Construct Ezafe Construction, which can be seen as the Kurdish equivalent of the NENA Neo-CSC. The marking of secondaries by the oblique case, present in Kurmanji dialects, is also discussed there. Section §9.5 discusses the Linker Ezafe Construction, which can be seen as the Kurdish equivalent of the NENA ALC. Section §9.6 discusses the usage of the Compounding Ezafe, especially productive in Sorani. Clausal secondaries ap-

[3]This system was developed by the Emir Djeladet Bedir Khan in the 1930's. Notice especially that in this system the vowel [æ] is rendered <e>, [e] is <ê> and [ɑ] is <a>. Thus, the suffix *-ek* which looks like an apocopated form of the definite determiner *-eke* in Sorani, is in fact the indefinite suffix in Kurmanji. To this system the following signs are added: The unaspirated (or pharyngealized) consonants are indicated by a lower dot, such as in <ṭ> (in the standard writing system this distinction is not marked). The trilled [r], indicated in Kurmanji orthography sometimes as a digraph <rr> is here rendered as <ř>. The Sorani [ʎ]~[ɫ] is rendered as <ł>. Stress is marked by means of an accent, when apparent in the source.

[4]This map can be found online (in a 1998 version) at http://geocurrents.info/wp-content/uploads/2012/10/Izady-Kurdish-Languages-map.png.

[5]I am grateful to Sebastian Nordhoff for preparing the map figuring in this book. The various maps use slightly different terminology regarding the Kurdish dialects and related languages. Izady refers to our Kurmanji as "North Kurmânji" while Sorani is "South Kurmânji". He attributes the Zazaki and Gorani languages to the "Pahlawâni group". Haig and Öpengin, on the other hand, treat our Sorani as "Central Kurdish" since their "Southern Kurdish" is reserved for the Kurdish varieties spoken in the Ilam and Kermanshah provinces of Iran, which are outside the scope of the current research (Izady, moreover, marks the latter as Gorani varieties). Zazaki and Gorani are marked by them as distinct from the above mentioned "Kurdish varieties", being instead "related varieties".

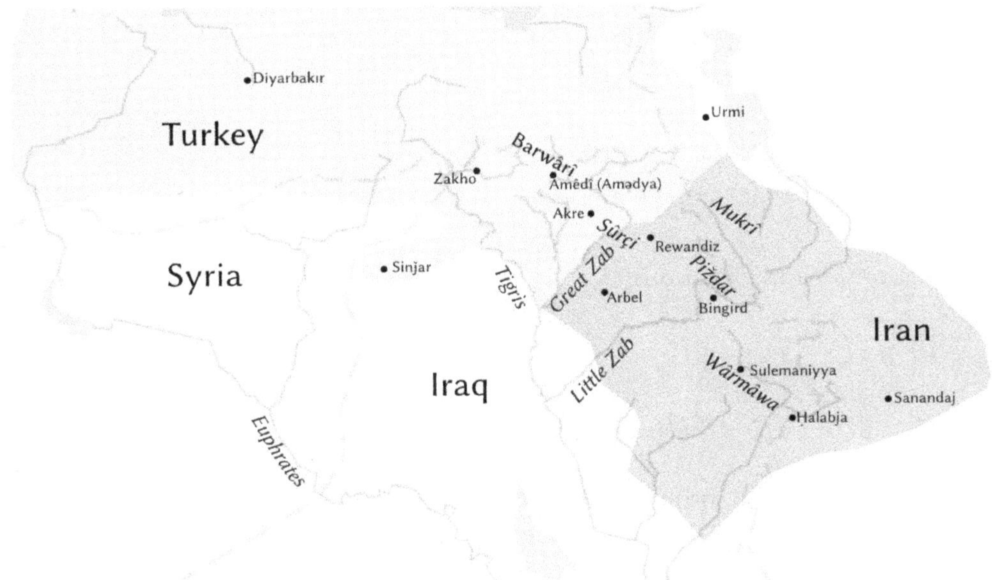

Figure 9.1: Map of surveyed Kurdish dialects and localities. Light grey = Kurmanji dialects; dark grey = Sorani dialects.

pear regularly in one of the Ezafe constructions, yet they can also appear in some alternative constructions, which are discussed in §9.7. The usage of the juxtaposition construction, as well as the rare inverse juxtapositioninverse juxtaposition construction, is presented in §9.8. Finally, §9.9 concludes this chapter with some general remarks and comparative prospects.

9.2 Possessive pronominal enclitics (X-y.POSS)

Sorani (but not Kurmanji) has a series of unstressed possessive pronominal morphemes. Thackston (2006b: 15) qualifies them as enclitics, while MacKenzie (1961: 76) treats them as suffixes. As these elements show promiscuous attachment, attaching indifferently to verbs (as objects; see Thackston 2006b: 37), to nouns, and to prepositions, I prefer to analyse them as clitics (see §4.2).[6]

The pronominal enclitics normally follow the definite or indefinite suffix, with the expected meaning:

[6]A thorough analysis of their status would require an investigation of their behaviour with verbal hosts, which is beyond the scope of this work. See, in this respect, Samvelian (2007b), who examines their attachment to verbs and prepositions and concludes, in a final account, that these elements are rather affixes.

(1) Sorani: **Noun–Pronoun**
کوڕەکەم
kuř-eké =m
son-DEF =POSS.1SG
'my son' (Thackston 2006b: 16)

(2) Sorani: **Noun–Pronoun**
کوڕێکم
kúř-êk =im
son-INDF =POSS.1SG
'a son of mine' (Thackston 2006b: 16)

When the noun is left unqualified, this typically yields a figurative or generic meaning:

(3) Sorani: **Noun–Pronoun**
کوڕم
kúř =im
son =POSS.1SG
'sonny (form of address for a young boy)' (Thackston 2006b: 16)

The possessive enclitics can appear after compound nominals consisting of a Noun+Adj. combination mediated by the compounding Ezafe (see §9.6).

(4) Sorani: **Compound Noun–Pronoun**
کوڕە کۆرپەکەم
[kuř-e- korpe]-ké =m
son-EZ- newborn-DEF =POSS.1SG
'my infant son' (Thackston 2006b: 53)

The same clitic placement is found when the compounding Ezafe is missing due to phonological conditions. The following Wârmâwa example can be compared to the NENA Sulemaniyya example (3) on page 227:

(5) Wârmâwa: **Compound Noun–Pronoun**
[bira-gewr]-ek =em
brother-big-DEF =POSS.1SG
'my elder brother' (MacKenzie 1961: 81 [204])

Finally, the possessive enclitics can follow the focus enclitic *-(î)ş* 'also'.

(6) Sorani: **Noun–Pronoun**
پارەکەشیان
par-eké =*ş* =*yan*
money-DEF =also =POSS.3PL
'their money too' (Thackston 2006b: 16)

(7) Sorani: **Noun–Pronoun**
رەفیقەکانیشم
refîq-ek-an =*îş* =*im*
friend-DEF-PL=also =POSS.1SG
'even my friends' (Thackston 2006b: 17)

Note that in Kurmanji, the lack of possessive pronominal enclitics entails the use of full pronouns which are marked by the oblique case (see example (15) on page 261).

9.3 The three Ezafe morphemes in Kurdish

In §4.3 I presented briefly the Persian Ezafe and the dispute regarding its morphemic status (suffix or clitic) and its syntactic attachment (with the primary or the secondary). Since the Persian Ezafe attaches phonologically to the primary, I concluded, with Samvelian (2007a; 2008), that the simplest account of the Persian Ezafe is to view it as a phrasal affix attaching morphologically and syntactically to its primary, marking the latter as being in construct state, i.e. wanting a complement.

The situation in Kurdish dialects is somewhat more complex. First, in Kurmanji, the Ezafe morpheme inflects for gender, number, and definiteness. More importantly, there are three distinct types of Ezafe markers, differing in their phonological attachment:

Construct Ezafe Devoid of stress, attaching phonologically to the primary (-EZ).

Linker Ezafe Can carry stress, and can appear without an immediate primary (LNK.EZ).

Compounding Ezafe Devoid of stress, forming part of a nominal compound (-EZ-).

The various forms of the Ezafe in standard Kurmanji and Sorani are shown in Table 9.1.

Table 9.1: The Ezafe forms in Standard Kurmanji and Sorani

		Kurmanji			Sorani
		MS	FS	PL	
Construct	DEF	*-ê*	*-a*	*-ên*[7]	*-î*
	INDF	*-î*	*-e*		
Linker		*yê*	*ya*	*yên*	*hî*
Compounding			*-e-*		*-e-*

Leaving aside for the moment the compounding Ezafe, I note that the (definite) construct Ezafe and the Linker Ezafe share the same form, except for a weak consonantal onset (Kurmanji: /*y-*/; Sorani: /*h-*/) marking the latter. In fact, in dialectal data this onset is absent at times. Thus, a natural assumption is to conflate the two sets, arguing these are prosodic variants of each other, one being an enclitic and the other (possibly) a proclitic. This is the approach taken by Haig (2008: 77) and elaborated upon in Haig (2011). Yet as Samvelian (2008) argues (for Kurmanji), there are distributional reasons for distinguishing the two series: The construct Ezafe is in complementary distribution with the oblique case marking of nouns (present only in Kurmanji), and thus cannot attach to oblique nouns, while the linker Ezafe is indifferent to the constitution of the primary.

(8) Kurmanji: **Noun Phrase–Adjective**
*[mal-a van jin-an] *-a / ya*
house-EZ.FS DEM.PROX.OBL.PL woman-OBL.PL *-EZ.DEF.FS / LNK.EZ.FS
biçuk
small
'these women's small house' (Samvelian 2008: 357, examples (47)–(48))

Since the construct Ezafe is in opposition to the oblique case suffix, Samvelian (2008: 358) analyses it as a suffix (or rather as a phrasal suffix), similar to the Persian Ezafe, while the linker Ezafe is analysed by her as an independent syntactic particle. A similar conclusion is reached by Schroeder (1999: 53). Recall that I used a similar approach to tease apart the NENA construct state suffix *-əd* and the proclitic linker *d-* (see §4.4).

[7] In the Kurmanji dialects overlapping with NENA, the regular marking of the plural Ezafe is in fact *-êd* or *-êt* (Öpengin & Haig 2014: 162).

Haig (2004: 79) objects to this type of analysis (and in particular to Schroeder 1999 noting that the complementary distribution of the (construct) Ezafe and the oblique case is not restricted to cases where the oblique case is realized by a suffix, but also in the relatively few nouns where the oblique case is realized by an internal stem mutation. Thus, one finds *cem şivan-ê me* [to shepherd-EZ1PL.OBL] meaning 'to our shepherd' and not **cem şivên-ê me* [to shepherd.OBL-EZ1PL.OBL]. While I concur with Haig that this demonstrates that the complementary distribution of the two markers is not due to "a low-level constraint on suffix-stacking", I disagree with his view that the Ezafe is not inflectional in nature. In fact, this evidence strengthen the position that the construct Ezafe is an inflectional element, as it shows the the oblique case marking and the construct Ezafe are part of the same abstract paradigm in the Kurmanji linguistic system (a case-cum-state paradigm, as it is), irrespective of the actual realisation of the members of the paradigm. Since the case marking (suffixal or by stem mutation) is clearly inflectional, the same must hold for the Ezafe.

In this study I adhere to Samvelian's analysis, and I shall treat the different types of Ezafe in different sections below. It should be noted, though, that this analysis is especially suitable for Kurmanji. In Sorani there are no inflectional case endings, and thus the above argument is not applicable.[8] Yet, as the Sorani construct Ezafe appears only after nominal elements (the linker Ezafe occurring only without an immediate primary), it can be seen as a nominal suffix, and therefore I treat it for simplicity's sake on a par with the Kurmanji construct Ezafe.

9.4 The construct Ezafe construction (X.CST Y)

9.4.1 Introduction

As explained above, all Kurdish dialects make use of the construct Ezafe, a suffix attaching to the primary phrase, marking it as construct state. The different varieties of Kurdish differ as to the number of inflectional forms the Ezafe exhibits, reflecting various number and gender distinctions. Generally speaking, the number of forms increases as one travels from the south-eastern extremity of Kurdish speaking areas to the north-western extremity. In this perspective, it is useful to take into account also dialects of languages close to Kurdish, such as Gorani in the south-east and Zazaki in the north-west.[9]

[8] In Sorani, on the other hand, nouns can be inflected by the possessive enclitics, discussed in §9.2. It would be interesting to see if the construct Ezafe is compatible with these enclitics, but unfortunately I have not found data regarding this question.

[9] See footnote 5 on page 254 for a discussion of various classifications of these languages.

In the southern part of my survey of Kurdish dialects, namely in the Sorani dialects, the construct Ezafe has a fixed form *-î~-i~-y*.[10] Note that the usage of an uninflected Ezafe is found also in the Gawrajū Gorani dialect, spoken in the southern extremity of the Kurdish speaking zone, near the city of Kerend (Mahmudweyssi et al. 2012: 16); this Ezafe has the form *-e~-y*, akin to the uninflected Persian Ezafe *-(y)e*.

(9) Sorani: **Noun–Noun**
كتاويەكانی قوتابخانەیەك
ktawî-ek-an-i *qutabkhane-yêk*
student-DEF-PL-EZ school-INDF
'the students of a school' (Thackston 2006b: 10)

(10) Silêmanî: **Noun–Noun**
ser-î *biniâdem*
head-EZ man
'men's heads' (MacKenzie 1961: 63 [49])

As example (9) on this page shows, the primary and secondary can be independently marked as definite or indefinite. If they are left unmarked, as in example (10) on the current page, the AC may be interpreted generically.

The same construction can be used with a full pronominal secondary, as an alternative to the usage of the possessive enclitics (see §9.2), for "special emphasis" (Abdulla & McCarus 1967: 179).

(11) Silêmanî: **Noun–Pronoun**
nàv-i *mín*
name-EZ 1SG
'*my* name' (Abdulla & McCarus 1967: 179)

As one travels northwards, roughly to the *Inter-Zab* region (between the Little Zab and the Great Zab rivers), more variation appears. In some Sorani dialects (namely, Mukrî and Rewandiz) the Ezafe may appear as *-(y)e* following a vowel (MacKenzie 1961: 62).

[10] Thackston transcribes the Ezafe as a lax *i*, separated from its host. Other authors, however, as well as the standard Sorani Arabic orthography, treat the Ezafe as a tense *î* (in Arabic script: ی), attached to its host. After vowels it is realised as the glide /*y*/. In line with my analysis of the Ezafe as a suffix, I transcribe it attached to its host, but I keep the formal variation intact.

(12) Rewandiz: **Noun–Pronoun**
kursî-(y)e min
seat-EZ 1SG
'my seat' (MacKenzie 1961: 62 [484])

This is purely a phonological variant of the Ezafe. More interesting is that some north-eastern Sorani dialects (Bingird, Piždar and Mukrî) exhibit an optional Ezafe form, *-ê*, reserved for feminine singular nouns (MacKenzie 1961: 61). This is shown by the following example:

(13) Mukrî: **Noun–Proper Noun**
xuşk-ê Mîr Zêndîn
sister-EZ.FS M. Z.
'Mir Zendin's sister' (MacKenzie 1961: 61 [30])

In the same dialects, whenever the primary has plural sense but no formal marking of this (as an unmarked noun can be interpreted singularly or plurally), an extra particle *de* may follow the Ezafe.[11]

(14) Bingird: **Noun–Noun**
pyaw-î de paşe
man-EZ PL king
'the king's men' (MacKenzie 1961: 62 [319])

The same marker is used whenever the primary consists of a conjunction of two singular nouns. In such cases, the Ezafe is attached phrase-finally.

(15) Bingird: **Conjoined nouns–Pronoun**
[dak û bab]-î de to
mother and father-EZ PL 2SG
'thy mother and father' (MacKenzie 1961: 62 [349])

Among the Kurmanji dialects, a distinction between the two genders is obligatory, as is shown in Table 9.1 on page 258. Most dialects also have a separate plural Ezafe, though sometimes it is assimilated with the masculine singular form. The usage of the plural form as well as the feminine form is shown in the following example, which shows also the possibility to embed the Ezafe construction:

[11] It is a curious fact that this plural Ezafe marker has a similar form to the Aramaic linker *d-*. Yet, as the Aramaic linker is not related in any way to marking of plurality, this is very likely a pure coincidence.

(16) Kurmanji: **Noun–Noun Phrase**
kitêb-ên [keç-a mirov]
book-EZ.DEF.PL girl-EZ.FS man
'the man's daughter's books' (Thackston 2006a: 13)

In some older literary texts, one finds the same plural particle as in the Sorani dialects mentioned above (see examples (14)–(15) on the previous page). Such is the case, for instance, in the poetry of the Kurdish poet Malaye Jaziri of Bohtan (1570-1640)[12]:

(17) Kurmanji: **Noun–Adjective**
چشمێن دِ سیَه
çeşm-ên di siyeh
eye-EZ.DEF.PL PL black
'black eyes' (Malaye Jaziri, *Diwân*, ed. Hartmann 1904: 217; MacKenzie 1961: 159, fn. 2)

The Kurmanji Ezafe, just like the Sorani Ezafe shown in example (15) on the preceding page, attaches phrase-finally to the primary, and has scope over the whole primary phrase. According to the description of Bedir Khan (1960), the inflectional features carried by the Kurmanji Ezafe suffix are, however, only dependent on the noun to which it directly attaches (this is also the case in example (58) on page 274, cited from Thackston):[13]

(18) Kurmanji: **Conjoined nouns–Pronoun**
[dê û bav]-ê min
mother and father-EZ.DEF.MS 1SG.OBL
'my mother and father' (Bedir Khan 1960: 2)

(19) Kurmanji: **Conjoined nouns–Pronoun**
[ker, hesp û mehîn]-a min
donkey, horse and mare-EZ.DEF.FS 1SG.OBL
'my donkey, horse and mare' (Bedir Khan 1960: 2)

[12] These years are given by Izady (1992: 176), who writes the poet's name as *Mullâ-i Jaziri*.

[13] One reviewer noted that this is not a strict rule but subject to dialectal variation, bringing the following example from the Zakho dialect: *kič u kur-ēt min* [daughter and son-EZ.PL 1SG.OBL] meaning 'my daughter and son'. Note that the plural Ezafe is used due to the plurality of the NP but attaches to a singular noun.

This behaviour indicates that the Kurmanji Ezafe should be analysed as a phrasal suffix: while morphologically it is tied to the nominal inflectional system and thus shows inflectional features of the noun it attaches to, syntactically it marks the entire NP as being in construct state and has thus wide syntactic scope (see §4.2 and in particular Table 4.1 on page 94).

Likewise, if the last noun of the primary has a plural sense by itself, it will receive the plural Ezafe suffix. In such cases the plural sense may be inferred pragmatically also for the other conjunct nouns of the primary, as in the following example:[14]

(20) Kurmanji: **Conjoined nouns–Noun**
[şexsiyet û rewşenbîr]-ên kurd-an
personality(FS) and intellectual-EZ.DEF.PL Kurdish-OBL.PL
'personalities and intellectuals of the Kurds' (Thackston 2006a: 15)

Bedir Khan notes that this pattern only arises with the conjunction *û* 'and'. When the primary NP consists of nouns joined using the disjunctive conjunction *(y)an* 'or', each element must belong to a separate AC.

(21) Kurmanji: **Disjoined Nouns–Pronoun**
hesp-ê min an mehîn-a min
horse-EZ.DEF.MS 1SG.OBL or mare-EZ.DEF.FS 1SG.OBL
'my horse or my mare' (Bedir Khan 1960: 2)

The Kurmanji Ezafe inflects also according to the definiteness of the noun. Yet, in contrast to its number and gender inflection, the (in)definiteness feature is not carried by the Ezafe suffix, but rather it co-varies with the presence of a singular indefinite suffix *-êk* (MacKenzie 1961: 158-160) or a plural indefinite suffix *-in* (Bedir Khan & Lescot 1970: 78).

(22) Kurmanji: **Noun–Noun**
hejmár-ek-e kovár-ê
issue(FS)-INDF-EZ.INDF.FS journal-OBL.FS
'an issue of that journal' (Thackston 2006a: 12)

[14] Note that a Kurmanji noun without Ezafe or oblique case marking is unmarked for number, and may be interpreted either as plural or as singular according to the context.

(23) Kurmanji: **Noun–Noun**
mehîn-in-e *keçk-ê*
mare-PL.INDF-EZ.INDF.PL girl-OBL.FS
'some mares of the girl' (Bedir Khan & Lescot 1970: 306)

Since these allo-forms depend on the explicit presence of an indefinite suffix, Samvelian (2008: 355-357) rejects the notion of the INDEFINITE EZAFE, analysing these forms instead as being conditioned by their post-affixal position. She shows that an indefinite plural noun not marked by the suffix *-in* takes the normal form of the Ezafe *-ên*:

(24) Diyarbakır: **Noun–Adjective**
pênc kur-ên ganc
five boy-EZ.PL young
'five young boys' (Samvelian 2008: 356, example (45))

This pattern, however, could equally well be analysed as a neutralisation of the definiteness feature of the plural Ezafe (as presented in Table 9.1 on page 258). Such a neutralisation may be motivated by the fact that the explicit marking of plural indefinite nouns by means of the suffix *-in* is quite rare (judging by the sources consulted), and that the indefinite plural Ezafe *-e* is identical in form to the indefinite feminine form, as is shown in examples (22)–(23) on the preceding page.

Samvelian (2008: 356) substantiates further her claim by citing MacKenzie (1961: 158), who mentions that in Sûrçi dialect, the indefinite form (termed by him SECONDARY EZAFE), follows "apparently" also the definite suffix *-eke*:

(25) Sûrçi: **Noun–Adjective**
mirow-eke-y xwarê
man-DEF-EZ.MS lower
'the lower man' (MacKenzie 1961: 160 [517])

Yet most Kurmanji dialects lack the definite suffix *-eke*, which is more typical of Sorani dialects. Thus, leaving aside such exceptional examples (whose status seems to be questioned by MacKenzie himself), it seems justifiable to regard the singular Ezafe forms *-î* (MS) and *-e* (FS) as allomorphic forms signalling indefiniteness of the primary noun.[15]

[15]Note, however, that *-î* is also used in some contexts where no indefiniteness is implied, such as with adverbial primaries (see §9.4.7).

The same cline of explicitness can also be found regarding the marking of the secondary by oblique case. This is treated in §9.4.2.

9.4.2 Oblique marking of secondaries

Kurmanji exhibits a bipartite case system, opposing the unmarked direct case with a marked oblique case, visible on nouns and pronouns. On nouns, the oblique case is normally marked by suffixes, which express moreover the gender and number features of the host noun. These suffixes are shown in Table 9.2.

Table 9.2: Kurmanji case endings

	MS	FS	PL
Direct		∅	
Oblique	∅ / *-î*	*-(y)ê*	*-(y)an*

A particularity of the masculine singular oblique suffix is that it appears only if the host noun is qualified by a determiner.[16] Yet a few masculine nouns show the oblique case by internal mutation, replacing an ultimate /*a*/ vowel by an /*ê*/ vowel (Thackston 2006a: 9; Haig 2004: 73). For example, *bajar* 'city' is *bajêr* in the oblique case (see example (74) on page 278).

The oblique case marks the dependents of both the attributive relation and the completive relation (see §2.1.1). It subsumes thus both the genitive case and the accusative case (and in the Kurmanji context, also the ergative case). Note, moreover, that similarly to the Ezafe the oblique suffixes can have phrasal scope, appearing on the final noun of conjoined nouns, and only optionally on the preceding nouns.[17] This is demonstrated by the following example, in which the oblique case takes the accusative role.

(26) Kurmanji: **Verb–Conjoined Nouns (objects)**
[jin-{ê} u kur-î] di-bîn-im
woman-{OBL.FS} and boy-OBL.MS IND-see-1SG
'I see the woman and the boy' (Samvelian 2008: 354, example (41))

[16]This is the rule in Standard Kurmanji. Yet in the Kurmanji dialects overlapping with the NENA speaking zone, there is a consistent suffix-marking of the oblique. See the discussion of Öpengin & Haig (2014: 162) and Haig & Öpengin (2018) regarding the "Southeastern" Kurmanji dialect group.

[17]In this respect it is also somewhat different to the Ezafe, as the Ezafe can only appear on the last conjoined noun, since it must be followed immediately by the secondary.

In this study, I am interested mainly in the genitive function of the oblique case, namely the marking of AC secondaries. This is shown in the following example (as for the oblique demonstrative, see Table 10.7 on page 327):

(27) Kurmanji: **Noun–Noun**
miróv-ek-î [w-î weláṭ-î]
man-INDF-EZ.INDF.MS DEM.DIST-OBL.MS country-OBL.MS
'a man of that country' (Thackston 2006a: 12)

For examples of feminine and plural oblique endings, see examples (20)–(22) on page 263.

It is important to note that the Ezafe suffix and the oblique marking (suffixal or by stem mutation) are morphologically in complementary distribution, although notionally they mark independent features, the Ezafe being related to the state category.[18] Thus, a secondary noun itself acting as primary is only marked by the Ezafe. An oblique suffix, if present at all, can only be marked in such cases at the end of the secondary phrase:

(28) Kurmanji: **Circumposition–Noun Phrase**
di [gund-ên kurd-ên Kurdistan-a Tirkiye-yê] de
in village-EZ.PL Kurd-EZ.PL Kurdistan-EZ.FS Turkey-OBL.FS in
'in the villages of the Kurds of Turkey's Kurdistan' (Thackston 2006a: 13)

Kurmanji dialects also have a series of full oblique pronouns, which can be used as secondaries. These are the functional equivalents of the Sorani possessive pronominal enclitics, described in §9.2. For example, the direct pronoun *ez* 'I' has the oblique form *min* (see its occurrence also in examples (18)–(19) on page 262):

(29) Kurmanji: **Noun–Pronoun**
kitêb-a min
book-EZ.DEF.FS 1SG.OBL
'my book' (Thackston 2006a: 18)

[18] *Pace* Thackston (2006a: 7) who speaks of construct "case". In the Zazaki language, related to Kurmanji, a noun can be marked both for oblique case and the construct state by means of a specially inflected Ezafe (Todd 2002: 43; and see further Larson & Yamakido 2006; Samvelian 2008; Plank 2012). See also the discussion at the end of §9.3.

In contrast to nouns, an oblique pronoun can further be marked by the Ezafe suffix:[19]

(30) Kurmanji: **Pronoun–Noun**
min-ê *bêçâra bibîna*
1.SG.OBL-EZ.MS poor look.IMP
'Look at me, poor thing' (Samvelian 2008: 353, example (39))

In contrast to Kurmanji, the south-eastern Sorani dialects (and notably the dialect of Sulemaniyya, which is the basis for standard Sorani) have no case system at all. The Sorani dialects to the north, however, show an oblique suffix for singular secondaries:[20]

(31) Bingird: **Noun–Noun**
lep-î *dest-î*
palm-EZ hand-OBL.MS
'palm of the hand' (MacKenzie 1961: 59)

(32) Bingird: **Noun–Noun**
zîn-î *maîn-ê*
saddle-EZ mare-OBL.FS
'saddle of the mare' (MacKenzie 1961: 59)

[19]Yet this may in fact be an instance of the linker Ezafe discussed in §9.5 phonologically encliticized to the primary, as it does not necessarily show the inflectional features of its host pronoun, as would be expected from the construct Ezafe. Thus, in the following example, the Ezafe suffix *-a* shows agreement with the primary *mal* 'house' rather than with the pronoun *min* (given that the speaker is a man):

(i) Kurmanji: **Pronoun–Noun**
mal-a *[bira-yê* *min]-a* *biçuk*
house.EZ.FS brother-EZ.MS 1.SG.OBL-EZ.FS small
'my brother's small house' (Samvelian 2008: 354, example (40))

See example (65) on page 277 for a clear case of the linker Ezafe following *min*.

[20]The plural is marked by a case-neutral suffix *-ân* (MacKenzie 1961: 58).

9.4.3 Adjectival secondaries

The Ezafe construction is used also with adjectival secondaries. In Kurmanji, adjectives differ from nouns by the fact that they never inflect and thus do not take an oblique suffix (MacKenzie 1961: 163).[21]

(33) Kurmanji: **Noun–Adjective**
mirov-ek-î *mezin*
man-INDF-EZ.INDF.MS big
'a big man' (Thackston 2006a: 14)

(34) Silêmanî: **Noun–Adjective**
tûtik-êk-î *piçkołe*
dog-INDF-EZ small
'a little dog' (MacKenzie 1961: 63 [69])

As the above examples show, the primary can be determined by the indefinite suffix in both Kurmanji and Sorani. In Kurmanji dialects, a definite sense is obtained by using the definite Ezafe:

(35) Kurmanji: **Noun–Adjective**
mirov-ê *mezin*
man-EZ.DEF.MS big
'the big man' (Thackston 2006a: 14)

In Sorani, however, a primary noun followed by an adjective is not normally combined with the definite suffix *-eke*. Instead, whenever a definite primary is needed, the compounding Ezafe is used (see §9.6). It seems, however, that the construct Ezafe construction is compatible with a definite primary, if the adjective has a descriptive, rather than restrictive, sense (see Thackston 2006b: 12, fn. 1).

(36) Sorani: **Noun–Adjective**
دەرسەکانی سەخت
ders-ek-an-i *sext*
lesson-DEF-PL-EZ hard
'the lessons, which are hard' (Thackston 2006b: 12)

[21]Note, however, that the denominal adjective derivational suffix *-î* is conspicuously similar to the masculine singular oblique ending, making an historical connection between the two possible. This recalls the situation in the Semitic domain, where a formal similarity can be observed between the Arabic adjectival ending *-iyy* and the genitive case *-i*. The usage of the oblique suffixes as derivational suffixes is much clearer in the case of the Kurmanji ordinals; see §9.4.5.

Whenever a primary is modified by more than one adjective, several alternative patterns are available. The adjectives may be conjoined to form one secondary phrase:

(37) Silêmanî: **Noun–Conjoined Adjectives**
minał-êk-î [pîs û poxił]
child-INDF-EZ dirty and filthy
'a filthy, dirty child' (MacKenzie 1961: 63)

(38) Kurmanji: **Noun–Conjoined Adjectives**
keç-ên [por-zer û çav-şîn û kesk]
woman-EZ.PL hair-yellow and eye-blue and green
'blonde and blue- and green- eyed women' (Thackston 2006a: 98)

Another possibility is to chain the subsequent adjectives by Ezafe suffixes, as the following Sorani examples show. In such cases one might expect the two adjectives to have different scopes (the first qualifying the primary noun only, while the second qualifies the N+Adj. combination), yet this is not apparent from the translations:

(39) Sorani: **Noun–Adjectives**
شارێکی گەورەی تازە
[shar-êk-î gewre]-y taze
city-INDF-EZ big-EZ modern
'a big modern city (*une grande ville moderne*)' (Blau 1980: 60)

(40) Silêmanî: **Noun–Adjectives**
[kiç-êk-î jwan]-î çwar-de =sał
girl-INDF-EZ pretty-EZ four-teen =year
'a beautiful, fourteen-year-old girl' (MacKenzie 1961: 63)

This latter possibility seems to be unavailable for Kurmanji dialects, which instead make use of the linker Ezafe construction in such cases (see §9.5).[22] This is correlated with the fact that the Kurmanji Ezafe is a nominal inflectional suffix, incompatible with adjectives, which never inflect. The Sorani Ezafe, on the other hand, does not *prima facie* form part of an inflectional system, and in this respect shows clitic behaviour (but see footnote 8 on page 259).

[22] See however the rare usage of the Kurmanji linker Ezafe *î* in examples (72)–(74) on page 278, which, notwithstanding the difference in analysis, is very similar formally to the construct Ezafe in the above cited Sorani examples.

9.4.4 Adjectival primaries

In Sorani, one finds that adjectives extended by nominal complements get the Ezafe suffix:

(41) Mukrî: **Adjective–Noun**
xerîk-î bezm-î (de-bû-n)
busy-EZ feasting-OBL(?) IND-be-PL
'(They would be) engaged in feasting.' (MacKenzie 1961: 65 [3[25]])

(42) Silêmanî: **Adjective–Noun**
tûş-î em derd-e
afflicted-EZ DEM.PROX trouble-DEF
'afflicted by this trouble' (MacKenzie 1961: 65 [67])

Note that example (41) on the current page is very similar to the NENA JSanandaj example (47) on page 239.

In Kurmanji, such examples are not expected to be found, as adjectives are normally not marked by the construct Ezafe (see discussion at the end of the previous section). Yet Samvelian (2008: 343) affirms the existence of this construction:

(43) Kurmanji: **Adjective–Noun**
Azâd âşiq-ê Narmîn-ê ya
A. in_love-EZ.MS N.-OBL.FS COP.3MS
'Azad is in love with Narmin.' (Samvelian 2008: 343, example (15))

Note, however, that Thackston (2006a: 197) lists this construction only in combination with the verb 'to be' (*'aşiq-e ... bûn*), rendering it possibly a fixed collocation.

9.4.5 Ordinal secondaries

Ordinals follow the Ezafe as regular secondaries. In standard Kurmanji they are derived from the cardinal numerals by a fixed oblique plural suffix *-yan*, except for the numeral 'first', which has a special form *ewel(î)* in which one can recognize the masculine singular oblique ending *-î*. Alternatively, ordinals (including 'first') may be derived by taking the suffix *-ê(m(în))* of Persian origin (Thackston 2006a: 25).[23]

[23] According to MacKenzie (1961: 170, §274.(a)), the Kurmanji dialects form ordinals by the suffix *-ê* (see example (85) on page 282), which he relates to the identically formed superlative suffix (MacKenzie 1961: 164, §268.(b)). In this case, it is the equivalent of Sorani suffix *-în*, serving as a superlative (MacKenzie 1961: 68, §190.(b)); see footnote 38 on page 291.

(44) Kurmanji: **Noun–Ordinal**
roj-a *sisi-yan*
day-EZ.DEF.FS three-OBL.PL
'(on the) third day' (Thackston 2006a: 25)

(45) Kurmanji: **Noun–Ordinal**
car-a *yeḳ-em*
time-EZ.DEF.FS one-ORD
'the first time' (Thackston 2006a: 25)

In Sorani, ordinals are similarly derived from the cardinal numerals by means of the suffix *-(h)em* (MacKenzie 1961: 72–73).

(46) Silêmanî: **Noun–Ordinal**
řêga-y *sê-hem*
third-EZ three-ORD
'the third road' (MacKenzie 1961: 72 [47])

Alternatively, Sorani uses a longer ordinal suffix *-(h)emîn* (borrowed in NENA JUrmi and JSanandaj; see example (27) on page 195 and example (46) on page 239). Yet when ordinals are derived by the full suffix *-emîn*, they are not used in the Ezafe construction, but rather in the inverse juxtaposition construction (see example (117) on page 291).

9.4.6 Adverbial secondaries

In Kurmanji, prepositional phrases can regularly occur as secondaries following the construct Ezafe:[24]

(47) Sorani: **Noun–Prepositional Phrase**
rojname-yek-e *[bi kurdî]*
newspaper-INDF-EZ.INDF.FS in Kurdish
'a newspaper in Kurdish' (Thackston 2006a: 14)

In Sorani, this construction is not mentioned in the sources consulted, except by Samvelian (2008: 346), who lists it as a regular construction:

[24]The usage of construct state marker followed by Prepositional Phrases is known also in the Aramaic domain. For Syriac, see examples (19)–(22) on page 55; for JZakho, see examples (12)–(13) on page 118; JUrmi: example (29) on page 195.

(48) Sorani: **Noun–Prepositional Phrase**
xânu-y [la sar şâx]
house-EZ at head mountain
'the house on the mountain' (Samvelian 2008: 346, example (19))

9.4.7 Adverbial primaries

Some nominals and adverbs can be used as prepositions. In Kurmanji, they may be marked by a frozen uninflected Ezafe *-î* termed by MacKenzie (1961: 200) the GENERIC EZAFE. Note, moreover, that complements of prepositions in Kurmanji are regularly marked by the oblique case.

(49) Akre: **Adverbial Noun–Noun**
nêzîk-î ḥakim-i
near-EZ judge-OBL.MS
'near the judge' (MacKenzie 1961: 161 [602])

See also example (58) on page 274 for the usage of the circumposition *ji ali-yê ... ve* [from side-EZ.MS ... from] introducing a passive agent.

In Sorani, an adverbial noun is similarly sometimes marked by the Ezafe (but see example (115) on page 290):

(50) Silêmanî: **Adverbial Noun–Pronoun**
la dwâ-y min
at last-EZ 1SG
'after me' (Abdulla & McCarus 1967: 75)

9.4.8 Verbal nouns as primaries

Verbal nouns, be they infinitives or nouns participating in complex predication (CP nouns), can be complemented by an argument following the construct Ezafe.[25] Note that Kurmanji infinitives have feminine gender and are hence marked by FS Ezafe (Thackston 2006a: 32).

[25] Compare this to the situation in Aramaic; Syriac participles: examples (22)–(23) on page 56; JZakho infinitives: §5.3.5; Qaraqosh infinitives: §6.2.7 JUrmi participles: example (31) on page 195; JSanandaj CP noun: example (71) on page 246.

(51) Kurmanji: **Infinitive–Pronoun (subject)**
çûyîn-a min
go.INF-EZ.DEF.FS 1SG.OBL
'my going' (Thackston 2006a: 33; see example (65) on page 277 for a fuller context)

(52) Sorani: **Infinitive–Noun Phrase (object)**
بۆ توانینی ئەم دیاری جێگای میر گەورەیە
bo twanîn-i [em dyarî kirdin-i [cêga-i Mîr
for be_able.INF-EZ DEM.PROX clarification do.INF-EZ position-ez M.
Gewre] =yé]
G. =DEF
'in order to enable this clarification of Mir Gawra's position' (Thackston 2006b: 12)

(53) Silêmanî: **CP Noun–Noun (object)**
swar-î řexş bû
horseman-EZ steed was
'He mounted his steed.' (MacKenzie 1961: 65 [66])

The argument occupying the secondary can also be an indirect object. Such is the case in the following example, in which the direct object *vê kaġez-ê* is governed directly by the verb, while the indirect object is governed by a CP noun.

(54) Akre: **CP Noun–Noun (indirect object)**
vê kaġez-ê teslîm-î [filan wezîr-î]
DEM.PROX.OBL letter-OBL.FS giving-EZ such_and_such vizier-OBL.MS
bi-k-e
SBJV-do-2SG
'Give this letter to such and such a vizier!' (MacKenzie 1961: 161; MacKenzie 1962: 274 [603])

9.4.9 Clausal secondaries and the use of the relativizer

Relative clauses, or, in other words, clausal secondaries, make use of the Ezafe construction as well, with the addition that normally a special particle, a relativizer, introduces the clause. Thus, the Ezafe signals that the primary is to be modified, while the relativizer marks the clause as a secondary.[26] In Sorani, the relativizer is کە *ke* while in Kurmanji it is *ḳu.*[27]

(55) Sorani: **Noun–Clause**
سەری کوڕەکەی کە نوستبوو
ser-i [kuř-eké-î ke nustibû]
head-EZ boy-DEF-EZ REL slept.3MS
'the head of the boy, who has fallen asleep' (Thackston 2006b: 73)

(56) Sorani: **Noun–Clause**
ئەو کراسەی کە تۆ کڕیوتە
ew kiras-e-y ke [to kiřî-w-t-e] (zor drêj
DEM.DIST dress-DEF-EZ REL 2SG bought-PRF-2SG-COP.3SG very long
=e)
=COP.3SG
'The dress that you bought (is very long).' (Blau 1980: 156)

(57) Kurmanji: **Noun–Clause**
wî ziman-ê ḳu [li ber mirinê ye]
DEM.DIST.OBL language-EZ.DEF.MS REL at fore die.INF.OBL.FS COP.3SG
'this language, which is on the verge of dying' (Thackston 2006a: 75)

(58) Kurmanji: **Noun Phrase–Clause**
[ew alfabe û rêziman]-a ḳu [ji ali-yê Celadet
DEM.DIST alphabet and grammar-EZ.DEF.FS REL from side-EZ.MS C.
Bedir-Xan ve haṭiye danîn]
B.-X. from PASS.PRF put_down.INF
'the alphabet and grammar that were established by Djeladet Bedir Khan' (Thackston 2006a: 75)

[26]In Sorani, Thackston distinguishes between the Ezafe introducing a relative clause, being a tense -*î*, and the regular Ezafe, being a lax *i*. As we have seen, other authors transcribe the regular Ezafe as a tense *î* as well, rendering this distinction apparently artificial.

[27]Haig (2011) treats *ḳu* as a complementizer, while Thackston (2006a) regards it as a relative pronoun. Since the current study deals here only with cases where *ḳu* is followed by a relative clause, I will treat it as a relativizer (glossed REL), without committing to its general status. Recall that the under-dot of /ḳ/ signals an unaspirated and/or pharyngealized consonant, a phonemic distinction that is normally not marked in standard Kurmanji orthography (Thackston: 4 marks it with an underscore and describes it as an unaspirated stop accompanied by pharyngealization [kˤ].

The relativizer can be omitted, especially (but not exclusively) when the primary refers to the object of the subordinated verb, according to Thackston (2006b: 73; 2006a: 77). Blau (1980: 157), however, relates its omission to the definite marking of the primary.

(59) Sorani: **Noun Phrase–Clause**
ئەو دوو فرمێسکە گەورەیەی ئەیانەوێ بکەونە خوارێ
[ew dû firmêsk-e- gewre-yé]-î [e-yan-ewê bi-kew-in-à
DEM.DIST two tear-EZ- big-DEF-EZ IND-3PL-want SBJV-fall-3PL-DIR
xwarè]
down
'those two large tears, which were about to dribble down' (Thackston 2006b: 75)

(60) Kurmanji: **Noun–Clause**
ṭişṭ-ên [min nivisîbûn]
thing-EZ.DEF.PL 1SG.OBL written
'the things I had written' (Thackston 2006a: 77)

(61) Sorani: **Pronoun–Clause**
ewe-y to dîwite
DEM-EZ 2SG seen
'that which thou hast seen' (MacKenzie 1961: 133)

See also the the discussion of MacKenzie (1961: 203–204) who presents various examples of Kurmanji relative clauses, with or without the relativizer.

9.5 The linker Ezafe construction (X LNK Y)

9.5.1 Introduction

In Kurmanji dialects alone, an independent (i.e. not suffixed) Ezafe may appear between a primary and a secondary. This happens most frequently whenever the primary is a noun phrase, rather than a simple noun. A nominal secondary is, as expected, marked with the oblique case (which is however ∅ for undetermined masculine singular nouns), while adjectives remain uninflected.

The linker Ezafe is very similar in form to the definite suffixed Ezafe, except that it is usually preceded by the segment *y-* (which can, however, be elided in certain dialects and certain phonological environments). Thus, as discussed in

§9.3, it is possible to consider the two forms as essentially one and the same morpheme, which cliticizes to the primary whenever it follows it immediately. Nonetheless, following the argumentation of Samvelian (2008), I distinguish between the two cases as manifesting different constructions. Moreover, in accordance with this study's framework the independent Ezafe has all the characteristics of a pronominal linker, as it can represent alone the primary (see §9.5.5), sharing with it, moreover, the number and gender features.

The linker Ezafe is used most often when the primary consists of a noun phrase, ending with an adjective[28] or another element which cannot take the construct Ezafe suffix (such as an oblique marked noun, see example (8) on page 258).

(62) Kurmanji: **Noun Phrase–Noun**
[dest-ê rast-ê] yê Cengî
hand-EZ.DEF.MS right-ADJ[29] LNK.EZ.MS C.
'Jengi's right hand' (Thackston 2006a: 15)

(63) Kurmanji: **Noun Phrase–Noun**
[hejmar-ek-e nû] ya kovar-ê
issue-INDF-EZ.INDF.FS new LNK.EZ.FS journal-OBL.MS
'a new issue of the journal' (Thackston 2006a: 15)

(64) Kurmanji: **Noun Phrase–Pronoun**
[kitêb-ek-e nû] ya min
book-INDF-EZ.INDF.FS new LNK.EZ.FS 1SG.OBL
'a new book of mine' (Thackston 2006a: 19)

In §9.4.8 we have seen that an infinitive may be connected to its argument by means of the Ezafe. When more than one such argument is expressed, the linker Ezafe can be used, as is shown in the following example:

[28] Note that in this respect the Kurmanji construct Ezafe is different from the Persian Ezafe, as the latter can appear following adjectives (see example (1) on page 94). In fact, the Persian system is more similar to the Sorani system.

[29] The *-ê* suffix seems to be a manifestation of the suffix deriving an adjective from a noun, as discussed by MacKenzie (1961: 164, §267b). In such a case *rast* could be understood as a noun or an adverb meaning 'the right side'.

(65) Kurmanji: **Infinitive Phrase–Noun (indirect object)**
[çûyîn-a min] [ya hotêl-ê]
go.INF-EZ.DEF.FS 1SG.OBL LNK.EZ.FS hotel-OBL.FS
'my going to the hotel' (Thackston 2006a: 33)

Note that the linker Ezafe follows the oblique pronoun *min* 'I'. Contrast this with example (30) on page 267, where it seems rather that it is the construct Ezafe that is used.

9.5.2 Adjectival and adverbial secondaries

Like the construct Ezafe, the linker Ezafe may be followed by adjectives:

(66) Akre: **Noun Phrase–Adjective**
[wakīl-ē xô] yē ʿām
agent-EZ.DEF.MS REFL LNK.EZ.MS general
'his own general agent' (MacKenzie 1961: 163 [685])

(67) Kurmanji: **Noun Phrase–Adjective**
(keç-a) [[xweh-a min] ya ciwan]
girl-EZ.DEF.FS sister-EZ.DEF.FS 1SG.OBL LNK.EZ.FS young
'my younger sister's daughter' (Bedir Khan 1960: 3)

(68) Kurmanji: **Noun Phrase–Adjective**
[darbe-yek-e mezin] ya ekonomîk
blow-INDF-EZ.INDF.FS great LNK.EZ.FS economic
'a great economic blow' (Thackston 2006a: 16)

(69) Kurmanji: **Noun Phrase–Conjoined Adjectives**
[heval-ê min] yê [delal û qênc]
friend-EZ.DEF.MS 1SG.OBL LNK.EZ.MS dear and good
'my dear good friend' (Bedir Khan 1960: 3)

Note the surprising scope relations in the last examples, whereby the secondary adjective headed by the linker Ezafe seems to have prior scope over the primary noun rather than over its direct pronominal or adjectival secondary (compare with examples (39)–(40) on page 269). This is not always the case, however, as the following examples show:

(70) Kurmanji: **Noun Phrase–Conjoined Adjectives**
[[keç û jin]-ên Ewrupî] yên [por-zer û çav şîn
girl and woman-EZ.DEF.PL European EZ.PL hair-yellow and eye blue
yan çav kesk]
or eye green
'blonde and blue- or green- eyed European girls and women' (Thackston 2006a: 16)

(71) Kurmanji: **Noun Phrase–Prepositional Phrase**
[rojname-yek-e rojane] ya [bi kurdî]
newspaper-INDF-EZ.INDF.FS daily LNK.EZ.FS in Kurdish
'a daily newspaper in Kurdish' (Thackston 2006a: 16)

Thackston (2006a: 16) notes that "[a]n optional – and fairly rare – alternative masc. sing. construct extender [=linker Ezafe] uses the same ending as the indefinite, *î*", but note that this form does not inflect:

(72) Kurmanji: **Noun Phrase–Adjective**
[şaîr-ek-î kurd] î bijarte
poet-INDF-EZ.INDF.MS Kurd LNK.EZ recognized
'a recognized Kurdish poet' (Thackston 2006a: 16)

According to Bedir Khan (1960: 3) (see also MacKenzie 1961: 158, §263.(c).(ii)), this is the standard way to modify a primary by a supplementary adjective (in addition to the possibility of conjoining two adjectives, as in examples (37)–(38) on page 269 or (69)–(70) above):

(73) Kurmanji: **Noun Phrase–Adjective Phrase**
[heval-ê min] [[yê delal] î qênc]
friend-EZ.DEF.MS 1SG.OBL LNK.EZ.MS dear LNK.EZ good
'my dear and good friend' (Bedir Khan 1960: 3)

(74) Kurmanji: **Noun Phrase–Adjective**
(taxe-yek ji) [taxe-yên bajêr] î
neighbourhood-INDF from neighbourhood-EZ.DEF.PL city.OBL LNK.EZ
dûr
far
'one of the city's far-away neighbourhoods' (Bedir Khan 1960: 3)

Note that this construction is quite similar to the construction used in Sorani, shown in examples (39)–(40) on page 269, except that in Sorani the *î* morpheme is analysed as the construct Ezafe.

9.5.3 Clausal secondaries

Clausal secondaries seem to appear especially frequently in the linker Ezafe construction when they are separated from the primary by intervening material, as in the following examples (compare to the NENA Qaraqosh example (65) on page 169). Note also the usage of the relativizer to mark the clausal secondary, as after the construct Ezafe (see §9.4.9):[30]

(75) Kurmanji: **Noun Phrase–Clause**
[tûr-ek mezin] (hebû), [yê ku di hindir-ê xwe de
bag-INDF big had LNK.EZ.DEF.MS REL in inside-EZ.DEF.MS REFL in
şekir ... dihewandin]
sugar ... contained
'(There was) a big bag, which contained in it sugar.' (Thackston 2006a: 75)

(76) Kurmanji: **Proper Noun–Clause**
(deng-ê seg-ên gund) [Şerko] (dîsa hişyar kir), [yê ku
voice-EZ.MS dog-PL.EZ village Sh. again awake do LNK.EZ.MS REL
ji kêfxweşi-yê hema hindik ma-bû bi-fir-e].
from happiness-OBL.FS thus little remain-PRF SBJV-fly-3SG
'(The sound of the village dogs once again awoke) Sherko, who was almost flying from happiness.' (Thackston 2006a: 75)

9.5.4 Aspectual usage of the Ezafe with verbal secondaries

A quite distinct usage of the linker Ezafe with clausal (or rather verbal) secondaries, standing outside the domain of the attributive system, is its usage as a tense/aspect marker. This usage is discussed extensively by Haig (2011), who terms it as the TENSE EZAFE, and who relates it to a reanalysis of the Ezafe in cleft sentences ("constructions where the initial NP was a left-dislocated topic" in his words) as an aspectual marker. As such, it can combine with a verb in the

[30]Interestingly, the primary, consisting of a noun followed by an adjective, lacks here an Ezafe. A reviewer noted that the Ezafe is often lacking after the indefinite suffix in spoken language, yet I have no further information confirming this.

present indicative to add a progressive aspect (MacKenzie 1961: 205) and generally occurs with the perfect in affirmative statements (MacKenzie 1961: 210). The Ezafe agrees in such cases with the non-oblique argument of the verb (typically the subject, but also the object in the ergative construction).

(77) Sinǰar: **Pronoun–Verb**
ez ê di-bêj-im
1SG LNK.EZ.MS IND-say-1SG
'I am saying (*Je suis en train de dire*).' (Blau 1975: 40 [210])

(78) Sinǰar: **Pronoun–Verb**
ez ê hat-im
1SG LNK.EZ.MS came-1SG
'I have come (*Je suis venu*).' (Blau 1975: 40 [284])

It is worth noting that similar constructions exists in the NENA Sardarid (NW Iran) and ʿAnkawa (NE Iraq) dialects, both of which are in contact with Kurmanji dialects. In these NENA dialects, the Aramaic *d-* linker is used as an aspectual marker. In Sardarid, it occurs only with a special form of the copula,[31] while in ʿAnkawa, it occurs more generally before present tense verbs.

(79) Sardarid: **Pronoun–Verb**
ana d-un bə-taya
1SG LNK-COP.1SG in-come.INF
'I am coming (*Ich komme gleich*).' (Younansardaroud 2001: 139)

(80) ʿAnkawa: **∅–Verb**
{ʾāy-lə} də= k-šaqəl
{COP-3MS} LNK= IND-take.3MS
'He is taking {right now}.' (Borghero 2013: 78)

[31] This analysis is suggested by Younansardaroud (2001: 138), who explains the form *du-* as a contraction of *d-aw* [LNK-3MS]. Napiorkowska (2015: 172), discussing a similarly formed copula in Diyana-Zariwaw, qualifies this etymology as "problematic", but her criticism relates to the presence of the 3MS pronoun following the linker rather than to the linker itself. In fact, she suggests that the deictic/presentative particles *du~do* found also in other dialects may share the same origin, namely the linker *d-* with an added round vowel *o*. The latter vowel could be explained as stemming from the copula base, found for instance as such in the Judi-dialects of Turkey (see Gutman 2015c: 310).

A thorough discussion of the ʿAnkawa construction is given by Borghero (2013: 77ff; 2015), who qualifies this construction as a PSEUDO-RELATIVE.[32] She compares it to the neighbouring Kurmanji dialects and relates it to a broader cross-linguistic and Semitic setting (yet she does not mention the Sardarid construction). She mentions that in other Semitic speaking areas it has been proposed as an areal feature (see details and references there).

9.5.5 Lack of primary

The Kurmanji linker Ezafe can head an NP by itself, without any preceding primary, as the following examples show. MacKenzie (1961: 162) terms it accordingly as a "demonstrative ezafe"; in the current terminological framework it falls neatly under the definition of a PRONOMINAL LINKER (linking in this case an implicit referent with the secondary). In such cases I treat the primary as a zero-marked, and in the examples I put a ∅ sign where an explicit primary phrase could appear (in the translation, the explicit primary, understood from the context, is sometimes given in parenthesis). The secondary, headed by the linker Ezafe is delimited by square brackets from further material.

(81) Akre: ∅–**Noun**
∅ [ya Haşim-î] maz-tir =e
∅ LNK.EZ.FS H.-OBL.MS big-er =COP
'Hashim's (daughter) is bigger.' (MacKenzie 1961: 163)

(82) Akre: ∅–**Pronoun**
ev kitêb-e ∅ [yêt min] =in
DEM.PROX book-DEF ∅ LNK.EZ.PL 1SG.OBL =COP.PL
'These books are mine.' (MacKenzie 1961: 163)

Appearing before adjectives or ordinals, the linker Ezafe without primary nominalizes them:

[32] She attributes this term and type of analysis to Pennacchietti (2007). In this article, Pennacchietti shows a parallel between the Kurmanji construction and a similar construction found in Modern South Arabian dialects. Since these languages have not been in contact, the parallel, in this case, must be seen as purely typological.

(83) Sûrçi: ∅–**Adjective**
gor-îa ∅ *[yê dî]*
turn-EZ.DEF.FS ∅ LNK.EZ.MS other
'the other one's turn' (MacKenzie 1961: 163 [530])

(84) Sûrçi: ∅–**Adjective**
mez ∅ *[yê xwar-ê]*
in_front ∅ LNK.EZ.MS down-ADJ
'in front of the lower one$_{MS}$' (MacKenzie 1961: 163 [517])

(85) Akre: ∅–**Ordinal**
∅ *[yê dw-ê]* ... ∅ *[yê sê-yê]*
∅ LNK.EZ.MS two-ORD ... ∅ LNK.EZ.MS three-ORD
'the second (man)... the third one' (MacKenzie 1961: 163 [562])

When it appears before a clausal secondary, it introduces a free relative clause (marked additionally by a relativizer):

(86) Kurmanji: ∅–**Clause**
∅ *[ya ḳu ji min re derî ve-ḳir] berdestḳ-a wê bû.*
∅ LNK.EZ.FS REL for 1SG.OBL for door open-do servant-EZ.DEF.FS 3FS.OBL was
'The one$_{FS}$ who opened the door for me was her servant.' (Thackston 2006a: 76)

Sorani too has a linker Ezafe, *(h)î*, but, in contrast to Kurmanji, it uses it exclusively to head independent NPs, i.e. ACs without an explicit primary.[33] MacKenzie (1961: 66) uses again the term DEMONSTRATIVE EZAFE, a label which may be more appropriate here due to the lack of a primary. Yet, for the sake of consistency, I treat this as a case of the linker Ezafe with a ∅ primary, on a par with the Kurmanji data (and gloss accordingly). Similarly to the Sorani construct Ezafe, it does not convey any gender or number features, though an optional plural marker can follow it.

[33] Without the weak consonantal onset /*h*/, it is in fact identical in form to the Sorani construct Ezafe. Indeed, in Sorani, the two may be one and the same morpheme appearing with or without primaries.

(87) Bingird: ∅–**Noun**
∅ î baxewan-eke-y
∅ LNK.EZ gardener-DEF-OBL.MS
'the gardener's' (MacKenzie 1961: 59 [304])

(88) Sorani: ∅–**Noun Phrase**
ئەسپە سوورەکە هی برا گەورەی منە
esp-e sûr-eke ∅ [hî bra gewre-y min] =e
horse-EZ.DEF red-DEF ∅ LNK.EZ brother big-EZ 1SG.OBL =COP
'The red horse is my elder brother's.' (Blau 1980: 64)

(89) Silêmanî: ∅–**Pronoun**
∅ hî kê
∅ LNK.EZ who
'whose?' (MacKenzie 1961: 66)

(90) Mukrî: ∅–**Pronoun**
∅ [î xo-m] le ∅ [î tû] pitir =e
∅ LNK.EZ REFL-1SG from ∅ LNK.EZ 2SG bigger =COP
'Mine is bigger than thine.' (MacKenzie 1961: 66 [242[29]])

(91) Sorani: ∅–**Pronoun**
کتێبەکە یا هی منە یا هی تۆیە
kitêb-eke ya ∅ [hî min] =e ya ∅ [hî to] =ye
book-DEF or ∅ LNK.EZ 1SG =COP or ∅ LNK.EZ 2SG =COP
'The book is either mine or thine.' (Blau 1980: 64)

Like the Kurmanji linker Ezafe, it is used as well to nominalize adjectives:

(92) Silêmanî: ∅–**Adjective**
∅ hî şîn
∅ LNK.EZ blue
'the blue one' (MacKenzie 1961: 66)

(93) Piždar: ∅–**Adjective**
∅ [î de dî] =ş =in hen
∅ LNK.EZ PL other =also =PL.A EX.PL
'We have other ones too.' (MacKenzie 1961: 67)

9.6 The compounding Ezafe construction

A special form of the Ezafe, *-e-* (=[æ]), can be used whenever the resulting AC should be treated syntactically as a single compound noun rather than an NP.[34] In Kurmanji dialects, this usage seems to be restricted to lexicalised compounds:[35]

(94) Akre: **Noun–Noun**
jan-e-ser
ache-EZ-head
'headache' (MacKenzie 1961: 215)

(95) Akre: **Noun–Adjective**
kêz-e-řeş
beetle-EZ-black
'cockchafer' (MacKenzie 1961: 216)

Such lexicalised compounds are also found in Sorani dialects. In these dialects, however, the usage of the compounding Ezafe is more widespread and not confined to lexicalised compounds. Indeed, it is used systematically (but not exclusively) whenever a definite primary is modified by an adjective. In such cases, the primary and secondary form a syntactic non-lexicalised nominal compound, as is evident by the fact that the definite suffix appears after the secondary.

[34] The terminology regarding this element varies. MacKenzie (1961: 64, §185) calls it "a compound vowel", while Blau (1980: 58) terms it "*particule de liaison*" (=linking particle). Thackston (2006b: 11), writing of Sorani, uses the term "the close *Izâfa* construction", but restricts it to cases of adjectival secondaries. Note that MacKenzie (1966: 18) describes the existence of the same "compound vowel" in the Gorani Hawrami dialect, but there it is restricted to definite compounds. It is also reported to be found in the Gorani Gawrajū dialect, where it is tentatively analysed as a compound marker (Mahmudweyssi et al. 2012: 16).

[35] Functionally, one may equate this to the historical construct state construction in some NENA dialects where it is only used for lexical compounds, such as Qaraqosh (see §6.2.1).

(96) Sorani: **Noun–Adjective**
هۆتێله باشه‌که
[hotêl-e- baş]-eké
hotel-EZ- good-DEF
'the good hotel' (Thackston 2006b: 11)

Normally, in such cases, the adjective is interpreted restrictively (or, in other words, intersectively). Contrast example (36) on page 268 with the following example:

(97) Sorani: **Noun–Adjective**
ده‌رسه سه‌خته‌کان
[ders-e- sext]-ek-an
lesson-EZ- hard-DEF-PL
'the hard lessons' (Thackston 2006b: 12)

While it may seem possible to analyse the compounding Ezafe in Sorani as an allomorph of the construct Ezafe conveying the feature of definiteness, as such a distinction exists in Kurmanji (see Table 9.1 on page 258), such an analysis cannot account for two use cases. First, as example (36) on page 268 shows, a definite primary can be followed by the construct Ezafe. Second, a non-definite primary can be followed by the compounding Ezafe, even when the resulting expression is not a lexicalised compound:

(98) Silêmanî: **Noun–Noun**
kilk-e- ker-êk
tail-EZ- donkey-INDF
'a donkey's tail' (MacKenzie 1961: 65 citing C.J. Edmond's unpublished description of Silêmanî)

Thus, it is more likely that the Sorani *-e* is simply an Ezafe-like morpheme which permits the creation of syntactic nominal compounds, which is furthermore frequently used with combinations of definite primaries with restrictive adjectives.

Note, finally, that the same morpheme is also used in some compounds where the order of the primary and secondary is reversed:

(99) Sorani: **Noun–Noun**
nergis-e- cař
narcissus-EZ- field
'field of narcissi' (MacKenzie 1961: 142)

(100) Sorani: **Noun–Adjective**
بەرزە پیاوێك
berz-e piyaw-êk
high-EZ man-INDF
'a great man' (Blau 1980: 61)

Judging by this and the other examples given by Blau (1980: 61), it may be that the reverse order in the case of adjectival secondaries is related to their evaluative nature.

9.7 Alternatives constructions for clausal secondaries

As discussed in §9.4.9 and §9.5.3, clausal secondaries regularly appear in the construct and linker Ezafe constructions, normally following a relativizer. Yet in Sorani the Ezafe morpheme can be replaced by other morphemes suffixed to the primary (Blau 1980: 156). These morphemes are related, formally or semantically, to the domain of determination.

First, the Ezafe may be replaced by a suffix *-ê(k)*, identical in form to the indefinite suffix, but without conveying any indefinite sense (glossed "INDF").

(101) Sorani: **Noun–Clause**
کراسێ کە تۆ کڕیوتە زۆر درێژە
kiras-ê [ke to kiřî-w-t-e] (zor drêj =e)
dress-"INDF" REL 2SG bought-PRF-2SG-COP.3SG very long =COP.3SG
'The dress that you bought (is very long).' (Blau 1980: 156)

This recalls the situation in Persian, where the suffix *-i* can be used both as an indefinite determiner and an Ezafe-like suffix introducing relative clauses. Samvelian (2006), who discusses this situation, concludes that these are two separate morphemes (regardless of a possible diachronic connection). The latter morpheme, moreover, should be distinguished from the Ezafe, as it conveys an intersective semantic value, appearing only before restrictive relative clauses. Judging by the Sorani examples, this may be true also for this language.

Syntactically, the *-ê(k)* suffix differs from the Ezafe, in that it does not require the secondary to follow it immediately:

(102) Sorani: **Noun–Clause**
کراسێ بکڕە کە پێت جوانە
[kiras-ê] bi-kiř-e [ke pê-t ciwan =e]
dress-"INDF" SBJV-buy-2SG REL for-2SG beautiful =COP.3SG
'Buy the dress that pleases you (*Achète-toi la robe qui te plaît*).' (Blau 1980: 157)

It is important to recall, moreover, that the indefinite suffix *-êk* by itself is compatible with the Ezafe (see for instance example (39) on page 269 and also discussion of Samvelian 2006: 27).

Alternatively, the Ezafe becomes redundant if the primary is determined by a demonstrative and the corresponding short definite suffix *-e*:

(103) Sorani: **Noun–Clause**
ئام پیاوە کە تۆ دەیبینی برا گەورەی منە
em piyaw-e [ke to de-y-bîn-î] (bira gawra-y min =e)
DEM.PROX man-DEF REL 2SG IND-P.3SG-see-A.2SG brother big-EZ 1SG =COP.3SG
'This man that you see (is my elder brother).' (Blau 1980: 156)

Also in this construction, the secondary can be separated from the primary by intervening material. This is the case in the following example, which differs from (102) only by the explicit definite determination of the primary:

(104) Sorani: **Noun–Clause**
ئەو کراسە بکڕە کە پێت جوانە
[ew kiras-e] bikiře [ke pê-t ciwan =e]
DEM.DIST dress-DEF SBJV-buy-2SG REL in-2SG beautiful =COP.3SG
'Buy the dress that pleases you.' (Blau 1980: 157)

Here too, it should be noted that the definite suffix *-e* is compatible with the Ezafe, as is shown in example (56) on page 274 (and contrast with example (101) on the preceding page).

Finally, descriptive relative clauses can be introduced solely by the relativizer:

(105) Sorani: **Noun Phrase–Clause**
باوکم کە سەرۆکی ئام خێڵە بوو
[bawk =im] [ke serok-î em xêł-e bû]
father =POSS.1SG REL head-EZ DEM.PROX tribe-DEF was.3SG
'my father, who was the head of the tribe' (Blau 1980: 156)

The exact usage conditions of these different constructions are, however, outside the scope of this work.

9.8 Juxtaposition (X Y)

One finds distinct cases where Kurdish dialects make use of the juxtaposition construction. In this construction no Ezafe is apparent, though the oblique case may still appear.

In some cases the lack of Ezafe is phonologically motivated. Some Kurmanji dialects, for instance, drop the Ezafe marker after a vowel-final primary. In such cases, one may analyse the Ezafe as having a ∅ allomorph:

(106) Akre: **Adjective–Noun**
tejî-∅ jêř
full-EZ gold
'full of gold' (MacKenzie 1961: 161 [567])

(107) Akre: **Noun–Noun**
cê-∅ germ-ê
place-EZ warmth-OBL.FS
'place of warmth' (MacKenzie 1961: 159 [545])

In the Sorani Wârmâwa dialect, on the other hand, one finds the juxtaposition construction without an apparent phonological trigger. Accordingly, I analyse such examples as lacking an Ezafe altogether:

(108) Wârmâwa: **Noun–Noun**
mel Ḥacî
house H.
'the house of Haji' (MacKenzie 1961: 62, fn. 2 [246])

This may be an areal phenomenon, as the juxtaposition construction is also found in Persian (Balaÿ & Esmaïli 2013: 209), as well as in Gorani, in particular in the Gawrajū dialect (Mahmudweyssi et al. 2012: 16), and in the Hawrami dialect, though in the latter it seems to be restricted to indefinite primaries (Holmberg & Odden 2008: 130–131).

9.8.1 Quantification expressions

The juxtaposition construction is also found in the special case where the primary can be analysed as quantifying the secondary. Such cases may be seen as being on the borderline of the AC system, since the relationship between the primary and the secondary is not a typical attributive relationship (see discussion in §7.7.3). The nouns used in the quantification expression can be compared with nominal classifiers found in some languages, albeit in the Kurdish case they are not grammaticalised as such.

For Sorani dialects, MacKenzie (1961: 63, §184.(c)) gives a wealth of examples of this construction (which he terms the PARTITIVE RELATION), including the following ones:[36]

(109) Silêmanî: **Q. Noun Phrase–Noun**
[yek hegbe] pare
one bag money
'a bag of money' (MacKenzie 1961: 63 [29])

(110) Wârmâwa: **Q. Noun Phrase–Noun**
[çwar fewc] ʿesker
four battalion soldier
'four battalions of soldiers' (MacKenzie 1961: 64 [265])

(111) Mukrî: **Q. Noun–Noun**
parw-êk nan û çor-êk ew
morsel-INDF bread and sip-INDF water
'a morsel bread and a sip of water' (MacKenzie 1961: 64 [93[33]])

For Kurmanji dialects, MacKenzie (1961: 161, §264.(e)) gives only three examples with the primary *hindek* 'a little', which may be seen as a fixed expression:

[36]The same construction is attested also in the Gorani Hawrami dialect (MacKenzie 1966: 20).

(112) Sûrçi: **Q. Noun–Noun**
hind-ek *pare*
measure-INDF money
'a little money' (MacKenzie 1961: 161 [514])

In a footnote, however, he cites Kurdoev (1956), who contrasts the following two examples, the first one instantiating the quantifying juxtaposition construction, while the second one is the normal Ezafe attributive construction:

(113) Kurmanji: **Q. Noun–Noun**
revok-ek *hesp*
herd-INDF horse
'one herd of horses' (MacKenzie 1961: 161, fn. 1 citing Kurdoev 1956: 34)

(114) Kurmanji: **Noun–Noun**
revok-a *hesp-a*
herd-EZ.FS horse-OBL.PL
'a horse-herd' (MacKenzie 1961: 161, fn. 1 citing Kurdoev 1956: 34)

9.8.2 Adverbial primaries

Edmonds (1955: 497) reports that nouns used as prepositions in Southern Kurdish (=Sorani) are used without the Ezafe (but see example (50) on page 272):

(115) Sorani: **Adverbial Noun–Noun**
nizîk *bewk* *=î* *=ewe* *(ra westa =bu).*
near[37] father =POSS.3SG =POSTPOSITION up stood =was
'(He was standing) near his father.' (Edmonds 1955: 497)

9.8.3 Compounds

Another case of juxtaposition is apparent in compounds. As discussed in §9.6, compounds are typically formed with the aid of the compounding Ezafe. Yet they can also occur without it:

[37] While the English gloss 'near' may be understood as primarily being a noun or an adverb, Edmonds (1955: 497) explicitly lists *nizîk* as a noun.

(116) Akre: **Noun–Adjective**
deḥle-řeş-ik
thorn-black-DIM
'blackberry bush' (MacKenzie 1961: 215)

To this one may add compound adjectival expressions like *por-zer* 'blond' (lit. hair-yellow) or *çav-şîn* 'blue-eyed' (lit. eye-blue) found in example (38) on page 269.

9.8.4 Inverse juxtaposition (Y X)

Inverse juxtapositioninverse juxtaposition construction is quite restricted in Kurdish dialects. MacKenzie (1961: 73) notes that Sorani ordinals formed by the suffix *-emîn* always precede the qualified noun (compare with examples in §9.4.5):

(117) Silêmanî: **Noun–Ordinal**
yek-emîn car
one-ORD time
'the first time' (MacKenzie 1961: 73)

This is expected insofar as the suffix *-emîn* is in fact composed of two parts: -*em*, being the ordinal suffix proper, and *-în*, being a superlative suffix (MacKenzie 1961: 68, §190.(b)).[38] Superlative adjectives regularly precede the head noun:

(118) Silêmanî: **Noun–Adjective (superlative)**
(bo) aza-tir-în serbaz
for brave-COMPR-SUPER soldier
'(for) the bravest soldier' (MacKenzie 1961: 68)

Also, in some nominal compounds the secondary precedes the primary noun:

(119) Silêmanî: **Noun–Noun**
osta-jin
craftsman-woman
'craftsman's wife' (MacKenzie 1961: 142)

Inverted compounds are also found in Kurmanji dialects, especially with adjectival secondaries; see MacKenzie (1961: 215) for some examples.

[38] The formal relationship between ordinals and superlatives is known also in other languages of the area, notably Arabic. See in this respect footnote 10 on page 123 and footnote 50 on page 383.

9.9 Conclusions and comparative prospects

In this chapter, I have surveyed the various ACs found in Kurmanji and Sorani dialects. As detailed grammars of specific Kurdish dialects are still scarce, many claims and examples are based on the standard varieties of these two dialect groups.

As we have seen, the AC system of the Kurdish dialects revolves around the various Ezafe constructions, which I have divided into three distinct types, as discussed in §9.3: the construct Ezafe, the linker Ezafe and the compounding Ezafe. This distinction, while independently motivated by the language structure, permits us to draw parallels between these constructions and similar NENA constructions. Especially the construct Ezafe construction can be seen in some respects as the equivalent of the NENA Neo-CSC, as both make use of a suffixal marker to flag the primary, while the linker Ezafe construction is the equivalent of the NENA ALC, as both make use of pronominal linkers.

The parallels between these constructions, however, are not perfect: In Kurdish the Ezafe morphemes are used to introduce all types of secondaries, be they nouns, adjectives, relative clauses, or prepositional phrases. Most NENA dialects, on the other hand, keep the Semitic distinction between adjectival modification, marked by juxtaposition-cum-agreement and nominal/clausal modification, marked by the construct state.[39] Yet another difference is the usage of adverbial primaries: In Kurdish, only prepositions formed from nouns can be marked by the Ezafe, while in NENA also core prepositions can be marked by the construct state suffix (the latter being true also of Persian, see Samvelian 2008: 345, example (16)).

As we have seen, the Ezafe morphemes of Sorani and Kurmanji are in some respects quite different:[40] In Standard Kurmanji, the construct Ezafe takes part in the nominal morphology, and as such is best treated as a nominal phrasal suffix. In addition to the construct Ezafe I distinguish an independent, pronominal linker Ezafe, which is typically used after NP primaries, but can also occur without a primary. In Kurmanji, moreover, only the linker Ezafe can regularly be used to chain several modifiers of one primary.

In standard Sorani, on the other hand, the Ezafe is a fixed, uninflected particle. While I treat this Ezafe too as a phrasal suffix mainly due to its selective

[39] An exception is the peripheral dialect of JSanandaj, which has borrowed the Iranic Ezafe together with its distribution; see §8.7.2.

[40] Looking at the dialectal map, one observes a continuum of change, as discussed in §9.4. The dialects located at the Inter-Zab region, Mukrî and Bingird included, present characteristics of transitional dialects. This is to a large extent also true of the Inter-Zab NENA dialects.

attachment to nominal hosts, it is more clitic-like than its Kurmanji counterpart. Indeed, in the Sorani case it is possible to argue that the linker Ezafe is simply an allomorph of the construct Ezafe, occurring when no explicit primary is present.

Comparing these facts to the situation in NENA shows that, by and large, most NENA dialects are similar in some respects to Kurmanji and in some respects to Sorani (and in some respects to neither). First, note that in all NENA dialects, the construct state suffix (be it of Aramaic origin or a borrowed Ezafe) is uninflected, like the Sorani Ezafe. On the other hand, as in Kurmanji, in most NENA dialects the construct state suffix occurs in complementary distribution with a similarly shaped linker, which can appear either with or without an explicit nominal primary.[41] Moreover, as discussed in §4.4, the NENA construct state suffix *-əd* can be analysed as a phrasal suffix in many dialects.

These partial similarities raise the question of the extent to which the NENA Neo-CSC is related to the construct Ezafe construction. This question is treated in depth in §10.4.2.

Another domain of possible contact is the emergence of NENA genitive marking (discussed in §4.5). This development may be related to the usage of the oblique case in Kurmanji dialects, although the latter is used in a wider syntactic domain. This question is discussed in §10.5.

Yet another plausible influence of Kurmanji dialects on some NENA dialects, discussed in §9.5.4, is the usage of the linker *d-* as a verbal aspectual marker in Sardarid and ʿAnkawa, on the model of the aspectual use of the Kurmanji Ezafe marker. This functional similarity has been previously observed by Borghero (2013: 77ff.).

In the Sorani-speaking region some NENA dialects, JSanandaj and Sulemaniyya in particular, have re-analysed their possessive enclitics as phrasal suffixes, very likely under influence of Sorani dialects (see §9.2 and compare with §8.2). The same dialects have generalized the usage of the juxtaposition construction as an AC. This too may be related to the influence of Sorani dialects. This possibility is explored in §11.3.2.2.

While trying to be exhaustive, the survey of the Kurdish AC systems given in the present chapter can certainly not do justice to the extent of dialectal complexity. Indeed, such an investigation would merit a monograph on its own. It is my hope that this chapter may provide an adequate seed for such a study.

[41] In some exceptional NENA dialects, notably JUrmi, the linker can co-occur with a construct state suffix, unlike the Kurmanji linker. See §7.3.2 regarding JUrmi, and §11.2 for a general discussion.

10 The development of D-markers in NENA dialects

10.1 Introduction

In the previous chapters I have surveyed some AC systems of certain NENA dialects from a synchronic perspective. We have seen that these dialects permit a wealth of constructions to mark the attributive relation, while at the same time some key strategies re-appear. In this and the following chapter I take a broad cross-dialectal view and compare the occurrence of the main constructions across all NENA dialects in the survey. This comparison will permit us to formulate some plausible hypotheses regarding the origin of these constructions. A key question in this regard is to evaluate the role language contact played in the NENA developments, as opposed to internal developments. Of course, both these factors play a role in the development of every language, but sometimes they can be shown to go hand in hand, while on other occasions they seem to block each other. As contact languages, I consider especially Kurdish dialects, whose AC system was presented in some detail in Chapter 9. To assess the internal development scenarios, I treat Syriac, whose AC system was presented in Chapter 3, as an approximative Proto-NENA stage, without entering into the methodological debate whether a Proto-NENA existed at all. Some allusions, moreover, will be made to other classical forms of Aramaic (notably Jewish Babylonian Aramaic), Early Jewish Neo-Aramaic (Nerwa), as well as other Neo-Aramaic varieties (Western Neo-Aramaic and Mīdin).

In this chapter I concentrate on the development of the D-MARKERS in NENA dialects, i.e. AC markers containing a /*d*/ segment which is a reflex of the Classical Aramaic *d-* linker or a cognate thereof. As such, the chapter is closely tied to Chapter 4, which presents the synchronic analysis of these markers in NENA dialects. While this chapter aims to track the development of these markers, it has a comparative part as well, as it presents the distribution of the various constructions cross-dialectally.

To situate the development of the D-markers, §10.2 discusses first the retention of the Classical Aramaic Analytic Linker Construction (=ALC, i.e. Syriac *bayta d=malkā* 'the house of the king', see §3.5) in NENA dialects. Section §10.3, on the other hand, discusses the non-retention of the Syriac Double Annexation Construction (=DAC, i.e. Syriac *bayt-ēh d=malkā*, see §3.6)

Section §10.4 discusses the arguably most prominent AC in NENA, namely the NEO-CONSTRUCT-STATE CONSTRUCTION (=Neo-CSC, i.e. Bēṣpən *bayt-əd malka*).[1] In particular, Section §10.4.1 discusses the origin of this construction, whether it is the Classical Aramaic ALC or rather the DAC. Section §10.4.2 discusses the role language contact might have played in its development.

Section §10.5 discusses the development of the genitive prefix *d-*, with a special emphasis on the role of language contact.

Section §10.6 discusses the distribution and development of alternative linkers in NENA. The usage of the linker *did* is discussed both as a basis for the attributive pronouns (§10.6.1) and as an independent linker (§10.6.2). Other linkers are discussed as well, notably *ad* or *od* (§10.6.3), and the JUrmi *ay* linker, in which the /*d*/ segment is arguably no more apparent (§10.6.4). Section §10.6.5 discusses the possible grammaticalisation of *mar-* 'owner' as a linker; while it is not related to the *d-* linker, it it treated here due to its possible functional equivalence.

10.2 The distribution of the inherited ALC: X *d*-Y

As seen in Chapter 3, the main AC in Syriac is the analytic linker construction (=ALC), a linker construction in which a linker *d-* mediates between the primary and the secondary, without any further marking on the primary. This construction, with the very same linker *d-* (sometimes realized /*də-*/ or even /*ʾəd-*/[2]) is retained in many NENA dialects, but often with various restrictions. I distinguish between cases where the *d-* linker mediates between two nouns, and cases where it mediates between a (pro)noun and clause. The dialectal distribution of these two possibilities is given in Table 10.1 on the facing page. Cases where the secondary is a pronoun, on the other hand, must be treated separately, as well

[1] I use the term NEO-CONSTRUCT differently from Mutzafi (2004b: 3, fn. 15), who uses it to refer to the innovated apocopated construct state formation, not being a reflex of the historical construct state formation. Since the distinction between the historical and the innovated apocopated construct state formations is not always obvious, I subsume both under the heading Apocopate-CSC, reserving the term Neo-CSC for the forms marked by the suffix *-əd*, stressing the fact that this is the main structural (head-marking) equivalent of the classical Semitic construct state in NENA dialects. A discussion of the development of the innovated Apocopate-CSC and the retention of the historical CSC is found in §11.1.

[2] While the form /*ʾəd-*/ can be seen as a phonetic variant of *d-*, with the schwa added as an epenthetic vowel, it may also represent an alternative linker form, similarly to *ad* or *od* discussed in §10.6.3. Since in all dialects, in which the form /*ʾəd-*/ is found, one finds also the basic form /*d-*/, this question does not affect the current discussion.

Table 10.1: Dialectal distribution of Noun + *d-* + Noun/Clause constructions. (+) indicates cases where the primary is ∅ or pronominal.

Region	Dialect	N *d*-Noun	N *d*-Clause
SE Turkey	Hertevin	(+)	+
	Bohtan		
	Bēṣpən		
	Gaznax		
	Baz	+	+
	Challa	+	(+)
	Jilu	+	+
NW Iraq	JZakho		+
	JAradhin		
	CAradhin	+	+
	Barwar	+	+
	Betanure		+
	Amədya	+	+
	Barzani		
	Alqosh	+	+
	Qaraqosh	+	+
NW Iran	JUrmi		
	Sardarid		
NE Iraq	Diyana-Zariwaw	+	?
	Arbel		+
	Koy Sanjaq		
	Sulemaniyya	+	(+)
W. Iran	JSanandaj		
	CSanandaj		

as cases where the primary is an adverbial. In the present discussion I exclude cases where I consider the *d-* segment to be re-analysed as a morphological genitive marker, i.e. preceding a vowel-initial determiner/pronoun (these cases are discussed in §10.5).

Out of the 24 dialects surveyed in Table 10.1 the *d-* appears as mediating between two nouns only in 10 dialects. Moreover, the usage of this construction is often qualified. Thus, Khan (2004: 192) reports that in Sulemaniyya this construction is used in "isolated instances". In Barwar it is reported to be in occasional use only (Khan 2008c: 398). In CAradhin an N *d*-N construction is not found (in my survey), but the construction [N+Adj] *d*-N is found once.[3] The usage of the construction is often motivated by morpho-phonological factors. In Challa it is used when the primary is a loanword, typically not adapted to Aramaic word-structure (Fassberg 2010: 46). In Jilu Fox (1997: 60) asserts that the linker appears after primaries ending in consonants, those being in fact also unadapted loanwords.

Taking into account also clausal secondaries, one finds this construction in three more dialects: JZakho, Betanure, and Arbel.[4] The most common type of clausal secondaries are those which start with a copula, which is typically vowel-initial. This phonological environment may have been favourable for the retention of the *d*- linker as a relativizer, as the linker could easily syllabify with the vowel-initial copula, creating an *optimal* CV syllable.[5] Support for this idea comes from JZakho, which has gone beyond mere retention of the *d*- linker, and has re-analysed the combination *d*+COP as an attributive form of the copula (Cohen 2010; see discussion in §5.5.2).

The construction is entirely lacking in Iranian-located dialects[6] as well as the peripheral dialects of Turkey (with the exception of Hertevin). In other words, the *d*- linker is better conserved in the central dialects, while it is lost in the periphery.

From the above, two conclusions arise. First, the use of the ALC, which was a major AC construction in Eastern Classical Aramaic has been greatly reduced in modern dialects. Second, the *d*- linker in its role as a relativizer proved to be

[3] In general there is a tendency to use the ALC with phrasal primaries, possibly due to the prosodic independence of the *d*- phrase. Nevertheless, phrasal primaries can appear also in other ACs, notably the Neo-CSC.

[4] It should be noted that these dialects make use of the ALC for nominal secondaries, but with other linkers. Thus, JZakho and Betanure use the linker *did* (see §10.6.2), while Arbel uses the linker *od* (§10.6.3).

[5] The retention of morphemic segments before vowels (including glottal stops, these being weak consonantal onsets) is a well-known phenomenon in NENA, especially in the verbal domain: In some dialects, the indicative marker *k*- is only conserved before vowel-initial (or /ʾ/-initial) verbal stems (e.g. Arbel: Khan 1999: 248).

[6] It is interesting to note that in Sardarid the *d*- marker survives only with the copula, as a verbal aspectual marker (see example (79) on page 280). This shows that the one of the last uses of the *d*- marker before its disappearance from the NENA AC system is with clausal secondaries, and more precisely with copular secondaries. In JSanandaj and JUrmi, on the other hand, the *d*- survives as a genitive marker on certain pronouns.

more durable, possibly due to the favourable role played by copular secondaries, as explained above.

The reason for the decline of the ALC in NENA can be attributed to two main reasons: 1) The replacement of the *d-* linker by other linkers (see §10.6); 2) The replacement of the linker construction by a head-marking construction, namely the Neo-CSC (§10.4).

10.3 The Syriac double annexation construction: X-y.POSS *d*-Y

While the use of the ALC has been reduced in NENA, its fate has been better than the Double Annexation Construction (=DAC). Recall that the DAC is a construction in which the secondary is indexed by a possessive pronoun on the primary, followed by the *d-* linker and the secondary itself (for example, *bayt-ēh d=malkā* 'the king's house'). This construction has completely disappeared from NENA dialects.[7] The only attested cases I could find of this construction in a modern NENA corpus are the Gospel translations in Qaraqosh, which clearly preserve the original Syriac wording (see §6.4.2).

10.4 Development of the Neo-Construct-State construction in NENA: X-*əd* Y

As stated above, the ALC and DAC, extant in Syriac, have been to a large extent replaced by the Neo-CSC of NENA, in which the primary is marked by a suffixed morpheme *-əd*. As Table 10.2 on the following page shows, this construction is extant in all surveyed NENA dialects, with the notable exception of JSanandaj. The extent to which the construction is used with primaries and secondaries other than nouns, however, varies quite a lot.[8] Some of the major categories are given

[7]This is not to imply that it died out. Rather, as shown in §10.4.1, it seems to have evolved into the Neo-CSC. Yet, in its Classical form, the DAC does not occur in NENA dialects (*Pace* Mengozzi (2005a: 383) who claims that "it is still used in certain varieties of NENA"). Only with pronominal secondaries does one find a similar construction in some dialects, used chiefly to disambiguate the usage of 3rd person possessors (see example (37) on page 335).

[8]Some of the variation, however, is probably attributable to variable corpus sizes available for each dialect.

Table 10.2: Distribution of the suffixed construct state. The entry (+) indicates clausal secondaries following only pronominal primaries or a construct state tautological infinitive (Hertevin only).

		Primaries			Secondaries		
Region	Dialect	Noun	Adj.	Inf.	NP	Ordinal	Clause
SE Turkey	Hertevin	+		(+)	+	+	(+)
	Bohtan	+			+		(+)
	Bēṣpən	+			+		
	Gaznax	+			+		
	Baz	+			+		
	Challa	+		+	+	+	+
	Jilu	+			+		
NW Iraq	JZakho	+	+	+	+	+	+
	JAradhin	+			+		(+)
	CAradhin	+		+	+	+	+
	Barwar	+	+		+	+	+
	Betanure	+		+	+	+	+
	Amədya	+			+	+	+
	Barzani	+					
	Alqosh	+			+	+	+
	Qaraqosh	+	+	+	+		+
NW Iran	JUrmi	+	+		+	+	+
	Sardarid	+			+	+	+
NE Iraq	Rustaqa						(+)
	Diyana-Z.	+	+		+	+	?
	Arbel	+			+		+
	Koy Sanjaq	+			+	+	+
	Sulemaniyya	+			+		(+)
W. Iran	JSanandaj						
	CSanandaj	+			+	+	

in Table 10.2, with the notable exclusion of adverbial primaries (i.e. prepositions and conjunctions), as these are lexically determined in each dialect.[9]

Two questions arise regarding this diachronic development of this marking:

1. What is the origin of the Neo-CSC? Is it the ALC, the DAC or both?
2. How did the Neo-CSC develop? Specifically, what is the role of language contact?

In the following sections, I shall attempt to answer these questions.

10.4.1 Origin of the Neo-CSC

Mengozzi (2005a: 378–380), following Khan (1999: 169), gives three possible hypotheses regarding the emergence of the Neo-CSC. In all accounts, it is clear that the suffixed segment */-d/* results from the encliticization of the Syriac proclitic *d-*. What is less clear is the source of the schwa vowel which precedes it, forming the suffixed morpheme */-əd/~/-ət/*. Recall that the schwa replaces as a vocalic nucleus the free state endings */-a/~/-e/* of words of Aramaic origin. Indeed, this replacement of the free state endings is one of the main reasons I have alluded to in considering the *-əd* ending as a morphologically integrated suffix of the noun stem (see §4.4.2.4).[10]

Mengozzi (2005a: 379f.), citing Khan (1999: 169), mentions three hypotheses regarding the origin of the schwa:

1. It results from a phonetic reduction of the */-a/~/-e/* free state suffixes appearing on the primary of the ALC.

[9]As for adjectival secondaries, these appear regularly in this construction only in Arbel (see example (22) on page 317) and to a limited extent, which is probably non-productive, in Barwar (e.g., *xəṭṭət romaye* 'roman wheat'; Khan 2008c: 523) and Barzani (*kalekūvid ʾuṛwa* 'the great wild ram'; Mutzafi 2004b: 4, fn. 33).

[10]Nouns of foreign origin ending in consonants can also get the *-əd* suffix in some dialects, such as the Kurdish loan *xadām* 'servant' in the following example:

(i) Arbel: **Noun–Noun Phrase**
xadā̃m-it [bā̃b-it ʾiyyà faqī̃r]
servant-CST father-CST DEM.PROX poor.SG
'the servant of the father of this poor man' (Khan 1999: 424 [S:31])

Foreign nouns whose final vowel is not seen as the free state ending may get a simple */-d/* suffix in the construct state (see §4.4.2.3). Recall also that in JUrmi the suffix may be */-ad/* under the influence of vowel harmony (see §7.2).

2. It is a reflex of a fossilized 3MS possessive pronoun *-ēh* originating in the DAC, which was phonetically attenuated to *-ə* (often realised as [ɪ] or [ɘ]).

3. It is a reflex of a demonstrative element *ə*<*ay*, originating in the ALC with an inserted demonstrative pronoun acting as determiner (i.e. primary + DEM + LNK + secondary; see §3.5.6 for Syriac examples).[11]

   To this one may add two supplementary hypotheses:

4. It is an epenthetic vowel added before a *-d* suffix (following the removal of the free state suffixes where present).

5. It is a reflex of the Sorani Ezafe suffix *-î* (=[i]~[ɪ]), or an fossilized and attenuated Kurmanji 3MS Ezafe suffix *-ê~-î* (=[e]~[i]).

Mengozzi (2005a: 380) prefers the second hypothesis, since it explains the occurrence of prepositional primaries with the *-əd* ending. Prepositions in Classical Aramaic cannot appear in the ALC, but rather must appear in the DAC (if a linker is present at all). Thus, only a DAC-origin hypothesis can explain their distribution with the *-əd* ending in NENA.[12] Mengozzi's examples are reproduced in Table 10.3 on the facing page.

A further fact substantiating this hypothesis is the fact the DAC is virtually absent in NENA dialects, as discussed in §10.3. This is easily explained if the DAC evolved into the Neo-CSC. The fact that the ALC remains to a certain extent in NENA, as shown in §10.3, indicates conversely that it was probably not the source of the Neo-CSC.

To round off the picture in favour of this hypothesis, note that Socin (1882: 122) (cited by Tsereteli 1965: 230) brings the Jilu example *šímm-o-d báxta* 'the name of the woman', in which the *-o-* element corresponds to the 3FS possessive suffix. This construction looks very much like the Neo-CSC, as the *d-* linker is encliticized to the primary, yet the FS possessive suffix is a clear indication of a DAC-origin. This example seems to reflect an earlier stage of NENA in which the

[11]This construction is probably the source of the NWNA Mīdin HEAVY POSSESSIVE SUFFIXES, which originated in the encliticization of the sequence *ay-ḏ*+POSS to a primary noun, yielding for instance *ʾu=bayt-ayḏe* 'his house'. See Jastrow (1985: 52, §47; 2002: 58), who offers, however, a different development path.

[12]As some prepositions, notably *l-* and *b-*, do not occur in the DAC in Syriac, one is obliged, moreover, to assume analogy across prepositions in order to explain their construct state marked forms, namely *ʾalləd* and *ʾabbəd*. According to Nöldeke (1875: 330, §231), in Classical Mandaic the preposition *b-* does occur very occasionally (*ganz vereinzelt*) in the DAC, but not the preposition *l-* (see also Pat-El 2012: 112).

Table 10.3: Mengozzi's argumentation regarding the origin of the Neo-CSC

	Classical Aramaic			NENA dialects	
ALC	*baytā* house.FREE **ʿammā* *with.FREE	*d=malkā* LNK=king *d=malkā* LNK=king			
DAC	*bayt-ēh* house-POSS.3MS *ʿamm-ēh* with-POSS.3MS	*d=malkā* LNK=king *d=malkā* LNK=king	> Neo-CSC	*bayt-əd* house-CST *ʾəmm-əd* with-CST	*malka* king *malka* king

possessive suffix was not yet fossilized and attenuated as an /ə/ segment. No such example, however, is attested in modern descriptions of NENA dialects (including Fox 1997 describing Jilu), so this example may rather reflect a certain purist or prescriptive approach to language (imitating the Syriac construction) rather than normal usage. Indeed, judging from the examples of Mengozzi (2005a: 374f.), already Early Christian NENA (manuscripts of the 17th century) had a fossilized, and possible phonetically attenuated, 3MS possessive suffix in the DAC.[13] Also some Neo-Aramaic writers using the 19th century Syriac script developed by missionaries in Urmi, notably Paul Bedjan, wrote a fossilized 3MS possessive suffix on the primary preceding a proclitic *d-* (Murre-van den Berg 1999: 192, §6.2.6; 198, §6.3.6, fn. 33).[14]

While the DAC-origin hypothesis seems thus highly plausible, it does not exclude the alternative explanations completely. First, as Mengozzi (2005a: 382) himself notes, this origin is problematic in explaining the use of the *-əd* suffix before clausal secondaries, since in Syriac these could only appear in the ALC. In order to explain the availability of the Neo-CSC construction in such cases, Mengozzi brings forth the first hypothesis, namely the ALC-origin hypothesis, and concludes that "the phonetic reduction that gave rise to the endings *-ed*, *-it*, etc.

[13] Confusingly, it was spelled sometimes as a final Syriac Aleph ܐ, rendering it orthographically similar to the free state suffix. Note that an Aleph has the consonantal value of a glottal stop /ʾ/, but it was likely not pronounced word-finally.

[14] Note, however, that Murre-van den Berg (1999: 175), who adopts an ALC-origin view of the *-əd* suffix, sees this fossilized 3MS possessive suffix as a *post-hoc* adaptation of the *-əd* suffix to grammar of Syriac.

neutralized the morpho-phonetic oppositions between two earlier constructions [the ALC and the DAC]".[15]

In order to reconcile the two origins, one can posit a double-origin hypothesis. In such a scenario, following the transformation of the DAC to the Neo-CSC, cases where the *d-* linker of the ALC is cliticized to the primary (as may happen due to prosodic reasons), are levelled by analogy to the Neo-CSC: e.g. ALC *bayt-a=d malka* > Neo-CSC *bayt-əd malka*. This would naturally also include cases with clausal secondaries.

One may wonder why the DAC (*bayt-ēh d=malkā*) was completely transformed into the Neo-CSC, while the ALC remains in complementary distribution with the latter. This is partially answered by the hypothesis that the transformation ALC>Neo-CSC is a later development, that may not yet have reached its culmination.[16] Yet also structural reasons may be called upon:

First, since the 3MS possessive suffix is normally realized in NENA as a vowel *-e* or *-u*, the encliticization of the *d-* to it is highly facilitated, being in fact a phonetic re-syllabification.[17] In the ALC, however, the primary may in principle end in a consonant (especially if it is an unadapted loanword[18]) thus preventing such a resyllabification, and conserving the availability of the ALC.

Second, from a more general point of view, the principle of ECONOMY seems to have played a role.[19] In Classical Aramaic, the marking of the primary by a possessive pronoun was part of a more general strategy of using PROLEPTIC

[15]He relates, moreover, the extended usage of the *-əd* suffix to the Kurdish Ezafe, a question which I shall examine in more detail below.

[16]In this respect, it would be interesting to follow the recent evolution of this construction in contemporary NENA dialects, now spoken for a large part in the diaspora.

[17]In Classical Aramaic a weak consonantal segment /*h*/ follows the vocalic nucleus yielding transc-ēh. Yet in most NENA dialects this segment has been elided, or conserved only in restricted morpho-phonological contexts (e.g. in in JZakho before a 3rd person copula; see Cohen 2012: 450). In some dialects it has been conserved or even strengthened to /*ḥ*/ segment (Coghill 2008: 96). The latter is the case for instance in Alqosh, yet this had no effect on the emergence of the Neo-CSC in the dialect. This hints that the elision of the /*h*/ segment in the possessive suffix of the DAC was independent of its development in other places, in line with the idea that the possessive suffix of the DAC was fossilized.

[18]In Syriac texts there are numerous Greek loanwords, for example.

[19]Recently, Cristofaro (2015) argued that ECONOMY should not be advanced as responsible for language change, but rather specific morpho-phonological processes of language change should be specified. Clearly, language change is driven by specific processes (as is detailed in this chapter), yet I believe that the principle of economy can give further insight about linguistic change as it relates to the general cognitive organisation of the linguistic system.

PRONOMINAL SUFFIXES to mark definiteness.[20] Yet over time the role of the proleptic pronoun as marking definiteness of the DAC must have eroded (probably hand-in-hand with the fossilization), as one finds in NENA the Neo-CSC used with indefinite nouns:[21]

(1) Amədya: **Noun–Noun**
xa šaqqiθ-əd ṃaye
INDF channel-CST water
'a channel of water' (Greenblatt 2011: 72)

The erosion of the definiteness value arose possibly due to the development of other means to mark definiteness (see §1.3), or since ACs are in general definite anyhow (cf. Haspelmath 1999: 231). Be that as it may, this led necessarily to the reanalysis of the proleptic pronoun as a pure primary-marker of the AC, on top of the linker, rendering the DAC a double-marked AC. But, by the principle of ECONOMY, it is preferable to transform the double-marked DAC to a single-marked Neo-CSC, thus reducing the cognitive burden of marking the construction on two separate loci.[22] The ALC, on the other hand, is single-marked (dependent-marked), thus showing equal structural complexity as the head-marked Neo-CSC.

What about the other hypotheses mentioned above? Regarding the third hypothesis, Mengozzi asserts that no evidence for the origin construction (X DEM LNK Y) is found in the Early NENA manuscripts he investigated. In Syriac, one finds instances of this construction (see §3.5.6 and most notably example (80) on page 74: *rawmā haw da= šmayyā* 'the height of heaven'), but not with prepositions as primaries. In any case, assuming this would be the origin of the Neo-CSC would require further explanation of the disappearance of the emphatic state suffixes (*-ā* in the cited example), unless it is assumed that they coalesced with the demonstrative pronoun. It is rather more probable that such a construction developed into an alternative linker such as *ad* or *od*, discussed in §10.6.3.

As for the fourth hypothesis, while the schwa segment in the *-əd* suffix arose from an attenuation of the 3MS possessive suffix, synchronically one could indeed argue that in most NENA dialects it has been re-analysed as merely an epenthetic vowel, enabling the syllabic addition of the *-d* suffix to the nominal

[20] This is still conserved in NENA dialects in the verbal domain, where definite objects are often indexed on the verb with proleptic pronouns. See Coghill (2014) for a discussion.

[21] An alternative explanation would be to assume that the indefinite usage of the Neo-CSC originated in the ALC, the latter not being tied to definiteness.

[22] This can be contrasted to the situation in Turkish, in which the double-marked construction is productive since it marks the definiteness of the AC (see example (1) on page 25).

stem.[23] Thus, in the Barwar dialect, whenever a primary noun ends in a vowel other than *-a* or *-e* serving as the Aramaic inflectional ending, only a /*-d*/~/*-t*/ suffix is added (Khan 2008c: 397).[24] The same phenomenon happens sometimes when the primary ends in a liquid, as in the following Gaznax example:

(2) Gaznax: **Noun–Noun**
ahl-d *Gaznax*
people-CST G.
'the people of Gaznax' (Gutman 2015c: 318 (7))

Thus, synchronically one could argue that the schwa is not a phonemic part of the *-əd* suffix, but rather an epenthetic vocalic nucleus needed due to the removal of the vocalic free state suffixes (but see the Qaraqosh example (25) on page 158, where the schwa is the sole exponent of the construct state).

What about the idea that the schwa is related to the Ezafe particle? Assuming that it results from the Kurmanji Ezafe raises analytical difficulties, since the latter shows gender and number inflection, so one would have to stipulate an extra step of fossilization of the Ezafe suffix, which is not observed in Kurmanji. The Sorani Ezafe, on the other hand, may be a better candidate, as it is an uninflecting particle. This idea gains further support from the fact that in some dialects, especially in NE Iraq, an Ezafe suffix *-i* stands in complementary distribution with an *-əd* suffix (see §11.4.1.1). Given the phonetic similarity of the schwa and this Ezafe (both roughly realized as [ɪ]), it may indeed be the case that bilingual speakers conflated the two. Yet, since the *-əd* suffix is found also in dialects which have not integrated any Ezafe marking, and also in the Kurmanji speaking area, it

[23] A similar claim is made by Spitaler (1938: 112, §107.f) regarding the schwa segment in the Western Neo-Aramaic Neo-CST suffix *-əl*. I am grateful to Ivri Bunis for drawing my attention to this reference.

[24] Khan (2008c: 397) reports one possible exception to this rule, occurring supposedly when *-əd* is suffixed to "[a]n unadapted loanword that has a final vowel that it has retained from the source language". In such cases the schwa is retained by an insertion of the glide /*y*/. He brings one example of this phenomenon:

(i) Barwar: **Noun–Noun**
ḥabba-y-ət *xəṭṭəθa*
seed-*glide*-CST wheat_grain
'a seed of grain' (Khan 2008c: 397)

Yet the validity of this analysis can be questioned, as in the Iraqi Arabic dictionary of Woodhead & Beene (1967: 89) *ḥabbāya* is listed as a variant of *ḥabba*. Thus, the /*y*/ segment is simply part of the lexical stem, and the schwa replaces the final *-a*.

seems rather implausible to place the origin of the schwa in a matter replication of the Ezafe. As for the different question of whether the Neo-CST suffix *-əd* developed due to pattern replication of the Kurdish Ezafe, this is dealt with in the next section (see in particular §10.4.2.2.1).

To conclude this section, I present the development of the Neo-CSC, as outlined above, in six distinct stages shown in Table 10.4 on the following page. To better apprehend the fossilization of the possessive suffix, the model Syriac expression is *bayt-āh d=malktā* 'house of the queen', as I assume that the plural possessive suffixes shifted to 3MS *-ēh*.

10.4.2 The role of language contact

According to the scenario outlined in Table 10.4, the key stages in the emergence of the neo-construct state suffix *-əd* were the encliticization of the linker *d-* to the primary (stage 3) and its subsequent reanalysis as a head-marking suffix (stages 4–5). The encliticization itself may be quite natural due to the syllabic structure (the primary ending in a vowel, either due to the emphatic state suffix, or the possessive suffix) as well as to the frequent prosodic boundness of the primary and secondary. Furthermore, Lahiri & Plank (2010) have suggested (from a Germanic perspective) that cross-linguistically there may be a tendency of encliticization of functional elements to preceding hosts. Yet encliticization does not necessarily mean reanalysis as a head-marking construction.[25] Thus, a natural question is: what led to the re-analysis?

A possible answer is to suppose that some external factor, such as language contact, may have played a role in this reanalysis. Indeed, such a proposal has been made by Cohen (2015: 121ff.). Cohen, examining data from JZakho, argues that its Neo-CSC emerged as a pattern replication (in the sense of Matras & Sakel 2007b) from co-territorial Kurmanji Kurdish. A similar proposal was made by Garbell (1965a: 171, §2.21.2) regarding JUrmi, attributing its Neo-CSC to Sorani influence ("Central Kurdish" in her terminology). Note, however, that also JUrmi is co-territorial with Kurmanji (see map of Izady 1992: 171).

In the following sections I shall present Cohen's proposal, and then evaluate it, taking into account data from different NENA dialects as well as Kurmanji and Sorani Kurdish and Syriac.[26]

[25] For example, while Lahiri & Plank (2010: 376) claim that the expression "drink a pint of milk a day" is prosodically organised as [drink a][pint of][milk a][day]. Yet the preposition "of" cannot be said to have been reanalysed as a head-marker.

[26] The argumentation in this section is similar to the presentation in Gutman (2017), but with some added details and arguments.

Table 10.4: Possible development path of the DAC and the ALC into the Neo-CSC, tracing the development of the model expression 'house of the queen'.

	Classical Aramaic	DAC	ALC
0	Initial state	*bayt-āh d=malktā*	*bayt-ā d=malktā*
1	The DAC possessive suffix is fossilized to the 3MS form *-ēh*, possibly losing its definiteness marking function.	*bayt-ēh d=malktā*	
2	The DAC possessive suffix loses its consonantal coda and is centralized to *-ə*.	*bayt-ə d=malktā*	
3	The *d-* linker of the DAC resyllabifies with the primary. This happens occasionally also in the ALC.	*bayt-ə=d malktā*	*bayt-a=d malktā*
4	The resulting *-əd* segment in the DAC is reanalysed as a unitary construct state suffix.	*bayt-əd malktā*	
5	By analogy, the *-ad* sequence in the ALC (*-ed* in plural) is levelled to the construct state suffix *-əd*.*		*bayt-əd malktā*
6	The /ə/ segment is reinterpreted as an epenthetic vowel, added only when the syllabic structure requires it.	*bayt-{ə}d malktā*	
*	The Neo-CSC construction coexists in complementary distribution with remnants of the ALC.	*bayt-əd malktā*	*bayt-ā d=malktā*
	NENA	Neo-CSC	ALC

10.4.2.1 Parallels between Kurmanji and NENA Attributive Constructions

Recall that in Kurmanji Kurdish the Ezafe morpheme marking attribution can be suffixed to the head noun (see (3) below=example (16) on page 262) or, when it does not directly follow the head noun, appear as an independent morpheme (see the morpheme in bold in (4) below=example (63) on page 276; see further §9.3 and the following sections).

(3) Kurmanji: **Noun–Noun Phrase**
kitêb-ên [keç-a mirov]
book-EZ.PL girl-EZ.FS man
'the man's daughter's books' (Thackston 2006a: 13)

(4) Kurmanji: **Noun Phrase–Noun**
[hejmar-ek-e nû] ***ya*** *kovar-ê*
issue-INDF-EZ.FS new LNK.EZ.FS journal-OBL.MS
'a new issue of the journal' (Thackston 2006a: 15)

Cohen (2015) argues that the independent Ezafe morpheme acted as a PIVOT in the pattern replication of the Neo-CSC. The proclitic pronominal linker *d-* was matched to the independent Ezafe, and consequently was encliticized to the construction's head and reanalysed as a head-marking suffix by analogy with the suffixed Ezafe.[27] Note that this proposal supposes that the *d-* was encliticized to a noun in the ALC, not the DAC.

As a further piece of evidence for the affinity between the two languages Cohen notes that both in Kurmanji and in NENA a head-marked noun can precede a clausal attribute, as in the following examples (=example (60) on page 275 and example (20) on page 120):

(5) Kurmanji: **Noun–Clause**
ṭiṣṭ-ên [min nivisîbûn]
thing-EZ.PL 1SG.OBL written
'the things I had written' (Thackston 2006a: 77)

[27]From a diachronic perspective, also within the Iranic language family the suffixed Ezafe arose from the encliticization of an independent element (Haig 2011). Haider & Zwanziger (1984) claim more specifically that it originates in a relative pronoun, which lost its case inflection and subsequently became the Ezafe.

(6) JZakho: **Noun–Clause**
xabr-ıt mír-rē-la
word-CST said-A3MS-DAT3FS
'the word(s) he told her' (Cohen 2012: 97 (24))

10.4.2.2 Mismatches between the Kurmanji and NENA constructions

Notwithstanding the appeal of the above explanation of the source of the NENA Neo-CSC, it presents some difficulties. First, it is worth noting that this is a somewhat unusual kind of pattern replication, as outlined in Matras & Sakel (2007b: 836). According to their model, it is the "functional scope" of the source construction which is replicated to the recipient language. Yet in this case, it is not the functional scope which is replicated (since the Ezafe and the *d-* linker have the same functions to begin with) but rather the distributional-prosodic properties of the Ezafe, namely its ability to occur as a head-marking suffix, rather than an independent morpheme, which is replicated.

Second, looking closely at the linguistic data from a cross-NENA perspective, one sees that there is no perfect match between the Kurmanji construction and the parallel NENA construction. It should be immediately emphasized that the observed mismatches, surveyed below, cannot preclude an imperfect pattern replication scenario. Indeed, Matras & Sakel (2007b: 836) clearly state that any pattern replication must be accommodated to constraints of the recipient language. Yet, given that in some respects the NENA construction is in fact more similar to the Sorani Ezafe construction (and in some respects to neither to Sorani nor Kurmanji), these mismatches may indicate that the Kurmanji Ezafe construction is not necessarily the sole or even the main source of this linguistic change.

Indeed, since the Neo-CSC is encountered both in the Kurmanji speaking-area and the Sorani speaking-area,[28] if one assumes that it results from language contact with one source language, one must further explain its propagation throughout the NENA speaking-zone (either by a wave model, or by assuming a common ancestor). Yet, given the partial similarity with each of the proposed source languages, such an assumption is not necessary. Accordingly, the aim of the following arguments is to show that the different facets of Neo-CSC cannot be attributed to contact with a single language, but they are better explained as an

[28] Arguably, in the Sorani speaking area, the Neo-CSC is somewhat less wide-spread, as some dialects, in particular JSanandaj and Sulemaniyya prefer the juxtaposition construction; see Chapter 8. However, as my sample of this area (NE Iraq and W Iran) is less comprehensive, I cannot draw firm conclusions out of this observation.

areal phenomenon related to the very long history of language convergence in this linguistic area.

10.4.2.2.1 Non-inflection of the NENA construct state marker In contrast to the Kurmanji linker Ezafe, the Classical Aramaic linker *d-* does not inflect. Moreover, the innovated construct state *-əd* suffix does not inflect as well, again in contrast to the Kurmanji construct Ezafe. Thus, any pivot matching between the two is partial at most.[29] Of relevance is the fact that Early Jewish Cis-Zab NENA (see §1.2.2) made use of inflecting demonstrative determiners joined to an enclitic *d-* linker, presenting a better parallel to the inflecting Ezafe. This can be observed in the Nerwa Texts, Jewish homilies from the 16th century written in Nerwa in NW Iraq, whose language is close to the ancestor stratum of JZakho:[30]

(7) Nerwa: **∅–Noun**
אוד אנואר [...] ואוד ג'מאם [...]
ʾaw =d anwār ... u= ʾaw =d ġamām
DEM.MS =LNK lights and= DEM.MS =LNK clouds
'that (the pillar) of fire ... and that of clouds' (*Pəšaṭ Wayəhî Bəšallaḥ* 22:5 ed. by Sabar 1976: 68)

(8) Nerwa: **Noun–Clause**
שבועה איד מומכלוך
šəḇûʿa,[31] *ʾay =d mōm-ax-lux*
oath(FS) DEM.FS =LNK put.PST-P1SG-A2MS
'the oath which you put us under' (*Pəšaṭ Wayəhî Bəšallaḥ* 4:3 ed. by Sabar 1976: 43)

[29] One may argue, as a reviewer of Gutman (2017) did, that there is a general tendency of the languages "of the area" to evolve towards morphological simplification and loss of nominal inflection, and thus it would be remarkable if the Aramaic linker were to gain inflection. Yet Kurmanji is one of the exceptional languages that have conserved a relatively rich nominal morphology, as attested also by the conservation of its case system. Thus, the mismatch in inflection is relevant when evaluating the specific hypothesis that Kurmanji served as the model for the development of the Neo-CSC, though it cannot by itself invalidate it.

[30] Arguably, the /-*d*/ segment in these examples is already re-analysed as the construct state suffix, as it regularly occurs also with nominal heads in Nerwa. Be this as it may, in some earlier state at least the demonstrative pronoun and the linker must have been conceived as independent morphemes.

[31] The comma, indicating a possible prosodic break, is added to the apparatus by Sabar and is not part of the original manuscript (see Sabar 1976: XLVII).

Thus, if Kurmanji was indeed the model language, one could expect a pivot match with these inflecting "linkers". However, although such inflecting elements are conserved in some NENA dialects such as C. Barwar or J. Arbel (see §10.6.3.1), they are never encliticized as such to the head-noun (see further the discussion in §10.6.3.1).[32]

From the point of view of inflection, The NENA Neo-CST suffix is in fact more similar to the Sorani Kurdish uninflecting Ezafe, which is always a fixed *-ī~y*, as in the following example (=example (10) on page 260):[33]

(9) Silêmanî: **Noun–Noun**
ser-î biniadem
head-EZ man
'men's heads' (MacKenzie 1961: 63)

As mentioned in §10.4.1, the phonetic similarity between the Sorani Ezafe and the /ə/ segment of the NENA construct state suffix *-əd* and their similar distribution, may have led bilingual speakers to conflate the two, but it is unlikely to have been the source of the schwa segment. It is equally unlikely that the Sorani Ezafe could have served as a pivot morpheme comparable to the Aramaic *d*-linker, given their different distribution: in contrast to the *d*- linker, the Sorani Ezafe cannot appear as an independent morpheme, except in those few cases in which it is not preceded by any nominal head at all (see examples (87)–(93) on page 283).[34]

10.4.2.2.2 Clausal secondaries and the usage of a subordinating particle In Kurmanji (as well as Sorani), clausal secondaries may to follow the subordinating particle *ḳu* (Sorani *ke*), as in the following example (=example (57) on page 274 and see further there):

(10) Kurmanji: **Noun–Clause**
[wî ziman]-ê [ḳu li=ber mir-in-ê ye]
DEM.DIST.OBL language-EZ.MS REL before die-INF-OBL.FS COP.3SG
"this language, which is on the verge of dying." (Thackston 2006a: 75)

[32]The fact that such an encliticization is in principle possible may be confirmed by the NWNA Mīdin dialect. See in this respect footnote 11 on page 302.

[33]In fact, there is no grammatical gender in Sorani.

[34]Due to its pronominal nature, the *d*- linker itself can also appear without a nominal antecedent preceding it (see examples (32)–(33) on page 60). Yet, judging by NENA examples, outside the predicative position it typically appears with a nominal antecedent or with a demonstrative/determiner preceding it, as in examples (7)–(8) on the previous page. Thus, it seems that the case of phrase-initial *d*- linkers are not frequent enough to drive this kind of language change scenario.

Most NENA dialects, on the other hand, do not have a dedicated relativizer in this position, but rely either on the construct state ending or on the linker *d-* (or derivative forms of it), example (20) on page 120 being typical. One dialect which does mimic completely the Kurdish pattern and particle is JUrmi, situated at the eastern periphery of the Kurmanji speaking area. This is shown in the following example (=example (99) on page 214):[35]

(11) JUrmi: **Noun–Clause**
naš-it [ki lóka wélu]
people-CST REL there COP.PST-3PL
'the people who were there' (Garbell 1965b: 55)

Another dialect which borrowed the particle, but without any construct state marking, is JSanandaj, located in the southern limit of the Sorani speaking area.[36] This construction is shown in the following example (=example (29) on page 235 and see further §8.6):

(12) JSanandaj: **Noun–Clause**
xá= ʿəda našé [ke= ga= xá meydā́n smix =èn]
INDF= few people REL= in= INDF square stood.RES =COP.3PL
'a group of people who were standing in a square' (Khan 2009b: 380 (1))

With the exception of these dialects, most NENA dialects do not replicate the relativizer-marked clausal attribution construction found in Kurmanji.[37]

10.4.2.2.3 Marking of prepositions with the construct state suffix In NENA, many prepositions can be optionally marked by the construct state suffix. This

[35]Yet as Garbell (1965b: 88) notes, clauses without an explicit subject NP can optionally appear directly after the construct state suffix.

[36]In general attribution is marked by mere juxtaposition in JSanandaj (see §8.3), so it should come as no surprise that no construct state marking is present. JSanandaj has also borrowed the actual Persian Ezafe morpheme which can co-occur with the relativizer following some conjunctions (see example (55) on page 241).

[37]A reviewer claimed that the usage of the relativizer is typical of "local Turkic, Persian, and a general areal feature of the languages of Urmi, western Iran and NE Anatolia" while Kurmanji dialects in SE Anatolia and northern Iraq tend to omit the relativizer and thus are more similar to the NENA spoken in these regions like JZakho. The evaluation of this claim would require a thorough corpus study of the relevant Kurmanji dialects; in the meanwhile, one can note that MacKenzie (1961: 203) gives numerous examples of the usage of the relativizer in Kurmanji dialects of northern Iraq, while the co-territorial NENA dialects lack such a construction, as stated above.

could be readily explained for prepositions of nominal origin, but it also holds true for pure prepositions which cannot be related to any noun, yielding variant forms such as *ʾəbb-əd~b-* 'in', *ʾəll-əd~ʾəll-~l-* 'to', *mənn-əd~m-* 'from' (Goldenberg 2000: 79). Recall that this fact was one of the main reasons for positing a DAC-origin for the Neo-CSC construction, following Mengozzi (2005a), whose argumentation is summarized in Table 10.3 on page 303.

In contrast to the situation in NENA, in Kurmanji only prepositions of nominal origin can be marked by the Ezafe. Cohen mentions in this respect the Kurmanji temporal conjunctions, namely *dema, gava, çaxê* and *wexta.* To this short list I could add some more prepositions of nominal character, which take invariably a un-inflecting Ezafe *-î.* The relation of this suffix to the inflecting Ezafe is somewhat obscure, since this form normally follows the indefinite suffix *-ek.* This is shown in the following examples ((13)=example (49) on page 272 and see further there):.

(13) Akre: **Adverbial Noun–Noun**
nêzîk-î ḥakim-i
near-EZ judge-OBL.MS
'near the judge' (MacKenzie 1961: 161 [602])

(14) Amêdî: **Adverbial Noun–Adverb**
pişṭ-î hingî
back(F)-EZ then
'after that' (MacKenzie 1961: 161)

In other words, in contrast to NENA, basic Kurdish prepositions such as *di* 'in' (taking part in circum-positional expressions) never take an Ezafe ending.

(15) Kurmanji: **Preposition–Noun**
di gund-an de
in village-PL.OBL in
'in the villages' (Thackston 2006a: 13)

To conclude, in NENA, construct state marking on prepositions is more readily available than in Kurmanji, and, moreover, this marking is morphologically more transparent. In this, NENA resembles in fact Persian, where one finds the Ezafe marking also on some prepositions which cannot be considered to be of nominal origin (Samvelian 2008: 345, example (16)).

10.4.2.2.4 Adjectival primaries In NENA adjectives can stand as the heads of an attributive construction, and consequently be marked by the construct state suffix. Such constructions can have several functions, such as marking the adjective as superlative or as emotive (see for example §5.3.4 regarding JZakho). Another usage, not necessarily the most frequent, is the specification of the adjectival lexeme itself, as in the following example (=example (35) on page 161):

(16) Qaraqosh: **Adjective–Noun**
góra xwár-əd kósa
man white-CST hair
'a white-haired man' (Khan 2002a: 281)

This last usage is typical of Semitic languages, and has been labelled in Semitic grammatical tradition IMPURE ANNEXATION.[38] It appears also in Syriac, in which one finds the adjective in the original construct state forms, as in the following example (=example (18) on page 54).

(17) Syriac: **Adjective–Noun**
ܐܢܬ ܗܘ ܡܪܝܐ ܢܓܝܪ ܪܘܚܐ. ܘܡܪܚܡܢܐ ܘܣܓܝ ܚܢܢܐ
ʾat =ʰu māryā ngir ruḥā wa= mraḥmānā w= saggi
2MS =3MS Lord long.CST spirit and= merciful and= great.CST
ḥnānā
compassion
'You are the Lord, long-suffering and merciful and of great compassion.' (*Peshiṭta*, Prayer of Manasseh, ed. Baars & Schneider 1972: A7; Gutman & Van Peursen 2011: 217 (7a))

In Kurmanji, however, such a construction is rarely found, as adjectives do not inflect in Kurmanji, and cannot receive an Ezafe suffix (but see example (43) on page 270 for a possible counter-example). It is rather in Sorani that one finds a similar construction, in which adjectives are head-marked by the Ezafe, as in the following example (=example (42) on page 270):

(18) Silêmanî: **Adjective–Noun**
tûş-î em derd-e
afflicted-EZ DEM.PROX trouble-DEF
'afflicted by this trouble' (MacKenzie 1961: 65 [67])

[38] See Goldenberg (2002) for an analysis of the phenomenon in Arabic, and Doron (2014) for a analysis of the phenomenon in Modern Hebrew, cast in formal semantics terminology.

Note, however, that the corresponding NENA construction (example (35) on page 161) occurs also in dialects which are in contact with Kurmanji dialects. Thus, two possibilities arise: either the construction was borrowed from Sorani and spread beyond the original contact zone; or, more likely, it is a retention of a construction that already existed in the language, but with new morphological marking.

10.4.2.2.5 Adjectival secondaries Another challenge for the pattern borrowing theory is the fact that, while adjectives may follow the Ezafe in Kurmanji (see example (63) on page 276), this is not the case in most NENA dialects. Adjectives in these dialects never follow a construct state noun. Rather, they stand in apposition with a free (non-construct) head noun, while agreeing in number and gender features. This is demonstrated in the following example (=example (95) on page 141):

(19) JZakho: **Noun–Adjective**
xa xamsa sqəl-ta
INDF maiden(FS) beautiful-FS
'a beautiful maiden' (Cohen 2012: 214)

Yet in Syriac, one finds an alternative structure, in which adjectives in absolute state (glossed ABS) can follow the *d-* linker:

(20) Syriac: **Noun Phrase–Noun**
ܪܘܚܗ ܕܐܢܫܐ ܕܬܒܝܪܐ
[ruḥ-ēh d= nāšā] da= tbirā
spirit(FS)-POSS.3MS LNK= man LNK= broken.ABS.FS
'the broken spirit of the person' (*Peshiṭta*, Sirach 4:2 *apud* Van Peursen 2007: 232)

As discussed in §3.5.3 the absolute state of adjectives in Syriac is typical of their predicative usage, and consequently the adjectival secondary in this construction is normally considered to be a nominal clause without an explicit subject argument, or alternatively a quasi-verbal predicate with a ∅ exponent of the subject.[39] Be that as it may, from the perspective of the overt constituents such examples are parallel to the following Kurmanji pattern:

[39] Recall that other nominal predicates, including emphatic state adjectives, require generally in Syriac a mention of the subject in the form of the enclitic personal pronoun. For a discussion of the use of the different states of the adjective, see Goldenberg (1991).

(21) Kurmanji: **Noun Phrase–Adjective**
[nav-ê wî mirov-î] yê rastîn
name-EZ.MS DEM.DIST.OBL man-OBL.MS EZ.MS real
'that man's real name' (Thackston 2006a: 15)

Examples such as the above could trigger in NENA the same pivot matching process Cohen describes in JZakho for adoption of the Neo-CSC with nominal and clausal attributes; however in most NENA dialects it does not occur with adjectives. An exceptional dialect in this respect is Arbel which has cases like the following (and see also example (43) on page 337):

(22) Arbel: **Noun–Noun**
brā̆t-it rubtá
daughter-CST big.FS
'the eldest daughter' (Khan 1999: 229 [Y:109])

Note that, similarly to the Syriac construction, but unlike the Kurmanji one, the adjective agrees with the head noun. The discrepancy is not surprising, given that adjectives in Kurmanji cannot inflect

Acknowledging the exceptional case of Arbel, how can the lack of this construction in the majority of dialects be explained? One possible reason may lie in the above mentioned claim that the adjectival attribute in Syriac is a minimal nominal clause, marked as predicate by the absolute state. In NENA, however, the absolute state is no longer productively used, and reduced clauses are in general not possible any more, due to the innovation of a quasi-mandatory copula paradigm (Goldenberg 2005; 2000).[40]

[40]Occasionally, nominal sentences without a copula are found, typically in introductory clauses (see the Diyana-Zariwaw examples in Napiorkowska 2015: 315, §13.3). Such clauses are also reported in the dialect of Tel-Kepe (Eleanor Coghill, p.c.). See also the apparently asyndetic relative clauses lacking a copula in JZakho example (108) on page 145 or Qaraqosh example (123) on page 184, though their clausal status is debated. As for the disappearance of the absolute state, the situation in NENA can be contrasted with that in Western Neo-Aramaic, where adjectives can still appear in absolute state (Arnold 1990: 363), and adjectival secondaries following a linker can be found:

(i) Maˁlūla: **Noun–Adjective**
hanna, ti ipxel
DEM.MS LNK stingy.ABS
'he who is stingy' (Arnold 2006: 16)

A second reason may lie in the inflecting nature of the Aramaic (indeed Semitic) adjective. In contrast to Kurdish, the Aramaic inflecting adjective can be referential and can stand by its own without an explicit nominal antecedent or linker (see Syriac example (107) on page 86). Thus, cases like Syriac example (20) or Arbel example (22) are superfluous, both with respect to the multiple-marking (AC marker + agreement), and with respect to the existence of a simpler juxtaposition + agreement pattern. Given that already in Syriac the usage-conditions of the ALC with adjectives are difficult to pinpoint (see discussion in §3.8.2), it is indeed natural that the NENA dialect ousted this construction rather than further grammaticalising it.[41]

Note that in both accounts, internally-motivated developments are more prominent than a possible contact-induced pattern replication scenario, thus blocking the occurrence of this construction in most NENA dialects.

10.4.2.3 Interim Conclusions

While the pattern borrowing hypothesis has merit in its simplicity and apparent elegance, it raises some difficulties in that the Kurmanji pattern is not exactly replicated in most NENA dialects. Indeed, taking a broad cross-dialectal perspective, one can establish parallels with various aspects of the Kurmanji pattern (such as the use of adjectives in Arbel, or the relativizer in JUrmi), but no single dialect seems to replicate entirely the Kurmanji pattern. While pattern replication is never expected to be perfect, it raises the question of whether Kurmanji is indeed the sole source language. In some respects, as stated above, the NENA pattern is in fact more similar to the Sorani pattern. Table 10.5 presents the features discussed above, contrasting 3 NENA dialects, Early J. Cis-Zab NENA (Nerwa), and the two main Kurdish varieties.

Clearly, there is a functional similarity between the Ezafe marking and the construct state marking, in that both are head-markers of attribution, and a diachronic similarity in that both originated in encliticization.[42] Cohen (2015: 121ff.) attributes the functional similarity to a specific Kurmanji pivot matching and pattern replication, but a viable alternative is to relate it to a more general phenomenon of areal linguistic convergence favouring head-marking of attributive constructions.

[41]As noted in footnote 25 on page 142, Eran Cohen (p.c.) suggested to me that it is rather constructions like *axōna aw rūwa* 'the older brother' (=example (97) on page 142), in which the determiner moves to the pre-adjectival position, that replicate the Kurmanji structure. Yet a similar construction existed already in Syriac (see example (109) on page 86).

[42]The functional similarity has been noted before, for instance by Mengozzi (2005a: 381), and by Mutzafi (2004b: 4, fn. 33).

Table 10.5: Comparison of the CSC and ALC across NENA dialects, Syriac and Kurdish. The example numbers refer to a Kurdish example of respective feature. Entries (+) or (-) indicate some reservations discussed in the appropriate section. (a) = JZakho, (b) = Arbel, (c) = JUrmi, (d) = Nerwa, (e) = Syriac, (f) = Kurmanji, (g) = Sorani

	Ex.	(a)	(b)	(c)	(d)	(e)	(f)	(g)
N(P) LNK N(P)	(63)	+	+	+	+	+	+	
N.CST N(P)	(16)	+	+	+	+	+	+	+
LNK inflects	(63)				(+)		+	
CST inflects	(16)						+	
N(P) LNK Cl.	(60)	+	+		+	+	(+)	
N.CST REL Cl.	(57)			+			+	+
Prep.CST N	(13)	+	+	+	+	+	(-)	
Adj.CST N	(18)	+		+	?	+		+
Adj. secondary	(21)		+		?	+	+	+

As stated above, the encliticization process itself, while being clearly an innovation in NENA, may be internally motivated, in line with a universal tendency of encliticization of functional elements to preceding hosts, as proposed by Lahiri & Plank (2010: 395). It is rather the re-analysis of the resulting */-əd/* segment as a construct state suffix which may need an external impetus. Yet in contact situations like the one discussed here, one cannot in fact reliably rule out one explanation in favour of the other. I concur with Cohen that the Kurmanji pattern probably played a role in the formation of the NENA Neo-CSC. Yet, following the encliticization process, it could also have risen out of internal analogy with the existing historical construct state marking, or due to contact with other languages of the area exhibiting construct state or head-marking morphology.[43] It seems that a reasonable position would be to relate the Neo-CSC to a linguistic feature present in the NENA/Kurdish Sprachbund, namely a preference to head-mark attributive constructions, without relating its source to any specific language.[44] Such a position can explain the partial similarities with Kurmanji and Sorani as well as ancient Aramaic strata. One can also go further and propose

[43]These may include Arabic, Syriac or Hebrew in liturgical use, other Iranic languages or Kurdish dialects using the Ezafe construction and even Turkish.

[44]One may argue that the preference of head-marking is going beyond the nominal domain, since in the verbal domain there is also a preference for indexing arguments on the verbs rather than marking the arguments by means of case or adpositions.

that the head-marked Iranic construction might have its origin in the original construct state construction of Aramaic (Classical Aramaic or possibly anterior strata), which was a language of high prestige in the region in antiquity.[45]

An argument in favour of this more general explanation is the rise of a Neo-CSC in Western Neo-Aramaic. In these dialects a similar suffixed construct state marker *-il* arose out of the Syriac dative linker construction (see §3.7).

(23) Maʿlūla: **Noun–Noun**
berč-il ǧabrōna
daughter-CST man
'the daughter of the man' (Arnold 1990: 301)

Since Western Neo-Aramaic was not in known contact with any Iranic language one must conclude that, in this case, the encliticization and reanalysis of the DLC yielding the *-il* suffix were mostly internal processes, possible influenced by the vernacular Arabic dialects, which, however, show construct state marking by stem reduction (and not by suffix). If such influence took place, it was purely a functional one, favouring a head-marked AC, in line with the hypothesis outlined above regarding a general areal preference for head-marking.

10.5 Development of the genitive prefix

Following the argumentation in §4.5, I treat a /*d*/ segment preceding certain demonstratives which begin with a glottal stop or a (semi)-vowel as a genitive marker.[46] In some dialects the justification for such an analysis is clearer, while in others still more research is needed, but as it occurs in quite distinct corners of

[45]While at the current state of knowledge this suggestion may sound speculative in nature, it is worthwhile to note in this respect that Middle Persian, in which the Ezafe construction started to stabilize, is contemporary with Classical Aramaic, and was clearly influenced by Aramaic by means of the Pahlavi (Aramaic-based) script. A somewhat similar suggestion was made by Utas (2005: 70f.), who notes that the *ZY* logogram used to write the Ezafe in Pahlavi stems from the Aramaic linker *ðī*. His account, however, suggests that the Ezafe construction is related to the analytic linker construction, rather than to the construct state construction. Further investigation is needed to elucidate this question.

[46]The JZakho interrogative pronoun *ēma* 'which', which exhibits the genitive form *dēma* can tentatively be analysed as being composed of a frozen demonstrative pronoun *ē* (identical to the feminine demonstrative pronoun) + interrogative *ma* 'what'. An alternative analysis in which the /*ē*/ segment is a reflex of the Semitic interrogative **ay* (cf. Biblical Hebrew אֵי) is less viable due to the presence of the interrogative element /*ma*/, while Biblical Hebrew אֵי normally combines with deictic elements (איזה, איפה etc.). Be it as it may, I assimilate *ēma* to the category of demonstratives in the current discussion.

the NENA speaking-area, it seems reasonable to conclude that it is a cross-NENA phenomenon, representing a possible shared feature of the NENA precursors.[47]

In Table 10.6 on page 323 I contrast four environments where one finds D-marked demonstratives (acting as determiners unless stated otherwise).[48] The D-markers in the first environment may be analysed either as genitive markers or as linkers, while in the other 3 environments their analysis as genitive markers is more straightforward, as a linker analysis is hardly tenable (see again §4.5):[49]

1. Following a noun in free state (e.g. Amədya *šula d-eyya ṣawaʾa* 'the job of this dyer'[50]): Such cases can simply be analysed as instances of the ALC, in which *d-* serves as a linker.[51] Of special interest are dialects which exhibit the N *d*-N construction (see Table 10.1 on page 297), but not the N *d*-[DEM+N] construction (Challa, Jilu, Alqosh and Qaraqosh),[52] and, conversely, dialects which do not have *d-* before nouns but preserve it before demonstrative pronouns (only JSanandaj).

2. Following a linker (e.g. JZakho *ʾōda dīd d-aw gōra* 'the room of the man'[53]): only a handful of dialects (with various linker shapes) show this pattern. Since this pattern exhibits a morpheme serving as a linker, the subsequent *d*-marker is naturally analysed as a genitive marker.[54]

3. Following a noun in construct state: the construct state may be marked by an *-əd* suffix (Jilu *xabr-əd d-a sawa* 'the word of this old man'[55]), by Eza-

[47]For the possibility that this development represents a wider areal phenomenon, encompassing also Neo-Mandaic, see footnote 42 on page 108.

[48]Recall that Cohen (2010: 90) identifies the same *d-* prefix as an ATTRIBUTIVE marker of the subordinated copula in JZakho (also §5.5.2). However, as similar copular forms in other dialects are yet to be investigated, I have not included them in the current comparative study.

[49]An empty cell in the table marks the absence of the corresponding construction in the database, but it does not completely exclude its existence in a given dialect, especially for the less-described dialects.

[50]Greenblatt 2011: 72.

[51]The dialects marked by (-) are those in which the available examples include only loan-nouns as primaries, lacking the distinct *-a* free state suffix, e.g. JZakho *sabab d-o ʾīzāla dīd-ax* 'the reason of your going' (=example (80) on page 137).

[52]In Diyana-Zariwaw, the latter construction is found, but Napiorkowska (2015: 95) mentions that "the independent relative particle [in fact, the genitive prefix] on its own is not always sufficient to express the genitive [=attributive] relation/possession, e.g.: ?*čtawa d-ʾawən*".

[53]Example (82) on page 138.

[54]In Gaznax, the genitive marking is not certain in this position; see Gutman (2015c: 316 (22)). In Diyana-Zariwaw I have found this pattern only with an independent demonstrative: *čtawa ʾəd= d-ʾawen* 'his book' (Napiorkowska 2015: 95).

[55]Example (7) on page 353.

fe (JSanandaj *fešár-e d-o màe* 'the pressure of the water'[56]) or by apocope (JZakho *bēs d-aw gōra* 'the house of the man'[57]).

4. Following a preposition: the preposition itself may be marked as construct state (Betanure *bəd d-ayya nūra* 'by this fire'[58]), or not (Betanure *gu d-é=dāna* 'at that time'[59]).

As in the development of the Neo-CST *-əd* suffix, in tracing the development of the genitive prefix *d-* one must clearly distinguish between 1) the phonological process leading to a retention of the *d-* prefix before the above-mentioned determiners, and 2) the morphological reanalysis of this segment as a genitive marker. Indeed, it is the second stage that may explain the differences in distribution of the genitive prefix in various NENA dialects.

Considering the first stage, recall that the *d-* prefix is retained before those determiners and pronouns that begin either with a weak consonantal onset (typically a glottal stop /ʾ/ but also the semi-vowels /*w*/ and /*y*/) or with a vowel. From an articulatory perspective, all these cases can be considered to be vowel-initial.[60] Thus, a natural hypothesis is to assume that the genitive prefix originated in the Classical Aramaic linker *d-*. As explained above, the linker *d-* of the ALC or DAC could re-syllabify with vowel-final primaries for syllabic reasons; yet this resyllabification was blocked whenever the secondary started with a vowel.[61] This tendency may be still operative in some NENA dialects, although exact statistics are hard to gather. As an illustration, in the grammar of Amədya, out of the 4 examples given by Greenblatt (2011: 72) representing the ALC, 3 have vowel-initial secondaries.[62]

This explanation readily explains the retention of the *d-* segment before the vowel-initial demonstratives, but it does not provide any reasons for its reanalysis as a genitive marker. Indeed, since the *d-* linker is retained as a proclitic in such a scenario, there is no change whatsoever in the construction: the ALC and the DAC remain the same. This corresponds to the first column of Table 10.6 (labelled FREE), but does not explain the occurrence of the *d-* prefix in the other columns.

[56]Example (60) on page 243.
[57]Example (79) on page 137.
[58]Mutzafi 2008a: 121 [500].
[59]Mutzafi 2008a: 120 [354].
[60]An initial glottal stop may in these cases be considered as a phonetic support for the initial vowel, rather than a phonemic segment.
[61]See footnote 5 on page 298.
[62]The fourth example has a /*t*/-initial secondary, leading to assimilation of the linker to /*t*/.

Table 10.6: Distribution of D-marked demonstrative following 1) Free state nouns 2) Linkers 3) Construct state nouns 4) Prepositions

Region	Dialect	FREE	LNK	CST	Prep.
SE Turkey	Hertevin	(-)		+	+
	Bohtan			+	
	Bēṣpən				+
	Gaznax		(+)	+	+
	Baz				+
	Challa				+
	Jilu			+	+
NW Iraq	JZakho	(-)	+	+	+
	JAradhin				
	CAradhin	+			+
	Barwar	+	+	+	+
	Betanure		+		+
	Amədya	+		+	+
	Barzani				+
	Alqosh				
	Qaraqosh			(-)	+
NW Iran	JUrmi	(-)	+	+	+
	Sardarid			+	+
NE Iraq	Rustaqa				
	Diyana-Z.	+	+	+	+
	Arbel			+	
	Koy Sanjaq				
	Sulemaniyya	+			+
W. Iran	JSanandaj	+		+	+
	CSanandaj	(-)		+	+
	Kerend				

A second hypothesis may solve this difficulty.[63] According to this hypothesis, the origin of the genitive *d-* is not in the *d-* linker but rather in the Neo-CST suffix *-əd*. Given a vowel-initial secondary, the final /*-d*/ of the *-əd* suffix would have a tendency to syllabify with the secondary. This would leave, however, a stranding schwa at the end of the primary. Since a schwa in an open syllable is phonologically undesirable (cf. Coghill 2003: 89), the speakers may rearrange the phonological material in two distinct ways:

1. Dropping the schwa altogether.[64]

2. Geminating the final /*-d*/ segment, leaving the schwa in a closed syllable.

In either case, the result is the same: the primary can be interpreted as being marked for construct state, either by apocope (first case) or by *-əd* suffix (second case), followed by the secondary marked by a prefix *d-*.

In the Qaraqosh dialect such a resyllabification is still operative. It is not restricted to determiners, and it happens not only before vowel-initial secondaries, but also before consonant clusters, as the following examples show (= example (20) on page 157 – example (21) on page 157):[65]

(24) Qaraqosh: **Noun–Noun**
yál *d=* *axòna*
child(ren) -CST= brother
'children of the brother' (Khan 2002a: 208 [F:3])

(25) Qaraqosh: **Noun–Noun**
ʾít-ə *-də=* *Šmòni*
church-
isischwa -CST= S.
'the church of Shmoni' (Khan 2002a: 208 [K:21])

[63]I'm indebted to my doctoral supervisor, Eleanor Coghill, for providing me with this idea.

[64]This is in line with a general phenomenon of eliding final schwas in some NENA dialects, especially when this does not result in a consonant cluster. See Khan (2002a: 49f.); Coghill (2003: 88f.).

[65]It may very well be the case that similar resyllabification processes are operative in other dialects as well, but due to transcript normalisation practised generally by linguists, this is not always evident in the corpus data. The grammars of Khan are exceptional in this respect, in that the transcription strives to reflect the prosodic structure of the language as accurately as possible.

In one example of Qaraqosh, one finds the gemination of the /*d*/ segment before an attributive demonstrative, providing the exact environment where it could be reanalysed as a genitive prefix, though this did not seem to happen in Qaraqosh (=example (102) on page 178 with a different gloss):

(26) Qaraqosh: **Noun–Noun**
b= *paqárt-əd* *d=* *áne* *ḥawāwi̇̀n*
in= neck-CST GEN(?)= DEM.DIST.PL animals
'on the neck of those animals' (Khan 2002a: 208 [B:72])

In other dialects, where the genitive prefix is better established, it is also possible to observe examples of the intermediate stage, where the primary is marked only be a schwa suffix, instead of a full *-əd* suffix or apocope. This is the case in Barwar:[66]

(27) Barwar: **Noun–Noun**
gu= *ṣádr-ə* *d-áwwa* *sùsa*
in= chest-CST GEN-DEM.MS horse
'in the chest of this horse' (Khan 2008c: 397 [A14:67])

In JUrmi this phenomenon is found with adverbial primaries (=example (81) on page 209):

(28) JUrmi: **Adverbial Noun–Noun**
⁺m-qulb-ə *d-o* *gora*
from-stead-CST GEN-DEM.DIST.SG man
'instead of that man' (Khan 2008b: 196)

As the above Qaraqosh examples show, the prosodic resyllabification of the /*d*/ segment with secondaries is not restricted to demonstrative secondaries. Yet only with demonstratives was this segment re-analysed as a genitive prefix, leading in

[66]In Barwar one also finds examples of resyllabification of the construct state suffix before the copula, which may be the first stage for the creation of a special subordinated copula, as in JZakho (see §5.5.2):

(i) Barwar: **Noun–Clause**
kú= *duk-ə* *-ṯ=* *íla* *mεθ-ə̀t-la-li.'*
every= place-
isischwa -CST= COP.3FS bring-A2MS-P3FS-DAT1SG
'Bring her to me wherever she is.' (Khan 2009a: 82)

turn to its occurrence in contexts where there was no *d-* segment initially, such as in the following example (=example (23) on page 111):

(29) Barwar: **Noun–Noun Phrase**
gnáy-ət [táwra d-o= gòṛa]
fault-CST ox GEN-DEF.MS= big.MS
'the fault of the big ox' (Khan 2008c: 517 [D2:19])

This leads to the following question: why was the *d-* segment reanalysed as a genitive marker only before demonstratives?[67] This question is even more pertinent, as the reintroduction of a genitive case marker goes against the above-discussed areal preference of head-marking and the lack of a case system in Aramaic since antiquity. Moreover, the fact that this marker is a prefix goes against the cross-linguistic dis-preference of prefixes.[68]

One possibility is that the vowel-initial demonstratives occur in high frequency amongst the vowel-initial secondaries. Since the number of these items is quite limited, their appearance with the *d-* marker is high enough to permit a reanalysis.

Setting aside pure frequency effects, one may seek a structural motivation for re-analysis. Thus, Khan (2009a: 71) suggests that the introduction of the *d-* segment in these contexts arises from an analogy to the genitive independent pronouns, some of which start with *d-*. As an example, he shows the analogy between Barwar *bɛθa diy-a* and *bɛθa d-ay*, both meaning 'her house'. This, however, would seem to explain only the occurrence of *d-* with independent demonstrative pronouns; its co-occurrence with attributive demonstratives would need a further step of analogy.

Another possible source of analogy is language contact. As is shown in Table 10.7 on the facing page, Kurmanji Kurdish possesses a series of oblique demonstratives, which, in contrast to the nominative demonstratives, are consonant initial (Thackston 2006a: 10).[69] Note that, similarly to the NENA demonstratives, the Kurmanji ones function both attributively and independently.

[67] As noted in footnote 46 on page 320, the interrogative pronoun *ēma* 'which' is analysed here as containing a demonstrative pronoun element *ē*. On the other hand, I do not treat here the question of the *d-* marked subordinated copula, which has only been clearly analysed as such in JZakho (but see previous footnote).

[68] Haspelmath (2011) claims that cross-linguistic generalisations about affixes are problematic due to the difficulty of defining the notion of affix as a COMPARATIVE CONCEPT. Dryer (2015), however, shows how to establish it as a comparative concept and affirms the above mentioned tendency.

[69] The series of the far-deixis demonstratives is the same, with the /v/ replaced by /w/.

Table 10.7: Kurmanji near-deixis demonstratives

	NOM	OBL
MS		*vî*
FS	*ev*	*vê*
PL		*van*

Kurmanji oblique case is used for 3 main functions:

1. Marking of complements of verbs, corresponding to an accusative use.[70]
2. Marking nominal complements (typically possessors) of Ezafe-marked nominal heads, corresponding to a genitive use.
3. Marking complements of adpositions, corresponding also to a genitive case (at least in the Semitic case-marking languages).

Note that the NENA innovated genitive prefix occurs in functions 2 and 3. In these environments the Kurmanji oblique demonstratives may have served as pivots for the reanalysis of the *d*+DEM complex as a case-marked demonstrative pronoun. The similar syllabic structure of the two elements (CV) may have been a further facilitating factor.

As Cohen (2015: 124) notes, such an hypothesis poses a difficulty, since the NENA *d-* marked demonstratives are not used for complements of verbs, i.e. in an accusative context.[71] One may solve this difficulty, however, by assuming that the NENA speakers did not generalize the occurrence of the *d-* segment outside its initial domain of appearance, but restricted its reanalysis to the AC domain.

A partial corroboration of the above hypothesis lies in the fact the usage of genitive demonstratives seems to be more restricted in the non-Kurmanji speaking areas (roughly North-East Iraq south of Arbel and West-Iran). Thus, while about 80% of the dialects surveyed in the Kurmanji-speaking area show genitive

[70]In the past tense, which exhibits an ergative alignment, the ergative argument is marked in the oblique case.

[71]An exceptional dialect in this respect is JSanandaj, which does use the *d-* marker to mark complements of verbs; see §8.8.4 and in particular example (74) on page 247. In other NENA dialects, the genitive case is sometimes used to mark complements of verbal nouns, i.e. infinitives (cf. Sabar 1976: 37, fn. 8) as well as complex-predicate nouns, but this is in all probability related to the nominal character of these heads.

case after prepositions, this is true only in about half of the dialects in the non-Kurmanji speaking area.[72] Similarly, marking of genitive case after the linker is present only in the Kurmanji-speaking area. Indeed, from Table 10.6 on page 323 one may tentatively conclude that the innovation of the genitive marker as such occurred at first in North-West Iraq, in the heart of the Kurmanji speaking zone, and spread out from there.

10.6 Development of alternative linkers

In §10.2 I have surveyed the distribution of the inherited Syriac linker *d-*. Many dialects, however, exhibit alternative linker forms, which may co-exist or supersede the *d-* linker. Table 10.8 summarizes the various alternative linkers which are found in each dialect. The first column, essentially identical to the first column of Table 10.1 on page 297, states whether the *d-* linker (*~/əd/~/də/~/t/*) is found in each dialect before nominal secondaries.[73] The second column gives alternative forms which function as linkers in each given dialect.[74] The third column gives the bases of the independent attributive pronouns (formed as base + possessive suffix, often termed INDEPENDENT GENITIVE PRONOUNS), which in some respects can be analysed as linkers (see discussion below).

10.6.1 Bases of independent attributive (genitive) pronouns

Before discussing the forms of the independent attributive pronouns' bases, we must clarify their relation to the (independent) pronominal linkers. Given a form like *did-i*, there are two distinct synchronic analyses available:

1. *did-* is a pronominal linker representing a primary; the possessive suffix *-i* represents a pronominal secondary. This is clearly the case in JZakho, where one finds examples such as the following (part of example (71) on page 134). To clarify the analysis, the two pronominal elements are represented in the literal translation by subscripts.

[72] The last figure should be taken with some caution due to the small sample of dialects in the non-Kurmanji area.

[73] Note that in Hertevin one finds the *d-* linker only without immediate primaries.

[74] Some of these linkers can appear both before clausal and nominal secondaries, while others select only nominal secondaries.

Table 10.8: Alternative linkers

Region	Dialect	*d-* linker	Alt. linker	Pronominal base
SE Turkey	Hertevin	(+)	*did*	*did-*, *d-* (alt. 2&3PL)
	Bohtan			*did-*, *d-* (2&3PL)
	Bēṣpən		*ad*	*diy-*
	Gaznax		*ad*	*diy-*
	Baz	+	*ʾəd*	*diyy-*
	Challa	+	*ʾəd*	*did-*, *d-* (1&2PL)
	Jilu	+		*diy-*
NW Iraq	JZakho		*dīd*, (*ʾōd*)	*did-* (SG), *d-* (PL)
	JAradhin			*did-* (SG), *d-* (PL)
	CAradhin	+		*dīy-*
	Barwar	+		*diy-*
	Betanure		*dəd*	*did-* (SG), *d-* (PL)
	Amədya	+	*dəd*	*did-* (SG), *d-* (PL)
	Barzani		*ʾod*	*did-*
	Alqosh	+		*diy-*
	Qaraqosh	+	*ʾəd*	*did-*
NW Iran	JUrmi		*ay*	*did-*
	Sardarid			*əd-*
NE Iraq	Rustaqa		*i*	*did-*
	Diyana-Z.	+	*ʾəd*	*did-*, *diy-*, *d-* (alt. 3pers.)
	Arbel		*ot*	*did-*
	Koy Sanjaq		*od*	*did-*
	Sulemaniyya	+		*did-*, *d-* (alt. 3pers.)
W. Iran	JSanandaj			*did-* (1&2), *d-* (3)
	CSanandaj			*did-*, *diy-*
	Kerend			?

(30) JZakho: **Preposition–Pronoun**
mən dīd-i
from LNK-POSS.1SG
'from mine, lit. from that$_1$ which belongs to me$_2$' (Cohen 2012: 95 (5))

2. *did-* is a semantically empty base, thus not representing pronominally a primary and having no semantic contribution. It is present only to enable the possessive suffix *-i* to stand as part of an independent word. For this function I use the term GENITIVE BASE, as the resulting word is the genitive counter-part of the independent (nominative) pronoun *ana* 'I'. This is the case in JUrmi, where one finds the following example (=example (83) on page 210):

(31) JUrmi: **Preposition–Pronoun**
bo-d= did-ew
because-CST= GEN-POSS.3MS
'because of him$_2$' (Khan 2008b: 192)

A priori, in dialects where the attributive pronominal base and the linker have the same form (ignoring allophony related to stress placement[75]), there is no reason to analyse them as two different morphemes, and the first analysis should be favoured. Thus, in these dialects, the pronominal linker, similarly to other nouns which it replaces, can be followed either by a noun or by a pronominal possessive suffix (see for instance the discussion of the JZakho linker in §5.4).

In other dialects, where the form of the linker differs from the attributive bases (such as JUrmi, where the linker *ay* is clearly distinct from the pronominal base *did-*), the motivation for such an analytical move is weaker, and the second analysis is probably more appropriate. Indeed, in some of these dialects the independent attributive pronouns occur after construct state marked prepositions or nouns; see JUrmi example (31) on the current page or Barzani example (8) on page 355. As this is atypical for a pronominal linker (see §2.3.4), it is a further indication that they should be analysed as separate morphemes semantically bleached of a pronominal primary. The dialectal distribution of this construction is given in Table 11.2 on page 354, and see also discussion in §11.2 there.

[75]Thus, *did-* is equivalent to *dəd*, and arguably also *diy-* is equivalent to *d-* with a glide inserted for phonological reasons (see footnote 80 on the facing page).

It should be noted, however, that in predicative position the difference between the two functions (linker vs. genitive) is neutralised, since predicates are in general non-referential and thus lack pronominal force.[76] Thus, an independent genitive pronoun, just as a pronominal linker, can appear in predicative position without an explicit primary. This is illustrated in JUrmi example (84) on page 211 and the following similar Arbel example:

(32) Arbel: ∅–**Pronoun**
kullà ∅ did-ṓx =ilu.'
all ∅ GEN-POSS.2MS =COP.3PL
'They all belong to you.' (Khan 1999: 220 [S:84])

Considering now the form of the these bases, it is clear that across the NENA dialects they present a coherent form being in general *did-* or *diy-* (with the rare exception of Sardarid *əd-*).[77] It is thus safe to assume that these forms stem back to the NENA precursors. The form *did-* as a pronominal base is present since antiquity in Jewish Babylonian Aramaic, where it is usually assumed to be a product of assimilation of the Official Aramaic pronominal base *dil-*, which is in turn retained in Syriac (Bar-Asher Siegal 2013b: 108).[78] Since no NENA dialect shows the base *dil-*, one can assume that in this respect the NENA precursor (or precursors) diverged from Syriac and was closer to Jewish Babylonian Aramaic. As for the form *diy-*, present especially in Turkey and some Iraqi dialects (as far south as Tel-Kepe[79]), this may result from a further phonetic mutation of *did-*, or as a phonetic extension of the simple linker *d(i)-* before possessive suffixes.[80] If the latter view is true, this may mean that the ancestors of these dialects never made use of a *did-* base, but rather contended with a *d-* base, identical to the erstwhile linker. Indeed, in many NENA dialects (mostly Jewish) the base *d-* is also used alongside a *did-* base, but it is normally restricted to some or all of the

[76] This is also true of adjectives, which in general lose their referential function, or covert pronominal head, in predicative position. Recall that in Syriac this is manifested by the use of the absolute state, as discussed in footnote 51 on page 87.

[77] In NWNA Mīdin one finds *did̤-* as well (Jastrow 1985: 43).

[78] For Nöldeke's explanation, see footnote 23 on page 64.

[79] Eleanor Coghill, p.c.

[80] The latter view is endorsed by Sinha (2000: 72). Evidence for this can be found in the fact that the 1SG form in Bēṣpən is *di'i~di*. Furthermore, other prepositions in the Judi-dialects of Turkey are extended in this way. For instance, the preposition *b-* in Gaznax is rendered *biy-* before pronominal suffixes (Gutman 2015c: 315). A similar analysis for Diyana-Zariwaw in NE Iraq is given as a possibility by Napiorkowska (2015: 93). She suggests, moreover, that *diy-* may originate in influence from the literary Christian Urmi NENA dialect (cf. Murre-van den Berg 1999: 198). The latter idea may also explain the occurrence of *diy-* in CSanandaj.

plural persons.[81] The reason for this seems to be syllabic: the plural pronominal suffixes are bi-syllabic, while the singular ones are mono-syllabic. Using alternatively the *d-* and *did-* bases guarantees bi-syllabicity across the paradigm. This is demonstrated in Table 10.9 with the paradigm from Amədya (Greenblatt 2011: 81), which is identical to the paradigm of JZakho (Cohen 2012: 453) except for the marking of length. A similar system is attested in Nerwa (Sabar 1976: 135), representing early J. Cis-Zab dialects. This corroborates the idea that the *d-* linker was available in Proto-Cis-Zab to act as a pronominal basis, and possibly also in other NENA precursors.

Table 10.9: Independent genitive pronouns in Amədya or JZakho

	SG	PL
1	*did-i*	*d-eni*
2M	*did-ux*	*d-oxun*
2F	*did-ax*	
3M	*did-e*	*d-ohun*
3F	*did-a*	

10.6.2 The *did* linker

In a group of dialects in North-West Iraq (JZakho, Betanure, Amədya), as well as Hertevin, the Syriac *d-* linker is replaced for the most part by the form *did* (~*dīd*~*dəd*) pre-nominally. In JZakho *did* also appears alongside *d-* in its role as a relativizer (as in Amədya), and as a complementizer.[82]

Assuming that the role of *did-* as a genitive pronominal base is prior to its use as a linker, a natural hypothesis would be that these dialects generalized its use from a pre-suffixal linker to a general linker, capable of appearing before any secondary (nominal as well as clausal). Indeed, in these dialects, there is no reason to analyse the pre-suffixal base and the linker *did* as two separate morphemes.

[81] In some dialects, namely JSanandaj, Sulemaniyya and Diyana-Zariwaw, the *d-* prefix is used with 3rd person genitive pronouns, singular and plural. Note though that in these cases these forms are identical or similar to the genitive demonstratives and do not incorporate the pronominal suffixes.

[82] This may be true also of Betanure and Hertevin, but I haven't found such occurrences in the available sources.

Another possibility is to relate the appearance of the *did* linker to the emergence of the Neo-CST suffix *-əd* discussed above. As we have noted in the previous chapters, the linker is functionally equivalent to a noun in construct state. With the emergence of the suffix *-əd* the speakers had the possibility to mark this explicitly by suffixing *-əd* to the linker itself, yielding */d(ə)/* + */-əd/* = */dəd/*~*/dīd/*.[83] Note that in all dialects which have the *did* linker the suffix *-əd* is highly productive. Further evidence may be adduced by the fact that in Early J. Neo-Aramaic, namely Nerwa this being the closest predecessor of JZakho, Amədya and Betanure, the *-əd* suffix is productive but no *did* linker is apparent, except as a pre-suffixal basis. Thus, it seems indeed that the development of the *-əd* suffix pre-dated the appearance of *did* as an independent linker, at least in the case of the Jewish dialects.[84]

The two above explanations are in fact not mutually exclusive but rather complementary. The development of the neo-construct suffix *-əd* may have eased the integration of the pre-suffixal basis *did-* as an independent linker, due to its reanalysis as */d+əd/*. This may also explain why in these dialects the usage of the original linker form *d-* has diminished, occurring in some dialects (such as JZakho) predominantly with clausal secondaries.

10.6.3 The *ad*, *od* and *ʾəd* linkers

Both in South-East Turkey and in Iraq one finds linkers consisting of a vowel followed by */-d/*. The forms *ad* and *od* stem in all probability from the demonstrative + linker construction present in Syriac (see §3.5.6). Note that, in Syriac, the pre-linker demonstrative, traditionally termed CORRELATIVE, appears especially (but not exclusively) before clausal secondaries, but in the NENA dialects where such linkers appear they are regularly followed by nominal secondaries. This may hint that the situation in Syriac was rather exceptional compared to the precursors of these NENA dialects.

As for the linker *ʾəd*, it may result from a phonetic reduction of the former linker forms, or it may be a phonetic variant of the simple linker */d(ə)-/*.[85] For

[83]The form */dīd/* is found frequently in JZakho. Note that */ī/* is simply the long counterpart of */ə/*. In some dialects closed mono-syllabic words are always realised with a long vocalic nucleus (cf. Gutman 2015c: 307, fn. 6). Thus the lengthening of the vowel in *dīd* is an automatic phonological process related to the fact that it becomes an independent stress-bearing word.

[84]The form *did* is also lacking from the Early Christian Neo-Aramaic poetry published by Mengozzi (2002; 2011), where only *di-*~*diy-* and *dil-* are present (see glossary of Mengozzi 2002: 205f.). These poems, however, originate in the region of Alqosh, where the *did* linker did not develop at all.

[85]See also footnote 2 on page 296.

the present discussion I leave this question open, and I shall concentrate on the clear forms *ad* and *od.*

10.6.3.1 J. Arbel contrasted with C. Barwar

Khan (1999: 224) analyses the Arbel linker *ʾot* as stemming from *ʾo + t* 'the one of', and Pat-El (2010: 67) relates it to the Syriac construction, explaining it as a "conflation of a Syriac-like **haw d-*". Indeed, the singular (far-deixis) demonstrative pronoun in Arbel is *ʾo*, with no number distinction (Khan 1999: 85). The emergence of the linker *ot* may be seen as product of the same process leading to the emergence of the Neo-CST *-əd* suffix, namely resyllabification of *d-* with the preceding element and their subsequent reanalysis as one morpho-syntactic unit (see §10.4.1). In this case, however, a further step of grammaticalisation took place, since the *ʾot* linker lost the SG number feature associated with the original demonstrative:

(33) Arbel: **Noun–Noun**
bšilmāne' ʾot= Ârbel'
Muslims LNK= A.
'the Muslims of Arbel' (Khan 1999: 224 [L:42])

Moreover, *pace* Pat-El, in contrast to the Syriac source construction, the *ʾot* linker does not induce a definite reading on the entire NP, and it can have an indefinite antecedent (possibly with a generic reading):[86]

(34) Arbel: **Noun Phrase–Noun**
[xanči masale] ʾot= ʾarbel
some stories LNK= A.
'some stories of Arbel' (Khan 1999: 224)

(35) Arbel: **Noun–Noun**
(xá= sinn-it dì̂b k-imr-í-wā-le,') káka ʾod= dì̂b'
INDF= tooth-CST wolf, IND-say-A3PL-PST-P3MS tooth LNK= wolf
'(It was called a wolf's tooth,) a tooth of a wolf.' (Khan 1999: 228 [L:209])

Furthermore, in contrast to demonstratives, the linker itself can serve as a generic indefinite head:

---

[86]Such examples, however, are relatively rare, possibly due to the general tendency of attribute constructions to be definite (Haspelmath 1999).

(36) Arbel: **∅–Clause**
ʾot= k-e-wa xa= čày k-míx-wā-leˈ
LNK= IND-come-PST INDF= tea IND-bring-PST-DAT3MS
'whoever came, we would bring tea for him' (Khan 1999: 170, 454 [L:229])

Thus, we can conclude that *ot* was grammaticalised as a general pronominal linker, losing the grammatical features and semantic weight associated with the original demonstrative pronoun element *ʾo*. This can be contrasted with Nerwa, representing Early J. Cis-Zab Neo-Aramaic, where the forms *ʾaw-d* and *ʾay-d* can still be analysed as inflecting demonstrative pronouns with a definite semantic value followed by an enclitic *-d* linker or construct state suffix (see examples (7)–(8) on page 311 and discussion there). A similar situation exists in Barwar, where an *ʾo-t* element is clearly segmentable into two distinct elements, an inflecting attributive demonstrative (which I analyse as a definite determiner in Barwar[87]) and a clitic linker:[88]

(37) Barwar: **Noun Phrase–Noun**
xón-e diy-e ʾo= t= Nìnweˈ
brother-POSS.3MS GEN-3MS DEF.MS= LNK= N.
'His brother from Nineveh' (Khan 2008c: 493 [A13:3])

(38) Barwar: **Noun–Noun**
yale ʾan= t= xal-i
children DEF.PL= LNK= uncle-POSS.1SG
'The children of my maternal uncle' (Khan 2008c: 493 (32))

(39) Barwar: **Noun Phrase–Clause**
(ʾə́θyɛ-le) [ʾo= gàwṛa díy-a],ˈ ʾo= t= [wéwa mùθyə-lla].ˈ
came-3MS DEF.MS man GEN-3FS DEF.MS= LNK= COP.PST.3MS bought-P3FS
'(He came back,) her husband, the one who had brought her.' (Khan 2008c: 957 [A12:53])

[87] See footnote 13 on page 11. Preceding a linker it marks the linker phrase as definite.

[88] The /*t*/ segment is bound phonologically both forward and backward in Khan's transcription. I assume that both the determiner *ʾo* and the linker *t* are proclitics.

(40) Barwar: **Noun Phrase–Clause**
m= [bnōn= mám-i] ʾan= t= [wɛ́wa gòṛe].'
from= sons.CST= uncle-POSS.1SG DEF.PL= LNK= COP.PST.3PL old.PL
'from my cousins, who were older' (Khan 2008c: 518 [B8:5])

The Barwar determiner can even be marked as genitive, if it occurs within a genitive NP:

(41) Barwar: **Noun–Noun–Clause**
bráta [d-o= Xáno Lapzèrin,' d-o= t= wewa
daughter GEN-DEF.MS X. L. GEN-DEF.MS= LNK= COP.PST.3MS
bə́nya Dəmdə̀ma]'
built D.
'the daughter of that Xano the Golden Hand, who had built Dəmdəma' (Khan 2008c: 957 [A11:17])

Khan (2009a: 83f.) notes that in Barwar this construction is available only for definite antecedents with non-restrictive relative clauses, while in Arbel the usage of *ʾot* is generalized to restrictive relative clauses as well. He considers, moreover, the Barwar situation to be "typologically more archaic", representing, in other words, an earlier stage of the development of these constructions.[89]

On the other hand, also in Arbel there are, alongside the linker *ʾot*, attributive demonstratives which can be marked by construct state suffix: the plural demonstrative pronoun *ʾinná-t* and the singular (near-deixis) demonstrative pronoun *ʾiyyá-t*. In contrast to the linker they conserve their definite reading:

(42) Arbel: **Pronoun–Clause**
mindí ʾiyyá-t zwìn-ni bāq-áw' nbìl-lu-lleu.'
thing DEM.SG.PROX-CST bought-1SG for-3FS took-A3PL-P3MS
'The thing that I bought for her - they took it' (Khan 1999: 388 [L:408])

[89]There is yet another distribution in Sulemaniyya, where *ʾot* heads only free (antecedent-less) relative clauses, whether they are definite or not (Khan 2004: 418). Note that the demonstrative pronoun *ʾo* in Sulemaniyya does not carry number or gender features (Khan 2004: 77). For the sporadic use of *od* in JUrmi, see §7.2.5.

(43) Arbel: **Noun Phrase–Noun Phrase + Clause**
sìmun,ˈ nāš-ít saràyˈ kul-lù qṭolún-nuˈ ˀínna-t rúww-ake ˀód
go.IMP people-CST S. all-3PL kill.IMP-3PL DEM.PL-CST great-DEF LNK
did-xùnˈ ˀínna-t itiwé-lu b= saràyˈ.
GEN-2PL DEM.PL-CST sit.PST-3PL in= S.
'Go and kill all the people of the *saray* (government office), your great men, who reside in the *saray*' (Khan 1999: 170, 510 [Y:174])

In some NENA dialects, Arbel included, adjectives can be nominalized by means of a demonstrative pronoun:[90]

(44) Arbel: ∅–**Adjective**
ˀó zurtá
DEM small.FS
'the small one' (Khan 1999: 229 [L:214])

Quite exceptionally in Arbel, however, the demonstrative pronoun in this environment is interchangeable with the linker *ˀot*:

(45) Arbel: ∅–**Adjective**
ˀot= rabtà
LNK= big.FS
'the big one' (Khan 1999: 230 [B:10])

Indeed, the latter possibility is available in Arbel as part of the general availability in this dialect of having adjectival secondaries following a construct state head (see example (22) on page 317). Yet the similarity with Sorani linker Ezafe construction used to nominalize adjectives (see example (92) on page 283) should not be overlooked. In Barwar a similar construction is also available, but only when the secondary "adjective is extended by an intensifier or by the comparative particle *biš*" (Khan 2008c: 509).

(46) Barwar: ∅–**Adjective Phrase**
ˀo =t biš= daqìqaˈ
DEF.MS =LNK more= thin.FS
'the one that is thinner' (Khan 2008c: 509 [B10:49])

[90] According to my survey, similar patterns exist in Amədya, Barwar, CAradhin, Diyana-Zariwaw, JZakho and Qaraqosh, and possible more dialects.

This is reminiscent of the situation in Syriac, in which the linker *d-* is used especially when preceding multi-word adjective phrases (see discussion in §3.8.2).

In Arbel, there are rare instances of construct state marked primaries preceding the linker. While these are marginal in Arbel, they may represent the first step of a process of grammaticalisation in which the construct state *-əd* suffix becomes obligatory in ACs, irrespectively of the appearance of the appearance of the *d-* linker or a derivative thereof. Synchronically, this may be analysed as an (optional) agreement-in-state pattern between the primary and the linker (see also §11.2):

(47) Arbel: **Noun–Noun**
jirān-ít ʾót hulaʾèʾ ga= Šaqlàwaʾ
neighbour-CST LNK Jews in= Š.
'the neighbour of the Jews in Shaqlawa' (Khan 1999: 224 [L:411])

In Koy Sanjaq, discussed below, this process has gone further.

10.6.3.2 J. Koy Sanjaq

The linker *ʾod* of Koy Sanjaq can similarly be analysed as a grammaticalised combination of the far-deixis demonstrative *ʾo* + construct state suffix *-d*. In this dialect the original linker *d-* is not used any more. A peculiarity of Koy Sanjaq is that the linker often follows a construct state primary, becoming effectively a construct state agreement marker. It can co-occur with (pro)nominal and clausal as well as ordinal secondaries:

(48) Koy Sanjaq: **Noun–Pronoun**
bel-a ʾod did-i
house-FREE LNK GEN-1SG
'my house' (Mutzafi 2004a: 62)

(49) Koy Sanjaq: **Noun–Noun**
b= wáxt-əd ʾod bāb-ew
in= time-CST LNK father-POSS.3MS
'in the time of his father' (Mutzafi 2004a: 63 [N 8])

(50) Koy Sanjaq: **Noun–Clause**
məndixā́n-əd ʾod ʾabe mən šār
items-CST LNK want.3MS from city
'the items that he wants from town' (Mutzafi 2004a: 63 [**N** 6])

(51) Koy Sanjaq: **Noun–Ordinal**
yarx-əd ʾod xamša
month-CST LNK five
'the fifth month' (Mutzafi 2004a: 168)

As in Arbel, the linker has lost the definite interpretation associated with the demonstrative, and can head generic-indefinite relative clauses:

(52) Koy Sanjaq: **∅–Clause**
ʾod šté-le mən yá= māʿe damudast míl-le
LNK drank-3MS from DEM.PROX.SG= water immediately died-3MS
'whoever drank from this water died immediately' (Mutzafi 2004a: 63)

In prepositional phrases, furthermore, the linker has entirely lost its pronominal status and has become a pure linker. It can only (optionally) follow construct state marked prepositions, establishing, as noted above, an agreement-in-state pattern between the prepositional primary and the linker:

(53) Koy Sanjaq: **Preposition–Noun/Pronoun**
gā́w {-əd {ʾod}} bela / did-ew
in -CST LNK house GEN-3MS
'in the house/in him' (Mutzafi 2004a: 174)

10.6.3.3 J. Barzani

Mutzafi (2004b: 3, fn. 15) mentions the existence of the linker ("independent particle of annexation") *ʾod* in this dialect. In the limited corpus available, there is only one clear example of its usage with a clausal secondary:[91]

[91]There is another example with a ∅ primary in the corpus, yet the translation is a bit strange: *ʾod gāwər ʾod hāwe* 'whoever [wishes] to marry or to be [something]' (Mutzafi 2004b: 6 (31)). An alternative is to understand the word *ʾod* as the imperative form of the verb *wāda* 'to do' (attested in the corpus), in which case the translation would be 'make him marry, make him be'. Another theoretical possibility is that *ʾod* is used in this example as a complementizer, but such a usage is not attested elsewhere in the corpus.

(54) Barzani: **Noun–Clause**
Xajoke, ʾod zəl-lan šūwá naqle ṭəlb-ā-lan
X. LNK went-1PL seven times asked-P3FS-A1PL
'Khajoke, to whom we went seven times and asked for her hand' (Mutzafi 2004b: 4 (7))

Additionally, there isan example with an adjectival secondary. In this case, the usage of the linker seems to be motivated by a contrastive focus on the adjective.

(55) Barzani: **Noun–Adjective**
(ʾə́t-wa-li xa xona), xon-i ʾod zora
EX-PST-1SG INDF brother brother-POSS.1SG LNK small.MS
'I had a brother, my youngest brother' (Mutzafi 2004b: 9 (13))

10.6.3.4 Judi-dialects

In the Judi-dialects (represented here by Bēṣpən and Gaznax) there is a similar linker *ad* which has almost entirely replaced the simple linker *d-*.

(56) Bēṣpən: **Noun–Noun**
suraye ad= kaldắn
Christians LNK= Chaldean
'Chaldean Christians' (Sinha 2000: 212 (179))

(57) Bēṣpən: **Noun–Ordinal**
bayta ad= tre
house LNK= two
'the second house' (Sinha 2000: 169)

(58) Gaznax: **Noun Phrase–Noun**
šula zaḥme ʾad d-awa zalame
work hard LNK GEN-DEM.MS man
'the hard work of this man' (Gutman 2015c: 316 (22))

In these dialects one finds a series of determiners (i.e. exclusively attributive demonstratives), all starting with *a-*, presented in Table 10.10 on the next page (adapted from Sinha 2000: 73). The linker form *ad* has thus effectively erased all gender/number information, in line with its grammaticalisation as a generalized linker.

Table 10.10: Determiners of Judi-Dialects

MS	*áw*
FS	*áy*
PL	*án*

10.6.3.5 J. Zakho

In JZakho there is generally no *ʾod* linker, but rather a *dīd* linker (see §10.6.2). In the context of Bible translations, however, the uninflecting form *ʾōd* is regularly used as a translational equivalent of the Hebrew relativizer אֲשֶׁר *ăšɛr* (Sabar 1983: ל; Goldenberg & Zaken 1990: 152)

(59) JZakho: **Noun–Clause**
(mpəq-la mən) d-ay dūka ʾōd [wēla tāma kutru
left-3FS from GEN-DEM.FS place LNK COP.PST.3FS there both
kalāsa dīd-a ʾəmm-a].
daughter_in_law.PL GEN-3FS with-3FS
'(She left) the place where she was with both her daughters-in-law.' (Ruth 1:7; Goldenberg & Zaken 1990: 153)

The usage of the form *ʾōd* may reflect some of kind of archaism, as similar (though inflecting) forms are present in Early J. Cis-Zab Neo-Aramaic (see examples (7)–(8) on page 311). Its composite form, moreover, may relate to a metalinguistic reflection on *ăšɛr* as a complex form.[92] In either case, the non-inflection of *ʾōd* parallels the fixed nature of *ăšɛr*, rather than originating in a process of grammaticalisation.

10.6.4 The J. Urmi *ay* linker

The JUrmi linker *ay* (see §7.3) poses a special problem regarding its origin, as it does not contain any /*d*/ element. The linker is identical in form with the demonstrative pronoun *ay*, which Garbell (1965b: 58) lists as an "archaic" variant of the singular proximal demonstrative pronoun *ya*. Like the Koy Sanjaq linker

[92]In fact, the common view today is that *ăšɛr* is ultimately derived from a construct state form of an Akkadian noun *ašru* 'place' (Klein 1987: 59). Yet its phonetic similarity to the relativizer שֶׁ *šɛ-* easily leads to the idea that it is a complex form containing the relative (cf. Gesenius 1909: 465, §138, fn. 1).

discussed above, most often than not it occurs after construct state marked primaries, in which case the /d/ segment of the construct state suffix re-syllabifies frequently with the linker, giving rise to the form *d-ay*, reminiscent of the genitive marking of demonstrative pronouns. When this does not happen, it is an indication that *ay* is indeed the linker, as in the following example (see further examples in §7.3.2):

(60) JUrmi: **Noun–Noun**
lél-ət ay= xlulà
night-CST LNK= wedding
'the night of the wedding' (Khan 2008b: 175 [93])

Unlike the demonstrative pronoun, the linker *ay* does not inflect for number, making it easily identifiable as such after plural primaries, such as 'children' in the following example:[93]

(61) JUrmi: **Noun–Noun Phrase**
dəmm-ə́t ay= [⁺yál-ət ay gomè]
blood-CST LNK= child(ren)-CST LNK Muslims
'the blood of the children of the Muslims' (Khan 2008b: 230 [101])

The demonstrative pronoun origin of the linker leads Khan (2008b: 8) to suggest that it is an "imitation of the Kurdish relational morpheme (*izafe*), which is demonstrative in origin" closely following the suggestion of Garbell (1965a: 171, §2.32.12). Later on, Khan (2008b: 176) elaborates on this idea, presenting effectively the adoption of the linker as a kind of pattern replication:

> It is likely to have developed under the influence of the *izafe* construction in Iranian languages. It appears not to be a direct loan from Iranian, in which the *izafe* is in principle monosyllabic (*e*, *i*, *a*), but rather an imitation of the *izafe* using Aramaic morphological material.

A difficulty, however, with the above proposal is found in the fact that the Ezafe arose out of a relative pronoun, not a simple demonstrative (Haider & Zwanziger 1984). Moreover, the pronominal origin of the Ezafe is quite old, going back at least to Middle Persian (spoken up to the 7th century) pre-dating the earliest attestation of NENA dialects by a millennium at least.

[93]Note that, due to the construct state suffix *-əd*, the morphological plural marking is erased, and the plural meaning is deduced from the textual context.

From a structural viewpoint, as discussed above in (§10.4.2.1), the Kurdish Ezafe is typically encliticized to the primary, which is rarely the case with the linker *ay* (see example (47) on page 200). Furthermore, in contrast to the Ezafe, the *ay* linker does not introduce a clausal secondary, but instead the relativizer *ki* is used (see also discussion in §10.4.2.2.2 on page 312). Similarly, adjectival secondaries are not introduced by the linker *ay* (although there are rare examples in which adjectives follow the homophonous determiner *ay*; see §7.3.4 and compare with §10.4.2.2.5 on page 316). One may wonder also regarding the form of the JUrmi linker: if the JUrmi speakers were indeed to borrow the Ezafe as a demonstrative pronoun element, wouldn't it be more natural to use the JUrmi demonstrative pronoun *ya* as a pivot, being identical in form to the Kurmanji FS Ezafe? Considering all these facts, it seems that the association of the *ay* linker to the Iranic Ezafe is hardly justified.[94]

A possible alternative explanation is to assume that the linker *ay* originated in a compound linker *ay-d*, analogical to the linkers discussed above. Subsequently, due to a phonological reduction, the linker became *ay*. The environment which promoted such a reduction may be exactly the same environment which led to the development of genitive marked demonstratives following the *-əd* suffix (see §10.5), as in the following example (=example (86) on page 211):

(62) JUrmi: **Noun–Noun**
⁺qayd-ət áy d-ò= tka
custom-CST LNK GEN-DEM.DIST.SG= place
'the custom of that place' (Khan 2008b: 176 [144])

Another minor factor may have been that the conflation of *ay-d* could lead to the form *ād~āt* which is identical to the independent 2SG pronoun. The desire to avoid ambiguity may have played a role in the dropping of the /*d*/.

Some support for this idea comes from comparing nominalized ordinal numbers. Comparing the following two examples (=example (65) on page 133 and example (65) on page 205), we see that JZakho *ay-d* corresponds closely to JUrmi *ay*:

[94] Garbell (1965a: 171, §2.32.12) notes that in J. Solduz and Šĭno the Ezafe particle *i* (apparently of Sorani origin) is borrowed, but this does not entail that *ay* is also borrowed, notwithstanding its functional similarity. Note that these localities, in contrast to Urmi, are on the border of the Sorani speaking area. Regarding borrowing of the *i* Ezafe see §11.4.1.1.

(63) JZakho: ∅–**Ordinal**
ʾay d= treʾ
DEF.FS LNK= two
'the second one (FS)' (Cohen 2012: 95 (7))

(64) JUrmi: ∅–**Ordinal**
ay arbi
LNK forty
'the fortieth' (Garbell 1965b: 88)

A similar piece of evidence in favour of this account comes from the Bible translation written in the Ruwandiz dialect, described by Rees (2008). In this translation, the particle אַי *ay* is used as a relativizer serving as the translation equivalent of Biblical Hebrew relativizer אֲשֶׁר *ăšɛr* (Rees 2008: 27).[95] Recall that in JZakho Bible translations the equivalent of *ăšɛr* is consistently *ʾod*, as described in §10.6.3.5. Thus, once again, we see that *ay* corresponds to a DEM+CST combination in JZakho. While these similarities are first and foremost functional and distributional, they corroborate the idea that *ay* as a linker (in JUrmi) or a relativizer (in Ruwandiz) originated in *ay-d*.

10.6.5 Emerging grammaticalisation of *mārā*

Quite distinct from the linkers that developed from the *d-* linker, in some dialects one finds reflexes of the construct state of the Aramaic word *mārā* 'owner, master', marking possession of qualities and goods.

(65) Alqosh: ***mara*–Noun**
mar= ʾérwe
owner.CST= sheep
'sheep owner' (Coghill 2003: 250)

(66) Qaraqosh: ***mara*–Noun**
gora mari šafqa
man owner.CST hat
'a man with a hat' (Khan 2002a: 211)

[95]In contrast to JUrmi, it is not used before nominal secondaries. In such context, the Ruwandiz translation uses consistently the Neo-CST suffix *-ət*, being the translation equivalent of the Biblical Hebrew construct state (Rees 2008: 82). Yet Rees (2008: 27) tentatively relates this use of *ay* to JUrmi influence.

(67) Sulemaniyya: **Noun–Noun**
baxta mara/mare pare
woman owner/owner.CST money
'a woman possessing money' (Khan 2004: 193)

Cohen (2012: 225) notes that when the secondary denotes a quality, the entire construction is similar to an adjective (similarly indeed to phrases headed by a linker):

(68) JZakho: ***mara*–Noun**
mare qūwəta
owner strength
'possessor of strength, strong' (Cohen 2012: 225 (60))

In JZakho one finds also an example where *mare* is followed by an interrogative pronouns:

(69) JZakho: ***mara*–Interrogative Pronoun**
mare mā wē-tən?
owner what COP-2MS
'What is on your mind' (Sabar 2002: 210)

In all these dialects *mar-* has lost its gender inflection, though in Alqosh and Sulemaniyya it inflects for number. In Qaraqosh and JZakho it is completely invariable. In these expressions *mar-* keeps to a large extent its original lexical semantics of ownership (clearly so in examples such as JZakho *mare bēsa* 'landlord'[96]), so we cannot properly speak of a grammaticalisation of *mar-*. Yet in some respects it shows the first signs of grammaticalisation, such as the loss of its inflectional features, and its usage as a grammatical head of adjectival-like phrases . If its usage became wider and more abstract it might emerge as a new linker.

10.7 Conclusions

In this chapter I have traced the development of the various D-markers in NENA dialects. I have showed that virtually all the developments involved can be explained by prosodic mechanisms of re-syllabification and cliticization. Yet the

[96]Cohen 2012: 224.

grammaticalisation of the resulting segmental material (be it the suffix *-əd*, the genitive prefix *d-*, or indeed linkers such as *od*) needs a further stage of morpho-syntactic re-analysis. It is in this last stage where language contact may play a crucial role. Nonetheless, as I have showed in the discussion of the emergence of the Neo-CST suffix *-əd* (§10.4.2), it is quite difficult to pinpoint the influence to a specific model language, due to the profusion of the features of these AC systems throughout the languages of the regions, forming effectively a Sprachbund.

To summarize my claims, I present the following model of development of the different D-markers. The division into stages helps conceptualize the process, but it should not be taken as a strict chronological ordering of the steps involved. As the beginnings of stage one are apparent in manuscripts of the 17th century (see §10.4) one may cautiously date the start of the process to that time, though it may in fact have started even earlier.[97]

Stage 1 The *d-* linker of the Classical Aramaic DAC transforms, by means of encliticization, into the Neo-CST suffix *-əd* (§10.4).

Stage 2 Due to analogy, the same process occurs to a limited extent with the *d-* linker of the ALC. In contrast to the DAC, the ALC remains in complementary distribution with the Neo-CSC.

Stage 3 The *-əd* suffix procliticizes to vowel-initial secondaries, being reanalysed as a genitive marker before vowel-initial demonstratives, possibly under the influence of Kurmanji (§10.5).

Stage 4 In some dialects, the emergence of the *-əd* suffix facilitates the generalisation of the pronominal base *did-* as an independent linker (§10.6.2).

Stage 5 In other dialects, combinations of DEM+LNK *d-* are grammaticalised to become new linkers such as Arbel *ot* (§10.6.3.1) or Gaznax *ad* (§10.6.3.4). In JUrmi, the /*d*/ segment is lost, giving rise to the linker *ay* (§10.6.4).

As we shall in the next chapter, these developments triggered further changes in the attributive systems of the NENA dialects.

[97] Such an estimate must be taken with a grain of salt, as manuscripts often lag behind the synchronic developments of language, due to a tendency of scribes to use archaic spelling conventions.

11 Further developments of attributive constructions

In the last chapter I have discussed the development of D-marked attributive constructions in NENA dialects. In this chapter I shall discuss further changes of the AC system, of which only some are related to the D-markers.

The first section deals with the apocopate construct state marking, functionally a variant of the *-əd* suffix, whose development may reflect both the retention of the historical construct state and innovative forms.

Section §11.2 discusses the re-introduction of various double-marked attributive constructions, following the loss of the DAC discussed in the previous chapter.

Section §11.3 presents a true innovation of NENA, very possible motivated by the influence of contact languages: the introduction of a productive zero-marked juxtaposition construction in the core of the AC system of various dialects.

Section §11.4 discusses further clear cases of contact influence, namely matter replication (borrowing of morphemes) from contact languages, notably the Iranic Ezafe (§11.4.1) and subordinator particle (§11.4.2).

In lieu of conclusions, I present in §11.5 a case study concerning a sub-domain of the AC system, namely nominal modification by ordinals. As we shall see, this sub-system is symptomatic of the entire AC system, as it shows both high variation and uniformity across dialects, model languages and anterior strata.

11.1 Apocopate construct state: Retention and renewal

Alongside the innovation of the Neo-CST suffix *-əd*, discussed in §10.4, in many NENA dialects one finds nominals marked exhibiting construct state by apocope, i.e. the omission of their free state suffix, usually *-a* or *-e*.[1] The apocope is occasionally extended to a preceding consonantal segment.

Mutzafi (2004b: 3, fn. 15; 2008a: 92) makes a distinction between innovated apocopated construct state nouns (which he terms “Neo-construct”) and reten-

[1]This is of course only possible with nous which exhibit the free state suffix; unadapted loanwords are thus excluded.

tions of the ancient construct state forms. For example, in Betanure he differentiates between *beθ* 'house of' and *be* 'household, family of', both derived from *beθa* 'house' (Mutzafi 2008a: 92). While some couplets can easily be distinguished due to irregular morpho-phonological processes which took place in the historical form (for instance, the free form *brona* 'son' is related both to the innovated construct state form *bron* and the historical construct state *bər*[2]), in general it is not always clear what the philological basis for this distinction it. Note, for instance, that Mutzafi (2004b: 3, fn. 15) asserts that *nāš* 'people of' is an innovated construct state form of *nāšā*, but Mutzafi (2008a: 92) lists it as a "possible old construct form".[3] Synchronically, moreover, the source of apocope plays no role: if a given dialect allows the regular usage of apocopate construct state nouns, the innovated and historical forms are morpho-syntactically equivalent, with the exception that some historical construct state nouns may only appear as part of lexicalised compounds (see examples (1)–(2) on page 350). Therefore, I prefer to subsume the two under one category of APOCOPATE CONSTRUCT STATE and reserve the term NEO-CONSTRUCT for the truly innovated suffix *-əd* discussed in the previous chapter.

The distribution of the apocopate CSC is given in Table 11.1, which should be compared to Table 10.2 on page 300, showing the distribution of the Neo-CSC.

As noted in §3.4, the Syriac CSC "tends to be confined to standing phrases verging on compound nouns" (Muraoka 1997: 61). This is in general quite true also for the historical CSC in many NENA dialects, which do not make productive use of the apocopate construct state, but in which one finds rather lexicalised compounds in which the primary is derived from an historical apocopate construct state. For instance, in Qaraqosh and Alqosh the historical construct state form *bar* 'son of' is only used as part of some lexicalised compounds (Khan 2002a: 211; Coghill 2003: 251).[4] Note the varying degree of lexicalization as manifested by the plural marking: In example (1) it is phrase final, while in example (2) it is also marked on the primary.

[2]The latter is the construct state of *brā* 'son', extant in Classical Aramaic, but not used as such in NENA. Diachronically, *brona* was derived from *brā* by addition of the diminutive suffix *-ona*, but in NENA it is the regular form of the noun.

[3]The situation for this noun is in fact more complex, as the form *nāš* appears sometimes in various dialects in contexts where a construct state is not regularly expected. In these cases it may represent a retention of the historical absolute state singular form (Khan 1999: 173), or possible a phonological process of final vowel elision, as it is found also in plural use: for instance, in Arbel one finds the expression *náš xriwé* 'bad people' (Khan 1999: 229 [B:13]), and in JZakho *ʾan nāš ʾımme* 'the people with him' (Cohen 2012: 117 (112)) (=example (13) on page 118).

[4]In these dialects *bar* does not represent a separate noun at all, and consequently it is not synchronically in construct state. However, I gloss it as such for the clarity of exposition.

Table 11.1: Distribution of apocopate construct state excluding compounds. The entry (-) marks dialects where only a handful of nouns can act as primaries.

Region	Dialect	Primaries			Secondaries		
		Noun	Adj.	Inf.	N/NP	Ordinal	Clause
SE Turkey	Hertevin	(-)			+		
	Bohtan						
	Bēṣpən						
	Gaznax						
	Baz						
	Challa	+			+	+	
	Jilu	(-)			+		
NW Iraq	JZakho	+	+	+	+	+	+
	JAradhin	(-)			+		
	CAradhin						
	Barwar	+	+		+		
	Betanure	+			+		
	Amədya	+			+		+
	Barzani	+			+		
	Alqosh						
	Qaraqosh	(-)			+		
NW Iran	JUrmi	+			+		
	Sardarid	+			+		
NE Iraq	Rustaqa						
	Diyana-Z.	(-)			+		
	Arbel	(-)			+		
	Koy Sanjaq						
	Sulemaniyya	(-)					
W. Iran	JSanandaj	(-)			+		
	CSanandaj	+			+		

(1) Alqosh: **Noun–Noun**
bar- zar-a, bar- zar-ə
son.CST- crop-SG son.CST- crop-PL
'seed, seeds' (Coghill 2003: 251)

(2) Alqosh: **Noun–Noun**
bar- nāš-a, bne- nās-ə
son.SG.CST- man-SG son.PL.CST- man-PL
'human, humans' (Coghill 2003: 251)

Such compounds are fixed phrases forming one conceptual unit, and the secondary is normally non-referential. Therefore, they cannot be considered as true productive ACs, and they are excluded from Table 11.1.[5]

Other dialects allow additionally a semi-lexicalised usage of the historical apocopate construct state. In these cases only a handful of nouns can act as primaries (typically kinship nouns such as *bər* 'son of',[6] and the construct state noun *be* 'house of'), but the secondary is referential (example (4)=example (33) on page 236).[7]

(3) CSanandaj: **Noun–Noun**
yoḥana bər ʿam-ī
Y. son.CST uncle-POSS.1SG
'my cousin John' (Panoussi 1990: 125 (7))

(4) JSanandaj: **Noun–Noun**
be= kalda
house.CST= bride
'house/family of the bride' (Khan 2009b: 201)

The last usage is also attested in Early J. Neo-Aramaic:

[5]For more information about compounds in Neo-Aramaic see Gutman (2014).

[6]Contrast with the usage of *bron*, which is also found as a grammatical head, but indicating age and not kinship (=example (11) on page 191):

(i) JUrmi: **Noun–Noun**
bron [ičči šinne]
son.CST sixty years
'a man 60 years old' (Garbell 1965b: 86)

For a kinship use of *bron*, see example (6) on page 352.

[7]Maclean (1895: 27–34, §16.(ii)) gives an extensive list of such expressions, including fixed compounds.

(5) Nerwa: **Noun–Noun**
בי ישראל
bē *yiśrā'ẹl*
house.CST I.
'the people of Israel' (*Pəšaṭ Wayəhî Bəšallaḥ* 1:25, Sabar 1976: 38; see there fn. 16)

Dialects which allow only such cases are marked with (-) in Table 11.1.[8]

However, even dialects which permit a productive use of apocope for marking construct state primaries (+ marking in the Table 11.1) make in fact a quite limited use of this possibility, both in terms of frequency and in terms of categorial diversity of primary and secondary. As Table 11.1 shows, most dialects allow only N+N combinations in this construction, which is less extensive than the Syriac usage, which allowed also adjectival and infinitival primaries. The extension to clausal secondaries, a clear innovation, is attested only in JZakho and the closely related Amədya dialect. Indeed, it seems that only JZakho generalized the usage of the apocopate construct state marking to be completely equivalent to the suffixed construct state marking. It is probably no coincidence that also the suffixed construct state marking is the most extensive in this dialect, as shown in Table 10.2 on page 300.[9]

How can the renaissance of apocopate construct state marking in JZakho and neighbouring dialects be explained? Judging by Nerwa, the apocopate construct state is hardly available in the Early Jewish Cis-Zab Neo-Aramaic, example (5) on this page being typical.[10] As in Nerwa the suffixed construct state marker is highly productive, one can tentatively conclude that the apocopate construct state is a recent innovation, appearing after the innovation of the *-əd* suffix as marker of construct state, rather than being a retention of the historical apocopate construct state. Moreover, the occurrences of the historical construct state

[8]Some dialects which are marked with + may in fact fall into this category, as the table is generally based on the explicit statement of such a limitation in the respective grammars.

[9]The data may contain a certain bias towards the JZakho data, as the attributive relation has been specifically investigated in this dialect by Cohen (2010; 2012: Ch. 2). Yet, at least amongst the well documented dialects, it is clear that no dialect matches its extensive usage of construct state-marking, both suffixed and apocopate.

[10]One may doubt whether Nerwa is truly representative in this respect. Yet, since there are no other comparable J. NENA sources of that time, and since in general the dialect is quite similar to an archaic form of JZakho, I regard this corpus tentatively as an approximation of the precursor of JZakho. Note also that Sabar (2002) writes that Nerwa "may be considered 'classical' JNA" [=J. Cis-Zab Neo-Aramaic].

cannot account for the renewal of this marking type, as they are constrained to specific expressions, and also since they often exhibit an irregular morphology, as the form *be* (construct state of *besa* 'house') shows.

Additionally, one can relate the renewed apocopate marking to the innovation of the genitive marking, discussed in §10.5. Recall that the development of the genitive prefix involved a resyllabification of the *-əd* suffix with a vowel-initial determiner, sometimes leaving behind a BARE PRIMARY, without any suffix at all, as in the following Barwar example:

(6) Barwar: **Noun–Noun**
brōn= *d-o=* *naša*
son.CST GEN-DEF.MS= man
'the son of that man' (Khan 2008c: 400 [A9:2])

After the *d-* prefix was reanalysed as a genitive marker, the bare form of the primary could have been reanalysed as a construct state form equivalent to the suffixed form *bron-əd*, and could consequently also occur without a genitive prefix following it. This hypothesis is corroborated by the fact that all those dialects that developed a productive apocopate construct state marking have also developed a genitive prefix, as is clear from comparing Table 11.1 on page 349 and Table 10.6 on page 323.[11] Moreover, this explains why most dialects restrict this development to N+N combinations.

Whatever the source of the apocopate CSC, it is clear, however, that the dialect of JZakho, and possibly also Amədya, went one step further, as they extended the usage of the apocopate construct state marking to more contexts, most notably clausal secondaries. In the context of JZakho, the latter development may be explained by the innovation of a *d-* marked subordinate copula, mirroring the *d-*marked genitive demonstrative pronouns in the clausal domain (see §5.5.2; also Cohen 2010: 90; 2012: 119ff.). As a consequence, the domain of usage of the apocopate construct state was extended and levelled by analogy with the usage domain of the suffixed construct state. As no neighbouring language shows a similar construct state marking, one must conclude that this was an internal development specific to JZakho and possibly neighbouring J. Cis-Zab dialects.

[11] All the dialects which have a productive apocopate CSC in my survey show the development of a genitive prefix *d-* in at least one environment (namely, after prepositions). On average, they exhibit 2⅓ plus-signs in Table 10.6. Conversely, those which have not developed a productive apocopate CSC may show no evidence at all of a genitive prefix, and exhibit on average less than 1½ plus-signs in this table.

11.2 Re-development of double marking

In §10.4.1 I have asserted that the Neo-CSC was preferred to the DAC due to the force of ECONOMY, since single head-marking is preferable to double-marking of head and dependent. Countering the force of economy is the force of CLARITY, which leads to a preference for more elaborate structures in order to ensure the correct transfer of the linguistic message. As is well known, these two forces shape language and cause cyclic changes in which marking is reduced and then re-introduced in another shape.[12] The NENA AC domain is no exception, as it exhibits the re-emergence of double-marked constructions.[13] Table 11.2 shows the possible ways of double marking of (pro)nominal secondaries following a construct state marked primary.

One type of double marking is the genitive case marking, which, by the very nature of case marking, marks the attributive relation on the secondary independently of the marking of the primary. However, in NENA the genitive case is normally not enough to instantiate an attributive relation, and therefore it appears typically alongside a construct state marked primary. One class of such genitive double marking is the *d-* prefix that appears on demonstrative pronouns (pre-nominal and independent), whose distribution is shown in the first column of Table 11.2. The development of this double marking has been discussed in §10.5.[14] Here one example should suffice:

(7) Jilu: **Noun–Noun**
xabr-əd d-a sawa
word-CST GEN-DEM old_man
'the word of this old man' (Fox 1997: 60)

Another class of genitive double marking is the use of independent attributive pronouns (e.g. *did-i~diy-i*) after construct state nouns, as shown in the second

[12]See in this respect the seminal paper of Slobin (1977: 186), who posits four "charges" which shape language: "(1) Be clear. (2) Be humanly processable in ongoing time. (3) Be quick and easy. (4) Be expressive." The first two fall under the the above notion of clarity, while the latter two relate to our notion of economy. In his words: "The first two charges – clarity and processibility – strive toward segementalization. The other two charges – temporal compactness and expressiveness – strive toward synthesis, however. As a result, Language constantly fluctuates between the poles of analyticity and syntheticity, since none of the charges can be ignored." (Slobin 1977: 192)

[13]Structurally, however, the NENA double-marking differs from the Classical Aramaic construction. In the Syriac DAC, the primary was marked by a pronoun indexing the secondary, while in the NENA double constructions, the primary is marked by a construct state marker.

[14]Note that the first column of Table 11.2 is identical to the third column of Table 10.6 on page 323.

Table 11.2: Double marked ACs. (-) = rare/doubtful occurrences; (Cl) = marginally occurring with clausal secondaries.

Region	Dialect	Secondary marking after CST primaries				
		GEN-DEM	*did/y*-POSS	LNK	LNK+GEN	REL
SE Turkey	Hertevin	+				
	Bohtan	+				
	Bēṣpən			(Cl)		
	Gaznax	+				
	Baz					
	Challa		+	(Cl)		
	Jilu	+				
NW Iraq	JZakho	+				
	JAradhin					
	CAradhin					
	Barwar	+	+	(-)		
	Betanure		+		+	
	Amədya	+	+	+		
	Barzani		+			
	Alqosh			(-)		
	Qaraqosh	(-)		(-)		
NW Iran	JUrmi	+	(-)	+	+	+
	Sardarid	+	+			+
NE Iraq	Rustaqa					
	Diyana-Z.	+	+			
	Arbel	+	+	(-)		
	Koy Sanjaq		+	+	+	+
	Sulemaniyya		+			(-)
W. Iran	JSanandaj	+	+			(-)
	CSanandaj	+				

column of Table 11.2. As discussed in §10.6.1, such pronouns can be analysed either as LNK+POSS or as GEN+POSS. In the latter case, they should follow construct state nouns, which is indeed the case for many dialects.

(8) Barzani: **Noun–Pronoun**
yāl-{əd} *did-i*
child(ren)-CST GEN-POSS.1SG
'my children' (Mutzafi 2002a: 66f.)

It is worthwhile noting that, with the exception of two dialects (Amədya and Betanure), the base *did-* is not used in such dialects as a linker (see Table 10.8 on page 329), which is coherent with the idea that it has been reanalysed as a genitive base, bleached of a pronominal reference.

The two exceptional dialects (Amədya and Betanure) are amongst those dialects which present a more profound structural change, namely they allow the independent linker itself (with nominal or pronominal secondaries) to occur after a construct state noun, against the logic of Classical Semitic languages, in which the linker is supposed to be in apposition with a free state noun (see §2.3.4.)

(9) Amədya: **Noun–Noun**
dar-ət *dəd xaye*
tree-CST LNK life
'the Tree of Life' (Greenblatt 2011: 73)

Consequently, the following example, while being formally similar to example (8), is analysed differently, in that *did-* is understood as a linker and not as a genitive marker.

(10) Amədya: **Noun–Pronoun**
beθ-əd *did-i*
house-CST LNK-POSS.1SG
'my house' (Greenblatt 2011: 81)

The occurrence of this construction with nominal secondaries is presented in the third and fourth columns of Table 11.2. As the table shows, it occurs regularly also in JUrmi (see §7.3.2) and in Koy Sanjaq (see examples (49)–(51) on page 338).

In these dialects it is difficult to analyse the linker as a genitive exponent, since it is sometimes followed by a separate genitive morpheme, as the following example shows.

(11) Betanure: **Noun–Noun**
ṃāy-əd did d-é= kθeθa
water-CST LNK GEN-DEM= chicken
'the broth of that chicken' (Mutzafi 2008a: 42 [548])

It seems rather that these dialects have generalized the usage of construct state marking to occur also before the linker, against the above mentioned logic of Classical Semitic languages. Note that in the dialects in which this is especially prominent, namely JUrmi and Koy Sanjaq, the linker is very probably derived from an erstwhile construct-state-marked demonstrative pronoun (see §10.6.3 and §10.6.4) standing in apposition to the primary. Moreover, in Amədya, Betanure and Koy Sanjaq the linker has a visible construct state form, as it ends with *-əd~-d*. It seems, therefore, that these dialects have developed an AGREEMENT IN STATE pattern, in which two nominal elements in apposition can optionally agree in their construct state marking. This is especially plausible in JUrmi in which two asyndetically coordinated nouns agree in state (see example (8) on page 190), considering that asyndetic coordination is formally similar to apposition.

Sporadic evidence of this construction is found also in Arbel (see example (47) on page 338), Qaraqosh (see §6.4.1), Alqosh, and Barwar. In these dialects this construction can at least partly be explained as resulting from some kind of *lapsus* or hesitation in speech, as in the following example.

(12) Barwar: **Noun–Noun**
qúww-ət ... t= ʾurusnàyeˈ
force-CST ... LNK= Russians
'the force ... of the Russians' (Khan 2008c: 399 [B7:8])

Indeed, even in Syriac there are rare occurrences of a similar construction with apocopate construct state, which are normally explained as errors (see example (35) on page 61 and the accompanying discussion).

Two dialects of Turkey, namely Bēṣpən and Challa restrict this construction to occur only with clausal secondaries (Bēṣpən and Challa).

(13) Bēṣpən: **Noun–Clause**
m= qam d-ayyá săhadut-əd d= wəd-la
from= before GEN-DEM testimony-CST LNK= made-3FS
'because of this sacrifice (lit. testimony) she made' (Sinha 2000: 212 [186])

In this case, we may tentatively relate it to the Kurmanji pattern, where a clause is introduced both by the Ezafe and the relativizer (see §9.4.9).[15] Yet the rarity of the construction in these dialects hinders a conclusive statement in this respect.

However, in other dialects we find direct evidence of such a relation, as a borrowed relativizer is used on top of a construct state marked primary or a linker (see for instance Koy Sanjaq example (51) on page 374 and Sardarid example (55) on page 375). The distribution of this construction is shown in the fifth column of Table 11.2 on page 354. This development may be seen as a case of pattern-cum-matter replication of the relativizers, which in the source languages (Kurmanji, Sorani and possible Persian) appear regularly after an Ezafe morpheme, paralleling the linker or the construct state marking (see §11.4.2). This development, moreover, may had an indirect influence on the development of CST+LNK construction discussed above, as the relativizer may have been perceived as the pre-clausal counterpart of the linker.

11.3 Loss of all marking: Juxtaposition constructions

In various dialects we find ACs that are not marked at all: The primary and secondary are simply juxtaposed one after the other. We consider here cases of Noun + Noun and Noun + Clause.[16] The distribution of these constructions is presented in Table 11.3, which shows that these constructions are often limited to a certain grammatical domain. In all cases, we must consider two main scenarios for the emergence of these constructions: the construction may originate in the loss of previous markers (for phonological or morphological reasons), or the construction as such may be innovated or borrowed into the language.

11.3.1 Clausal secondaries

Clausal secondaries juxtaposed to their primaries are typically called ASYNDETIC RELATIVE CLAUSES. As Table 11.3 shows, in the majority of dialects this construction is restricted to cases where the antecedent noun is indefinite.[17] The following is a typical example:

[15] I am grateful for Eran Cohen for this idea.

[16] We exclude adjectival secondaries, since these are normally marked by agreement of the adjective with the primary noun. While some loan-adjectives do not inflect, and thus attach to the noun in a pure juxtaposition construction, this is better seen as lexical property of these adjectives rather than the emergence of a new AC strategy.

[17] It should be noted that even in those dialects marked as INDF exceptions to the rule may occur.

Table 11.3: Distribution of juxtaposition constructions. Q = quantification primaries; INDF = indefinite primaries.

Region	Dialect	Secondaries	
		Noun	Clause
South-East Turkey	Hertevin	(+)	INDF
	Bohtan	+	+
	Bēṣpən		
	Gaznax		+
	Baz		
	Challa	(-)	
	Jilu		+
North-West Iraq	JZakho		INDF
	JAradhin		
	CAradhin		INDF
	Barwar	Q	INDF
	Betanure		
	Amədya		+
	Barzani		
	Alqosh		
	Qaraqosh		INDF
North-West Iran	JUrmi	Q	INDF
	Sardarid		
North-East Iraq	Diyana-Zariwaw	(-)	
	Arbel	Q^{+}	INDF
	Koy Sanjaq		
	Sulemaniyya	+	INDF
West Iran	JSanandaj	+	+
	CSanandaj		

(14) Barwar: **Noun–Clause**
ʾiθ-wa' xa= ràbban,' tíwɛ-wa gu= xa= gəppìθa.'
EX-PST INDF= monk sit-PST in= INDF= cave
'There was once a monk who lived in a cave.' (Khan 2008c: 961 [A15:1])

This example presents a typical usage situation an asyndetic relative clauses: the antecedent is introduced by the particle of existence and an indefinite determiner, and subsequently qualified by a clause. In such cases one may reasonably doubt the validity of the relative clause analysis, as an alternative analysis in terms of two separate clauses is viable as well ('There was once a monk. He lived in a cave.'). Thus, the relative wide distribution of this construction should be taken with a grain of salt, as in some cases the examples can be disputed.[18]

Cohen (2012: 138) raises the possibility that these constructions are a replication of an Arabic pattern. Indeed, Arabic innovated a pattern in which asyndetic relative clauses can occur after indefinite nouns (Badawi et al. 2004: 494; for the historical development see Pat-El 2014). This idea is corroborated by the fact that most of the dialects which exhibit this construction are located in Iraq, at most 100km away from the Arabic-speaking urban center of Mosul.[19]. We may similarly assume there were connections between the speakers of JUrmi and the J. communities in Iraq.[20] As for the C. Hertevin dialect in Turkey, this was in close geographical proximity to an Arabic vernacular.

Yet Arabic is not the only possible source. An alternative source may be a Sorani construction, in which the primary is marked by an *-êk* suffix before a clausal secondary (this suffix is often reduced to *ê*, but is clearly distinct from the Ezafe *-i*). The secondary may furthermore be marked by the relativizer *ke*, but this is not always the case.

As discussed in §9.7, the *-êk* suffix is identical to the indefinite suffix, and may very well be historically related to it, although synchronically it does not convey an indefinite sense (i.e. the primary may be definite). If we assume that in a prior stage of the language it was simply the indefinite marker, we get the following

[18]Paradoxically, the less-disputable cases are those where the secondary is a reduced clause, as these cannot occur as matrix clauses; see JZakho example (108) on page 145 and Qaraqosh example (123) on page 184.

[19]The Jewish NENA speakers of the region had regular contacts with the J. community of Mosul, which was predominantly Arabic speaking but had also bilingual NENA-speaking Jews originating in Kurdistan (Sabar 1976: XXV; 1984a; 1990: 54) Moreover, in the region we find also other Arabic speaking J. communities; see the map of Jastrow (1990: 4)

[20]As anecdotal evidence I can mention the case of Rabbi Ḥaim Yeshurun, whom I interviewed in Israel, who moved from Nerwa to Urmi around 1940.

formal construction: N-INDF {REL} Clause. Since the relativizer is optional to some extent, it is easy to see how this construction could be the source of the NENA construction. Furthermore, even if the *-êk* was never functionally identical to the indefinite suffix (or cognate with it), a speaker of NENA with knowledge of Sorani might mistakenly analyse it as the indefinite suffix, leading effectively to the same kind of contact influence.

A difficulty is presented by those dialects which do not restrict the use of asyndetic relative clauses to indefinite primaries, but allow it also with definite primaries, as in the following Jilu example:

(15) Jilu: **Noun–Clause**
ġzi-li o naša qem mexi-li təmmal
saw-1SG DEF.MS man PST hit.A3MS-P1SG yesterday
'I saw the man that hit me yesterday.' (Fox 1997: 81)

In JSanandaj (see examples (14)–(15) on page 230) this may be understood as part of the larger tendency to omit all AC markers in this dialect (see §11.3.2.2). In the other dialects, mostly present in Turkey with the exception of Amədya, the source of this generalized construction is not clear. It should be noted, moreover, that amongst these dialects, only Bohtan makes use of the generalized juxtaposition construction regularly and extensively. Since the speakers of Bohtan lived through several stages of immigration, and came in contact with various languages (Fox 2009: 3–5), the exact source (and time of appearance) of this construction is difficult to pinpoint.[21]

11.3.2 Nominal secondaries

11.3.2.1 Quantification expressions

In general, the juxtaposition construction with nouns as secondaries is less common in NENA. Yet, h ere again, we have to identify a special sub-type which reoccurs in several dialects, namely the case where the primary quantifies the secondary, as in the following examples:

(16) Barwar: **Q. Noun Phrase–Noun**
[xa= reša] tuma
one= head garlic
'one head of garlic' (Khan 2008c: 494 [B10:19])

[21]For instance, currently Bohtan speakers reside in Russia, and speak Russian as well. As some varieties of Russian allow asyndetic relative clauses (Murelli 2011: 397), this could theoretically be the source of the construction in Bohtan.

(17) Arbel: **Q. Noun Phrase–Noun**
[tré tannakè]' xiṭṭe'
two tins grain
'two tins of grain' (Khan 1999: 239 [B:116])

These cases are in the borderline of the AC domain, as semantically the secondary is in fact the head of the expression (see discussion in §7.7.3). Syntactically, we may prefer to analyse the primary as a phrasal realisation of the quantifier slot, which we assume is generally available in the NENA NP (see the QUANT slot in Table 1.2 on page 13 and the preceding discussion). Given such an analysis, it is no surprise that no AC marking is found.

Another possibility is to relate it to the Classical Arabic تمييز *tamyīz* construction, in which a counted or measured noun appears in the accusative, rather than genitive, case (Schulz 2004: 157). In Classical Arabic this construction is also used for the specification of material, and indeed, we find the last usage also in sporadic examples of NENA:

(18) Arbel: **Noun–Noun (material)**
ṣĭqilyé dehwà'
rings gold
'rings of gold' (Khan 1999: 239 [L:466])

While a direct influence of Classical Arabic on NENA might seem implausible,[22] the classical construction may have been mediated through the vernacular Iraqi Arabic dialect, which lost case markings but retained the general structure of this construction (though allowing optional marking of construct state on the primary).

(19) Iraqi Arabic: **Q. Noun–Noun**
ḥafna-{t} timman
handful-{FS.CST} rice
'a handful of rice' (Erwin 2004 [1963]: 375)

[22] One cannot completely rule out an influence of written Arabic on NENA, as the Early J. NENA homilies available to us (Nerwa) might have been redacted from Judeo-Arabic sources (Sabar 1984a: 201). Be that as it may, Sabar (1984a: 202) notes that the Arabic elements in these texts belong to the northern Iraqi Arabic *qeltu* dialects, which are of course different from the standard Classical Arabic.

(20) Iraqi Arabic: **Noun–Noun (material)**
sāʿa ðahab
watch gold
'a gold watch' (Erwin 2004 [1963]: 375)

Alternatively, we may postulate this as a common Semitic feature, which is preserved in NENA although not present in Syriac.[23]

Another alternative motivation is the fact that in some Kurdish dialects we also find the juxtaposition construction expressing quantification (the PARTITIVE RELATION of MacKenzie 1961: 63f.). As discussed in §9.8.1, in Kurmanji dialects this usage seems to be quite limited, while in Sorani dialects it is widespread. The following example is from the dialect of Sulemaniyya (=example (109) on page 289):

(21) Silêmanî: **Q. Noun Phrase–Noun**
[yek hegbe] pare
one bag money
'a bag of money' (MacKenzie 1961: 63 [29])

Thus, this construction may reflect an areal phenomenon rather than a specifically Semitic heritage.

11.3.2.2 General usage

A more general usage of the juxtaposition construction is found in two regions: Turkey and the Iraqi-Iranian border area (that is, outside the historical core of the NENA dialects). In Turkey, only Bohtan seems to use this construction regularly, in alternation with D-markers:

(22) Bohtan: **Noun–Noun**
tara gumota
door stables
'the door of the stables' (Fox 2009: 93)

Fox (2009: 92) postulates that this construction "may be the result of complete assimilation followed by simplification of the resulting geminate cluster: **tarəd gumota* > **tarəg gumota* > *tara gumota*." The difficulty with this explanation is

[23]It is interesting to note that we find a similar construction in Modern Hebrew. Thus, we find the ubiquitous colloquial example מנה פלאפל *mana falafel* 'one portion of falafel', in which no construct state marking is present.

that it does not explain the restoration of the Aramaic free state suffix *-a*. One may try to save this explanation by suggesting that the *d* marker assimilated to the following consonant when it was still procliticized to the secondary (i.e. before the emergence of the construct state suffix *-əd*), yet it is unclear why this happened specifically in this dialect. Given the complex immigration history of the Bohtan speakers (see end of §11.3.1 on page 360) we cannot preclude some unknown language contact motivating this construction.

In the other NENA dialects of Turkey, the construction is quite limited: In Challa we find it in a few expressions (notably *yoma šapsa* 'the Sabbath day'), and in Hertevin it occurs only when the primary is a loan-noun without an Aramaic inflectional ending. In the latter dialect, given that many of the Hertevin examples given by Jastrow (1988: 26) have primaries of Arabic origin, such as example (23), it may be more specifically a matter-cum-pattern replication of the Arabic CSC, in which the primary is normally left unaltered (unless it is a feminine noun).

(23) Hertevin: **Noun–Noun**
šekl ḥa zalama
appearance INDF man
'the appearance of a man' (Jastrow 1988: 26 [576])

A productive and extensive usage of the juxtaposition construction is found in my survey only in Sulemaniyya and JSanandaj in the Iraqi-Iranian border area.[24] See §8.3 for examples of JSanandaj, and the following examples for Sulemaniyya ((24)=example (9) on page 229). Note that, in these dialects, the *-a* ending of native Aramaic nouns cannot be analysed any more as designating the free state.

(24) Sulemaniyya: **Noun–Noun**
šəmma brona
name son
'the name of the boy' (Khan 2004: 192)

[24]The same construction is also found in the Iranian J. Saqqəz dialect, which is however not included in my survey. Goldenberg (1997: 11) brings the example *belá šultaná* 'king's house' from this dialect. In Iraq we find this construction also in Diyana-Zariwaw, but apparently only with the primary *šəmma* 'name':

(i) Diyana-Zariwaw: **Noun–Noun**
šəmma sawun-i
name grandfather-POSS.1SG
'my grandfather's name' (Napiorkowska 2015: 315)

(25) Sulemaniyya: **Noun–Noun**
brona mălək
son king
'the son of the king' (Khan 2007: 202)

It is not entirely clear how this construction developed. The limited geographical extent of this constructions points to a language contact origin, possibly from Sorani. Indeed, Khan (2007: 202) suggests that this construction results from the identification of the compounding Ezafe *-e* (see §9.6) with the Aramaic inflectional ending *-a*.[25] Thus, he compares example (25) with the following Silêmanî example:

(26) Silêmanî: **Noun–Noun**
kuř-e- paşa
son-EZ- king
'the king's son' (MacKenzie 1961: 64 [25])

This idea, however, poses some difficulties. First, as discussed in §9.6, the compounding Ezafe creates a nominal compound consisting of the two members of the construction. Consequently, the bond between the two members cannot be interrupted by other grammatical elements. For instance, a demonstrative pronoun can envelop such a phrase, but not intervene in the middle, judging by the examples at my disposal:

(27) Sorani: **Noun–Noun**
ئام هۆتێله باشه
em [hotêl-e- baş]-é
DEM.PROX hotel-EZ- good-DEM
'this good hotel' (Thackston 2006b: 11)

In Sulemaniyya, by contrast, we find intervening demonstrative pronouns and even complex secondaries, as in the following example:

(28) Sulemaniyya: **Noun–Noun Phrase**
bába [ʾó= brona [ga= libl-á-le ḥajì]] =yele.
father DEM= son REL= took-P3FS-A-3MS haji =COP.PST
'The father of the boy who took her away was a ḥāji.' (Khan 2004: 261 [R:146])

[25]Both are pronounced [æ]. The difference in transcription results from my decision to use the Kurdish Latinized orthography for Kurdish dialects (see footnote 3 on page 254).

Another difficulty relates to the fact that the compounding Ezafe itself is not borrowed in Sulemaniyya, nor in JSanandaj. If it were borrowed, we would expect it to appear on non-Aramaic loanwords (which normally lack an Aramaic inflectional ending) acting as primaries, but this is not the case. A scenario in which the Aramaic inflection ending is confounded with Ezafe seems implausible without the borrowing of the actual morpheme.

One could assume that the Ezafe was quickly reanalysed as ∅ marking in the NENA dialects concerned, and then extended to nouns not ending in *-a*. Yet in this case we would have to assume that the borrowed morpheme did not leave any trace. Indeed, in some neighbouring Kurdish dialects the compounding Ezafe is omitted following nouns ending in certain vowels, such as [a] or [e] (MacKenzie 1961: 64). This means that, even if it was borrowed and used following a native Aramaic noun, it would be realised as a ∅ rather than confounded with the Aramaic inflectional ending. This would provide an easy explanation for the juxtaposition construction used with plural primaries ending in *-e*:

(29) Sulemaniyya: **Noun–Noun**
bate Šlomo
houses Š.
'the houses of Shlomo' (Khan 2004: 192)

An alternative and arguably simpler hypothesis is to directly relate the NENA juxtaposition construction to a similar unmarked construction which is extant in some Sorani dialects, in particular Wârmâwa, which is geographically close to Sulemaniyya.[26] This is shown in the following example (=example (108) on page 288):

(30) Wârmâwa: **Noun–Noun**
meł Ḥacî
house H.
'the house of Haji' (MacKenzie 1961: 62, fn. 2 [246])

Such cases, if frequent enough, may provide a seed for the juxtaposition construction in Sulemaniyya, without positing a borrowing and reanalysis of the compounding Ezafe as equivalent to the Aramaic free state ending, though such a possibility cannot be completely excluded.

[26]The Wârmâwa juxtaposition construction seems to be most frequent with primaries marked by the indefinite suffix *-êk* (MacKenzie 1961: 62, fn. 2), which may in some contexts replace the Ezafe (see §9.7, but it does not exclude unmarked definite primaries.

On a broader view, as mentioned in §9.8, the juxtaposition construction is possibly an areal phenomenon, as it also attested in Gorani and in Persian. These languages may more easily account for the existence of the juxtaposition construction in JSanandaj, due to their closer geographical proximity to the latter dialect.

11.4 Matter replication

The constructions discussed above all make use of native Aramaic morphemic material, irrespective of the question of whether the development of these structures was influenced by language contact. In some dialects, however, we see clear BORROWING of morphemic material from Iranic languages, termed by Matras & Sakel (2007b) MATTER REPLICATION. As Table 11.4 on the next page shows, two types of morphemes are borrowed as grammatical markers of ACs: the Ezafe marker (in two shapes: *e* and *i*) and a subordinating particle of the general form /*kV*/. Moreover, the table makes clear that most of the matter replications took place in North-East Iraq and the Iranian regions. North-West Iraq is practically immune from this type of borrowing. This may indicate a more intensive contact situation in the former regions.

11.4.1 Borrowing of the Ezafe

Only in two dialects, Rustaqa and JSanandaj, is the Ezafe truly generalized. It is probably no coincidence that these dialects have by and large lost the inherited D-marking of ACs. Judging moreover by the data of JSanandaj (§8.7.2), it seems that the introduction of the Ezafe is relatively recent, as its usage is still to some extent privileged with loan-expressions. Moreover, it is quite probable that the Ezafe, which was first introduced into the language by way of loan-expressions, has expanded its usage domain due to the loss of the inherited D-marker.[27] A case in point in Sulemaniyya, which shows an intermediate stage of development: It has abandoned to a large extent the D-markers in favour of a juxtaposition construction (see §11.3.2), but the Ezafe markers are still constrained to loan-expressions.

In the following subsections we survey the occurrence of the Ezafe in the different geographical regions of the NENA-speaking area.

[27]For an elaboration of this idea in terms of FORGETTING the construct state marking, see Gutman (2015a).

Table 11.4: Borrowed AC markers. Parentheses indicate restricted or marginal use.

Region	Dialect	Ezafe	Subordinator
South-East Turkey	Hertevin		
	Bohtan		
	Bēṣpən		
	Gaznax	(*e*)	
	Baz		
	Challa	(*e*, *i*)	
	Jilu		
North-West Iraq	JZakho		
	JAradhin		
	CAradhin		
	Barwar		
	Betanure		
	Amədya		
	Barzani		
	Alqosh		
	Qaraqosh		
North-West Iran	JUrmi		*ki-{t}*
	Sardarid		*qäd*, *či*
North-East Iraq	Rustaqa	*i*	
	Diyana-Zariwaw		
	Arbel	(*i*)	
	Koy Sanjaq		*ka*
	Sulemaniyya	(*i*)	*ga~ka*
West Iran	JSanandaj	*e*	*ke*, *ya*
	CSanandaj		

11.4.1.1 North-East Iraq: *i* Ezafe

Three out of five dialects in the North-East Iraq region exhibit usage of the Ezafe particle *-i*, in all probability borrowed from the co-territorial Sorani dialects (cf. Khan 2002b: 408).

Khan (1999: 169) speculates that the *-i* morpheme is a reduction of the *ay* demonstrative, which is used as a linker in JUrmi, and as a relativizer in the Bible translation of Ruwandiz (see §10.6.4). We maintain, however, that the two morphemes should not be confounded, not least since a reduction of *ay* would normally yield an *ē* vowel.[28]

Another hypothesis given by Khan (1999: 168) is that the *-i* segment results from the elision of the *d* segment of the construct state *-əd* suffix, following the assimilation of the latter to the initial consonant of the subsequent word (i.e. the secondary).[29] The fact that the *i* morpheme can occur following an *-əd* suffix is counter-indicative of this idea. Yet the phonetic similarity between the vocalic nucleus of the *-əd* suffix (namely, the /ə/ segment) and the /i/ segment may have led bilingual speakers (of Sorani and NENA) to perceive the /ə/ segment as being the *-i* Ezafe, thus enhancing the availability of the latter morpheme. Indeed, Khan (1999: 169) tentatively suggests such a link: "It may be more than a coincidence, however, that *-i* is also the *izafe* particle in the Kurdish dialects of the region (MacKenzie 1961: 61–64) and this may have had an influence on the Neo-Aramaic form." Weighing the (admittedly meagre) evidence, it seems that a purely internal phonological process cannot account for the distribution of the *-i* suffix. Rather, it must have been initially borrowed from Sorani, and only subsequently could there be a reanalysis of a stranding /ə/ of the *-əd* suffix as the Ezafe.

11.4.1.1.1 Rustaqa In this dialect the Ezafe suffix has replaced the native D-markers, except following some interrogative pronouns discussed below (Khan 2002b: 408f.). In most cases it is appended after the Aramaic *-a* ending, but in some cases it replaces it, similarly to the native *-əd* suffix.[30]

[28]See in this respect also footnote 94 on page 343.

[29]Ideally, an /i/ and an /ə/ should be distinct phonetically, but in lax pronunciation both may be produced as [ɪ].

[30]I have conducted some interviews with elderly Rustaqa speakers in Israel, November 2012. Due to the complexity of the material and time constraints I have not yet been able to transcribe it in full, so my data relies mostly on Khan (2002b). I could however verify the existence of the Ezafe suffix.

(31) Rustaqa: **Noun–Noun**
ṣiwa-i xabuše
tree-EZ apples
'an apple tree' (own fieldwork)

(32) Rustaqa: **Noun–Noun**
baxt-i Šlomo
wife-EZ Š.
'the wife of Shlomo' (Khan 2002b: 409)

As in Sorani, the Ezafe can appear before a clausal secondary:

(33) Rustaqa: **Noun–Clause**
ʾo gora-y [timmal idye-le] (dost =e)
DEF man-EZ yesterday came-3MS friend =COP
'The man who came yesterday (is my friend).' (Khan 2002b: 409)

Khan (2002b: 409) does not mention cases of the Ezafe mediating between a noun and an adjective. He does however give a case where the Ezafe is used to nominalize an adjective:

(34) Rustaqa: ∅–**Adjective**
(šáqil) i rabta
take.IMP EZ big.FS
'(Take) the big one!' (Khan 2002b: 409)

This usage is analogous to the independent Ezafe in Sorani (see example (92) on page 283).

The historical *d-* linker is only conserved as apparent construct state marking after some interrogative pronouns preceding clausal secondaries, in which case it transforms them to indefinite pronouns:

(35) Rustaqa: **Pronoun–Clause**
manni-t [ade bel-an] (paṣix)
who-CST come house-POSS.1PL please.SBJV.3MS
'Whoever comes to our house (will be pleased).' (Khan 2002b: 409)

(36) Rustaqa: **Pronoun–Clause**
ma-t *[kayf-ox* *made]* *(ʾol)*
what-CST pleasure-POSS.2MS bring.3MS do.IMP
'(Do) what brings you pleasure!' (Khan 2002b: 409)

The fact that the erstwhile construct state *-d* suffix is conserved in this context hints that the *-əd* construct state suffix was operative in a precursor of Rustaqa. The indefinite pronouns *mannit* 'whoever' and *mat* 'whatever' must have conserved this segment since they have been grammaticalised as such.[31] Yet the */-d/* segment does not operate any more as a true construct state suffix, and indeed it can be followed by the Ezafe suffix.

(37) Rustaqa: **Pronoun–Clause**
manni-t-i *abe* *(maṣe* *hade)*
who-CST-EZ SBJV.want.3MS can.3MS come.SBJV.3MS
'Whoever wants (can come).' (Khan 2002b: 409)

(38) Rustaqa: **Pronoun–Clause**
ma-t-i *abet* *(ʾol)*
what-CST-EZ SBJV.want.2MS do.IMP
'(Do) what you want!' (Khan 2002b: 409)

Additionally, we find the historical *did-* pronominal base. In the following example it appears after the Modern Hebrew loan-expression עולה חדש *ʿole ḥadaš* 'new immigrant to Israel'.

(39) Rustaqa: **Noun Phrase–Pronoun**
hole *hadaš did-an*
immigrant new GEN-1PL
'our new immigrants' (own fieldwork)

11.4.1.1.2 Arbel In Arbel, we find the *i* Ezafe virtually only in the speech of one informant of Khan (1999), originating from the town of Batas (50 km northeast of Arbel). Occasionally, the Ezafe appears after the native *-əd* suffix, as in the following example:

[31] The same indefinite pronouns are found in other dialects as well. See JZakho examples (22)–(23) on page 120 and JUrmi examples (37)–(38) on page 197.

(40) Arbel: **Noun–Noun**
kullà mamlakát-it =*i*[32] *Kurdistán*
all towns-CST EZ= K.
'all the towns of Kurdistan' (Khan 1999: 169 [B:146])

More frequently, however, it replaces it:

(41) Arbel: **Noun–Noun**
kolā́n-ĭ mšilmāne
street-EZ Muslims
'the streets of the Muslims' (Khan 1999: 168 [B:47])

(42) Arbel: **Noun–Pronoun**
ʾízl-ĭ díd-i
wool-EZ GEN-1SG
'my wool' (Khan 1999: 219 [B:127])

(43) Arbel: **Noun–Adjective**
b= *ṣalm-ĭ́ komé*
in= face(PL)-EZ black.PL
'with a dark face' (Khan 1999: 229 [B:111])

Khan (1999: 168) attributes the latter occurrences to the elision of the /*d*/ segment of the *-əd* suffix, and transcribes the ending as <*ĭ*> which phonetically should be understood as [ə] or [ɪ]. As discussed at the introduction of §11.4.1.1 we prefer to treat all these cases as borrowing of the Ezafe.[33] The co-occurrence of the Ezafe with an adjective ((43) above) is typical of the Iranic construction, but extant in Arbel also with the native *-əd* suffix (see example (22) on page 317).

Note also the following example, where Khan analyses the *-i* as the Ezafe, most probably because the *-i* suffix does not replace the primary's *-a* ending:[34]

[32]Khan transcribes this example with the Ezafe *i* attached to *Kurdistán*. Listening to the example, it sounds to me rather syllabified with the preceding word.

[33]Listening to the available recordings, moreover, I could not hear a clear difference between the *-ĭ* and *-i* suffixes. Thus, in Khan (1999: 540 [B:145]) we find the expression *b-dáwr-ĭ Pā́ša-i Kòra* 'In the time of P. K.'. To my ear, the two *-i* suffixes sound identical, notwithstanding the fact that the first one replaces an *-a* ending. Note the second one is clearly a Kurdish Ezafe as it is part of a Kurdish proper noun.

[34]This example is exceptional also in that it is produced by another informant, resident of Girdmāla, 20 km south of Arbel.

(44) Arbel: **Pronoun–Noun Phrase**
hemà-i [xà ṭpurt-it hula'à]
which-EZ INDF fingernail-CST Jew
'whatever fingernail of a Jew' (Khan 1999: 170 [Y:182])

11.4.1.1.3 Sulemaniyya In Sulemaniyya the Ezafe seems to occur only after loanwords, both nouns and prepositions (Khan 2004: 192–193).[35]

(45) Sulemaniyya: **Noun–Noun**
ḥukmát-i 'Iráq
government-EZ I.
'the government of Iraq' (Khan 2004: 192 [A:5])

(46) Sulemaniyya: **Noun–Pronoun**
maktab-i did-an
school-EZ GEN-1PL
'our school' (Khan 2004: 253)

(47) Sulemaniyya: **Adverbial–Noun**
ga-báyn-i 'o= guḏá =w 'o= lo'à
in-between-EZ DEF= wall =and DEF= room
'between the wall and the room' (Khan 2004: 214 [V])

As discussed in §11.4.1, the usage of the Ezafe only with loan-expressions in these dialects may indicate that in general the Ezafe found in NENA dialects was imported through loan-expressions, and only subsequently its usage was extended to native primaries in some dialects, such as JSanandaj discussed in the next paragraph.[36]

[35]The preposition *báyn-* 'between' appearing in (47) is listed by Khan (2004: 598) as originating in Kurdish. Of course, it must be ultimately borrowed from Arabic بَيْنَ *bayna.* While Aramaic has a cognate preposition *ben* the diphthong */ay/* seems to indicate a foreign origin, or at least a merger of the two.

[36]It is interesting to note that also in the Turkic languages of Iran the Persian Ezafe is normally borrowed only as part of Persian expressions, and only rarely with native Turkic words. See Kıral (2006) for a discussion.

11.4.1.2 West Iran: J. Sanandaj

Among the sampled dialects of Iran, we find the Ezafe only in JSanandaj, as detailed in §8.7.2.[37] The form of the Ezafe *-e* is indicative of its Persian origin, as well as its typical occurrence inside Persian phrases. Its usage, however, has been extended beyond the domain of fixed Persian phrases, as discussed there.

11.4.1.3 South-East Turkey

In South-East Turkey, the usage of the Ezafe is sporadically attested, in very particular usage. Thus, in Challa we find the following loan-phrase. While the nouns are of Arabic origin, the usage of the Ezafe indicates the expression must have been borrowed from Kurmanji.

(48) Challa: **Noun–Noun**
ʾawlād-e rasū́l
children-EZ Messenger
'descendant of the Messenger' (Fassberg 2010: 56)

A possible productive use can be found in the following example:

(49) Challa: **Adverbial–noun**
tuxm-i xalwa la pāyəš go xədyawás did-u
kind-EZ milk NEG remain in breasts.CST GEN-3PL
'No trace of milk remains in their breasts.' (Fassberg 2010: 56, fn. 46)

An interesting development is presented by the Judi-dialects, where the Ezafe ending has been grammaticalised to become a lexical ending meaning 'descendant of'.[38] This indicates that the Ezafe was only borrowed as part of proper names in these dialects.

(50) Gaznax: **Noun–Noun**
Yaqo-ye Musa
Y.-EZ M.
'Yaqo son of Musa' (Gutman 2015c: 317 (25))

[37] Garbell (1965a: 171, §2.32.12) mentions the usage of the Sorani Ezafe *i* in J. Solduz and Šĭno, but we have no further information on this. See footnote 94 on page 343.

[38] I am grateful to Joseph Alichoran, for pointing this out for me.

11.4.2 Borrowing of subordinating particles

11.4.2.1 North-East Iraq

In Sulemaniyya and Koy Sanjaq we find the Sorani subordinator *ka* borrowed. The Sorani particle can act both as a relativizer and as a complementizer (much like the NENA linker *d-~did*), and it appears in the two roles also in the recipient NENA dialects. In Koy Sanjaq it is borrowed simply as *ka*, while in Sulemaniyya it often appears as *ga*.[39] In both dialects, it can co-occur as a relativizer with any other available AC marking (such as the Koy Sanjaq linker *od* or the Sulemaniyya construct state ending).

(51) Koy Sanjaq: **Noun–Clause**
ʾo ʿaqubrona ʾod ka xlíṣwāle
DEM.DIST.SG mouse LNK REL saved-PST-3MS
'that mouse who had been saved' (Mutzafi 2004a: 63 [N 20])

(52) Sulemaniyya: **Noun–Clause**
bába ʾó= brona ga= libl-á-le ḥajì =yele.ˈ
father DEM= son REL= took-P3FS-A3MS ḥaji =COP.PST.3MS
'The father of the boy who took her away was a ḥāji.' (Khan 2004: 414 [R:146])

(53) Sulemaniyya: **Pronoun–Clause**
ʾó-d ga= k-imr-án-wa zarandà =y
DEM-CST REL= IND-say-1SG-PST tough =COP
'the one whom I was just saying was tough' (Khan 2004: 418 [R:135])

As a complementizer we find the following example:

(54) Sulemaniyya: **Verb–Clause**
kăyén-wa ga= ʾó bratá il= d-o= bróna gbà.ˈ
know.3PL-PST COMP= DEM girl to= GEN-DEM= boy want.3FS
'They would know that the girl loved the boy.' (Khan 2004: 440 [R:29])

[39] The reason for this shift is not clear. It may stem from an analogy to the existing preposition *ga* 'in'.

11.4.2.2 North-West Iran

In North-West Iran we find various forms of the relativizer which may be borrowed from Kurmanji *ḳu*[40], from Persian که *kæ* or from Azeri *ki*. Younansardaroud (2001: 180) relates the Sardarid form *či* to the Persian relativizer *kæ*,[41] while Garbell (1965a: 172, §2.32.1.(5)) relates the JUrmi form *ki* to the Azeri source. The only evidence for a Kurmanji influence may be the use of the uvular /*q*/ segment in Sardarid *qad*, which may correspond to the unaspirated *ḳ* of the Kurmanji relativizer. Yet it may also be related to preposition *qa, qāt* 'for' present in the dialect.

The /*d*/ segment of Sardarid *qäd* is probably a retention of the Aramaic *d-*, and can be analysed as an explicit construct state marking of the relativizer. This marking can be optionally found in JUrmi as well, in the form *kit* (see §7.6.4).

Various examples of the relativizer in JUrmi are given in §7.6. The usage in Sardarid is quite similar. Note that it can optionally co-occur with construct state marking on the primary:

(55) Sardarid: **Noun–Clause**
⁺o čtav-{əd} qad/či at zvin-ət len mačuḥa
DEF book-{CST} REL 2MS bought-2MS NEG.COP.1SG found
'The book that you bought, I cannot find (it).' (Younansardaroud 2001: 181)

11.4.2.3 West-Iran

In West-Iran we find the relativizer *ke* only in JSanandaj, and not in adjacent CSanandaj. In this case, a Persian as well as a Sorani origin is possible. Given the great impact of Persian on this dialect, the former option seems preferable. Alongside the *ke* relativizer we find also a *ya* relativizer, which may be related to the Persian Ezafe, the latter sometimes appearing with an initial glide. We note indeed that while *ke* is compatible with the primary-marking Ezafe, this is not the case with *ya*. Various usage examples of both are given in §8.6.

11.5 Case study: The marking of ordinal numbers

To show the diversity of NENA dialects in a nutshell, it is illuminating to study a system on the fringes of the AC system, namely the qualification of nouns by

[40] This is the form of standard Kurmanji, but the Urmia dialect may show some variation.
[41] It is not clear whether she relates the form *qad* as well to a Persian origin.

ordinal numbers. Ordinal numbers ('first', 'second', etc.) are akin to adjectives in many languages, in contrast to the cardinal numbers ('one', 'two', etc.) which relate directly to quantification. In Semitic languages, and in NENA in particular, ordinals show a special behaviour, mixing characteristics of adjectives with those of nominal attributes.[42] The NENA ordinal system is interesting in that it conserves some characteristics of ancient strata (as shown by its affinity to Syriac), while at the same time it shows similarities to contact languages.

As the ordinal 'first' behaves specially in some respects, it deserves a separate discussion in the next section, followed by a treatment of the higher ordinals.

11.5.1 The ordinal 'first'

A particularity of the ordinal 'first' in Semitic languages is that every Semitic language-branch has a unique form to express it, and it is thus not part of a shared Semitic heritage, but rather an independent innovation of each branch (Loewenstamm 1955). The ordinal 'first' shows often, moreover, a special morpho-syntactic behaviour as compared to the other numerals, and NENA is no exception.

In many NENA dialects we find an adjectival ordinal *qamāya* 'first', related to Syriac ܩܕܡܝܐ *qaḏmāyā*. Like other adjectives, it usually appears after the qualified noun and agrees with it in number and gender, as in the following example (=example (71) on page 380).

(56) Alqosh: **Noun–Ordinal (first)**
yóma qamā́ya
day(MS) first.MS
'the first day' (Coghill 2003: 293 [A:137])

This ordinal can be nominalized like other adjectives, namely by putting a determiner before it:

(57) CAradhin: ∅–**Ordinal (first)**
aw qamāya
DEF.MS first.MS
'the first' (Krotkoff 1982: 22 [112])

[42]For example, in the Biblical Hebrew phrase יום הששי *yōm haš-šišši* 'the sixth day' (Genesis 1:31), the ordinal *šišši* agrees in gender and number with the head *yōm* as an adjective, but the placement of the definite article *ha-* is typical of the Hebrew CSC. Incidently, a similar construction is found in Iraqi Arabic; see example (61) on page 378.

Some dialects have borrowed the Arabic ordinal أَوَّل *ʾawwal* ‘first’. In Arabic, both the written standard and the Iraqi Arabic vernacular, this ordinal (like others) can appear after the qualified noun as an inflecting adjective, or preceding the qualified noun while forming with it a CSC, invariably in the MS form (Schulz 2004: 224; Erwin 2004 [1963]: 366f.).[43] The adjectival usage of *ʾawwal* has not been adopted in NENA, but in several NENA dialects we find the uninflecting ordinal *ʾawwal* (or a similar form) preceding the qualified noun, mimicking the structure of the Arabic CSC.

(58) Arbel: **Noun–Ordinal (first)**
ʾáwwal baxtá
first woman
‘the first woman’ (Khan 1999: 181)

Fassberg (2010: 92, fn. 102) notes that the form *ʾawwal* is attested in Palestinian Aramaic since the Middle Ages, and also in NENA it is found in the earliest strata, namely Nerwa, as shown in the examples below. Note, however, that these are very particular occurrences, having in common the adverbial meaning of ‘first time’.[44]

(59) Nerwa: **Noun–Ordinal (first)**
אאהין וילא אול גאר דפלטלא מנד קוותי
ʾāhin we-la ʾawwal jār d= pləṭ-la mənn-əd quwətt-i
3FS COP.PST-3FS first time LNK= left-3FS from-CST strength-POSS.1SG
‘It was the first time that it came out of my potency.’ (*Midraš Parašat Wayḥi* 29:3 ed. by Sabar 1984b: 85, line 27)

(60) Nerwa: **Adverbial Clause–Ordinal (first)**
אוול מאד מירתי
ʾawwal ma-d mīrr-ət-ti
first what-CST said-P2MS-A1SG
‘at first when I told you’ (*Midraš Parašat Wayḥi* 27:29 ed. by Sabar 1984b: 51, line 2)

[43]To be sure, in the written standard language the ordinal ‘first’ can inflect in the pre-nominal position as well, but the MS form is frequently used with disregard for gender agreement (Badawi et al. 2004: 271).

[44]Fassberg (2010: 92, fn. 102) apparently did not consult the actual examples but only the occurrence of *ʾawwal* in the glossary of Sabar (1984b: 248). For this reason he relates it to the somewhat different construction in example (63). Note that a similar restricted use of *ʾawwal* is found also in contemporary NENA, such as in Alqosh, where it is found only in the expressions *ʾáwwal-ga* ‘the first time’ and *ʾáwwal-məndi* ‘firstly’ (Coghill 2003: 284).

In vernacular Iraqi Arabic we find additionally a construction in which the ordinal appears as a secondary of the CSC.

(61) Iraqi Arabic: **Noun–Ordinal**
yōm il-ʾawwal
day(MS) DEF-first.MS
'the first day' (Erwin 2004 [1963]: 367)

(62) Iraqi Arabic: **Noun–Ordinal**
san-t il-ʾūla
year-FS.CST DEF-first.FS
'the first year' (Erwin 2004 [1963]: 367)

A similar construction is found in some NENA dialects, but the ordinal *ʾawwal* never inflects. Both in Iraqi Arabic and in NENA this construction is in fact not limited to the ordinal 'first'.

(63) Challa: **Noun–Ordinal (first)**
yom ʾawwal
day.CST first
'the first day' (Fassberg 2010: 92)

(64) Arbel: **Noun–Ordinal (first)**
tré= yom-it ʾàwwal
two= day-CST first
'two first days' (Khan 1999: 181 [B:72])

While this construction seems thus to be a pattern-cum-matter replication from vernacular Arabic, we find in Arbel the Kurdish Kurmanji form *ʾawwalí* alongside *ʾáwwal* (cf. Khan 1999: 181).[45]

(65) Arbel: **Noun–Ordinal (first)**
gor-it ʾawwalí
man-CST first
'the first man' (Khan 1999: 181)

The above example may further hint at a Kurmanji influence, if we consider the *-əd* suffix to be the functional equivalent of the Kurdish Ezafe, since in Kur-

[45]In Kurmanji orthography it is written *ewel(î)*. As discussed in §9.4.5 the final *-î* ending probably reflects a lexicalised Kurmanji oblique ending.

dish (both Kurmanji and Sorani) ordinals follow the Ezafe (see §9.4.5). Instead of arguing decisively in favour of one option or another, it seems that similarly to other domains of the AC system, this pattern (head-marked primary followed by an ordinal) represents an areal phenomenon (see further discussion of this in the next section).

Finally, in the dialects of Sulemaniyya and JSanandaj we find the Arabic ordinal 'first' (borrowed through Sorani *(h)eweḷ*[46]) following the noun without any further marking.[47] This is expected in these dialects, given their widespread usage of the juxtaposition construction (see §11.3).

(66) Sulemaniyya: **Noun–Ordinal (first)**
gorá hawwál
first man
'the first man' (Khan 2004: 277)

In Sulemaniyya, but not in JSanandaj, a native inflecting ordinal *qamayna* 'first.MS' may be used instead (Khan 2004: 206).

11.5.2 Higher ordinals

In most NENA dialects, the remaining ordinals are formed by putting a cardinal numeral after a construct state noun or a linker. In some dialects the numeral agrees, moreover, with the head noun in number and gender (at least for the numerals 2–10).[48] This system is clearly inherited from prior strata of Aramaic, as it appears in Syriac as well (see §3.5.5).

Recall that in Syriac the numeral must appear after the linker *d-*, as described in §3.5.5. In NENA dialects, however, we find the numerals after different kinds of linkers, as well as the Neo-CSC (*-əd* suffix) and apocopate CSC. Thus, in NENA we see a generalisation of the Syriac pattern in that all types of construct state heads, irrespective of their forms, can govern a numeral acting as an ordinal. This is shown in the following examples ((69)=example (60) on page 131).

[46]In Sorani we find the forms ئەوەڵ *ʾeweḷ* and هەوەڵ *heweḷ* (Hakem 2012: 48) alongside the regularly formed یەکەم *yêkem* (Thackston 2006b: 18).

[47]In JSanandaj an Ezafe may intervene, or alternatively the ordinal may precede the head. Compare examples (45) on page 239, (13) on page 230 and (25) on page 234.

[48]In general, this happens in the dialects which have conserved a gender distinction in the cardinal system.

(67) Challa: **Noun–Ordinal**
yom *tre*
day.CST two
'the second day' (Fassberg 2010: 92)

(68) Challa: **Noun–Ordinal**
yarx-əd *ʾarba*
month-CST four
'the fourth month' (Fassberg 2010: 45)

(69) JZakho: **Noun–Ordinal**
ē *baxta* *dīd* *ṭḷāha*
DEF.FS woman LNK three
'the third wife' (Cohen 2012: 95 (8))

The closest resemblance to Syriac is shown by the Qaraqosh dialects, where an agreeing numeral is preceded by the linker *d-*, as in the following example (=example (93) on page 176). Note that Qaraqosh has also borrowed an Arabic pattern; see example (82) on page 384.

(70) Qaraqosh: **Noun–Ordinal**
báxta *d=* *tə́ttə*
woman LNK= second.FS
'the second woman' (Khan 2002a: 225)

As a linker is pronominal, it suffices to nominalize the ordinal, yet it is often preceded by a determiner. Consider the following two Alqosh examples:

(71) Alqosh: **Noun–Ordinal**
yóma *qamā́ya* *lɛ̀θ* *=u'* ***de=*** ***trḗ*** *lɛ̀θ* *=u'*
day(MS) first.MS NEG.EX =and LNK= two.MS NEG.EX =and
'The first day there was nothing, and the second (day) there was nothing.' (Coghill 2003: 293 [A:137])

(72) Alqosh: **∅–Ordinal**
ʾɛ= t= xámmeš
DEF.FS LNK= five.FS
'the fifth one' (Coghill 2003: 293 [A])

See also the similar JZakho examples (65)–(66) on page 133.

While these constructions clearly show continuity with Syriac, they are also structurally similar to constructions in neighbouring languages. As we saw in examples (61)–(62) on page 378, the Iraqi Arabic CSC is also used with inflecting ordinals as secondaries.

(73) Iraqi Arabic: **Noun–Ordinal**
marr-t iθ-θānya
time-FS.CST DEF-second.FS
'the second time, the next time' (Erwin 2004 [1963]: 367)

Note that in contrast to the NENA and Syriac constructions, the secondary is a true adjectival ordinal, distinct from the corresponding cardinal form, e.g. *θnēn* 'two' (see Erwin 2004 [1963]: 268).

The NENA construction is, moreover, similar to the construction found in the neighbouring Iranic languages. Thus, both in Kurmanji and Sorani, as well as in Persian, we find the ordinal numbers follow an Ezafe marked head noun, which is functionally equivalent to a construct state noun in Aramaic. Similarly to example (71), the ordinals can also be nominalized by appearing after an independent Ezafe (example (74)=example (44) on page 271; example (75)=example (46) on page 271; example (76)=example (85) on page 282):

(74) Kurmanji: **Noun–Ordinal**
roj-a sisi-yan
day-EZ.DEF.FS three-OBL.PL
'(on the) third day' (Thackston 2006a: 25)

(75) Silêmanî: **Noun–Ordinal**
řêga-y sê-hem
third-EZ three-ORD
'the third road' (MacKenzie 1961: 72 [47])

(76) Akre: ∅–**Ordinal**
yê dw-ê ... yê sê-yê
EZ.MS two-ORD ... EZ.MS three-ORD
'the second... third one' (MacKenzie 1961: 163 [562])

Morphologically, the Kurdish numerals show a number of differences in comparison to native Aramaic numerals. First, in accordance with some NENA dialects but in contrast with the Syriac construction and the more conservative NENA dialects, the numerals do not show gender or number features. In contrast to all NENA dialects and the ordinals appearing in the Syriac linker construction, the ordinals are clearly marked as distinct from the corresponding cardinals by a dedicated suffix.[49] In this respect they show a certain affinity with the Syriac adjectival ordinals which are marked by the derivational suffix *-āyā*, but recall that these ordinals are used in the adjectival juxtaposition-cum-agreement construction (see example (105) on page 85).

Given the partial similarities with Syriac, vernacular Arabic, as well as with Kurdish dialects, should the NENA construction be related to internal developments or to language contact? Some authors prefer the latter option. Garbell (1965a: 172) thus asserts that the NENA construction is an "exact parallel to the K[urdish] construction." Noorlander (2014: 214) claims that the Syriac linker construction was used only in a "chronological sense" (i.e. for enumerating days, months etc.) and that in NENA its scope was "extended and [it] ultimately replaced the originally [Syriac-like] productive ordinal adjectives [...] most likely due to contact with Kurdish." Yet, just as in the case of the adoption of the Neo-CSC suffix *-əd* (see §10.4.2), we cannot be sure what the precise role of language contact was, or even what the direction of borrowing was: from Kurdish to Aramaic or vice versa (or both, in different periods). Even the disappearance of agreement features of the numerals, which may be attributed to a Kurdish origin, reflect an areal (and possibly universal) tendency to erode inflectional features with time.

While pattern replication is thus difficult to ascertain, we find clear cases of matter borrowing, namely the borrowing of the Sorani derivational affix *-emîn*. In

[49] As discussed in §9.4.5, in standard Kurmanji the suffix *-yan* represents the plural oblique case suffix, which is grammatically expected due to the syntactic position of ordinals following the Ezafe. In the dialectal data (as in Akre above), MacKenzie (1961: 170) reports rather on the usage of the suffix *-ê*, which is possibly related to the superlative suffix (see footnote 23 on page 270). In Sorani, on the other hand, the oblique case is no longer productive, and the suffix *-hem*, while historically possibly related to the plural oblique case marker, must be seen as an ordinal derivational suffix.

Sorani, an ordinal thus marked must precede the head noun, as in the following example (=example (117) on page 291):[50]

(77) Silêmanî: **Noun–Ordinal**
yek-em-în jar
one-ORD-SUPER time
'for the first time' (MacKenzie 1961: 73)

The suffix *-em(in)* is also found in Persian, where it behaves similarly to Sorani (Balaÿ & Esmaïli 2013: 262), and is in fact also borrowed into Kurmanji (Thackston 2006a: 25), but without changing the post-nominal position of the ordinal.

Some NENA dialects (Arbel, Koy Sanjaq, Sulemaniyya, JUrmi and JSanandaj) have borrowed the Sorani ordinal suffix as *-min*, either directly from the latter or through Kurmanji (see also Garbell 1965a: 166, §1.22.3). In JUrmi and JSanandaj the ordinals thus formed can appear before the qualified noun (see examples (80) on the next page and (127) on page 222),[51] while in Arbel and Koy Sanjaq the ordinals must follow a construct state noun or a linker, thus showing greater affinity with the Kurmanji construction, as well as with the native Aramaic construction.[52]

(78) Arbel: **Noun–Ordinal**
báxt-ət tre-mín
woman-CST two-ORD
'the second woman' (Khan 1999: 181)

(79) Koy Sanjaq: **Noun–Ordinal**
yā́ləd ʾod tre-min
child LNK two-ORD
'the second child' (Mutzafi 2004a: 168)

[50]As discussed in §9.8.4, this suffix is composed of two parts: *-em*, the ordinal suffix proper, and *-în*, which is normally used to form superlative adjectives. Superlative adjectives thus marked precede their head noun. *In passim*, we note here two further areal phenomena: 1) The relationship between superlative form and ordinals exists also in Arabic, though only for the ordinal 'first'. 2) The positioning of superlative adjectives before the qualified noun is found also in Arabic, as well as in NENA; see JZakho examples (32)–(33) on page 123 and footnote 10 there.

[51]In JUrmi we find the suffix *-mənji*. Garbell (1965a: 166) explains the ending *-ji* as a further ordinal suffix borrowed from Azeri.

[52]In JUrmi the ordinal suffix may be absent when numerals higher than ten are used, and then the numeral must appear in the CSC or ALC (Khan 2008b: 187).

In JSanandaj we find in fact both the pre-nominal and post-nominal positions for derived ordinals, the latter optionally following an Ezafe. Although arguably JSanandaj is the NENA dialect most influenced by Iranic language contact, it permits the optional suffixation of an Aramaic inflectional suffix on top of the Iranic derivational suffix (example (80)=example (26) on page 234; example (81)=example (46) on page 239 and example (21) on page 232).

(80) JSanandaj: **Noun–Ordinal**
tre-min-{ta} baxta
two-ORD-{FS} woman
'the second women' (Khan 2009b: 213)

(81) JSanandaj: **Noun–Ordinal**
baxtá-{e} tre-min-{ta}
woman-{EZ} two-ORD-{FS}
'the second woman' (Khan 2009b: 213)

The JSanandaj ordinal is thus adjectival in nature and resembles the Syriac adjectival ordinals structurally, notwithstanding the use of a loan-morpheme. When following the Ezafe, it approaches moreover the Syriac ordinal linker construction; recall, however, that in Syriac the secondaries of the latter construction are inflecting cardinals (which have a special inflection pattern), rather than the adjectival ordinals.

Finally, in Qaraqosh, being in close contact with the Arabic-speaking city of Mosul, we find a pattern-cum-matter replication of the Arabic CSC headed (syntactically) by ordinal adjectives. Compare the following two examples (example (82)=example (111) on page 181):

(82) Qaraqosh: **Noun–Ordinal**
ʾu= θáləθ yóma
and= third day
'the third day' (Khan 2002a: 640 [F:72])

(83) Iraqi Arabic: **Noun–Ordinal**
θāliθ šahar
third.MS month
'the third month' (Erwin 2004 [1963]: 368)

Note that both in the Arabic vernacular and in the Qaraqosh example the ordinal is invariably in the MS form, and also that this construction yields a definite meaning, although no definite marker is present.

11.5.3 Case study conclusions

To conclude, in the sub-system of ordinal numbers the NENA dialects exhibit constructions that continue classical Aramaic strategies while resembling patterns from contact languages. The interaction between these two sources lead to high dialectal variation, each dialect showing a unique combination of constructions and features, as shown in Table 11.5.

Table 11.5: Ordinal constructions in select NENA dialects and model languages. A (+) or non-blank entry denotes a construction is available, with following {optional} qualifications: ORD=numerals marked as ordinals (distinct from cardinals); AGR=numeral agrees with primary; 1st = restricted to ordinal 'first', Arabic = Arabic loan-ordinals.

		N Ord	Ord N	N.CST Ord	LNK Ord
Syriac		ORD.AGR			AGR
Iraqi Arabic		ORD.AGR	ORD	ORD.AGR	
Kurmanji				ORD	ORD
Sorani			ORD	ORD	
NENA dialects					
SE Turkey	Challa			+	
NW Iraq	JZakho	1st.AGR		+	+
NW Iraq	Qaraqosh	1st.AGR	=Arabic		AGR
NW Iran	JUrmi		ORD	{ORD}	{ORD}
NE Iraq	Arbel		1st	{ORD}	
NE Iraq	Sulemaniyya	{1st.AGR}	1st	1st	
W Iran	JSanandaj	ORD.{AGR}	ORD.{AGR}	ORD.{AGR}	

At the same time, a comparison of the various dialects and contact languages reveals also recurring patterns, notably the CST-marked construction with numeral secondaries. This situation is symptomatic of the entire AC system of NENA dialects: While each dialect permits idiosyncratic constructions and variations, the usage of a head-marking construction reoccurs again and again, both in the NENA dialects and in the contact languages.

12 General conclusions

The current study aims at a morpho-syntactic comparison of a particular grammatical domain, the attributive system, across NENA dialects. It is worthwhile noting that this is the first monograph-sized comparison of Neo-Aramaic dialects ever produced, to the best of my knowledge. As such, it is my hope that it will open the way to further broad comparative studies of various grammatical phenomena in this fascinating language group. In order to appeal to a broad linguistic audience, the approach taken in this study combined methodology and insights from various fields of linguistics, namely typology, contact linguistics and historical linguistics.

This study had as its starting point the Semitic ANNEXATION construction, used primarily to modify nominals by other nominals, but also by prepositional phrases and clauses. Following Goldenberg (1995), I identified this construction as the exponent of the attributive relationship, and consequently I defined the notion of ATTRIBUTIVE CONSTRUCTION as any construction marking this relationship. This permits us to move beyond the specific morphological marking associated with the annexation construction (namely the historical construct state) and examine a wider range of constructions sharing a common functional denominator.

In the following sections, I shall summarize the major ideas and contributions advanced by this study. The first three sections discuss contributions to general linguistic theory or linguistic typology: §12.1 discusses the construct state as a cross-linguistic category. §12.2 emphasizes the importance of a complex typology of attributive constructions, while §12.3 discusses encliticization and cyclicity as possible universals of language change.

The following sections, conversely, are specific to the study of NENA dialects: §12.4 re-discusses the various morphemic markers developed from Classical Aramaic *d-*, while §12.5 gives a short summary of the variation found within the NENA AC systems. §12.6 re-traces in broad lines the developments of these systems.

§12.7 concludes again on a more general tone, addressing the difficulty of establishing the direction of language contact within linguistic convergence zones

(Sprachbunds). §12.8 ends the chapter with some suggestions for further research questions and directions.

12.1 The construct state as a cross-linguistic category

In the domain of linguistic theory, this study emphasizes the importance of recognizing STATE MORPHOLOGY, and in particular the construct state, as a cross-linguistic category. As discussed in §2.3.1, the recognition of the notion of construct state as a valid cross-linguistic category has been suggested before (notably by Creissels 2009). In this work, I proposed to define the category of STATE as a non-projecting morphological category which marks the SYNTACTIC VALENCY of nominals: Construct state nominals require a complement, while free state nominals can do without. The syntactic valency should be kept apart from the SEMANTIC VALENCY of nouns, which corresponds to their inherent argument structure. The latter is encoded morphologically in some languages by an ALIENABILITY split present in the nominal system (Bickel & Nichols 2013), but this is quite different from state morphology, as the latter encodes the *ad-hoc* valency of a nominal. By way of analogy, I proposed to see the construct state as the nominal counterpart of causative morphology in verbs: both add one argument to the argument structure of their host in a given syntactic context.

The construct state thus defined is the mirror-image of genitive case. The latter marks (*inter alia*) a nominal as a dependent of another nominal, while the former marks a nominal as governing another nominal. Intrinsically state morphology is a head-marking device (cf. Nichols & Bickel 2013). For this reason, state morphology is invisible outside the domain of its NP, i.e. it is non-projecting. Notwithstanding its non-projecting property, we have seen that some NENA dialects, notably JUrmi, have possibly developed an optional AGREEMENT IN STATE rule, by which a pronominal linker, being syntactically in construct state, induces construct state marking on its antecedent, being the primary of the construction (see §7.3.2). As such constructions form cohesive NP units, under this analysis too the construct state feature does not project beyond the domain of the NP.

I have claimed, moreover, that the three-way state system present in Early Aramaic should be seen as an idiosyncrasy of these languages. These Aramaic strata distinguish construct state, absolute state and emphatic state. The latter two are instances of the free state, and the opposition between them relates to the domain of determination: the emphatic state was used in the Early Aramaic strata for definite nouns while the absolute state was in general used for indefinite nouns. The three-way state distinction is justified in that a construct state noun is by itself not determined, but rather the entire NP takes its determination from the complement. As such, the three-state system can be seen as a particular Semitic case of the confounding of possessors and determination (cf. Haspelmath 1999). At the semantic level, however, nominal valency and determination are logically independent.

The usefulness of the category of state becomes clear when examining the debate regarding the Persian Ezafe, presented in §4.3. The notion of construct state provides a clear notional framework to analyse this particle, thus avoiding much of the controversy surrounding this construction. Moreover, the recognition of a functional category of construct state has permitted us to make comparisons between languages which realize this category differently, be it by the Ezafe suffix, the *-əd* suffix or apocope. At the same time, the construct state is differentiated from pronominal cross-reference head-marking, thus rendering it different to a mere synonym of the notion of head-marking.

12.2 Complex typology of attributive constructions

Building on the works of Plank (1995) in typology and Goldenberg (2013a: Ch. 14) in Semitic linguistics, I have shown that establishing a simple head- vs. dependent-marking typology of adnominal modification is often too simplistic. Rather, as discussed in Chapter 2, it is profitable to distinguish additionally between two types of markers, namely simple AC markers (construct state and genitive case) and pronominal markers, the latter indexing one member of the construction on the other. The recognition of these different types of markers provides a better account of the diversity of constructions found in NENA dialects (and in all probability across the languages of the world). It permits one, moreover, to better trace language change, as a pronominal marker can easily fossilize, thereby losing its pronominal value and becoming a simple marker. As discussed in §10.4, this is very probably what happened in NENA, whereby the double-marked DAC, containing pronominal primary and secondary markers was simplified to become the head-marked Neo-CSC, exhibiting only a simple primary marker.

12.3 Universal tendencies of language change

This study did not take an *a priori* approach regarding linguistic universals. Yet the observations regarding the changes in the NENA attributive systems corroborate certain claims regarding universal tendencies of language change. The emergence of the Neo-CSC (see §10.4) supports the idea that encliticization of functional elements to a preceding host (disregarding their syntactic scope) is a universal tendency, which could also explain the general preference of suffixation over prefixation (cf. Dryer 2015). In this respect, the expectations put forward by Lahiri & Plank are indeed borne out:

> There is probably something to be said for the wider validity of the trochaic/dactylic phrasing preference beyond Germanic and these other families; but we won't say it here. It would be of considerable interest, though, because it would help explain the near-universal preference for suffixing over prefixing. If it does not matter where grammatical words are positioned relative to the lexical words which they belong with syntactically, before or after, since phonologically they will always prefer to associate leftwards; and if cliticisation is what eventually leads to affixation – then the result will be suffixation rather than prefixation whatever the syntactic point of departure. (Lahiri & Plank 2010: 395)

An important point I have stressed in this regard, however, is that encliticization by itself is not enough for language change, but it must be accompanied by a subsequent step of re-analysis in order to have a lasting change on the linguistic system. Such a re-analysis may be motivated by external reasons (language contact) or internal factors, such as the force of ECONOMY.

Another observation, stemming from the study of re-emerging double-marked constructions (see §11.2), is the cyclic nature of language change. While the emergence of the Neo-CSC may have been partially motivated by the economic reduction of a double-marked construction to a single-marked construction, later developments re-introduce double-marked constructions, though in a different guise. I attributed these changes to the meta-linguistic force of CLARITY, favouring more elaborate structures, but one can equally well relate this to the dynamic nature of linguistic systems, always being in a state of transition. This is due to the CREATIVITY of speakers, who constantly create new linguistic constructions, whether consciously or unconsciously.

12.4 Morphemic differentiation of NENA attributive construction markers

As we have seen in Chapter 4, many scholars bundle together the various attributive constructions present in the NENA dialects, especially these that contain a reflex of the Classical Aramaic linker *d-*, as one construction exploiting the "annexation particle *d-* ". Building on the work of Cohen (2010) who discusses JZakho, I have claimed that at least two, if not three, distinct D-markers should be clearly differentiated across NENA dialects. Most importantly, the suffix *-əd* is analysed as a construct state suffix, instantiating a construction different to that of the linker *d-* (or various alternative linkers). Similarly, the /*d*/ segment itself should be analysed as two distinct morphemic markers: the pronominal linker *d-*, and the genitive prefix *d-*, present before certain demonstratives and determiners. While the genitive prefix is more difficult to ascertain across all NENA dialects (for instance, its presence is debatable in the Qaraqosh dialect; see Chapter 6), it is nonetheless useful to recognize its potential occurrence in various NENA dialects, in order to trace the development of these constructions.

12.5 Variation and uniformity in NENA dialects

In the introduction I set out two research questions directly related to the study of NENA dialects:

1. What is the extent of the variation among attributive constructions in the documented NENA dialects? Which different constructions exist in the various dialects to express the attributive relationship?

2. How do these constructions relate to the contact languages of NENA *vis à vis* the historical background of NENA? In other words, what was the role of language contact in shaping the synchronic manifestations of the attributive constructions in NENA dialects?

The research clearly demonstrates that the various NENA dialects present a wealth of different constructions and sub-constructions within the attributive domain. The richness of these systems (within each dialect and across the group as a whole) is due to the wide geographic spread of these dialects, allowing for different source constructions for each dialect's system: On the one hand, one finds numerous diverging contact languages potentially affecting each dialect. On the other hand, the various dialects may themselves be descendants of diverging anterior dialects, representing an ancient undocumented dialectal continuum not necessarily originating in a unique Proto-NENA dialect. Indeed, the high diversity found in the study corroborates rather the view that no unique Proto-NENA dialect of the Classical Aramaic period existed.[1]

[1]Such a view is also advocated by Kim (2008). It is interesting to note that Hoberman (1988: 558f.), while acknowledging the existence of such an ancient dialectal continuum, nonetheless posits the existence of a Proto-NENA dialect, possibly for methodological reasons.

Yet, glossing over some of the finer details, there are two constructions (in a broad sense) that re-occur again and again in the various dialects:

The construct state construction: In this construction the primary is marked morphologically by the construct state. In the vast majority of dialects this is achieved by the Neo-CST suffix *-əd*, but some dialects have revived the use of apocopate CST while others have borrowed the Iranic Ezafe as a construct state marker.

The analytic linker construction: In this construction type a linker is joined syntactically with the secondary, while representing pronominally the primary. In some dialects the linker is a direct reflex of the Classical Aramaic linker *d-*, while in other dialects alternative linker forms are used, typically reflexes of a DEM+LNK combination or of the pronominal base *did-* present in Jewish Babylonian Aramaic.

It is fascinating to see that while the morphemic material of these two constructions is very often innovated in NENA (such as the ubiquitous Neo-CST suffix *-əd*), they actually represent continuity with older strata of Aramaic, and indeed with the Semitic language family as a whole, since these two construction types are documented in Semitic languages since their earliest attestations (see §2.3). Indeed, as Cohen (2010) notes, the NENA dialects have re-introduced structural features present in ancient Semitic languages but lost in the Classical Aramaic stratum, notably the possibility of having clausal secondaries in the CSC. Evaluating the role of language contact in these developments, I gave a nuanced picture, pointing out that they can be conceived both as products of language contact with diverse languages and as internal developments. The general difficulty with ascertaining language contact is re-iterated in §12.7.

Alongside these two construction types, one finds two minor construction types occurring in some NENA dialects:

The juxtaposition construction: In a typical grammar of a Semitic language, apposition is expressed by the juxtaposition-cum-agreement construction, which typically occurs with adjectival secondaries. Some NENA dialects, however, have extended the use of juxtaposition (without agreement) to be a genuine marker of the attributive relation, both with nominal and clausal secondaries (see §11.3).

The relativizer construction: In dialects which are in intensive contact with Iranic languages, a matter-cum-pattern replication of the Relativizer Construction can be found, yielding a construction in which a subordinating particle introduces clausal secondaries (§11.4.2).

In contrast to the two former constructions, the two latter constructions can be qualified as true innovations of NENA dialects with respect to anterior strata of Aramaic. The relativizer is clearly an instance of matter replication, but the research also corroborates the hypothesis that the juxtaposition construction is a case of pattern replication, as it occurs especially in areas where intensive language contact with Iranic languages took place. Indeed, the examination of the co-territorial dialectal Kurdish and Gorani data establishes a direct connection with the juxtaposition constructions extant in these languages.[2]

Another innovation found across NENA dialects is the introduction of the *d-* prefix as a genitive case marker of certain determiners and pronouns (mostly demonstratives). I noted that this major innovation in the grammar of Aramaic goes against the supposed universal dispreference of prefixation. Consequently, I attributed it to the effect of language contact, and more specifically to pattern replication of the Kurmanji oblique demonstratives (see §10.5).

12.6 Historical development of the NENA attributive constructions

In Chapters 10–11 I have advanced several hypotheses regarding the development of the NENA attributive constructions. These amount to the conception of a "Domino model" or a CHAIN REACTION: The initial point for the re-shaping of the NENA AC system was the re-analysis of the DAC (*bayt-ēh d=malkā* 'house of the king') as the Neo-CSC (*bet-əd malka*). This pivotal change in the system led to further phonological reshuffles, which eventually brought about the genitive case prefix (§10.5) as well as the innovated apocopate CSC (§11.1). The latter point is especially worth emphasizing, as I reject the view that the apocopate CSC is a re-generalisation of the historical apocopate CSC.

Also the emergence of new linkers can be related to this 'chain reaction'. I claimed, for instance, that the linker *did*, originally serving only as a pronominal base (e.g. in Jewish Babylonian Aramaic), could be generalized due to its apparent construct state suffix *-d* (§10.6.2). As for other linkers, such as *od* or *ad*, these

[2]As noted in §2.3, the usage of the juxtaposition construction with clausal secondaries and indefinite primaries is very probably related to contact with Arabic vernaculars, and indeed this kind of usage (in contrast to the generalized use of juxtaposition to mark the attributive relation) is more widespread across NENA dialects.

too are the result of the encliticization of the original linker *d-* to its primary, a development in line with the emergence of the Neo-CST suffix *-əd* (§10.6.3). Finally, the emergence of the linker *ay* in JUrmi (and related dialects) originates in a further deletion of the *-d* segment (§10.6.4).

Certainly, these claims can be challenged, and to a certain extent they should be seen as hypotheses rather than firm facts. Yet the study's model has the advantage of giving a unified account to the majority of changes in the NENA attributive systems, thus explaining the striking similarity between many NENA dialects, without necessarily postulating a putative Proto-NENA. The fact that the initial change was motivated by the encliticization of the linker *d-* to the primary, a change which is in line with the claimed universal tendency of encliticization of functional elements (see §12.3), means moreover that this change could have happened independently in several pre-NENA dialects, without necessarily sharing a common ancestor of the Classical Aramaic period. This is to some extent corroborated by the fact that also Western Neo-Aramaic shows a similar re-structuring. Yet the fact that in Western Neo-Aramaic the subsequent changes did not take place may hint that at least some of the subsequent reanalysis occurred under the influence of language contact.

12.7 Language contact and linguistic convergence

A major research question posed at the outset was to identify which NENA constructions are due to language contact, and which are due to internal developments. It was hoped that clear differences in the geographic distribution of certain patterns would allow the discovery of clear language contact effects. This expectation was borne out only partially. Indeed, according to the data gathered, it seems that the dialects in the south-eastern periphery of the NENA speaking zone, i.e. the dialects in the Sorani Kurdish speaking area (roughly from Arbel southwards), show greater susceptibility to contact effects, as is apparent from the numerous cases of matter replication in these dialects, be it the Ezafe suffix or the Iranic relativizer (see Table 11.4 on page 367). In this vein, it seems reasonable to conclude that the generalized juxtaposition construction found in JSanandaj and Sulemaniyya is a product of language contact (see §11.3.2.2).

Yet, as discussed in §10.4.2, such a clear assertion becomes more difficult when dealing with the most important construction of NENA, namely the Neo-CSC. Part of the problem lies in the fact that this construction is widespread and occurs in virtually all corners of the NENA speaking zone (see Table 10.2 on page 300). Another difficulty lies in the fact that it shows affinity not only with various

Kurdish dialects (both Sorani and Kurmanji) but also with Classical Aramaic languages such as Syriac (see Table 10.5 on page 319). Moreover, the development of the Neo-CST suffix seems to follow from the universal tendency of encliticization of functional elements. The last two factors go against language contact as the source of this construction, yet the great functional and structural similarity with contact languages seems to indicate that some sort of contact must be involved. I concluded that the Neo-CSC is an instance of a linguistic convergence, in line with the areal preference to head-mark attributive constructions, but without positing a specific source language.

This conclusion places the inquiry into the development of the Neo-CSC in a wider context, namely the dynamics of linguistic convergence zones, known also as Sprachbunds.[3] Since the languages in such areas show high structural similarity due to a long history of contact, it is very difficult for any specific grammatical construction to ascertain the direction of contact and consequently whether a given construction is native to a certain language or not. A somewhat similar difficulty is addressed by Pat-El (2013a), who wishes to distinguish between internal developments and language contact between "genetically related languages". Methodologically, this is apparently a different question, since a convergence area brings together non-related languages, yet in both cases one is faced with the difficulty of reconstructing the historical development of languages with abundant structural similarities. Pat-El suggests to remedy the difficulty by scrutinizing 1) intermediate stages of language change processes and 2) the generalization of a construction across categories. As we have seen in the study of the Neo-CSC, these measures are not helpful in this case, since both in NENA and in Iranic languages one can observe intermediate stages and generalisation across categories.

To conclude this point, in convergence zones language contact clearly plays a role, yet it is difficult, and in some cases maybe even impossible, to relate a specific structural feature to one source language. In §10.4.2.3 I formulated the (still speculative) hypothesis, that the preference for head-marking of ACs (i.e., construct state morphology) is originally an Aramaic feature transferred into

[3]The recognition of the impact of linguistic convergence areas on the NENA grammar has been highlighted in numerous recent publications. Noorlander & Stilo (2015) discuss the verbal system of NENA dialects as part of the Araxes-Iran Linguistic Area, while Gandon (2017) discusses the relativization strategy of Iranian NENA dialects as part of the Caucasus-Western Iran area. See also the preface of Khan & Napiorkowska (2015: VII): "[T]he historical development of Neo-Aramaic cannot be fully understood without taking into account the structures of the languages with which the dialects have been in contact. [...] the parallels have developed in the Neo-Aramaic dialects by varying degrees of convergence with other languages".

Iranic languages, and then re-transferred into Neo-Aramaic. If this is true, the Neo-CST is effectively both a product of contact and of native Aramaic grammar.

12.8 Further research questions

The aim of this study was to describe and compare the attributive systems of various NENA dialects, attempting as well to reconstruct their development. Special emphasis was given to the question of the effect of language contact in the emergence of these systems. Yet, from a more general typological point of view two further questions can be asked:

1. Are the NENA AC systems typical or exceptional amongst the languages of the world? Do they show typical patterns of head-marking languages? What do they teach us about head-marking languages?

2. In the study I have traced several changes in the AC systems over time. For instance, I claimed that the emergence of the genitive case was subsequent to the emergence of the Neo-CST suffix. Are these claims in line with known universals of language change? Do they corroborate exiting implicational universals? Do they allow deducing new implicational scales from them?

Another further direction of study regards the methodology of the research. Methodologically, the analysis used in this study is purely a qualitative one. The data gathered could be exploited instead in a quantitative approach, relying on the recent advances in the production of phylogenetic trees in linguistic typology. The availability of constructions in the various dialects, presented in tabular format in Chapters 10–11, could be seen as FEATURES fed into this type of analysis. These results may elucidate the question of classification of the NENA dialects, and could be compared with classification done using the traditional comparative method (e.g. Hoberman 1988; Mutzafi 2008b). Moreover, as discussed in the last section, the question of the importance of language contact still remains somewhat ambivalent. One could try to disentangle this question using a phylogenetic tree, by taking into account also data from the contact languages surveyed, and observe whether they cluster with specific NENA dialects. In this respect, while the study has not resolved all the questions raised, it provides a wealth of ready-made data useful for further investigation.

Finally, the AC system is just one part of the NP domain. In §1.3 I have touched briefly upon the question of determination and quantification of the NENA NP, but these questions would in fact profit from a dedicated comparative research.

As we have seen, this topic is not disconnected from the AC system: in Semitic languages in general, determination interacts with state morphology (§2.3.3), and in NENA in particular some of the linkers are clearly related to determiners (notably JUrmi *ay*). Thus, the study of the determination system of NENA would be the natural continuation of the current study. Indeed, as I stated above, it is my hope that this study would provide an example for further in-depth and broad comparative studies of Neo-Aramaic dialects.

References

Abdulla, Jamal Jalal & Ernest N. McCarus. 1967. *Kurdish basic course: Dialect of Sulaimania, Iraq*. Ann Arbor: The University of Michigan Press.

Acuña-Fariña, Juan Carlos. 1999. On apposition. *English Language and Linguistics* 3. 59–81.

Alichoran, Joseph & Jean Sibille. 2013. L'araméen. In Georg Kremnitz (ed.), *Histoire sociale des langues de France*, 869–875. Presses universitaires de Rennes. *(Edité) avec le concours de Fañch Broudic et du collectif HSLF.*

Arnold, Werner (ed.). n.d. *SemArch – Semitisches Tonarchiv*. Technical realization Hafis El-Ghannam. Archive of recordings of living Semitic languages, curated at the University of Heidelberg. http://www.semarch.uni-hd.de.

Arnold, Werner. 1990. *Das Neuwestaramäische*. Vol. V. *Grammatik* (Semitica Viva 4/V). Wiesbaden: Otto Harrassowitz. Audio: http://www.semarch.uni-hd.de/dokumentgruppen.php43?ST_ID=5&DT_ID=8.

Arnold, Werner. 2006. *Lehrbuch des Neuwestaramäischen. Zweite, revidierte und erwiterte Auflage* (Semitica Viva - Series Didactica 1). Wiesbaden: Harrassowitz Verlag.

Arnold, Werner & Hartmut Bobzin (eds.). 2002. *„Sprich doch mit deinen Knechten aramäisch, wir verstehen es!": 60 Beiträge zur Semitistik: Festschrift für Otto Jastrow zum 60. Geburtstag*. Wiesbaden: Harrassowitz Verlag.

Assemanus, Josephus Simonius (ed.). 1719. *Bibliotheca orientalis Clementino-Vaticana: De scriporibus syris orthodoxis*. Rome. Reprinted 1975 by Georg Olms Verlag, Hildesheim.

Assemanus, Stephanus Evodius (ed.). 1743. *Sancti Ephraem Syri: Opera omnia*. Rome.

Assemanus, Stephanus Evodius (ed.). 1748. *Acta martyrum orientalium et occidentalium*. Rome.

Avinery, Iddo. 1988. הניב הארמי של יהודי זאכו *[The Aramaic dialect of the Jews of Zākhō]*. Jerusalem: The Israel Academy of the Sciences & Humanities. In Hebrew.

Baars, W. & H. Schneider. 1972. Prayer of Manasseh. In the Peshiṭta Institute (ed.), *The Old Testament in Syriac according to the Peshiṭta version*, vol. IV/6 *Canticles or Odes, Prayer of Manasseh, Apocryphal Psalms, Psalms of Solomon, Tobit, I (3) Esdras.* Leiden: Brill.

Badawi, Elsaid, Michael G. Carter & Adrian Gully. 2004. *Modern Written Arabic: A comprehensive grammar.* London: Routledge.

Bakker, Dirk. 2011. *Bardaisan's book of the laws of the countries: A computer-assisted linguistic analysis.* Leiden University dissertation.

Balaÿ, Christophe & Hossein Esmaïli. 2013. *Manuel de persan: Le persan au quotidien.* 3rd edn. (Langues Inalco). Paris: Langues & Mondes - L'Asiathèque.

Bar-Asher Siegal, Elitzur A. 2013a. Adnominal possessive and subordinating particles in Semitic languages. In Colette Bodelot, Hana Gruet-Skrabalova & François Trouilleux (eds.), *Morphologie, syntaxe et sémantique des subordonnants*, 133–150. Clermont-Ferrand: Presses Universitaires Blaise-Pascal.

Bar-Asher Siegal, Elitzur A. 2013b. *Introduction to the grammar of Jewish Babylonian Aramaic* (Textbooks of Near Eastern Languages III/3). Münster: Ugarit-Verlag.

Barker, Chris. 1995. *Possessive descriptions.* Stanford, CA: CSLI Publications.

Becker, Karl Ferdinand. 1830. *A grammar of the German language.* London: John Murray, Albemarle Street.

Bedir Khan, Djeladet & Roger Lescot. 1970. *Grammaire kurde (dialect kurmandji).* Paris: Librairie d'Amérique et d'Orient.

Bedir Khan, Kamuran Aali. 1960. *Lanuge kurde: Eléments de grammaire extraits des cours donnés à l'Ecole Nationale des Langues Orientales Vivantes.* 2nd edn. Paris.

Benedictus, Petrus (ed.). 1740. *Sancti Ephraem Syri: Opera omnia.* Rome.

Benmamoun, Elabbas. 2005. Construct state. In Kees Versteegh (ed.), *Encyclopedia of Arabic language and linguistics*, vol. 1, 477–482. Leiden: Brill.

Ben-Rahamim, Yosef. 2006. שפה אחת ודברים אחדים *[One language and one speech]:* טקסטים בארמית מזרחית חדשה - להגי אורמיא ונע'דא *[Texts in the Jewish Neo-Aramaic dialect of Azerbaijan (Urmia and Naġda)].* Jerusalem: Ben-Zvi Institute.

Beyer, Klaus. 1986. *The Aramaic language: Its distribution and subdivisions.* Trans. from German by John F. Healey. Göttingen: Vandenhoeck & Ruprecht.

Bickel, Balthasar & Johanna Nichols. 2013. Obligatory possessive inflection. In Matthew S. Dryer & Martin Haspelmath (eds.), *The world atlas of language structures online.* Leipzig: Max Planck Institute for Evolutionary Anthropology. http://wals.info/chapter/58.

Blau, Joyce. 1975. *Le kurde de ʿAmādiya et de Djabal Sindjār: Analyse linguistique, textes folkloriques, glossaires* (Travaux de l'Institut d'Études Iraniennes de l'Université de la Sorbonne Nouvelle 8). Paris: Librairie C. Klincksieck.

Blau, Joyce. 1980. *Manuel de kurde: Dialecte sorani* (Institut d'Études Iraniennes de l'Université de la Sorbonne Nouvelle, Documents et Ouvrages de Reference 2). Paris: Librairie C. Klincksieck. Re-edited as *Methode de Kurde. Sorani* سۆرانی. Paris: L'Haramattan, 2000.

Bögel, Tina & Miriam Butt. 2013. Possessive clitics and Ezafe in Urdu. In Kersti Börjars, David Denison & Alan Scott (eds.), *Morphosyntactic categories and the expression of possession* (Linguistics Today 199), 291–322. Amsterdam: John Benjamins.

Bögel, Tina, Miriam Butt & Sebastian Sulger. 2008. Urdu Ezafe and the morphology-syntax interface. In Miriam Butt & Tracy Holloway King (eds.), *Proceedings of LFG08*, 129–149. Stanford, CA: CSLI Publications.

Borer, Hagit. 2008. Compounds: The view from Hebrew. In R. Lieber & P. Stekauer (eds.), *The Oxford handbook of compounds*, 491–511. Oxford: Oxford University Press.

Borghero, Roberta. 2013. Aspects of grammaticalization in North Eastern Neo-Aramaic. *Annali dell'Istituto Orientale di Napoli* 73. 67–89.

Borghero, Roberta. 2015. The present continuous in the Neo-Aramaic dialect of ʿAnkawa and its areal and typological parallels. In Geoffrey Khan & Lidia Napiorkowska (eds.), *Neo-Aramaic and its linguistic context* (Gorgias Neo-Aramaic Studies 14), 187–206. Piscataway, NJ: Gorgias Press.

Bozdémir, Michel. 1991. *Méthode de turc*. Vol. 1 (Langues de L'Asie - INALCO). Paris: L'Asiathèque.

Broadwell, George Aaron. 2008. Turkish suspended affixation is lexical sharing. In Miriam Butt & Tracy Holloway King (eds.), *Proceedings of LFG08*, 198–213. Stanford, CA: CSLI Publications.

Brock, Sebastian P. 1997. Some remarks on the use of the construct in Classical Syriac. In Elie Wardini (ed.), *Built on solid rock: Studies in honour of professor Ebbe Egede Knudsen on the occasion of his 65th birthday April 11th 1997* (Serie B: Skrifter 98), 44–60. Oslo: Instituttet for sammenlignende kulturforskning / Novus forlag.

Brown, Dunstan & Marina Chumakina. 2013. What there might be and what there is: an introduction to canonical typology. In Dunstan Brown, Marina Chumakina & Greville G. Corbett (eds.), *Canonical morphology and syntax*, 1–19. Oxford: Oxford University Press.

Brown, Dunstan, Marina Chumakina & Greville G. Corbett (eds.). 2013. *Canonical morphology and syntax*. Oxford: Oxford University Press.

Bulakh, Maria. 2009. Nota genitivi *Za-* in Epigraphic Geez. *Journal of Semitic Studies* 54(2). 393–419.

Burkitt, F. C. (ed.). 1904. *Evangelion da-mepharreshe.* Cambridge.

Butt, Miriam & Tracy Holloway King (eds.). 2008. *Proceedings of LFG08.* Stanford, CA: CSLI Publications.

Christophe, Anne, Séverine Millotte, Savita Bernal & Jeff Lidz. 2008. Bootstrapping lexical and syntactic acquisition. *Language and Speech* 51. 61–75.

Chyet, Michael L. 1995. Neo-Aramaic and Kurdish: An interdisciplinary consideration of their influence on each other. *Israel Oriental Studies* XV. 219–252.

Chyet, Michael L. 1997. A preliminary list of Aramaic loanwords in Kurdish. In Asma Afsaruddin & A. H. Mathias Zahniser (eds.), *Humanism, culture, and language in the Near East: Studies in honor of Georg Krotkoff*, 283–300. Winona Lake, IN: Eisenbrauns.

Coghill, Eleanor. 2003. *The Neo-Aramaic dialect of Alqosh.* University of Cambridge dissertation.

Coghill, Eleanor. 2008. Some notable features in North-Eastern Neo-Aramaic dialects of Iraq. In Geoffrey Khan (ed.), *Neo-Aramaic dialect studies: Proceedings of a workshop on Neo-Aramaic held in Cambridge 2005* (Gorgias Neo-Aramaic Studies 1), 91–104. Piscataway, NJ: Gorgias Press.

Coghill, Eleanor. 2014. Differential object marking in Neo-Aramaic. *Linguistics* 52(2). 335–364.

Coghill, Eleanor. 2016. *The rise and fall or ergativity in Neo-Aramaic: Cycles of alignment change.* Oxford: Oxford University Press.

Coghill, Eleanor. 2018. North-Eastern Neo-Aramaic and language contact. In Anthony Grant (ed.), *The Oxford handbook of language contact.* Oxford: Oxford University Press, to appear.

Cohen, Eran. 2008. Adjectival *ša* syntagms and adjectives in Old Babylonian. *Bulletin of the School of Oriental and African Studies* 71(1). 25–52.

Cohen, Eran. 2010. Marking nucleus and attribute in North-Eastern Neo-Aramaic. In *Proceeding of the VIII Afro-Asiatic Congress (September 2008, Naples)* (Studi Maghrebini (Nuova Serie) VII), 79–94.

Cohen, Eran. 2012. *The syntax of Neo-Aramaic: the Jewish dialect of Zakho* (Gorgias Neo-Aramaic Studies 13). Piscataway, NJ: Gorgias Press.

Cohen, Eran. 2013. Attribute. In Geoffrey Khan (ed.), *Encyclopedia of Hebrew language and linguistics*, vol. 1, 235–239. Leiden: Brill.

Cohen, Eran. 2015. Head-marking in Neo-Aramaic genitive constructions and the *ezafe* construction in Kurdish. In Aaron M. Butts (ed.), *Semitic languages in contact* (Studies in Semitic Languages and Linguistics 82), 114–125. Leiden: Brill.

Cohen, Eran. 2018. The determination system in the dialect of Jewish Zakho. To appear in a *Festschrift* for Ariel Shisha-Halevy.

Comrie, Bernard, Martin Haspelmath & Balthasar Bickel. 2008. *The Leipzig glossing rules: Conventions for interlinear morpheme-by-morpheme glosses* (revised version of February 2008). http://www.eva.mpg.de/lingua/resources/glossing-rules.php.

Comrie, Bernard & Sandra A. Thompson. 2007. Lexical nominalization. In Timothy Shopen (ed.), *Language typology and syntactic description*. Vol. 3: *Grammatical categories and the lexicon*, 2nd edn., 334–381. Cambridge: Cambridge University Press.

Creissels, Denis. 2009. Construct forms of nouns in African languages. In Peter K. Austin, Oliver Bond, Monik Charette, David Nathan & Peter Sells (eds.), *Proceedings of Conference on Language Documentation and Linguistic Theory 2*, 73–82. London: SOAS.

Cristofaro, Sonia. 2015. Synchronic vs. diachronic explanations of typological universals: redefining the role of frequency. Paper presented at the conference Diversity linguistics: retrospect and prospect, Max Planck Institute for Evolutionary Anthropology Leipzig, 1–3 May 2015. http://www.eva.mpg.de/fileadmin/content_files/linguistics/conferences/2015-diversity-linguistics/Cristoforo_handout.pdf.

Croft, William. 2011. *Radical construction grammar: Syntactic theory in typological perspective*. Oxford: Oxford University Press.

Danon, Gabi. 2008. Definiteness spreading in the Hebrew construct state. *Lingua* 118(7). 872–906.

Dion, Paul-E. 1978. The language spoken in ancient Sam'al. *Journal of Near Eastern Studies* 37(2). 115–118.

Dixon, R. M. W. 2010. *Basic linguistic theory*. Vol. 2: *Grammatical topics*. Oxford: Oxford University Press.

Doron, Edit. 2014. The adjectival construct in Hebrew. In Nurit Melnik (ed.), *Proceedings of IATL 2013* (MIT Working Papers in Linguistics 72), 15–32.

Doron, Edit & Irit Meir. 2013. Construct state: Modern Hebrew. In Geoffrey Khan (ed.), *Encyclopedia of Hebrew language and linguistics*, vol. 1, 581–589. Leiden: Brill.

Drijvers, Han J.W. (ed.). 1965. *The book of the laws of the countries: Dialogue on fate of Bardaiṣan of Edessa*. Assen: Van Gorcum. Reprint 2007 by Gorgias Press, with new introduction by Jan Willem Drijvers.

Dryer, Matthew S. 2013a. Order of adjective and noun. In Matthew S. Dryer & Martin Haspelmath (eds.), *The world atlas of language structures online*. Leipzig:

Max Planck Institute for Evolutionary Anthropology. http://wals.info/chapter/87.

Dryer, Matthew S. 2013b. Order of genitive and noun. In Matthew S. Dryer & Martin Haspelmath (eds.), *The world atlas of language structures online*. Leipzig: Max Planck Institute for Evolutionary Anthropology. http://wals.info/chapter/86.

Dryer, Matthew S. 2013c. Order of relative clause and noun. In Matthew S. Dryer & Martin Haspelmath (eds.), *The world atlas of language structures online*. Leipzig: Max Planck Institute for Evolutionary Anthropology. http://wals.info/chapter/90.

Dryer, Matthew S. 2015. Affix as a comparative concept. Paper presented at the conference Diversity linguistics: retrospect and prospect, Max Planck Institute for Evolutionary Anthropology Leipzig, 1–3 May 2015. www.eva.mpg.de/fileadmin/content_files/linguistics/conferences/2015-diversity-linguistics/Dryer_handout.pdf.

Dryer, Matthew S. & Martin Haspelmath (eds.). 2013. *The world atlas of language structures online*. Leipzig: Max Planck Institute for Evolutionary Anthropology. http://wals.info.

Duval, Rubens. 1881. *Traité de grammaire syriaque*. Paris: F. Vieweg, libraire-éditeur.

Edmonds, C. J. 1955. Prepositions and personal affixes in Southern Kurdish. *Bulletin of the School of Oriental and African Studies* 17. 490–502.

Erwin, Wallace M. 2004 [1963]. *A short reference grammar of Iraqi Arabic* (Georgetown Classics in Arabic Language and Linguistics). Washington, D.C.: Georgetown University Press.

Fabri, Ray. 1996. The construct state and the pseudo-construct state in Maltese. *Rivista di Linguistica* 8(1). 245–274.

Fairbanks, Gordon H. 1979. The genitive case, its nature, origins and replacements. *University of Hawai'i at Mānoa: Working Papers in Linguistics* 11(2). 35–43.

Fassberg, Steven E. 2010. *The Jewish Neo-Aramaic dialect of Challa* (Studies in Semitic Languages and Linguistics 54). Leiden: Brill.

Faust, Noam. 2014. Where it's [at]: A phonological effect of phasal boundaries in the construct state of Modern Hebrew. *Lingua* 150. 315–331.

Fitzmyer, Joseph A. 1979. *A wandering Aramean: Collected aramaic essays*. Missoula, MT: Scholars Press.

Fox, Samuel E. 1997. *The Neo-Aramaic dialect of Jilu* (Semitica Viva 16). Wiesbaden: Otto Harrassowitz Verlag.

Fox, Samuel E. 2009. *The Neo-Aramaic dialect of Bohtan* (Gorgias Neo-Aramaic Studies 9). Piscataway, NJ: Gorgias Press.

Frankenberg, W. 1912. *Euagrius Ponticus* (Abhandlungen der Königlichen Gesellschaft der Wissenschaften zu Göttingen and Philologisch-Historische Klasse, n.f. XIII.2). Berlin: Weidmannsche Buchhandlung.

Freedman, David Noel. 1972. The broken construct chain. *Biblica* 53(4). 534–536.

Gai, Amikam. 1993. High-load nominal attributes in some Semitic languages. *Journal of the American Oriental Society* 113(2). 269–270.

Gai, Amikam. 2013. Kəpurtə d Atalja - Ellat puratti: A rare syntactic construction in Modern Syriac and Akkadian. *Le Muséon* 126(1–2). 21–28.

Gandon, Ophélie. 2017. Convergence areas in the Caucasus–Western Iran area with respect to relativization strategies. 18e Rencontres Jeunes Chercheurs en Sciences du Langage, Jun 2015, Paris, France. In *Actes des 18e rencontres jeunes chercheurs en sciences du langage*. https://hal-univ-paris3.archives-ouvertes.fr/hal-01495136.

Garbell, Irene. 1965a. The impact of Kurdish and Turkish on the Jewish Neo-Aramaic dialect of Persian Azerbaijan and the adjoining regions. *Journal of the American Oriental Society* 85(2). 159–177.

Garbell, Irene. 1965b. *The Jewish Neo-Aramaic dialect of Persian Azerbaijan: Linguistic analysis and folkloristic texts* (Janua linguarum, Series practica 3). The Hague: Mouton & Co.

Gesenius, Wilhelm. 1909. *Hebräische Grammatik: Völlig umgearbeitet von E. Kautzsch*. Leipzig: F.C.W. Vogel.

Gil, David. 2013. Genitives, adjectives and relative clauses. In Matthew S. Dryer & Martin Haspelmath (eds.), *The world atlas of language structures online*. Leipzig: Max Planck Institute for Evolutionary Anthropology. http://wals.info/chapter/60.

Glinert, Lewis. 1989. *The grammar of Modern Hebrew*. Cambridge: Cambridge University Press.

Goldberg, Adele E. 1995. *Constructions: A construction grammar approach to argument structure* (Cognitive Theory of Language and Culture). Chicago: The University of Chicago Press.

Goldenberg, Gideon. 1979. Review of Edward Ullendorff, *The Ethiopians: an introduction to country and people*. *Journal of Semitic Studies* 24(2). 321–326.

Goldenberg, Gideon. 1983. On Syriac sentence-structure. In Michael Sokoloff (ed.), *Arameans, Aramaic and the Aramaic literary tradition* (Bar-Ilan Studies in Near Eastern Languages and Culture), 97–140. Ramat Gan: Bar-Ilan University Press. Reprinted in *Studies in Semitic linguistics: Selected writings*, 525–568. Jerusalem: Magnes Press, 1998.

Goldenberg, Gideon. 1987. יחסים תחביריים וטיפולוגיה בלשונות שמיות [Syntactic relations and typology in semitic languages]. In עיונים בעקבות מפעלו של פולוצקי: דברים שנאמרו בערב לכבוד יעקב פולוצקי בהגיעו לגבורות *[Following Polotsky's teachings: Lectures in honour of H. J. Polotsky on the occasion of his eightieth birthday]*. Delivered at the Israel Academy of Sciences and Humanities in a meeting held on the 21st of January 1986, 7–18. Jerusalem: Israel Academy of Sciences & Humanities. Translated to English by Shmuel Bar in *Studies in Semitic linguistics: Selected writings*, 138–147. Jerusalem: Magnes Press, 1998.

Goldenberg, Gideon. 1991. On predicative adjectives and Syriac syntax. *Bibliotheca Orientalis* 48. 716–726. Reprinted in *Studies in Semitic linguistics: Selected writings*, 579–590. Jerusalem: Magnes Press, 1998.

Goldenberg, Gideon. 1995. Attribution in Semitic languages. *Langues Orientales Anciennes: Philologie et Linguistique* (5–6). 1–20. Reprinted in *Studies in Semitic linguistics: Selected writings*, 46–65. Jerusalem: Magnes Press, 1998.

Goldenberg, Gideon. 1997. Conservative and innovative features in Semitic languages. In Alessandro Bausi & Mauro Tosco (eds.), *Afroasiatica Neapolitana: Contributi presentati all'8° Incontro di Linguistica Afroasiatica (Camito-Semitica). Napoli, 25-26 Gennaio 1996 (Papers from the 8th Italian Meeting of Afroasiatic (Hamito-Semitic) Linguistics. Naples, January 25-26, 1996)* (Studi Afrianistici, Serie Etiopica 6), 3–21. Napoli: Instituto Universitario Orientale. Reprinted in *Further studies in Semitic linguistics* (Alter Orient und Altes Testament 405), 29–46. Münster: Ugarit-Verlag, 2013.

Goldenberg, Gideon. 1998. *Studies in Semitic linguistics: Selected writings*. Jerusalem: Magnes Press.

Goldenberg, Gideon. 2000. Early Neo-Aramaic and present-day dialectal diversity. *Journal of Semitic Studies* 45(1). 69–89. Reprinted in *Further studies in Semitic linguistics* (Alter Orient und Altes Testament 405), 235–252. Münster: Ugarit-Verlag, 2013.

Goldenberg, Gideon. 2002. Two types of phrase adjectivization. In Werner Arnold & Hartmut Bobzin (eds.), *„Sprich doch mit deinen Knechten aramäisch, wir verstehen es!": 60 Beiträge zur Semitistik: Festschrift für Otto Jastrow zum 60. Geburtstag*, 193–208. Wiesbaden: Harrassowitz Verlag. Reprinted in *Further studies in Semitic linguistics* (Alter Orient und Altes Testament 405), 123–139. Münster: Ugarit-Verlag, 2013.

Goldenberg, Gideon. 2005. Pronouns, copulas and a syntactical revolution in Neo-Semitic. In Alessandro Mengozzi (ed.), *Studi Afroasiatici (Afro-Asiatic Studies):*

XI Incontro Italiano di Linguistica Camitosemitica (11th Italian Meeting of Afro-Asiatic Linguistics) (Materiali linguistici 52), 239–252. Milano: FrancoAngeli. Reprinted in *Further studies in Semitic linguistics* (Alter Orient und Altes Testament 405), 97–108. Münster: Ugarit-Verlag, 2013.

Goldenberg, Gideon. 2013a. *Semitic languages: Features, structures, relations, processes.* Oxford University Press.

Goldenberg, Gideon. 2013b. *Further studies in Semitic linguistics* (Alter Orient und Altes Testament 405). Münster: Ugarit-Verlag.

Goldenberg, Gideon & Mordekhay Zaken. 1990. The book of Ruth in Neo-Aramaic. In Wolfhart Heinrichs (ed.), *Studies in Neo-Aramaic* (Harvard Semitic Series 36), 151–157. Atlanta, GA: Scholars Press.

Grassi, Giulia Francesca. 2013. Analytical and synthetic genitive constructions in Old, Imperial and Epigraphic Middle Aramaic. In Reinhard G. Lehmann & Anna Elise Zernecke (eds.), *Schrift und Sprache: Papers read at the 10th Mainz international collquium on Ancient Hebrew (MICAH), Mainz, 28–30 October 2011*, vol. 15 (KUSATO), 375–434. Kamen: Hermut Spenner.

Greenblatt, Jared. 2011. *The Jewish Neo-Aramaic dialect of amədya* (Studies in Semitic Languages and Linguistics 61). Leiden: Brill.

Gutman, Ariel. 2008. Reexamination of the bare preterite base in the Jewish Neo-Aramaic dialect of Zakho. *Aramaic Studies* 6(1). 59–84.

Gutman, Ariel. 2014. *Construct state constructions in Neo-Aramaic: are these compounds?* http://www.academia.edu/7804086/Construct_State_Constructions_in_Neo-Aramaic_Are_These_Compounds. Presentation given at the International Conference on the Cross-linguistic Comparison of Indo-Germanic and Semitic Languages, University of Konstanz, 21–23 July 2014.

Gutman, Ariel. 2015a. Forgetting language: Language change and language death as cases of forgetting. In Giovanni Galizia & David Shulman (eds.), *Forgetting: An interdisciplinary conversation* (Martin Buber Society of Fellows Notebook Series), 99–112. Jerusalem: Magnes Press.

Gutman, Ariel. 2015b. Review of *Semitic languages: Features, structures, relations, processes*, by Gideon Goldenberg (Goldenberg 2013a). *Linguistic Typology* 19(1). 131–139.

Gutman, Ariel. 2015c. Some features of the Gaznax dialect (South-East Turkey). In Geoffrey Khan & Lidia Napiorkowska (eds.), *Neo-Aramaic and its linguistic context* (Gorgias Neo-Aramaic Studies 14), 305–321. Piscataway, NJ: Gorgias Press.

Gutman, Ariel. 2016. *Attributive constructions in North-Eastern Neo-Aramaic: Areal, typological and historical perspectives.* University of Konstanz dissertation. http://nbn-resolving.de/urn:nbn:de:bsz:352-0-352520.

Gutman, Ariel. 2017. Can pattern replication be easily established? the case of the Neo-Aramaic Neo-Construct. 18e Rencontres Jeunes Chercheurs en Sciences du Langage, Jun 2015, Paris, France. In *Actes des 18e rencontres jeunes chercheurs en sciences du langage.* https://hal-univ-paris3.archives-ouvertes.fr/hal-01495125.

Gutman, Ariel, Isabelle Dautriche, Benoît Crabbé & Anne Christophe. 2015. Bootstrapping the syntactic bootstrapper: Probabilistic labeling of prosodic phrases. *Language Acquisition* 22(3). 285–309.

Gutman, Ariel & Willem Th. van Peursen. 2011. *The two Syriac versions of the Prayer of Manasseh* (Gorgias Eastern Christian Studies 30). Piscataway, NJ: Gorgias Press.

Gzella, Holger. 2011. Northwest Semitic in general. In Stefan Weninger (ed.), *The Semitic languages: An international handbook* (Handbooks of linguistics and communication sciences 36), 425–451. Berlin: De Gruyter Mouton.

Häberl, Charles G. 2007. The relative pronoun d̠- and the pronominal suffixes in Mandaic. *Journal of Semitic Studies* LII(1). 71–77.

Häberl, Charles G. 2009. *The Neo-Mandaic dialect of Khorramshahr* (Semitica Viva 45). Wiesbaden: Harrassowitz Verlag.

Haider, Hubert & Ronald Zwanziger. 1984. Relatively attributive: The "ezāfe"-construction from Old Iranian to Modern Persian. In Jacek Fisiak (ed.), *Historical syntax* (Trends in Linguistics: Studies and Monographs 23), 137–172. Berlin: Mouton Publishers.

Haig, Geoffrey. 2004. *Alignment in Kurdish: A diachronic perspective.* Christian-Albrechts-Universität zu Kiel Habilitation thesis.

Haig, Geoffrey. 2008. *Alignment change in Iranian languages: A construction grammar approach* (Empirical approaches to language typology 37). Berlin: Mouton de Gruyter.

Haig, Geoffrey. 2011. Linker, relativizer, nominalizer, tense-particle: On the Ezafe in West Iranian. In Foong Ha Yap, Karen Grunow-Hårsta & Janick Wrona (eds.), *Nominalization in Asian languages: Diachronic and typological perspectives*, 363–390. Amsterdam: Benjamins.

Haig, Geoffrey & Ergin Öpengin. 2014. Kurdish: A critical research review. *Kurdish Studies* 2(2). 99–122.

Haig, Geoffrey & Ergin Öpengin. 2018. Kurmanji Kurdish in Turkey: Structure, varieties and status. In Christiane Bulut (ed.), *Linguistic minorities in Turkey and Turkic speaking minorities of the peripheries* (Turcologica 111). Wiesbaden: Harrassowitz Verlag, to appear.

Hakem, Halkawt. 2012. *Dictionnaire kurde-français (sorani).* Paris: L'Asiathèque.

Hartmann, Martin (ed.). 1904. *Der kurdische Diwan des Schēch Aḥmed von Ğezīret Ibn ʿOmar genannt Mäla'i Ğizri: Fotolithografie einer handschrift.* Berlin: S. Calvary & Co.

Haspelmath, Martin. 1999. Explaining article-possessor complementarity: Economic motivation in noun phrase syntax. *Language* 75(2). 227–243.

Haspelmath, Martin. 2010. Comparative concepts and descriptive categories in crosslinguistic studies. *Lanuage* 86(3). 663–687.

Haspelmath, Martin. 2011. The indeterminacy of word segmentation and the nature of morphology and syntax. *Folia Linguistica* (54). 31–80.

Haspelmath, Martin. 2015. Defining vs. diagnosing linguistic categories: A case study of clitic phenomena. In Joanna Błaszczak, Dorota Klimek-Jankowska & Krzysztof Migdalski (eds.), *How categorical are categories?* (Studies in Generative Grammar 122). Berlin: De Gruyter Mouton.

Heinrichs, Wolfhart (ed.). 1990. *Studies in Neo-Aramaic* (Harvard Semitic Series 36). Atlanta, GA: Scholars Press.

Heinrichs, Wolfhart. 2002. Peculiarities of the verbal system of senāya within the framework of north eastern Neo-Aramaic (nena). In Werner Arnold & Hartmut Bobzin (eds.), *„Sprich doch mit deinen Knechten aramäisch, wir verstehen es!": 60 Beiträge zur Semitistik: Festschrift für Otto Jastrow zum 60. Geburtstag*, 237–268. Wiesbaden: Harrassowitz Verlag.

Heller, Daphna. 2002. Possession as a lexical relation: Evidence from the Hebrew construct state. In Line Mikkelsen & Christopher Potts (eds.), *Proceedings of the 21st West Coast Conference on Formal Linguistics*, 127–140. Somerville, MA: Cascadilla Press.

Hoberman, Robert D. 1988. The history of the Modern Aramaic pronouns and pronominal suffixes. *Journal of the American Oriental Society* 108(4). 557–575.

Hoberman, Robert D. 1993. Chaldean aramaic of Zakho. In Riccardo Contini, Fabrizio A. Pennacchietti & Mauro Tosco (eds.), *Semitica: Serta philologica constantino tsereteli dicata*, 115–126. Torino: Silvio Zamorani Editore.

Hoffmann, Johann Georg (ed.). 1880. *Julianos der Abtrünnige, syrische Erzählungen.* Leiden.

Holmberg, Anders & David Odden. 2008. The noun phrase in Hawrami. In Simin Karimi, Vida Samiian & Donald Stilo (eds.), *Aspects of Iranian linguistics*, 129–151. Newcastle: Cambridge Scholars Publishing.

Hopkins, Simon. 1997. On the construction *šmēh l-gaḇrā* "the name of the man" in Aramaic. *Journal of Semitic Studies* 152(1). 23–32.

Hopkins, Simon. 2009. "That Monster of a Man" and the emotive genitive. In Gideon Goldenberg & Ariel Shisha-Halevy (eds.), *Egyptian, Semitic and general grammar: Studies in memory of H. J. Polotsky*, 363–389. Jerusalem: The Israel Academy of Sciences & Humanities.

Izady, Mehrdad R. 1992. *The Kurds: A concise handbook*. Washington, D.C.: Taylor & Francis.

Jastrow, Otto. 1985. *Laut- und Formenlehre des neuaramaeischen Dialekts von Mīdin im Ṭūr ʿAbdīn*. 3. ergänzte Auflage. Wiesbaden: Otto Harrassowitz.

Jastrow, Otto. 1988. *Der neuaramäische Dialekt von Hertevin (Provinz Siirt)* (Semitica Viva 3). Wiesbaden: Otto Harrassowitz Verlag. Audio: www.semarch.uni-hd.de/tondokumente.php43?ORT_ID=27.

Jastrow, Otto. 1990. *Der arabische Dialekt der Juden von ʿAqra und Arbīl* (Semitica Viva 5). Wiesbaden: Otto Harrassowitz.

Jastrow, Otto. 2002. *Lehrbuch der Ṭuroyo-Sprache* (Semitica Viva - Series Didactica 2). Wiesbaden: Harrassowitz Verlag.

Jastrow, Otto. 2005. Der bestimmte Artikel im Aramäischen: Ein Blick auf 3000 Jahre Sprachgeschichte. In Bogdan Burtea, Josef Tropper & Helen Younansardaroud (eds.), *Studia Semitica et Semitohamitica: Festschrift für Rainer Voigt anläßlich seines 60. Geburtstages am 17. Januar 2004* (Alter Orient und Altes Testament 317). Münster: Ugarit Verlag.

Jenni, Ernst. 2003. *Lehrbuch Der Hebräischen Sprache Des Alten Testaments: Neubearbeitung des „Hebräischen Schulbuchs" von Hollenberg-Budde*. Basel: Schwabe & Co AG Verlag.

Jespersen, Otto. 1992 [1924]. *The philosophy of grammar: With a new introduction and index by James D. McCawley*. Chicago: The University of Chicago Press.

Joosten, Jan. 1996. *The Syriac language of the Peshitta and old Syriac versions of Matthew: Syntactic structure, inner-syriac developments and translation technique* (Studies in Semitic Languages and Linguistics 12). Leiden: Brill.

Kabak, Bariş. 2007. Turkish suspended affixation. *Linguistics* 45(2). 311–347.

Kahnemuyipour, Arsalan. 2003. Syntactic categories and Persian stress. *Natural Language & Linguistic Theory* 21(2). 333–379.

Karimi, Simin, Vida Samiian & Donald Stilo (eds.). 2008. *Aspects of Iranian linguistics*. Newcastle: Cambridge Scholars Publishing.

Kaufman, Stephen A. 1997. Aramaic. In Robert Hetzron (ed.), *The Semitic languages*, 114–130. Routledge.

Khan, Geoffrey (ed.). n.d. *The north eastern Neo-Aramaic database project.* http://nena.caret.cam.ac.uk.

Khan, Geoffrey. 1999. *A grammar of Neo-Aramaic: The dialect of the Jews of Arbel* (Handbook of Oriental Studies I-47). Leiden: Brill. Audio: www.semarch.uni-hd.de/dokumentgruppen.php43?ST_ID=5&DT_ID=124.

Khan, Geoffrey. 2002a. *The Neo-Aramaic dialect of Qaraqosh* (Studies in Semitic languages and linguistics 36). Leiden: Brill. Audio: www.semarch.uni-hd.de/tondokumente.php43?ORT_ID=137.

Khan, Geoffrey. 2002b. The Neo-Aramaic dialect of the Jews of Rustaqa. In Werner Arnold & Hartmut Bobzin (eds.), *„Sprich doch mit deinen Knechten aramäisch, wir verstehen es!“: 60 Beiträge zur Semitistik: Festschrift für Otto Jastrow zum 60. Geburtstag*, 395–410. Wiesbaden: Harrassowitz Verlag.

Khan, Geoffrey. 2004. *The Jewish Neo-Aramaic dialect of Sulemaniyya and Ḥalabja* (Studies in Semitic Languages and Linguistics 44). Leiden: Brill. Audio: www.semarch.uni-hd.de/tondokumente.php43?ORT_ID=138.

Khan, Geoffrey. 2007. Grammatical borrowing in North-Eastern Neo-Aramaic. In Yaron Matras & Jeanette Sakel (eds.), *Grammatical borrowing in cross-linguistic perspective* (Empirical approaches to language typology 38), 197–214. Berlin: Mouton de Gruyter.

Khan, Geoffrey. 2008a. The expression of definiteness in North-Eastern Neo-Aramaic dialects. In Holger Gzella & Margaretha L. Folmer (eds.), *Aramaic in its historical and linguistic setting* (Veröffentlichungen der Orientalischen Kommisssion der Akademie Mainz 50), 287–304. Wiesbaden: Harrassowitz Verlag.

Khan, Geoffrey. 2008b. *The Jewish Neo-Aramaic dialect of Urmi* (Gorgias Neo-Aramaic Studies 2). Piscataway, NJ: Gorgias Press.

Khan, Geoffrey. 2008c. *The Neo-Aramaic Dialect of Barwar.* 3 vols. (Handbook of Oriental Studies I-96). Leiden: Brill.

Khan, Geoffrey. 2009a. The genitive and relative clauses in the North-Eastern Neo-Aramaic dialects. Supplement 25. 69–87.

Khan, Geoffrey. 2009b. *The Jewish Neo-Aramaic dialect of Sanandaj* (Gorgias Neo-Aramaic Studies 10). Piscataway, NJ: Gorgias Press.

Khan, Geoffrey (ed.). 2013. *Encyclopedia of Hebrew language and linguistics.* Leiden: Brill.

Khan, Geoffrey & Lidia Napiorkowska (eds.). 2015. *Neo-Aramaic and its linguistic context* (Gorgias Neo-Aramaic Studies 14). Piscataway, NJ: Gorgias Press.

Kim, Ronald. 2008. “Stammbaum” or continuum? the subgrouping of modern aramaic dialects reconsidered. *Journal of the American Oriental Society* 128(3). 505–531.

Kıral, Filiz. 2006. Izafet constructions in Turkic varieties of Iran. In Hendrik Boeschoten & Lars Johanson (eds.), *Turkic languages in contact* (Turcologica 61), 158–165. Wiesbaden: Harrassowitz Verlag.

Klavans, Judith L. 1985. The independence of syntax and phonology in cliticization. *Language* 61(1).

Klein, Ernst. 1987. *A comprehensive etymological dictionary of the Hebrew language for readers of English.* Jerusalem: Carta & The University of Haifa.

König, Eduard. 1901. The emphatic state in Aramaic. *The American Journal of Semitic Languages and Literatures* 17(4). 209–221.

Koptjevskaja-Tamm, Maria. 2003. Possessive noun phrases in the languages of Europe. In Frans Plank (ed.), *Noun phrase structure in the languages of Europe* (Empirical Approaches to Language Typology Eurotyp 20(7)), 621–722. Berlin: Mouton de Gruyter.

Krotkoff, Georg. 1982. *A Neo-Aramaic dialect of Kurdistan: Texts, grammar and vocabulary* (American Oriental Series 64). New Haven, CT: American Oriental Society. Audio: www.semarch.uni-hd.de/tondokumente.php43?ORT_ID=59. [A description of C. Aradhin dialect].

Kurdoev, Kanat Kalashevich. 1956. Numerativnye slova v kurdskom jazyke (number terms in Kurdish). *Kratkie Soobščenija Inst. Vostok.* (XXII). 28–36.

Lahiri, Aditi. 2003. Hierarchical restructuring in the creation of verbal morphology in Bengali and Germanic: Evidence from phonology. In Aditi Lahiri (ed.), *Analogy, levelling & markedness: Principles of change in phonology and morphology*, Second and revised edition, 71–123. Berlin: Mouton de Gruyter. First published in 2000.

Lahiri, Aditi & Frans Plank. 2010. Phonological phrasing in Germanic: The judgement of history, confirmed through experiment. *Transactions of the Philological Society* 108(3). 370–398.

Land, Jan Pieter Nicolaas (ed.). 1870. *Anecdota Syriaca.* Vol. 3 *Zachariae Episcopi Mitylenes.* Leiden: Brill.

Larson, Richard K. & Hiroko Yamakido. 2006. Zazaki "Double Ezafe" as double case-marking. Paper presented at the Linguistic Society of America annual meetings, Albuquerque, January, 2006.

Lee, Samuel (ed.). 1842. *Eusebius, bishop of Cæsarea, on the Theophania or divine manifestation of Our Lord and Saviour Jesus Christ: A Syriac version edited from an ancient manuscript recently discovered.* London: Society for the Publication of Oriental Texts.

Lewis, A. S. (ed.). 1910. *The Old Syriac Gospels or Evalngelion da-Mepharreshê.* London.

Lewis, Geoffrey L. 1967. *Turkish grammar.* Oxford: Clarendon Press.

Lewis, M. Paul, Gary F. Simons & Charles D. Fennig (eds.). 2013. *Ethnologue: Languages of the world.* Seventeenth edition. Dallas, TX: SIL International. www.ethnologue.com.

Loewenstamm, Shmuel E. 1955. על התהוותו של המושג "ראשון" בשפות השמיות [The development of the term "first" in the Semitic languages]. *Tarbiz* 24(3). 249–251.

Lyons, Christopher. 1999. *Definiteness* (Cambridge Textbooks in Linguistics). Cambridge: Cambridge University Press.

MacKenzie, David Neil. 1961. *Kurdish dialect studies.* Vol. I (London Oriental Series 9). London: Oxford University Press. Reprinted by the School of Oriental and African Studies 1981.

MacKenzie, David Neil. 1962. *Kurdish dialect studies.* Vol. II (London Oriental Series 10). London: Oxford University Press.

MacKenzie, David Neil. 1966. *The dialect of Awroman (Hawrāmān-ī Luhōn): Grammatical sketch, texts, and vocabulary.* Vol. 4 (Historisk-filosofiske Skrifter 3). København: Det Kongelige Danske Videnskabernes Selskab (The Royal Danish Academy of Sciences & Letters).

Maclean, Arthur John. 1895. *Grammar of the dialects of vernacular Syriac: As spoken by the Eastern Syrians of Kurdistan, North-West Persia, and The Plain of Mosul, with notices of the vernacular of the Jews of Azerbaijan and of Zakhu near Mosul.* Cambridge University Press.

Macuch, Rudolf. 1965. *Handbook of Classical and Modern Mandaic.* Berlin: Walter de Gruyter & Co.

Mahmudweyssi, Parwin, Denise Bailey, Ludwig Paul & Geoffrey Haig. 2012. *The Gorani language of Gawrajū, a village of West Iran: Texts, grammar, and lexicon* (Beiträge zur Iranistik 35). Wiesbaden: Dr. Ludwig Reichert Velag.

Marogulov, Konstantin I. 1976. *Grammaire néo-syriaque pour écoles d'adultes (dialecte d'Urmia).* Trans. from Neo-Aramaic by Olga Kapeliuk (*Comptes rendus de g.l.e.c.s, Supplément* 5). Paris: Geuthner. Original title: *Grammatiqij qə mədrəsi d gurь*, Moscow, 1935.

Martin, Paulin (ed.). 1876. *Chronique de Josué le Stylite: Écrite vers l'an 515* (Abhandlungen für die Kunde des Morgenlandes VI/1). Leipzig: F. A. Brockhaus.

Matras, Yaron & Jeanette Sakel (eds.). 2007a. *Grammatical borrowing in cross-linguistic perspective* (Empirical approaches to language typology 38). Berlin: Mouton de Gruyter.

Matras, Yaron & Jeanette Sakel. 2007b. Investigating the mechanisms of pattern replication in language convergence. *Studies in Language* 31(4). 829–865.

McPherson, Laura & Paul Caldani. 2013. *Leshaan senaaye: the senaya language.* http://www.senaya.org.

Meltzer-Asscher, Aya & Tal Siloni. 2013. Inalienable possession: Modern Hebrew. In Geoffrey Khan (ed.), *Encyclopedia of Hebrew language and linguistics*, vol. 2, 253–254. Leiden: Brill.

Mengozzi, Alessandro (ed.). 2002. *Israel of Alqosh and Joseph of Telkepe, a story in a truthful language: Religious poems in vernacular Syriac (North Iraq, 17th century).* Vol. I: Text and Glossary (Corpus Scriptorum Christianorum Orientalium 589). Louvain: Peeters.

Mengozzi, Alessandro. 2005a. Extended prepositions in Neo-Aramaic, Kurdish and Italian. In Alessandro Mengozzi (ed.), *Studi Afroasiatici (Afro-Asiatic Studies): XI Incontro Italiano di Linguistica Camitosemitica (11th Italian Meeting of Afro-Asiatic Linguistics)* (Materiali linguistici 52), 371–390. Milano: FrancoAngeli.

Mengozzi, Alessandro (ed.). 2005b. *Studi Afroasiatici (Afro-Asiatic Studies): XI Incontro Italiano di Linguistica Camitosemitica (11th Italian Meeting of Afro-Asiatic Linguistics)* (Materiali linguistici 52). Milano: FrancoAngeli.

Mengozzi, Alessandro (ed.). 2011. *Religious poetry in vernacular Syriac from Northern Iraq (17th-20th centuries)* (Corpus Scriptorum Christianorum Orientalium 627–628). Louvain: Peeters.

Meyer, Mark. 2012. *A comparative dialectical study of genitive constructions in Aramaic translations of Exodus* (Perspectives on Linguistics and Ancient Languages 2). Piscataway, NJ: Gorgias Press.

Miller, Philip H. 1992. *Clitics and constituents in phrase structure grammar.* New York: Garland.

Muraoka, Takamitsu. 1997. *Classical Syriac: A basic grammar with a chrestomathy* (Porta Linguarum Orientalium - Neue Serie 19). Wiesbaden: Harrassowitz Verlag.

Muraoka, Takamitsu. 2013. *Classical Syriac for Hebraists.* 2nd edn. (Subsidia et Instrumenta Linguarum Orientis 6). Wiesbaden: Harrassowitz Verlag.

Murelli, Adriano. 2011. *Relative constructions in European non-standard varieties* (Empirical approaches to language typology 50). Berlin: De Gruyter Mouton.

Murre-van den Berg, Helene L. 1999. *From a spoken to a written language: The introduction and development of literary Urmia Aramaic in the nineteenth century* (Publication of the "De Goeje Fund" No. XXVIII). Leiden: Nederlands Instituut voor het Nabije Oosten. Extended version of her doctoral thesis from 1995.

Mutzafi, Hezy. 2000. The Neo-Aramaic dialect of Maha Khtaya d-Baz: Phonology, morphology and texts. *Journal of Semitic Studies* XLV(2). 293–322.

Mutzafi, Hezy. 2002a. Barzani Jewish Neo-Aramaic and its dialects. *Mediterranean Language Review* 14. 41–70.

Mutzafi, Hezy. 2002b. On the Jewish Neo-Aramaic dialect of Aradhin and its dialectal affinities. In Werner Arnold & Hartmut Bobzin (eds.), *„Sprich doch mit deinen Knechten aramäisch, wir verstehen es!": 60 Beiträge zur Semitistik: Festschrift für Otto Jastrow zum 60. Geburtstag*, 479–488. Wiesbaden: Harrassowitz Verlag.

Mutzafi, Hezy. 2004a. *The Jewish Neo-Aramaic dialect of Koy Sanjaq (Iraqi Kurdistan)* (Semitica Viva 32). Wiesbaden: Harrassowitz Verlag. Audio: www.semarch.uni-hd.de/tondokumente.php43?ORT_ID=71.

Mutzafi, Hezy. 2004b. Two texts in Barzani Jewish Neo-Aramaic. *Bulletin of the School of Oriental and African Studies* 67(01). 1–13. Audio: www.semarch.uni-hd.de/tondokumente.php43?&GR_ID=&ORT_ID=115&DOK_ID=1437.

Mutzafi, Hezy. 2008a. *The Jewish Neo-Aramaic dialect of Betanure (province of Dihok)* (Semitica Viva 43). Wiesbaden: Harrassowitz Verlag. Audio: www.semarch.uni-hd.de/tondokumente.php43?ORT_ID=159.

Mutzafi, Hezy. 2008b. Trans-Zab Jewish Neo-Aramaic. *Bulletin of SOAS* 71(3). 409–431.

Mutzafi, Hezy. 2015. Christian Salamas and Jewish Salamas: Two separate types of Neo-Aramaic. In Geoffrey Khan & Lidia Napiorkowska (eds.), *Neo-Aramaic and its linguistic context* (Gorgias Neo-Aramaic Studies 14), 289–304. Piscataway, NJ: Gorgias Press.

Napiorkowska, Lidia. 2015. *A grammar of the Christian Neo-Aramaic dialect of Diyana-Zariwaw* (Studies in Semitic Languages and Linguistics 81). Leiden: Brill.

Nichols, Johanna. 1986. Head-marking and dependent-marking grammar. *Language* 62(1). 56–119.

Nichols, Johanna & Balthasar Bickel. 2013. Locus of marking in possessive noun phrases. In Matthew S. Dryer & Martin Haspelmath (eds.), *The world atlas of language structures online.* Leipzig: Max Planck Institute for Evolutionary Anthropology. http://wals.info/chapter/24.

Nikolaeva, Irina & Andrew Spencer. 2013. Possession and modification – a perspective from canonical typology. In Dunstan Brown, Marina Chumakina & Greville G. Corbett (eds.), *Canonical morphology and syntax*, 207–238. Oxford: Oxford University Press.

Nöldeke, Theodor. 1875. *Mandäische grammatik.* Halle: Verlag der Buchhandlung des Waisenhauses.

Nöldeke, Theodor. 1898. *Kurzgefasste Syrische Grammatik.* 2nd edn. Leipzig: Chr. Herm. Tauchnitz. In English: *Compendious Syriac Grammar.* Trans. by James A. Crichton. London: Williams & Norgate, 1904.

Noorlander, Paul M. 2014. Diversity in convergence: Kurdish and Aramaic variation entangled. *Kurdish Studies* 2(2). 201–224.

Noorlander, Paul M. & Donald Stilo. 2015. On the convergence of verbal systems of Aramaic and its neighbours. In Geoffrey Khan & Lidia Napiorkowska (eds.), *Neo-Aramaic and its linguistic context* (Gorgias Neo-Aramaic Studies 14), 426–484. Piscataway, NJ: Gorgias Press.

Öpengin, Ergin & Geoffrey Haig. 2014. Regional variation in Kurmanji: A preliminary classification of dialects. *Kurdish Studies* 2(2). 143–176.

Ornan, Uzzi. 1964. הצירופים השמניים בלשון-הספרות העברית החדשה, בייחוד ע"פ הפרוזה של ח"נ ביאליק *[The nominal phrase in Modern Written Hebrew, especially according to the prose of H. N. Bialik].* Hebrew University of Jerusalem dissertation. Re-edited 2011 by Karmel, Jerusalem.

Panoussi, Estiphan. 1990. On the Senaya dialect. In Wolfhart Heinrichs (ed.), *Studies in Neo-Aramaic* (Harvard Semitic Series 36), 107–129. Atlanta, GA: Scholars Press.

Pat-El, Na'ama. 2009. The development of the Semitic definite article: A syntactic approach. *Journal of Semitic Studies* LIV(1). 19–50.

Pat-El, Na'ama. 2010. The origin and function of the so-called "correlative" in Classical Syriac. *Folia Orientalia* 45–46. 61–69.

Pat-El, Na'ama. 2012. *Studies in the historical syntax of Aramaic* (Perspectives on Linguistics and Ancient Languages 1). Piscataway, NJ: Gorgias Press.

Pat-El, Na'ama. 2013a. Contact or inheritance? Criteria for distinguishing internal and external change in genetically related language. *Journal of Language Contact* (6). 313–328.

Pat-El, Na'ama. 2013b. Inalienable possession: Biblical Hebrew. In Geoffrey Khan (ed.), *Encyclopedia of Hebrew language and linguistics*, vol. 2, 252–253. Leiden: Brill.

Pat-El, Na'ama. 2014. The morphosyntax of nominal antecedents in Semitic, and an innovation in Arabic. In Lutz Edzard & John Huehnergard (eds.), *Proceedings of the Oslo-Austin workshop in Semitic linguistics: Oslo, May 23 and 24, 2013* (Abhandlungen für die Kunde des Morgenlandes 88). Wiesbaden: Harrassowitz Verlag.

Payne Smith, Jessie. 1903. *A compendious Syriac dictionary: Founded upon the Thesaurus Syriacus by R. Payne Smith.* Oxford: Clarendon Press.

Pennacchietti, Fabrizio A. 1968. *Studi sui pronomi determinativi semitici* (Pubblicazioni del Seminario di Semitistica – Ricerche 4). Napoli: Istituto Orientale di Napoli.

Pennacchietti, Fabrizio A. 2007. L'impiego di frasi pseudorelative come verbi finiti. In F. Venier (ed.), *Relative e pseudorelative tra grammatica e testo*, 133–148. Alessandria: Edizioni dell'Orso.

Pennacchietti, Fabrizio A. & Alessandro Orengo. 1995. Neoaramaico, Curdo e Armeno: Lingue a contatto. *Egitto e Vicino Oriente* 18. 221–233.

van Peursen, Willem Th. 2007. *Language and interpretation in the Syriac text of Ben Sira: A comparative linguistic and literary study* (Monographs of the Peshitta Institute Leiden 16). Leiden: Brill.

van Peursen, Willem Th. & Terry C. Falla. 2009. The particles ܟܝܬ and ܕܝܢ in Classical Syriac: Syntactic and semantic aspects. In P. J. Williams (ed.), *Foundations for Syriac lexicography ii: Colloquia of the international Syriac language project* (Perspectives on Syriac Linguistics 3), 63–98. Piscataway, NJ: Gorgias Press.

Plank, Frans. 1995. (Re-)introducing suffixaufnahme. In Frans Plank (ed.), *Double case: Agreement by suffixaufnahme*, 3–110. New York: Oxford University Press.

Plank, Frans. 2012. Suffixaufnahme: Dix-sept ans après. http://ling.uni-konstanz.de/pages/home/plank/for_download/presentations_2/32_FP_Suffixaufnahme_x2012.pdf. Paper presented at Konst-anz–Essex–JNU New Delhi Genitive Workshop, Konstanz, 11-13 October 2012.

Poizat, Bruno. 2008. *Manuel de soureth: Initiation à l'araméen d'aujourd'hui, parlé et écrit. Avec la collaboration de Yawsep Alichoran et Yohanan Binouissa.* Paris: Geuthner.

Polotsky, Hans J. 1961. Review of R. Schneider, *L'expression des compléments de verbe et de nom et la place de l'adjectif épithète en guèze. Journal of Semitic Studies* 6(2). 251–256.

Rees, Margo. 2008. *Lishan didan, targum didan: Translation language in a Neo-Aramaic Targum tradition* (Gorgias Neo-Aramaic Studies 3). Piscataway, NJ: Gorgias Press.

Retsö, Jan. 1984–1986. State, determination and definiteness in Arabic: A reconsideration. *Orientalia Suecana* 33–35. 341–346.

Retsö, Jan. 1997. State and plural marking in Semitic. In Elie Wardini (ed.), *Built on solid rock: Studies in honour of professor Ebbe Egede Knudsen on the occasion of his 65th birthday April 11th 1997* (Serie B: Skrifter 98), 268–282. Oslo: Instituttet for sammenlignende kulturforskning / Novus forlag.

Rießler, Michael. 2016. *Adjective attribution* (Studies in Diversity Linguistics 2). Berlin: Language Science Press.

Riester, Arndt. 2001. *A cross-linguistic perspective on attributive possession*. Amsterdam: Universiteit van Amsterdam master thesis.

Sabar, Yona. 1976. *Pəšaṭ Wayəhî Bəšallaḥ: A Neo-Aramaic Midrash on Beshallaḥ (Exodus). Introduction, phonetic transcription, translation, notes and glossary*. Wiesbaden: Otto Harrassowitz.

Sabar, Yona. 1983. *The book of Genesis in Neo-Aramaic* (Publications of The Hebrew University Language Traditions Project IX). Jerusalem: Magnes Press.

Sabar, Yona. 1984a. The Arabic elements in the Jewish Neo-Aramaic texts of Nerwa and ʿAmādīya, Iraqi Kurdistan. *Journal of the American Oriental Society* 104(1). 201–211.

Sabar, Yona. 1984b. מדרשים בארמית יהודי כורדיסטאן לפרשיות ויחי, בשלח ויתרו *[Homilies in the Neo-Aramaic of the Kurdistani Jews on the Parashot Wayḥi, Beshallaḥ and Yitro]*. Jerusalem: The Israel Academy of Sciences & Humanities.

Sabar, Yona. 1990. General European loanwords in Jewish Neo-Aramaic dialect of Zakho, Iraqi Kurdistan. In Wolfhart Heinrichs (ed.), *Studies in Neo-Aramaic* (Harvard Semitic Series 36), 53–66. Atlanta, GA: Scholars Press.

Sabar, Yona. 2002. *A Jewish Neo-Aramaic dictionary: Dialects of Amidya, Dihok, Nerwa and Zakho, northwestern Iraq* (Semitica Viva 28). Wiesbaden: Harrassowitz Verlag.

Sabar, Yona. 2007. Agonies of childbearing and child rearing in Iraqi Kurdistan: a narrative in Jewish Neo-Aramaic and its English translation. In Tali Bar & Eran Cohen (eds.), *Studies in Semitic and general linguistics in honor of Gideon Goldenberg* (Alter Orient und Altes Testament 334), 107–145. Münster: Ugarit-Verlag.

Sakel, Jeanette. 2007. Types of loan: matter and pattern. In Yaron Matras & Jeanette Sakel (eds.), *Grammatical borrowing in cross-linguistic perspective* (Empirical approaches to language typology 38), 15–30. Berlin: Mouton de Gruyter.

Samiian, Vida. 1994. The Ezafe construction: some implications for the theory of X-bar syntax. In Mehdi Marashi (ed.), *Persian studies in North America: Studies in honor of Mohammad Ali Jazayery*, 17–41. Bethesda, MD: Iranbooks.

Samvelian, Pollet. 2006. L'enclitique -i introducteur de relative en persan : déterminant, allomorphe de l'ezāfe, ou autre chose encore? *Studia Iranica* 35. 7–34.

Samvelian, Pollet. 2007a. A (phrasal) affix analysis of the Persian Ezafe. *Journal of Linguistics* (43). 605–645.

Samvelian, Pollet. 2007b. What Sorani Kurdish absolute prepositions tell us about cliticization. In Frederick Hoyt, Nikki Seifert, Alexandra Teodorescu & Jessica

White (eds.), *Texas linguistic society ix: The morphosyntax of underrepresented languages*, 263–283. Stanford, CA: CSLI Publications.
Samvelian, Pollet. 2008. The Ezafe as a head-marking inflectional affix: evidence from Persian and Kurmanji Kurdish. In Simin Karimi, Vida Samiian & Donald Stilo (eds.), *Aspects of Iranian linguistics*, 339–361. Newcastle: Cambridge Scholars Publishing.
Samvelian, Pollet. 2012. *Grammaire des prédicats complexes: Les constructions nom-verbe.* Paris: Lavoisier.
Schaller, Nurit. 2007. *Grammatische Skizze des Jüdisch Nordostneuaramäischen Dialekts aus Sanandağ (Iranisch Kurdistan).* Hochschule für Jüdische Studien Heidelberg Magisterarbeit.
Schroeder, Christoph. 1999. Attribution im Kurmancî (Nordkurdisch). In Karl Heinz Wagner & Wolfgang Wildgen (eds.), *Studien zur Phonologie, Grammatik, Sprachphilosophie und Semiotik* (Bremer Linguistisches Kolloquium 6), 43–63. Bremen: Institut für Allgemeine und Angewandte Sprachwissenschaft.
Schulz, Eckehard. 2004. *A student grammar of Modern Standard Arabic.* Cambridge University Press.
Shelzinger, Yitzhak & Dorit Ravid. 1998. הסמיכות הכפולה בעברית החדשה: עודפות או קיום עצמאי? [The double compound in Modern Hebrew: Redundancy or independent existence?] בלשנות עברית *[Hebrew Linguistics]* 43. 85–97.
Sinha, Jasmin. 2000. *Der neuostaramäische Dialekt von Bēṣpən (Provinz Mardin, Südosttürkei): Eine grammatische Darstellung.* Wiesbaden: Herassowitz Verlag. Audio: www.semarch.uni-hd.de/tondokumente.php43?ORT_ID=15.
Slobin, Dan I. 1977. Language change in childhood and in history. In John Macnamara (ed.), *Language learning and thought* (Perspectives in Neurolinguistics and Psycholinguistics), 185–214. New York: Academic Press.
Socin, Albert. 1882. *Die neu-aramäischen Dialekte von Urmia bis Mosul: Texte u. Uebers.* Tübingen: Laupp.
Sokoloff, Michael. 2002. *A dictionary of Jewish Babylonian Aramaic of the Talmudic and Geonic periods.* Ramat-Gan: Bar Ilan University Press.
Spencer, Andrew & Ana Luís. 2013. The canonical clitic. In Dunstan Brown, Marina Chumakina & Greville G. Corbett (eds.), *Canonical morphology and syntax*, 123–150. Oxford: Oxford University Press.
Spitaler, Anton. 1938. *Grammatik des neuaramäischen Dialekts von Maʿlūla (Antilibanon).* Vol. 23 (Abhandlungen für die Kunde des Morgenlandes 1). Leipzig: Deutsche Morgenländische Gesellschaft. Reprinted 1966 by Kraus Reprint Ltd., Nendeln.

Talay, Shabo. 2008. *Die neuaramäischen Dialekte der Khabur-Assyrer in Nordostsyrien: Einführung, phonologie und morphologie* (Semitica Viva 40). Wiesbaden: Harrassowitz Verlag.

Thackston, W. M. 2006a. *Kurmanji Kurdish: A reference grammar with selected readings.* http://www.fas.harvard.edu/~iranian/Kurmanji.

Thackston, W. M. 2006b. زمانی کوردی سۆرانی *Sorani Kurdish: A reference grammar with selected readings.* http://www.fas.harvard.edu/~iranian/Sorani.

Todd, Terry Lynn. 2002. *A grammar of Dimili: Also known as Zaza.* Stockholm: Iremet Förlag. Re-edited 2008 as an electronic edition, available at www.zazaki.de/english/T.L.Todd-AGrammarofDimli.pdf.

Tsereteli, Konstantin. 1965. A type of nominal syntagm in Modern Aramaic Dialects. *Bulletin of the School of Oriental and African Studies, University of London* 28(2). 227–232.

Ultan, Russel. 1978. Toward a typology of substantival possession. In Joseph H. Greenberg (ed.), *Universals of human language.* Vol. 4: *Syntax*, 11–50. Standford, CA: Standford University Press.

Utas, Bo. 2005. Semitic in Iranian: Written, read, and spoken language. In Éva Ágnes Csató, Bo Isaksson & Carina Jahani (eds.), *Linguistic convergence and areal diffusion: Case studies from Iranian, Semitic and Turkic*, 65–78. London & New York: RoutledgeCurzon.

Van Hecke, Pierre. 2013. Construct state: Biblical Hebrew. In Geoffrey Khan (ed.), *Encyclopedia of Hebrew language and linguistics*, vol. 1, 579–580. Leiden: Brill.

Van Peursen. 2007–2009. See under Peursen.

Verhej, Arian J. C. 1989. The genitive construction with two *nomina recta. Zeitschrift für Althebraistik* 2. 210–212.

Waltke, Bruce K. & M. O'Connor. 1990. *An introduction to Biblical Hebrew sytnax.* Winona Lake, IN: Eisenbrauns.

Wardini, Elie (ed.). 1997. *Built on solid rock: Studies in honour of professor Ebbe Egede Knudsen on the occasion of his 65th birthday April 11th 1997* (Serie B: Skrifter 98). Oslo: Instituttet for sammenlignende kulturforskning / Novus forlag.

Wertheimer, Ada. 2001. The functions of the Syriac particle *d-*. *Le Muséon* 114(3–4). 259–289.

Williams, Peter J. 2001. *Studies in the syntax of the Peshitta of 1 Kings* (Monographs of the Peshitta Institute Leiden 12). Leiden: Brill.

Woodhead, D. R. & Wayne Beene (eds.). 1967. *A dictionary of Iraqi Arabic: Arabic-English* (The Richard Slade Harrell Arabic Series 10). Washington, D.C.: Georgetown University Press.

Wright, William (ed.). 1871. *Apocryphal acts of the apostles: Edited from Syriac manuscripts in the British Museum and other libraries.* London: Williams & Norgate.

Younansardaroud, Helen. 2001. *Der neuostaramäische Dialekt von Särdä:rïd* (Semitica Viva 26). Wiesbaden: Harrassowitz Verlag. Audio: www.semarch.uni-hd.de/tondokumente.php43?ORT_ID=14.

Zwicky, Arnold M. 1987. Supressing the Z's. *Journal of Linguistics* 23(1). 133–148.

Zwicky, Arnold M. & Geoffrey K. Pullum. 1983. Cliticization vs. inflection: English *n't*. *Language* 59. 502–513.

Name index

Language index

Subject index

www.ingramcontent.com/pod-product-compliance
Lightning Source LLC
Chambersburg PA
CBHW081112160426
42814CB00035B/290
* 9 7 8 3 9 6 1 1 0 0 8 2 8 *